"The providential role of the heretics in ancient Christianity was to challenge the worshiping community to return to the classic doctrinal consensus on scriptural teaching. The task is to mark boundaries to teachings that are other than the right teaching according to the best minds of the church. Wilhite has made these boundaries much clearer, enabling readers today to better grasp the Word of God the Father incarnate in the Son by the power of the Spirit."

—**Thomas C. Oden**, general editor, Ancient Christian Commentary on Scripture; Drew University Graduate School

"This is an unusual book, aimed at communicating the dynamics of the development of Christology to an audience not steeped in late antique thought. It draws from contemporary scholarship and primary texts and conveys key ideas and evidence to support a reading of the christological 'center' working itself out in different contexts over many centuries. Wilhite allows a narrative to emerge, aware that telling the story may be the best way to begin an induction into the Christologies of early Christianity. I commend this book to the motivated Christian determined to understand the significance and achievement of christological development."

—**Andrew Teal**, Pembroke College, Oxford

"This fascinating tour of early christological heresies belongs in the library of anyone interested in Christian theology. With winsome clarity and impressive brevity, David Wilhite demonstrates how these heresies have often been misrepresented and misunderstood, masterfully summarizing a wealth of historical research. This is not an apologetic for heresy, but it is an appeal for charity. Each chapter illustrates how much we stand to gain when we move beyond caricature and appreciate the real complexity involved in these debates."

—**Marc Cortez**, Wheaton College

THE GOSPEL

ACCORDING TO

HERETICS

Discovering Orthodoxy
through Early Christological Conflicts

DAVID E. WILHITE

B
Baker Academic
a division of Baker Publishing Group
Grand Rapids, Michigan

© 2015 by David E. Wilhite

Published by Baker Academic
a division of Baker Publishing Group
P.O. Box 6287, Grand Rapids, MI 49516-6287
www.bakeracademic.com

Printed in the United States of America

Library of Congress Cataloging-in-Publication Data
Wilhite, David E.
  The gospel according to heretics : discovering orthodoxy through early christological conflicts / David E. Wilhite.
      pages cm
  Includes bibliographical references and index.
  ISBN 978-0-8010-3976-8 (pbk.)
  1. Christian heresies—History—Early church, ca. 30–600. 2. Christian heretics. I. Title.
  BT1319.W54 2015
  273—dc23   2015010415

15 16 17 18 19 20 21   7 6 5 4 3 2 1

Contents

Preface

John, my neighbor, knocked on my door; he was not happy. He had just seen in the news that then–presidential candidate and Texas governor Rick Perry had been introduced at a rally by the pastor of First Baptist Dallas. The pastor disparaged Perry's opponent for adhering to the "cult" of Mormonism. My neighbor, a lifelong Mormon, knew my Baptist affiliation, and he wanted to know, "You don't think my church is a cult, do you?!" My response involved a lot of hemming and hawing and trying to explain how not all Baptists are alike and how I research early Christian history. Finally, I got around to saying, "I don't think you're a member of a cult. I just think you're a heretic." He seemed to like that answer, and we're still friends. This book is dedicated to my neighbors and to all of the heretics in my life.

This project began when a student and fellow church member (and now friend) named Chris Kuhl asked me to "teach heresy" in Sunday school. His point was that he better appreciated his own faith after taking my Christian history class, where I very sympathetically surveyed the heretics. I agreed to teach the class on the condition that Chris teach it with me. Every week, I gave the history of a heretic, Chris pointed us to relevant biblical passages, and then we recruited Hannah Starkey (now Smith), a college student (now a medical student), to lead the discussion. The class went very well—although explaining to my tenure review committee why I was "teaching heresy" in Sunday school was a bit awkward. One Friday I was in my office preparing my Sunday school lesson when James Ernest from Baker Academic knocked on my door. He had been meeting with the real scholars on campus, but stopped to meet me and asked, "What are you working on?" "The gospel according to heretics," I answered. "That would make a great book!" he said. So here we are. Chris and Hannah, thanks for letting me steal this idea. This book is also dedicated to them and to the many potential heretics who took this class at church (I taught it twice at University Baptist in Waco).

Thanks of course must also go to my wife and children for putting up with me during this project. It went on far too long, and I like to think out loud, so my apologies to them for having to put up with heresy in the home. My son liked to point out that I'm doing "that boring theology stuff" every time he saw me at the computer. On a happier note, he told me this week that he is ready to be baptized. My hope for him is that he will always hold to the orthodox faith, while also having the freedom of a heretic's curiosity—a *fides quaerens intellectum*, or, "boring theology stuff."

On the professional level, this work is heavily indebted to a long list of people. First, I thank James Ernest and my friends at Baker Academic for their support, guidance, and patience. Frankly, without James's expertise both in the realm of publishing and in early Christian studies, I would not have trusted myself to undertake this precarious project. Also, for his help throughout much of this project, Josh Thiering deserves much more than the meager hourly pay offered to graduate assistants. Countless little things needed to complete a project like this add up fast, and I owe him a huge debt of gratitude. Next, I thank Baylor University for supporting this project with a research leave. I also thank the dean and the faculty of Truett Seminary, who allowed me to teach this as an elective. The students who took my class also deserve a lot of credit for shaping my thinking. Our Master of Divinity students have got to be some of the best in the country. They are amazing and make this job a blast.

Several people graciously gave of their time and helped with various chapters at various stages. Lest I go on too long in listing them chapter by chapter, I will simply name them in alphabetical order: Richard Bauckham, Scott Bertand, Natalie Carnes, Denny Clark, Ronald Heine, Andrew McGowan, Scot McKnight, Kelley Spoerl, Todd Still, Andrew Teal, Sergey Trostyanskiy, Daniel Williams, and Michael Williams. They certainly deserve more mention than time will allow, for they kept me from making some serious mistakes. Obviously, they are not to blame for any problems remaining in this work, as I am sure they would each write this work or particular chapters very differently than I have done. Their feedback, nevertheless, greatly improved the project. Clare Rothschild read another essay of mine on Marcion that is as yet unpublished. Her detailed insights have been very helpful to me, even if I did not directly address them all in this work. In addition to reading my chapter on the Gnostics, Michael Williams shared copies of forthcoming essays with me that helped to supplement and inform some of my understandings of Gnostic cosmogony. I also wish to thank Fr. Nichalas March for sharing his translation of Gregory of Nyssa's *Antirrheticus adversus Apolinarium* (thesis for Holy Cross Greek Orthodox School of Theology, 2013). The work was still waiting to be bound by Hellenic College Holy Cross's library, and Fr. March graciously shared an electronic copy with me just before the completion of this manuscript. Kelley Spoerl not only read and offered feedback on my Apollinarianism chapter; she also graciously shared as-yet-unpublished work on Apollinaris that helped correct some of my assumptions about the sources and historical development of this important figure. Thanks also go to Abjar Bankhou for conversations that helped me to think more deeply about his own Syrian Christian tradition as well as the Christian encounter with Arabian expansion. This brings me to the last chapter, on Islam, which proved especially challenging. I am deeply indebted to Imam Yusuf Ziya Kavakci for his time in talking with me at length. The same goes for Zeki Saritoprak, who also was of great assistance to me with some of the primary and secondary literature. He shared some of his essays with me that proved very influential to my thinking about the dialogue between the two faiths that has taken place in the past (and could take place in the future).

Finally, let me conclude my acknowledgments with a prayer. Today, August 15, 2013, as I complete this manuscript, the morning news reports that the Egyptian military has declared a state of emergency and has marched against supporters of the ousted president. In doing so, the military opened fire on protesters. According to the Associated Press, the Egyptian Health Ministry has listed the death toll at 421. *Kyrie eleison!* Part of the backlash includes violence directed against the Copts in Egypt. The pressure and attacks against this minority Christian community have steadily increased under the recent waves of political turmoil. The Al Jazeera website has pictures this morning of St. Mary's Church in flames. The same page has a picture of Muslims standing hand in hand around another Christian church, protecting it from extremists. *Kyrie eleison!* I do not mention any of this to point fingers. Violence begets violence, and such a cycle has been going on in Egypt for a long time. Of course, there is more than sectarian violence here, and yet this scene is a staggering reminder of how serious the subject of heresy can be. I do, therefore, wish to add my voice to the prayers offered up on behalf of our sisters and brothers in Egypt. The secularists who may deny being God's children, the Muslims who deeply honor Jesus in their tradition, and the Christians who have been labeled monophysite heretics all deserve our prayers and much more. Over my desk I see a Coptic icon of Madonna and Child given to me by a friend of Egyptian descent. In my ears I hear the voice of Rachel weeping for her children.

Kyrie eleison!

Abbreviations

ACCS	Ancient Christian Commentary on Scripture
ACW	Ancient Christian Writers
ANF	*Ante-Nicene Fathers*
AThR	*Anglican Theological Review*
BRIIFS	*Bulletin of the Royal Institute for Inter-Faith Studies*
BSOAS	*Bulletin of the School of Oriental and African Studies*
ByzZ	*Byzantinische Zeitschrift*
CCSL	Corpus Christianorum: Series latina. Turnhout, 1953–
CH	*Church History*
CHRC	*Church History and Religious Culture*
CSEL	Corpus scriptorum ecclesiasticorum latinorum
DOP	*Dumbarton Oaks Papers*
EC	*Early Christianity*
ER	*Ecumenical Review*
ExpTim	*Expository Times*
FC	Fathers of the Church
FH	*Fides et Historia*
GCS	Die griechische christliche Schriftsteller der ersten [drei] Jahrhunderte
GOTR	*Greek Orthodox Theological Review*
HTR	*Harvard Theological Review*
ICMR	*Islam and Christian-Muslim Relations*
IJFM	*International Journal of Frontier Missions*
JAAR	*Journal of the American Academy of Religion*
JECS	*Journal of Early Christian Studies*
JEH	*Journal of Ecclesiastical History*
JRH	*Journal of Religious History*
JSNT	*Journal for the Study of the New Testament*
JTS	*Journal of Theological Studies*

LCL	Loeb Classical Library
NHL	*The Nag Hammadi Library in English*. Edited by J. M. Robinson. 4th rev. ed. Leiden, 1996
NHMS	Nag Hammadi and Manichaean Studies
NovT	*Novum Testamentum*
NPNF¹	*Nicene and Post-Nicene Fathers*, Series 1
NPNF²	*Nicene and Post-Nicene Fathers*, Series 2
OrChr	*Oriens Christianus*
PBR	*Patristic and Byzantine Review*
PG	Patrologia graeca. Edited by J.-P. Migne. 162 vols. Paris, 1857–86
PO	Patrologia orientalis
ProEccl	*Pro Ecclesia*
PTS	Patristische Texte und Studien
r.	reigned
R&T	*Religion and Theology*
SC	Sources chrétiennes. Paris, 1943–
SJT	*Scottish Journal of Theology*
SocAnth	*Social Anthropology*
SR	*Studies in Religion/Sciences Religieuses*
STK	*Svensk Teologisk Kvartalskrift*
StPatr	*Studia Patristica*
SVTQ	*St. Vladimir's Theological Quarterly*
ThTo	*Theology Today*
TS	*Theological Studies*
TUGAL	Texte und Untersuchungen zur Geschichte der altchristlichen Literatur
USQR	*Union Seminary Quarterly Review*
VC	*Vigiliae Christianae*
VCSup	Supplements to Vigiliae Christianae
WUNT	Wissenschaftliche Untersuchungen zum Neuen Testament
ZAC	*Zeitschrift für Antikes Christentum*

Introduction

Defining Heresy,
Revising Orthodoxy

But I examined the works and traditions of the heretics, defiling my mind for a little time with their abominable opinions, but receiving this benefit from them, that I refuted them by myself, and detested them all the more.

—Dionysius of Alexandria

The rejection of heretics brings into relief what your Church holds and what sound doctrine maintains.

—Augustine

The "Gospel according to . . ." theme stems back to the earliest collection of Gospel texts. That there were four canonical Gospels, that readers had to understand that any one "Gospel" had to be clarified as "according to" someone in particular, bothered some ancient Christians. Around 170 a Christian writer named Tatian called into question the validity of having multiple Gospels—after all, could not God have given one authorized version?—and in order to solve the problem Tatian created a supergospel (called the "Diatessaron") that harmonized all four. To be sure, Tatian was not the first or only Christian to see the Gospels as texts that could

1

be reworked, and so we will return at times to Tatian and the treatment of the Gospel texts later in this book. But for now let us acknowledge that, unlike Tatian, most Christians saw no problem with the "according to" aspect of "the gospel." For the majority of Christian tradition, any retelling or recording of "the gospel" will always be a version "according to" someone. Jesus apparently set up what we call evangelism (notice the borrowed Greek word for "gospel," *euangelion*; i.e., "gospelization") so that the good news would be dispersed in this "according to" strategy (see Acts 1:8). The gospel would always be according to various witnesses.

The four canonical Gospels were not the only ones, and beyond Gospel texts there were numerous expressions of the good news of Jesus Christ, such as oral proclamation, letters, and apocalyptic literature. What about the so-called heretics, who may or may not have written a gospel text, but who nevertheless always had their own particular understanding of the gospel? This book is an attempt to hear what the heretics preached about Jesus.

What If . . . ?

What if (as some say) the "orthodox" version of the story has misled us? What if people like Arius were misrepresented and maligned? At least sometimes that has certainly happened! What if the Gnostics were not wolf-like philosophers in sheep's clothing, but well-intended disciples who utilized a different conceptual and imaginative approach to their theology? I could go on and on with such what-ifs.

These questions are not simply intellectual gymnastics; much less are they conspiracy theories in the making. The best historical studies of the last century have found evidence to suggest that our understanding of the "heretics" is so one-sided as to need revising. This book attempts to take this scholarly reassessment seriously, extensively revising our understanding of each heresy. Beyond an understanding of the heresies themselves, such a study of the various unorthodox alternatives that shaped traditional Christian thinking offers those who wish to understand their own orthodoxy a more complete picture.

If our orthodoxy was forged in the fires of heretical debate, then we had better understand who and what these heresies were. Otherwise, our "orthodoxy" may be a doctrinal equivalent of the emperor's new clothes. On the other hand, what-ifs are hypotheticals that cannot be answered. Therefore some clarifications need to be made about this project of listening to the heretics.

Revising Orthodoxy? Mistake #1: Sensationalism

Let us list some things that this book is *not* trying to do. First, it is not trying to be sensational. Every Easter, the popular media offers specials on "what really happened to Jesus." Even historians who know better can easily be tempted to be sensational for the sake of being sensational, and it must be admitted that a book entitled *The Gospel according to Heretics* looks dangerously close to playing that game. This title, however, was chosen because it captures the dynamic found in the ancient christological debates: the good news of salvation found in Jesus Christ depends very much on how one understands orthodoxy and heresy. Instead of catchy titles and simplistic answers, we are trying to read the ancient Christian writers, acknowledging all their diversity and complexity. The "gospel" is understood here to be the intersection of Christology and soteriology (the doctrine of salvation).

It may also alleviate some fears if I spoil the ending of this book: I think the "heretics"—even if they were not evil, wicked deviants—were wrong. At times, I am almost persuaded by certain so-called heretical doctrines (e.g., monophysitism), and at still other times I have to admit that I belong to a tradition that holds to a certain "heretical" practice (e.g., iconoclasm). Nevertheless, at the end of the day, I see the heresies as heresies because the teachings are inadequate and unconvincing.

To be sure, not all the "heretics" were heretics: many did not say what their opponents claimed they said. Nevertheless, in the chapters that follow, the teachings known as heresies will be found to fall short of the orthodox answers. On the one hand, I am trying to "take the heretics seriously," as Majella Franzmann put it, and even to inquire what can be learned from their silenced voices.[1] On the other hand, while the heretics do need to be reincorporated into the history of early Christianity, reincorporating them into the theology of current Christianity may be another matter altogether. Franzmann concludes by asking, "Why should the paradigm of one Christian group be axiomatic for the history and analysis of the entire movement?" The obvious answer is that it should not be, and neither should the orthodox paradigm be replaced by the heretical, which Franzmann acknowledges: "To allow minority heretical groups a voice that overwhelms the voice of the orthodox would present a similar lack of balance as pertains currently."[2] What follows in this book is not new and improved orthodoxy, but a supplement to our understanding. There is a place for studying orthodoxy, or traditional

1. Majella Franzmann, "A Complete History of Early Christianity: Taking the 'Heretics' Seriously," *JRH* 29, no. 2 (2005): 117–28.
2. Ibid., 128.

views of Christ.[3] The current study, however, is not simply asking the straight-forward questions, who was and is Jesus? Instead, we are asking why certain Christian groups understood Jesus the way they did.[4]

Revising Orthodoxy? Mistake #2: (Hyper-)Skepticism

Second, this book is not undertaking historical criticism just to be critical. To answer this question about why the heretics said what they said, we must go against the grain of traditional Christian thinking, and this certainly will cause some to balk, and perhaps with good reason. Can we simply dismiss everything reported about the heretics? No. Obviously not. The rationale for when and how to revise our history needs some ground rules.

That one of the orthodox made a claim about a certain heretic does not mean we can dismiss said claim and assert the opposite. For example, if an orthodox writer claims a certain heretic was immoral, denied the resurrection, and rejected the practice of baptism, we cannot simply assume that the heretic in question lived a morally perfect life, believed in physical resurrection, and practiced full immersion. It is possible that any combination of those three accusations is true or false or is less than the whole truth or something other than the truth. We are not looking to undo the orthodox claims about her-etics; we are trying to read them closely. The need is not for an antagonistic reading of "orthodox" sources, but an honest and critical reading of them.

This need for a critical reading arises simply because of the admitted bias of the orthodox sources. They explicitly claim to be attacking what they think is a false and even dangerous teaching. The orthodox writers, therefore, have tried to tip the scales in their favor as much as possible—something everyone did at that time. Their heretical opponents, it should be noted, were usually using the same tactic. The current study, however, hopes to rebalance the scales. Since we have heard the orthodox side of the story, and since in many

3. Classic studies include J. N. D. Kelly, *Early Christian Doctrines*, rev. ed. (San Francisco: HarperSanFrancisco, 1978); Aloys Grillmeier, *Christ in Christian Tradition*, vol. 1, *From the Apostolic Age to Chalcedon (451)*, trans. J. S. Bowden (London: Mowbray, 1965), 456–91, and vol. 2, *From the Council of Chalcedon to Gregory the Great (590–604)*, trans. Pauline Allen and John Cawte (London: Mowbray, 1965). A helpful "new map" (as the author calls it on p. x) is Christopher A. Beeley, *The Unity of Christ: Continuity and Conflict in Patristic Tradition* (New Haven: Yale University Press, 2012), for Beeley not only finds many heretics to have been more orthodox than previously thought; he also finds more diversity among the orthodox than is often admitted.

4. For a broader, but less critical, example of such an approach, see Harold O. J. Brown, *Heresies: The Image of Christ in the Mirror of Heresy and Orthodoxy from the Apostles to the Present* (New York: Doubleday, 1984).

instances the heretical side has been deleted from the historical records, let us instead scrutinize the so-called orthodox account.

Revising Orthodoxy? Mistake #3: Subjectivism

Another word of caution. When the modern Protestant liberal movement attempted to uncover the historical Jesus, it used a set of criteria that resulted in a picture of a Jesus who remarkably resembled a modern Protestant liberal. As Albert Schweitzer famously critiqued, these scholars looked down the long well of history only to find their own reflection staring back at them.[5] The current revisionist trend of reading the heretics in a sympathetic light is in danger of making the same mistake.

We cannot read the reports of heretical mistakes and think, "Surely, [*insert heretic here*] did not think that! That would have been foolish." This will be tempting, for example, when we read about the myths of the "Gnostics": surely people of average intelligence did not believe that different aeons emanated down over and over again until one of them shed a tear, which dried into eye crust, which formed the material gunk that later became earth (see chap. 3). While this sentiment represents our intuitive response, such assumptions prove to be wrong. Our best studies suggest some so-called Gnostics did in fact believe exactly that. Our incredulous impulse is driven by our modern preconceptions of what a "person of average intelligence" (i.e., me) would or would not believe. To make such psychological assumptions is entirely unacceptable in a historical study. Such assumptions risk anachronism, ethnocentrism, and egocentrism. Times are different; people are different. We need another set of criteria besides "WWID?" (What Would I Do?).

Since I have brought up the subject of liberalism, allow me to compare the sometimes notorious German liberal method of historical criticism and the present project. Whereas liberalism subjects the Scriptures to what has been labeled a hermeneutic of suspicion, the approach of the current project is not *just* a hermeneutic of suspicion. I make the distinction because of the

---

5. Albert Schweitzer, *The Quest of the Historical Jesus: A Critical Study of Its Progress from Reimarus to Wrede*, trans. W. Montgomery (London: Adam and Charles Black, 1910). To be sure, more evenhanded "quests" are still ongoing; see the criteria for such an endeavor that have received widespread acceptance in John P. Meier, *A Marginal Jew: Rethinking the Historical Jesus*, vol. 1, *The Roots of the Problem and the Person* (New York: Doubleday, 1991), 167–83. For a moderately optimistic view as to how much data can be uncovered, even if the data stems from the "Christ of faith," see the approaches of James D. G. Dunn, *Jesus Remembered* (Grand Rapids: Eerdmans, 2003), esp. 335–36; and Richard Bauckham, *Jesus and the Eyewitnesses: The Gospels as Eyewitness Testimony* (Grand Rapids: Eerdmans, 2006), esp. 114–47, 472–508.

problems in which the historical-critical approach to Scripture has mired itself. Many, even many self-described liberals (or now "postliberals"), have bemoaned the hermeneutic of suspicion as not so much a method as a blank check to question whatever one wants to call into question. In such a climate, the main point of scriptural study gets lost.[6]

The primary difference between applying a hermeneutic of suspicion to Scripture and applying it to the orthodox opponents of the heretics is that the orthodox writers attempted to portray the heretics in the worst possible light. Any uncritical reading of these sources, any hermeneutic of trust, will inevitably be misled. Therefore, given the drastic difference in tone between the orthodox writers and the Gospel writers (for example), the former corpus merits a more critical stance.

Just how the hermeneutic of suspicion can be utilized in a more methodologically consistent way is beyond the scope of what can be said here. It should be used (and is used in what follows), but for now suffice it to say that any approach to the early Christian writings that simply calls into question whatever it wants to call into question is doomed to lack credibility.[7] Instead of simply questioning the traditionalist view for the sake of questioning, I will attempt to show why any given item needs to be called into question.

Reinterpreting Orthodoxy: A Theoretical Practice

To explain how we can read the heretics, we need a few words about facts and a critical interpretation. First, a critical examination of such central tenets does not necessarily require a "true objectivity," as if such a thing were possible, as if one could become an agnostic and start from a blank slate. Although I admittedly start from a subjective position (the position of faith), my faith still questions. As a wise man once told me, "It's okay to doubt your beliefs, but it's not okay to believe your doubts" (thanks, Dad).[8] In short, this work is a free and open examination of those central tenets of the faith by a person of faith. In the classical Christian tradition of Augustine and Anselm, this

6. See esp. Hans Frei, *The Eclipse of Biblical Narrative* (New Haven: Yale University Press, 1974).

7. This is often the critique, for example, of Gerd Lüdemann, *Heretics: The Other Side of Early Christianity*, trans. John Bowden (Louisville: Westminster John Knox, 1996).

8. For doubt as a structural necessity for faith, see both Karl Barth, *Evangelical Theology: An Introduction*, trans. Grover Foley (New York: Holt, Rinehart and Winston, 1963), 131–32; and Paul Tillich, *Dynamics of Faith* (New York: Harper & Row, 1957), 18–19. Also cf. the paradoxical wisdom of Augustine, *On the Trinity* 9.1: "Let us doubt without unbelief of things to be believed."

endeavor is called "faith seeking understanding." What is not normal in the classical tradition is to lean past the authoritative voices of the early church and listen to those early groups who have been labeled "heretics" by the winners, but who simply called themselves "Christians." Can we learn anything from them? We certainly can try.

When we try to reread texts in a new light, we face certain challenges. There is simply no owner's manual for how to do this. To borrow a pop-culture analogy, in the film *The Matrix*, characters can easily learn how to fly a helicopter: since their brains are plugged into a computer, they simply download a digital copy of the pilot's manual. Philosophically, this same concept was articulated by the Enlightenment thinker John Locke (not to be confused with the guy from the television drama *Lost*). Locke argued that our minds are a blank slate, or a *tabula rasa*, and when we see, hear, smell, read, and so on, we more or less download that information onto our minds (not his description, of course).

In a post-Enlightenment era, Locke's view is no longer credible. That is, unless Morpheus frees you from the Matrix; but remember, that has not happened to most of us. All of us are trapped in what Paul calls "this body of death" (Rom. 7:24) or what Jean François Lyotard (a more recent philosopher) called "the postmodern condition."[9] We do not download "facts"; rather, we interpret them. The famous critic of modernity Friedrich Nietzsche confidently concluded that there are no such things as facts, only interpretations. When you read the Bible, for example, you read it through the lens of your experiences. If you are rich or poor, black or white, male or female, Egyptian or American, the chances are you will read the very same text in a very different way. The same occurs when we read our earliest Christian texts.

I mention this "postmodern condition" in order to make clear what this project is doing. This is an attempt to *reinterpret* the heretics in a different light. I do not begin with this pessimistic view of what one can (not) know so as to cause despair. When one encounters the wall of interpretations and accepts that we will never scale it to find "facts," it is tempting to give up. Why try to say anything, if anyone can say whatever anyone wants? Such a cry of dereliction, while understandable, is not the final word.

Even if we accept Nietzsche's claim that "there are no facts, only interpretations," we can also move past him with Clifford Geertz and insist that some interpretations are better than others.[10] Another proponent of the postmodern

9. Jean François Lyotard, *The Postmodern Condition: A Report on Knowledge* (Minneapolis: University of Minnesota Press, 1984).

10. David N. Gellner, "Religion, Politics, and Ritual: Remarks on Geertz and Bloch," *SocAnth* 7, no. 2 (1999): 136.

condition is Jacques Derrida, who championed deconstruction, according to which every meaning and interpretation is open to being dismantled and reinterpreted—if not ad infinitum, then ad nauseum![11] For this approach, he was often accused of nihilism, the notion that there is *no* meaning to anything. To be fair to poor Derrida, he never claimed this himself; instead, he claimed that there was always *more* meaning than any one interpretation lets on. What is usually missed in critiques of Derrida is how Derrida went on to insist that despite the inevitable insufficiency of any interpretation, an interpretation must be made nonetheless. One must "go for it," or to use Derrida's preferred, controversial terminology, one must "make the cut" (i.e., like circumcision).

Interestingly, Derrida toward the end of his life reclaimed his own circumcision; that is, he reclaimed his own Jewish heritage and confessed to his secret life of "prayers and tears." In said "confession" (or, again in his Derridean way, his "Circumfession"), Derrida chose to interact with none other than a writer from the early church, a former heretic turned heresy hunter, Augustine.[12] If Derrida can do it, so can you!

If all of this philosophical justification is a bit too abstract for our purposes, perhaps the reader will indulge me as I retell a joke I heard from my friend Jon Harrison, a mathematical physicist (Baylor University).

> Once upon a time, a politician, a statistician, and a mathematical physicist were riding on a train through Scotland. They all looked out the window and saw a black sheep. The politician said, "Look, Scottish sheep are black!" The statistician said, "No, one Scottish sheep is black." The mathematical physicist corrected them both: "No, at least one side of one Scottish sheep is black."

The point of this mathematical attempt at humor (sorry, Jon) is to clarify what methodology we wish to use. The method of a politician (generalizing from specifics) will certainly get it wrong. On the other hand, the temptation to limit ourselves to some sort of mathematical precision (talking only about one side of one sheep) will render us virtually unable to say anything, if not

---

11. For the understanding of Derrida given here, see John D. Caputo, *The Prayers and Tears of Jacques Derrida: Religion without Religion* (Bloomington: Indiana University Press, 1997).

12. In the book with Geoffrey Bennington, *Jacques Derrida*, trans. G. Bennington (Chicago: University of Chicago Press, 1993). Interestingly, many so-called postmodern thinkers made the same "religious turn": Hannah Arendt, *Love and Saint Augustine*, ed. Joanna Vecchiarelli Scott and Judith Chelius Stark (Chicago: University of Chicago Press, 1996); John D. Caputo, *On Religion* (London: Routledge, 2001); Michel Foucault, *The History of Sexuality*, vol. 4 (unavailable to the public; see Elizabeth A. Clark, "Foucault, the Fathers and Sex," *JAAR* 56, no. 4 [1988]: 619–41); and Jean-François Lyotard, *The Confessions of Augustine*, trans. Richard Beardsworth (Stanford, CA: Stanford University Press, 2000), to name a few prominent examples.

make us look just plain cowardly—after all, the odds are good both sides of that sheep were black. The middle way of interpreting "facts" (which is still different from the statistician, who was simply less mathematically precise) is not a science but an art.

While the task of undertaking history as an artful interpretation may seem daunting, the reader should take comfort. The recent trend toward revisionist history has produced surprisingly fruitful results. While this debate is still ongoing and may appear (or even be) somewhat chaotic at the moment, I ask the reader to jump into this stream of thought and join in the attempt to reinterpret the early Christian period.

Reinterpreting Orthodoxy: A Traditional Practice

While there is no rulebook for how to reread the early church, as evidenced by the lack of consensus on any given point in the discipline of early Christian studies, some who have gone before us have blazed trails we can follow. Christianity has always recognized how any new expression of the gospel must be tethered to the historical tradition that came before. This began with the original Jesus community, which claimed to be witnesses to Jesus, but within which conflict quickly arose between various Christian groups that claimed to be heirs to the apostles. Through this period of contested claims, all parties fought to show how their own view aligned with the traditional one, and during the period of the ecumenical councils this claim to tradition grew even more pronounced.

Even in the Protestant Reformation, the emphasis on *sola scriptura* was never meant to replace the classic expression of the Christian faith.[13] Instead, Protestants claimed that late medieval Catholicism had somewhere steered off course. It is true that much unfortunate rhetoric against the pope as antichrist resulted in confusion among Protestants about the role of Christian history. Luther himself brought this historical revision to the forefront in his work *On the Councils and the Church* (1539). Luther underscored how the church's traditions sometimes need to be, and often have been, corrected. This historical approach set a new trajectory for Reformation and even Enlightenment thinking.

In 1699 Gottfried Arnold, himself a good Lutheran, boldly entitled his book on church history *The Impartial History of the Church and the Heretics*. His attempt to be "impartial" and listen to the heretics was not as objective as

---

13. For this view, see D. H. Williams, *Evangelicals and Tradition: The Formative Influence of the Early Church* (Grand Rapids: Baker Academic, 2005).

Arnold thought, for he was criticized for being too sympathetic to the heretics, and so his "unbiased" history was in fact still biased, only in the opposite direction from that of the traditional telling of the story. Nonetheless, Arnold set the stage for modern historians to endeavor to reread the early church.[14] In the wake of an Arnoldian era of church history, Walter Bauer later became a leading voice in this discussion. Bauer rejected the older model of a united and unambiguous orthodoxy from which heretics deviated. Alternatively, Bauer hypothesized, "Perhaps—I repeat, perhaps—certain manifestations of Christian life that the authors of the church renounce as 'heresies' originally had not been such at all, but, at least here and there, were the only form of the new religion—that is, for those regions they were simply 'Christianity.'"[15] Today, most scholars have replaced Bauer's caution with confidence: instead of early orthodox Christianity, we must speak of numerous, heterogeneous Christian*ities*.

Reinterpreting Orthodoxy: A Transparent Practice

Following in the wake of Luther, Arnold, and many others, we will reexamine ten major heresies and attempt to take seriously an "impartial" approach. Since true objectivity is impossible, I have tried to be as transparent as possible about my interpretations and rationale in each chapter that follows. I have cited the primary sources as much as possible, but since the debate is how to read the given primary sources, I have also referred to secondary sources about matters that are contested. Two factors constrained my use of these sources. First, space would not allow inclusion of all of the secondary literature, and so I have kept the scholarly debates and references to a minimum. My use of these sources has also been truncated by the desire to make this work as accessible as possible for those new to the academic debates. It is hoped, however, that the secondary discussions have been adequately heard and represented. Where secondary sources are cited, either they provide the reader with helpful further discussion on the issue at hand or they credit a scholar with a particular interpretation. Second, and again because the audience in mind will include nonspecialists, the sources are almost strictly in English. I

14. For an excellent review of Christian historians such as Arnold, see Philip Schaff and David S. Schaff, *History of the Christian Church* (New York: Scribner's Sons, 1910), 1:27–54. For an excellent review of Christian historians such as the Schaffs, see Elizabeth A. Clark, *Founding the Fathers: Early Church History and Protestant Professors in Nineteenth-Century America* (Philadelphia: University of Pennsylvania Press, 2011).

15. Walter Bauer, *Orthodoxy and Heresy in Earliest Christianity*, ed. Robert A. Kraft and Gerhard Kroedel (Philadelphia: Fortress, 1979), xxii.

have consulted the critical editions of the primary sources (see bibliography), but where possible I have used and listed the English translation. Hopefully, the following chapters have heard the primary sources afresh, or at the least offered the readers the opportunity to do so on their own.

As much as we want to avoid some of the extremes of revisionist history and sensationalism mentioned above, there is no escaping the need to rethink our understanding of the ancient heretics. Some history needs revising. Rethinking the traditional version of things, however, can be difficult. For example, in a 1976 essay revisiting Athanasius's teachings, G. C. Stead cautiously addressed the subject:

> To an extraordinary degree the faith of Athanasius has become the faith of the Church, and to criticize him must look as if we wished to shatter the rock from which we were hewn. Nevertheless I have come to think that the methods used by Athanasius in defending his faith will not serve to commend eternal truths to the present age; and it is for the Church's ultimate good that we seek to show where their weakness lies.[16]

While many today still sympathize with Stead, his cautioning also sounds somewhat outdated. For one thing, virtually the whole guild of early Christian studies has embraced the so-called revisionist approach. Furthermore, Stead's statement merely begs the question: is Athanasius—or are any of the fathers of the church—the church's "rock"? Of course not, and Stead knows it. His point is that such respected voices may seem disrespected when read with a critical eye. Disrespect, however, is not the intent. Instead, the point is honesty. When we talk about orthodoxy, let's be honest. To do so, we need to be clear in what we mean by "orthodoxy," and so we must define a few terms.

Rethinking Orthodoxy: Specifying Terms

The reader may have already noticed that I have had to put certain terms like "orthodoxy" and "heresy" in quotation marks. I will avoid this annoying practice as much as possible, but it has to be acknowledged that terms like these do need qualification.

Definitions of Heresy

The Greek word *hairesis* simply means "faction" or "party." Ancient philosophy students would claim to be "of Plato" or "of Pythagoras," to name

16. G. Christopher Stead, "Rhetorical Method in Athanasius," VC 30 (1976): 136–37.

but two examples. They were of that "heresy," or faction. Later Christian authors, however, began using the term in opposition to the "catholic," or universal, church. They, the "heretics," were of the wrong party because they broke away and formed their own "faction" and taught wrong teachings. This use of the word, however, was an accusation against the so-called heretical group, and that group most likely disputed the charges.

For example, in the early second century, Ignatius, the bishop of Antioch, admitted, "For there are some who are accustomed to carrying about the Name maliciously and deceitfully while doing other things unworthy of God. You must avoid them as wild beasts."[17] In other words, the people Ignatius labeled heretics identified themselves by "the Name," calling themselves followers of Christ, or Christians. Similarly, Augustine bemoaned the fact that "heretics . . . have the Christian name . . . they too at any rate are called Christians."[18]

Both the orthodox and the heretics called themselves Christian. We will see in many of the chapters that follow that the so-called heretics call themselves orthodox and call their opponents heretics. Since these terms are contested, they become very difficult to define.

Definitions of Orthodoxy

The term "orthodoxy" itself needs to be defined, or at least disambiguated. This word can mean any one of the following:

1. The Eastern Orthodox Church, as opposed to the Roman Catholic Church or any Protestant denomination—a meaning rarely used in this book.

2. The orthodox church or party, as opposed to the heretical, false church— this meaning is often used in this book. The problem for this definition has to do with who gets to decide which party can claim to be the true church and which party gets labeled the wrong or heretical church.

3. The correct doctrine, as opposed to false teaching, or "heresy"—this meaning is often used in this book. The Greek word *orthos* means "straight," "right," or "correct," and the word *doxa* means "opinion" or "teaching." Add these two together and we have *ortho-doxy*. The problem for this definition is the same as above. Who gets to decide which teaching is the correct and which is the false?

17. *To the Ephesians* 7.
18. *City of God* 18.51.

Because terms like "orthodoxy" and "heresy" are contested, it becomes impossible to offer objective and stable definitions. Perhaps we could find alternative categories.

One attempt at new terminology occurs when scholars distinguish proto-orthodoxy from orthodoxy to indicate the early Christians who taught correctly before correct doctrine had been defined by the ecumenical councils. For our study, however, this practice gives too much preference to those later periods. Another attempt to find new categories is the common practice of differentiating between orthodox, heretical, and heterodox views. This last term implies the writers whose teachings did not meet approval later, but who could not have known that they were saying something unorthodox in their own day. Again, this is a step in the right direction, but it still gives too much authority to later voices.

Perhaps we are asking the wrong question. Instead of asking, "What is orthodoxy?" we should ask, "Who gets to define what is orthodox?" As for this last question, the now-cliché answer is, "The winners." In the present book, we would like to hear how orthodoxy was defined by "the losers." To hear the losers, or heretics, is admittedly an impossible task in most cases—after all, they are all dead and their books were mostly burned. As a starting point, historians now assume that even the most pious and dogmatic statements from church history, such as the acts of the ecumenical councils, were "propaganda."[19] To be sure, this is only to say that all views are biased, and so this observation cannot be used to dismiss those councils. Historians also assume that the theological declarations contained within those acts represent the sincere faith of those who espoused them. The issue today is whether the declarations about who is orthodox and who is heretical can be reassessed.

We want to reread certain sources because there are problems in those sources. First, not all texts mean the same thing when using the word "heresy." As already discussed, the term originally meant a party or faction, but it later came to imply something more sinister. The very fact that the concept of heresy has a history should cause us to pause and reevaluate the sources. Can earlier writers be held accountable to a later standard? For example, New Testament authors never used the word "Trinity." Does that make them untrinitarian? Not necessarily. It does, however, beg the reader to attempt to read those texts on their own terms and in their own context. The same can and should be done for all primary sources.

19. See Thomas Graumann, "'Reading' the First Council of Ephesus (431)," in *Chalcedon in Context: Church Councils 400–700*, ed. Richard Price and Mary Whitby (Liverpool: Liverpool University Press, 2009), 28.

Another reason that some texts need rereading is that—to put it bluntly—some texts cannot be trusted. History is written by the winners, and too often the winners are violent and oppressive.[20] This claim suggests that we should define orthodoxy as violence. Even when the orthodox were not physically violent, they were rhetorically violent.[21] This claim, in turn, suggests that we should define orthodoxy as rhetoric. Even if the orthodox were not malicious but products of their time, they were part of a violent culture.[22] This third claim suggests that we should define orthodoxy as culture. While these definitions need to be supplemented, the benefit of all of them is that they avoid the older understanding of orthodoxy as a static thing, like right statements. The sources are clear that terms like "Trinity" were late and developed their own meaning. What is more, this older definition is not old enough: it is a modern definition of orthodoxy, not the ancient definition that the early Christians themselves used.

In short, no single definition of heresy was ever fixed, agreed on, and therefore stable enough to use in a critical analysis. Perhaps we could learn more about defining heresy by defining its opposite. Let us look at a few of the ideas that ancient Christians used to define "orthodoxy."

Characteristics of Orthodoxy

For many early Christian writers, a key characteristic of being orthodox was to be ancient. "Ancient" was variously defined as apostolic (i.e., the same as the original apostles) or traditional (i.e., the same as that which has always been handed down from generation to generation). Paul admitted to being a latecomer. He was a last and least apostle, the "last of all, . . . one untimely born" (1 Cor. 15:8), but he insisted that "the good news [*euangelion*] that I proclaimed to you" (1 Cor. 15:1) was the same as that which had been "handed

20. According to Averil Cameron, "The Violence of Orthodoxy," in *Heresy and Identity in Late Antiquity*, ed. Eduard Iricinschi and Holger M. Zellentin (Tübingen: Mohr Siebeck, 2008), 102–14.
21. See the following influential works: Elizabeth A. Clark, *The Origenist Controversy: The Cultural Construction of an Early Christian Debate* (Princeton: Princeton University Press, 1992); Rebecca Lyman, "A Topography of Heresy: Mapping the Rhetorical Creation of Arianism," in *Arianism after Arius: Essays on the Development of the Fourth-Century Trinitarian Conflicts*, ed. M. R. Barnes and D. H. Williams (Edinburgh: T&T Clark, 1993), 45–62; and Virginia Burrus, *The Making of a Heretic: Gender, Authority, and the Priscillianist Controversy* (Berkeley: University of California Press, 1995).
22. Rebecca Lyman, "Natural Resources: Tradition without Orthodoxy," *AThR* 84 (2002): 67–80; Lyman, "Hellenism and Heresy," *JECS* 11 (2003): 209–22; along different lines, Lewis Ayres, *Nicaea and Its Legacy: An Approach to Fourth-Century Trinitarian Theology* (Oxford: Oxford University Press, 2004).

on" since the beginning (1 Cor. 15:3). The noun from the Greek verb translated "handed on" is *paradosis*, the equivalent of the Latin *traditio*—tradition. Orthodoxy is traditional.

The content of this apostolic tradition is the same gospel (*euangelion*) and the same preaching (*kērygma*) that Paul's colleagues preached elsewhere (see Gal. 1–2). This content can be summarized: "that Christ died for our sins in accordance with the scriptures, and that he was buried, and that he was raised on the third day in accordance with the scriptures" (1 Cor. 15:3–4). This summary, however, cannot be understood as exhaustive. Surely, Paul preaches about the God that Jesus called Father! Surely Paul preaches about the Spirit of Christ sent to the believers! Of course, the point is that such summaries are exactly that: the summary of the whole gospel preached since the original apostolic times and still preached by those who hold to the tradition. Anyone who deviates—even from seemingly ancillary parts of this gospel, such as the *koinōnia*, fellowship or communion, that results from it—is to be considered "accursed" (Gal. 1:8). Paul's Greek term for accursed, *anathema*, will be used against all who deviate from this tradition in the generations that follow.[23]

Later Christians will develop this kind of thinking to respond to various teachings deemed deviant. The classical creeds, such as the Nicene, were understood to stand in a direct line of succession from the earliest *kērygma*. Before there were precise creeds, formulated by official teachers and councils of the church, many Christian writers invoked the Rule of Faith.

This rule looks to us like a creed. It is triune in outline—belief in "God the Father Almighty . . . and Jesus Christ . . . and the Holy Spirit"—but was not a creed for those who used it. At least, it was not an official declaration of any council, and the precision of the statements themselves was not the issue. Many second- and third-century Christians cited this same rule but with slightly altered wording and emphases. The claim that this rule was believed by everyone everywhere since the apostolic times is certainly an exaggeration. It was a compelling argument against unorthodox teachers who did not align with this rule. What may be more accurate is that Paul's "tradition," the later "rule," and the creeds all refer to the same content: the gospel.

What about the Bible? Counterintuitive to many modern Christians, especially Protestants, is the fact that the gospel, the tradition, and the creeds all preceded the Bible. Of course, by "the Bible" we mean the bound book of specific Jewish and Christian Scriptures. If, instead of the Bible, we asked about

---

23. It is worth noting that the only group later deemed "heretics" mentioned in the New Testament is the Nicolaitans (Rev. 2:6, 15). But very little is known of this group (see Kenneth A. Fox, "The Nicolaitans, Nicolaus, and the Early Church," *SR* 23, no. 4 [1994]: 485–96).

"the Scriptures," then we would find more overlap and mutually informed content. The fact remains that the books that made it into the church's Bible were the ones that met the "rule" of the church, orthodoxy. The Greek writers preferred to call the Rule of Faith by the name "the Canon of Truth." The "canon" as we think of it today—the books that made it into the Bible—is inverted from the order in the ancient Christian thought: the canon was the rule, the standard of orthodoxy that had to be met, in order for certain books to be included in the church's practice and preaching.

To be sure, this is a complex issue and raises a lot of questions, but the point is that in the earliest Christian centuries one couldn't simply say orthodoxy is the teaching that is true to the Scriptures, because both the Scriptures and their interpretation were being contested.[24] The often-ill-defined core of the Christian faith—not a creed, not a set of Scriptures, but the gospel of Jesus Christ as known in the apostolic preaching and tradition—was the stated difference between orthodox and unorthodox. These characteristics of orthodoxy have their opposite in the stated characteristics of heresy. (If the reader feels like we are going back and forth between orthodoxy and heresy, that's because we are. But we're almost done, so bear with me.)

Characteristics of Heresy

If orthodoxy is classically defined as ancient and traditional, then heresy by default is novel and deviant.[25] The alleged motivations of heretical deviation are numerous and usually malicious. The most innocent explanation is that heretics were overly curious.[26] Only slightly better is the claim that heretics were simply stupid.[27] They are still curious, but are too stupid to find the orthodox answers.

The more sinister accusations include claims about the heretics' immorality. For example, Valentinus was jealous of not being selected bishop (Tertullian, *Against Valentinus* 4.1), and the Gnostics on the whole were libertines (see chap. 3). Similarly, the heretics never suffered martyrdom (according to

24. For those concerned about this approach being taken too far, see the counterarguments of Alister McGrath, *Heresy: A History of Defending the Truth* (New York: HarperCollins, 2009).
25. Best summarized by Tertullian, *Prescript against Heretics* 29.
26. E.g., Hippolytus, *Against Noetus* 16.6: "Are you not satisfied to be told that the Son of God was made manifest for your salvation, if you would have but faith? But in your meddling curiosity do you look for how he was born according to the Spirit?"
27. E.g., Gregory of Nazianzus, *Letter* 102: "What could be more unreasonable than this . . . [i.e., Apollinarianism—see chap. 6]? . . . For though it has a certain sophistical grace through the quickness of its antithesis, and a sort of juggling quackery grateful to the uninstructed, yet it is the most absurd of absurdities and the most foolish of follies."

Eusebius, *Ecclesiastical History* 5.16.12)—except for when they did (e.g., Eusebius, *Ecclesiastical History* 5.16.21). The devil is working behind the scenes when it comes to heretics, as he did with Judas (cf. John 13:2).[28] Tragically, the rhetoric of the church sometimes quickly devolved into using anti-Semitisms (cf. John 8:44), claiming that heretics were a "second Judaism."[29] The hyperbolic nature of such accusations is obvious, for the same heretics are often accused of "hellenizing," or using Greek philosophy. The accusations are undoubtedly unfair caricatures, but they all illustrate the deviancy inherent in any heresy. Heresy is a deviation from the truth.

The problem with such characterizations of heresy is that the heretics themselves would likely claim they were traditional and not novel—see the Bauer thesis, mentioned above. This is especially the case when certain questions were unclear in earlier sources. Therefore, while these characterizations do help us clarify what the early Christians meant by "heresy," they still do not define the content of that heresy, or its orthodox alternative. At this point, we have seen the generalizations made by the early Christian writers about orthodoxy and heresy. The discussion can now proceed to look to the specific heresies themselves to see how these terms were used on a case-by-case basis.

Rethinking Orthodoxy: Specifying Claims

Since we cannot begin our investigation with a predetermined and undisputed definition of either orthodoxy or heresy, we will have to proceed by looking to see how each heretic and teaching came to be seen as unorthodox. Every case is different. While strategies of refuting heresy are borrowed and repeated, there is no simple pattern for how to recognize and attack heresy, writ large. The same emphasis must be made about how to analyze each heresy. Some heretics are almost entirely unattainable to us except in the version of their opponents (e.g., the Ebionites and Eutyches). Others left a surprising number of sources for us to hear their views firsthand (e.g., the so-called Gnostics and Nestorius). Therefore, each chapter will have to begin afresh with another person and another context.

In order to aid the reader, each chapter begins with a simple summary. This is usually the view expressed about the heretic by the orthodox opponents. Each summary is then supplemented with a closer investigation into the accused heretic and the alleged heresy. The heretic in most cases probably did

28. E.g., Cyprian, *On the Unity of the Church* 1.3; Athanasius, *Defense of the Nicene Definition* 2.
29. E.g., Gregory of Nazianzus, *Letter* 101.

not actually teach the heresy named after him. For example, Nestorius most likely did not teach "Nestorianism." An alternate name is given, therefore, for the actual teaching in order to differentiate what Nestorius himself said (according to our best sources) from the Nestorian heresy (known from the hostile sources). Again, every case is different: Arius probably taught the heretical doctrine of subordinationism, but even then the term needs to be used instead of "Arianism" because many, if not most, of those deemed "Arians" never read anything by Arius. The heretical doctrine is the main issue, even if it was attached to a certain "arch-heretic" (as the founders of heresy were called), and even if historians doubt the credibility of the accusation against the accused heretic.

Just as it is tempting to abandon the categories of orthodoxy and heresy altogether, it will be tempting to abandon labels like "Ebionites," "Gnostics," and "Arians" (each for unique reasons). To erase these labels altogether, however, will cause more problems than it solves in the current study. Since we are reviewing the primary sources to see how they can be reinterpreted, we must begin with the terms used by these sources, only we will try to unpack them and see past the veneers of misrepresentation and libel. Also, while the labels themselves may do a disservice to the history of the controversy in question, the labels came to have a life of their own in later theological discussions. The term "adoptionism" as used of the Ebionites, as best I can tell, is a complete misnomer. Nonetheless, both the category of adoptionism and that of Ebionism need to be retained because they are used against later heretics like Paul of Samosata. A similar phenomenon can be found with docetism and the much later Manichaeans, and other teachings also seen to compromise the full humanity of Christ.

Lastly, since this work is a work of reinterpretation, others may not agree with all of my interpretations. Wherever possible, I have tried to represent views on which a majority of scholars agree. At times, however, I have ventured away from the flock and offered my own reading. I have tried to indicate these moments in each chapter with the various notes, since the nonspecialist still deserves to have these admitted up front. Some will want more nuance and more sources, and others fewer or different sources. For these shortcomings, I can only plead for patience and point to the limitations of space and time.

In all of the chapters that follow, the parameters are set by the question of Christology. Christology, of course, cannot be completely disentangled from other doctrines, and so other questions do arise. For example, Christology does not simply ask who Jesus is but also seeks to know what Jesus does. Therefore, the other major doctrine that remains in the purview of this study is soteriology, or the doctrine of salvation. I do not, however, undertake a full investigation into atonement theory, because that takes us beyond the scope of these sources. Theological questions about the nature of God and anthropological questions about the nature of humanity are unavoidable and often take center stage, but they always do so because Christ's divine nature and/or human nature is in question. Other larger doctrines, such as ontology, cosmology, and epistemology, are discussed, but not exhaustively. These major themes, despite their far-reaching ramifications in our thinking and despite the dizzying display of diverse forms in the sources, all nicely intersect in the theme of the gospel. It is the gospel of Jesus Christ, but it is according to heresy.

Recommended Bibliography

Bauer, Walter. *Orthodoxy and Heresy in Earliest Christianity*. Edited by Robert A. Kraft and Gerhard Kroedel. Philadelphia: Fortress, 1979.

Brown, Dan. *The Da Vinci Code*. New York: Doubleday, 2003. Just kidding . . . but you know you wanted to see it listed here!

Dehandschutter, Boudewijn. "Heresy and the Early Christian Notion of Tradition." In *Heretics and Heresies in the Ancient Church and in Eastern Christianity*, edited by Joseph Verheyden and Herman Teule, 7–21. Leuven: Peeters, 2011.

Edwards, Mark. *Catholicity and Heresy in the Early Church*. Farnham, UK: Ashgate, 2009.

Iricinschi, Eduard, and Holger M. Zellentin, eds. *Heresy and Identity in Late Antiquity*. Tübingen: Mohr Siebeck, 2008.

**Summary:
Marcionites**

**Key Doctrine:
Supersessionism**

- Jesus = God 2.0
- The God of the Old Testament = bad, mean, judging; but the Jesus-God of the New Testament = good, nice, loving

Key Date

- 144: Marcion is condemned by Christians in Rome

1

Marcion

Supersessionism

Marcion . . . a wolf from Pontus.
—Justin Martyr

Marcion . . . a mouse from Pontus.
—Tertullian

We should not mistake the accusations of Marcion's opponents for the substance of his opinions.

—Joseph R. Hoffman

In the middle of the second century, Marcion approached the highly revered bishop Polycarp, asking for approval and "recognition." In response, Polycarp retorted, "I 'recognize' you. You're the firstborn of Satan!"[1]

---

1. As reported by Irenaeus, *Against Heresies* 3.3.4 (my loose translation). It should be noted that many recent scholars reject the historicity of this scene.

What did Marcion do or teach to deserve such a biting one-liner? From Polycarp's perspective (and the perspective of the orthodox party that would emerge), Marcion blasphemed God, meaning he taught the following.

1. Marcion denounced the God of the Old Testament; and so he
2. rejected the Jewish Scriptures, and so he also
3. claimed creation to be evil.

Such teachings, however, must not have been seen as blasphemy or heresy by all. For example, many Christians—called "Marcionites" by their opponents—followed Marcion. In fact, some in the early church bemoaned the spread of Marcion's teachings over the whole earth.[2] It is telling that an outsider would hardly be able to distinguish "catholic" churches from "Marcionite" churches.[3] For that matter, long after Marcionism had been rejected by the catholic party, bishops worried that new converts would not be able to tell the difference between a Marcionite church and a "catholic" one.[4] Our outline of Marcion's "blasphemies," of course, is the version told by the non-Marcionite Christians. We must, then, try to hear Marcion's side of the story. Before we can do so, let us begin with what we know of Marcion's life.

Just the "Facts," Marcion, Just the "Facts"

Marcion comes from the town of Sinope in the region of Pontus, which was located on the southern shore of the Black Sea (modern-day Turkey), but his impact on Christian history occurs when he arrives in Rome.[5] Exactly when he was born and died cannot be known, but he arrived in Rome by 144.[6] As for his background, we can list not so much facts as accusations, since all we know of him comes from his opponents. The "facts" are as follows.

2. Justin Martyr, *1 Apology* 26.5–6; Tertullian, *Against Marcion* 5.19.2. In the middle of the fourth century Epiphanius claims "Marcionites" can be found in Italy, Egypt, Palestine, Arabia, Cyprus, Thebaid, and Persia (*Panarion* 42.1.2).

3. See, e.g., the non-Christian Celsus's accusations in Origen, *Against Celsus* 2.27; 6.52–53, 74; and cf. the accounts of Marcionite martyrs below.

4. See Cyril of Jerusalem, *Catechetical Lectures* 18.26; cf. Theodoret of Cyrrhus, *Letter* 113.

5. The town of Sinope and the account of Marcion's debate in Rome are known only in the later sources (although cf. Tertullian, *Against Marcion* 1.1.5), and so they are debatable. It is hard to see why anyone would invent Sinope in particular, however, and so most scholars accept it.

6. The date of 144 is based on Tertullian, *Against Marcion* 1.19.2.

"Catholic"

In the early Christian centuries, the term "catholic" did not mean Roman Catholic. The word more simply meant "universal" or, literally, "according to the whole" (Greek *kata* + *holos*). Early Christian writers claimed to belong to the whole church in order to distinguish themselves from the heretics, who were understood as belonging to rogue sects. Before long, "catholic" becomes the precise title for churches that are non-Marcionite, or non-Gnostic, or some other such distinction. The catholic party is said to be the one true church. On the other hand, these sects claim the opposite: they belong to the true church, and their opponents have deviated from the true teachings of the true church. In general the term "catholic" will be used here to refer to those who were considered such by later generations, although there will be times when the problems with the label will be called to the reader's attention.

a. He was wealthy. Or, this may be a way to discredit him (cf. Matt. 19:16–22; James 5:1).

b. His wealth came from being a shipowner. Or, this too could be a contrast with Jesus's first disciples (cf. Mark 1:20).

c. He gave a very large gift to the church in Rome on his arrival there. Or, this could be portraying Marcion as one who bribes (cf. Exod. 23:8; Acts 8:20).[7]

d. His mentor was a renowned heretic named Cerdo. Or, Marcion's ideas sound like Cerdo's ideas, and this connection is the surest way to discredit him.[8]

e. His father was a bishop, who excommunicated him in Sinope for raping a virgin.[9] Or, Marcion's teachings violated the "virgin Bride" (i.e., the church)—later Christians simply misunderstood.

7. But of course the Christians gave the money back (see Tertullian, *Against Marcion* 4.4.3; 5.17.1)—or, Tertullian does not wish to make unnecessary enemies, and so he will assume that the money was returned to Marcion. This accusation is also problematic because the sources do not agree as to the details of this account: Epiphanius (*Panarion* 42.1.7–8) insists that no one in Rome received him into the fellowship but that he was instead recognized as a heretic from the beginning and there was a later debate between him and the elders.

8. Unlike later sources, Justin (*1 Apology* 26) does not know Cerdo, but he nevertheless offers the common accusation that Marcion descended from earlier heretics, namely Simon the Magician and Menander.

9. Pseudo-Tertullian, *Against All Heresies* 6.2. Notice this information was not known to Tertullian himself, who certainly would have capitalized on it (see where Tertullian makes similar claims against Apelles in *Prescript against Heretics* 30). The same can certainly be said of Irenaeus and Clement of Alexandria, if not also Justin.

f. Marcion repented of his teachings late in life, but died before making things right with the church. Or, no one knows what happened to him, and reports of Marcion's own rejection of Marcionism would refute any who might be tempted by this heresy.

g. Marcion was a pescetarian.[10] Or, . . . well, there is no "or" this time. What motive could someone have for making this up? Perhaps, since Christians are "little fish" (i.e., they have the fish symbol of ICHTHUS on their chariots),[11] Marcion gobbles them up.[12] No "orthodox" opponent, however, used this "fact" against him.

Most scholars accept points (a)–(c) as facts, while (d) is debated, leaving (e) and (f), which are generally assumed to be slander. The last point, (g), is just mentioned here because it might one day win the reader a game of Church History Trivial Pursuit.

In Rome Marcion may have been accepted into the church, only later being declared a heretic when he presented his teachings to the leaders of the church. Why and how he presented these matters is unclear. Whether Marcion himself was even "excommunicated" (or for that matter, whether anyone could function as a "pope" or "bishop" of some sort in order to excommunicate him at this time) is itself debatable at best. Perhaps Marcion simply left Rome when his teachings were attacked by others. We cannot be sure. What we do find in the sources, however, is an immediate and outright rejection of his teachings as "heresy."

The Heresy: A Portrait or Caricature?

When it comes to his teaching, we can proceed on firmer ground for the following reason. While his opponents attempt to show the absurdities in his thinking, they nevertheless portray Marcion as having his own consistent logic. Since Marcion's teachings make sense on their own terms, we can understand both why he would have held such beliefs and why his opponents rejected them.

Because the anti-Marcionite writers used rhetorical flourish to discredit Marcion, we must take a critical stance toward their claims. For example, we

10. Cf. Tertullian, *Against Marcion* 1.14.5; Hippolytus, *Refutation of All Heresies* 7.18.

11. *Ichthus* is the Greek word for fish. Christians found the letters to be an acronym for Christ: *Iesous CHristos THeou hUios Soter*, which means "Jesus Christ God's Son Savior."

12. This may sound like a stretch, but compare Tertullian, *On Baptism* 1, regarding another heretic.

Tertullian (ca. 160–220)

Tertullian wrote the most extensive work against Marcion (uncreatively entitled *Against Marcion*). He writes from Carthage in North Africa and is famous for his wit and biting rhetoric. He was formerly understood to have been a Roman lawyer, a priest, one who despised philosophy, and he was even said to have converted to the Montanist heresy later in life. This picture of Tertullian, however, has been heavily revised in recent decades. Because he writes so extensively against Marcion and because he is relatively close to Marcion's time, he is the primary source for our understanding of the Marcionite heresy. Most other "orthodox" opponents of Marcion provide only a few paragraphs about him and his teaching. Thus, Tertullian's work will be used repeatedly throughout this chapter.

will explore how Marcion allegedly cut and pasted the New Testament to fit his teachings. When Tertullian—the most elaborate source on Marcion—first reports this in his work *Against Marcion*, he does so in highly embellished terms: after reporting how cold the climate of Pontus is, and how barbaric the people of Pontus are, he exclaims, "Even so, the most barbarous and melancholy thing about Pontus is that Marcion was born there . . . !"[13] He then likens Marcion to the vermin said to infest the region, claiming Marcion is a "Pontic mouse" that "gnaws" away at good things, namely the holy books. Clearly, Tertullian ridicules Marcion in order to discredit him. Of course, we need not fault Tertullian; this approach represents the norm for debate in the ancient world; we can probably assume that Marcion would have used similar rhetoric in response. We can ignore Tertullian as far as Marcion's barbarity. Can we also dismiss Tertullian's claim that Marcion—like a mouse—"gnawed away" at the Scriptures? Should we not question whether Marcion ever edited the New Testament as the anti-Marcionite writers claim? Here, as we will see below, the problem is more complex. Tertullian, it is widely assumed, had copies of Marcion's texts at hand, and so he may be a reliable source for Marcion's actions, a matter that will be debated below.

On the other hand, the earliest respondents to Marcion, such as Justin, Irenaeus, and Tertullian, could not have fabricated pure lies, since Marcion's followers were still around to object. So what do we really know about Marcion's teaching?

13. *Against Marcion* 1.1 (the translation is from Evans [p. 5], but I have added a punctuation mark).

Marcion's "Bible"

Marcion's Bible probably had only two books in it: the *Euangelion* and the *Apostolikon*. The *Euangelion*, which simply means "Gospel" in Greek, is the Gospel according to Luke, only much shorter than our version of Luke. In general, Luke's references to the Old Testament have been deleted. Marcion's version begins with Luke 3:1 and then skips to Luke 4:31 and following. In other words, there is no birth narrative, and nothing of Jesus's life before he began preaching. The *Apostolikon*, or Apostle's Writings, is a book of Paul's letters. Only ten are included in it, and they are—in order—Galatians, 1 and 2 Corinthians, Romans, 1 and 2 Thessalonians, Laodiceans (= our Ephesians), Colossians, Philemon, and Philippians. Marcion also wrote a work called *Antitheses*, which probably functioned as a preface to his Bible. This work contrasted examples of God's actions in the Old Testament with Christ's teachings. The point was to demonstrate how the Old Testament view of God was incompatible with a Christian view.

Marcion's Canon: Reduce, Reuse, Reject

The traditional view is that Marcion's key mistake was rejecting the Old Testament and parts of the New Testament that rely heavily on it, including three of the Gospels. Luke is the only Gospel he uses, but he still must edit certain parts (i.e., those that quote Jewish Scripture). Or, as Irenaeus claimed, Marcion "mutilated" or "circumcised" the Gospel of Luke—quite an ironic charge![14] Marcion's apostle is Paul, who is, after all, "the apostle to the gentiles," or non-Jews. However, even with Paul's letters, Marcion had to censor references to the Old Testament, which to Irenaeus was to "dismember" or "castrate" Paul—even more ironic (cf. Gal. 5:12).[15] Also, Marcion rejected Acts, perhaps because Acts claims too much of the Old Testament and shows the Jewish roots of the early church.[16]

14. *Against Heresies* 1.27.2. "Mutilate" is the word choice of the *ANF* translation. The Latin manuscript preserves the word *circumcidens*. Cf. Tertullian, *Against Marcion* 4.2.4: *caederet*.

15. Tertullian, *Against Marcion* 4.2.4. *ANF* = "dismember"; the Latin is *abscidit*. Tertullian, *Against Marcion* 5.1.9, claims, "That these [Paul's epistles] have suffered mutilation [*mutilatas*] even in number, the precedent of that gospel [of Luke], which is now the heretic's, must have prepared us to expect."

16. See Tertullian, *Against Marcion* 5.2.7. The notion that being Jewish was the problem is misleading: Marcion constantly attacks the actions of the Jews' God, not the Jews themselves, leaving no grounds on which to accuse him of anti-Semitism. See John G. Gager, *The Origins of Anti-Semitism: Attitudes toward Judaism in Pagan and Christian Antiquity* (Oxford: Oxford

Therein, it is said, Marcion has compiled the first Christian canon. No Hebrews (of course!). No James, Peter, John. No Revelation. What remained was an abridged Luke and ten edited letters of Paul. From Marcion's slimmed-down canon, one might assume that his heresy lay in rejecting the church's Bible. That assumption, however, may be the reverse of his logic.

The earliest Christians simply had no Bible—at least they had no modern, bound book with a set number of books in it. Instead, the earliest Christians often differed as to which books (or better: "writings" [Latin = *scripturae*]) they read, sang, and celebrated in their gatherings. In comparison, Marcion's "narrow canon" is not all that different from the "canon" of some other Christians from his time.[17] There is some debate as to whether Marcion selected and edited *the* canon (as Irenaeus and Tertullian thought he did), or whether he simply made logical conclusions from a "canon" he had received.[18] For the current discussion, the question of Marcion's "heresy," rather than being about the canon, is better understood in terms of theology and Christology.

The Gospel according to Marcion

Christians from his time understood Marcion's heresy not so much in terms of a rejection of Scriptures but in terms of Christology. The principle matter for the anti-Marcionist writers lay in the question of whether the Creator-God of the Old Testament was one and the same as the Christ of the New Testament. In other words, Marcion's primary mistake, or heresy, was in terms of his doctrine of Christ.[19]

Question: What does Marcion understand to be the character of Jesus? *Answer*: Love.[20] A love so complete it is self-sacrificial. So far, so good. From

University Press, 1983), 171–72; and Heikki Räisänen, "Marcion and the Origins of Christian Anti-Judaism: A Reappraisal," *Temenos* 33 (1997): 121–35.

17. Cf., e.g., the writings of Ignatius and Polycarp, whose known "canons" are roughly the same as Marcion's.

18. A view championed by John Knox, *Marcion and the New Testament: An Essay in the Early History of the Canon* (Chicago: University of Chicago Press, 1942). The trend in scholarly debate is certainly moving toward the latter option. For bibliography, see Judith M. Lieu, "'As Much My Apostle as Christ Is Mine': The Dispute over Paul between Tertullian and Marcion," *EC* 1 (2010): 43–45; Lieu, "Marcion and the Synoptic Problem," in *New Studies in the Synoptic Problem*, ed. P. Foster, A. Gregory, J. S. Kloppenborg, and J. Verheyden (Leuven: Peeters, 2011), 740–44.

19. A similar argument was made by Barbara Aland, "Marcion-Marcionites-Marcionism," in *Encyclopedia of the Early Church*, ed. Angelo Di Berardino (Oxford: Oxford University Press, 1992), 1:523–24.

20. Marcion's lost work *Antitheses* apparently began with this fundamental contrast between the God of love in Christ and the Creator-God (the "demiurge"). See Tertullian, *Against Marcion*

this starting point, Marcion devotes himself to this God of love revealed in Christ. After he has started with Christ, Marcion then looks to the Old Testament and finds a very different God: a God who demands retaliation (e.g., Exod. 21:24; cf. Matt. 5:21) and even genocide (e.g., in 1 Sam. 15), allows polygamy (e.g., with Jacob), requests child sacrifice (esp. see Gen. 22), summons she-bears on children (e.g., 2 Kings 2:24), and does countless other deplorable—or at least unloving—acts. Marcion's understanding of the gospel is one of love and acceptance sent from heaven, and so any God who acts contrary to this must be foreign to the God met in Christ, or as Marcion put it, "beneath" the God of Christ.

So far, we can readily sympathize with Marcion: no close reader of the two Testaments in a Christian Bible has failed to recognize certain themes that seem incompatible. Also, if Paul made it clear that gentiles do not need to adhere to Jewish laws (circumcision, food laws, holy days, etc.), then the law (or at least the Jewish scriptures' witness to God) and the gospel (or at least the "New Testament" or "New Testimony") are antithetical.

Marcion has concluded both that Christ is not the Creator-God and that Christ is better than the Creator-God. The claim that Christ is better, good, and loving seems to demand that the Creator-God is less good, if not evil. After this conclusion, there arises another series of questions for Marcion.

1. If Jesus is not the evil Creator-God, then what does this mean about creation itself? Is it also evil?
2. If Jesus is not the Creator-God and creation is evil, what about our created bodies? Did Jesus take up a real body?
3. If Jesus is not the Creator-God and creation is evil, what about the things we do in our bodies?

Marcion's followers, we are told, ridiculed creation. Marcion's own stance is not so clear. Let us discuss each question in more detail.

What about Creation Itself?

As to whether God created the world, Marcion finds as many evils in the world as he does in the Old Testament. Therefore, he blames creation itself on a different god (called the "demiurge"—meaning "one who makes"). After all, so the logic goes, this mess we call the cosmos cannot be the fault

---

4.6.1. A reconstruction of this work can be found in Wayne A. Meeks and John T. Fitzgerald, *The Writings of St. Paul*, 2nd ed. (New York: Norton, 2007), 286–88.

Are the Old and New Testaments Incompatible?

Readers should be wary of simplistic assertions as to whether the Old and New Testaments are incompatible. This idea seems to suffer from the same fallacy as Marcion's view: if two things seem incompatible, then they must be incompatible. The vast majority of early Christians could not accept such a notion after believing in the incarnation of God. The temptation to reject the Old Testament and its view of God has persisted to the modern era in thinkers like Adolf von Harnack, who tried to delete the entire Old Testament from Protestant theology. Tertullian's response to Marcion still rings true: "Antitheses for the most part are produced by diversity of purposes, not of authorities" (*Against Marcion* 4.24.1). In other words, different purposes or actions were carried out by the same God. Whereas the "orthodox" interpreted the Scriptures' alleged contradictions as God working in different ways at different times, Marcion understood the contradictions as reflecting two different gods.

of the loving God known in Christ. Marcion allegedly prooftexted the Gospel of Luke, where Jesus teaches that bad fruit comes only from bad trees (Luke 6:43). All of the bad things that the creator/demiurge "made"—nay, even claimed to make (cf. Isa. 45:7; Jer. 18:11)—must imply that the creator/demiurge is bad.

Once again, we must pause to consider whether this traditional reading of Marcion does him justice (pun intended). According to Marcion, the Creator-God is concerned with righteousness. Is the Creator-God "just" or just plain evil? For the orthodox writers, however, there is no separating justice/judgment from goodness/mercy. To be just is to be good. Marcion was not so sure. It is likely that Marcion himself preferred the God of love known in Christ over the evil Creator-God known in the Old Testament. Later, followers found this unconvincing, since parts of the Old Testament show God being just. It is later Marcionites, not Marcion, who concerned themselves with the Creator's future judgment.[21] As for the past creation, we can conclude that Marcion believed it at best flawed and imperfect, and perhaps downright "evil." The good news, according to Marcion, is that Christ has come to rescue us from the trap (i.e., the created order) in which the evil Creator-God has us. The world is a trap, not just because God made it and us in it, but because this world leads to death of the body and of the soul.[22]

21. Sebastian Moll, *The Arch-Heretic Marcion* (Tübingen: Mohr Siebeck, 2010), 49–54.
22. Epiphanius, *Panarion* 42.3.5.

Marcion's "-isms" #1: Docetism

"Docetism" comes from the Greek *dokeō*, "to seem or appear." It teaches that Christ only appeared to have a body and that he was in fact a hologram, a ghost (or "phantasm"). This heresy is generally associated with Gnosticism (see chap. 3), but Marcion is usually assumed to hold to this teaching as well. This assumption, however, is like so many other traditional depictions of Marcion in that it is an accusation made against him by his earliest opponents (see the next section).

Although Marcion believed Christ was a God of love and not judgment, there is no evidence that Marcion taught universalism. According to an early account, he believed that Jesus descended into hell and saved all those condemned by the Creator-God (Cain, the Sodomites, etc.).[23] The rest (i.e., the Jews) distrusted this manifestation of a Savior and thought it a test of the Creator-God. They remained in hell, waiting in vain for the Creator-God to be good. Rather than "Love wins," Marcion says, "Love tried." It is the way in which Christ "tried" that provides us with a glimpse of how Marcion answered the next question.

What about Created Bodies, Especially Jesus's Body?

Marcion believed created matter was evil, and so he must have said the same for human bodies, including Christ's body—according to the traditional view. The premise about creation itself being evil, however, has now been nuanced: creation is not so much evil as not-good/imperfect. Should we not rethink Marcion's view of the body as well?

Third-century Christian writers repeatedly assert that Marcion denied the incarnation and preferred to think of Jesus as simply pretending to appear in the flesh (something known as "docetism," which we will discuss in chap. 3), and so scholars generally assume this to be the case.[24] These writers, however, have less firsthand information than is often thought, and they all depend on Irenaeus's brief statements about Marcion, in which he conflates Marcion with other docetists.[25]

There is credible evidence that Marcion:

23. Irenaeus, *Against Heresies* 1.27.3; Epiphanius, *Panarion* 42.4.4.
24. E.g., Clement of Alexandria, *Stromata* 3.3.12; Tertullian, *Against Marcion*; Hippolytus, *Refutation of All Heresies* 10.15; Pseudo-Tertullian, *Against All Heresies* 6.1–2.
25. *Against Heresies* 1.27.2; 3.11.3; 4.32.2; cf. 5.1.2.

1. denied Christ's birth and asserted that Christ instead "came down" straight from heaven to Capernaum (see Luke 4:31, which begins Marcion's Luke), and

2. denied a bodily resurrection and preferred a "spiritual body" (cf. 1 Cor. 15:44) in the afterlife.[26]

Orthodox opponents could use these two denials to assume that Marcion also denied that Christ had a body. These same opponents further add motive to Marcion's denial.

In graphic terms, Tertullian blamed Marcion for abhorring human bodies, which Marcion thought were simply "full of &$*#!"[27] Marcion, therefore, must have been repulsed by the notion of Christ being "formed from a woman's blood . . . [and his being] spilt upon the ground through the sewer of a body, with a sudden attack of pains along with the uncleanness of all those months."[28] Clearly, Marcion thinks that the flesh is disgusting. While the logic sounds sound, the problem is that Marcion himself never said the body was a sewer. This is Tertullian's rhetoric about Marcion, not a quote from Marcion himself. Tertullian also claimed, "If, being the Son of man, he is of human birth, there is body derived from body. Evidently you could more easily discover a man born without heart or brains, like Marcion, than without a body, like Marcion's Christ. Go and search then for the heart, or the brains, of that man of Pontus."[29] This obviously charged rhetoric has been taken as unfair regarding Marcion's brain, but accurate concerning Jesus's body. Why? We can no longer depend uncritically on Tertullian's rhetoric, for we may as well accept that Marcion's own body was brainless—the original zombie! The reason for doubting such rhetoric as historically accurate is found in several conflicting statements made by Marcion's opponents: Marcion did in fact believe in the crucifixion of Christ in the flesh.[30] Although not born of woman, and not raised in a physical body, Christ came in a real (not docetic) body.[31]

Once again, it is worth setting Marcion's thoughts within their wider context of the early to mid-second century. That one could draw the same conclusion about Christ's lack of birth and lack of a physical resurrection

26. Irenaeus, *Against Heresies* 1.27.2; Hippolytus, *Refutation of All Heresies* 10.15.

27. Tertullian, *Against Marcion* 3.10.1. Evans's translation, "packed with dung," is the G-rated version.

28. *Against Marcion* 4.21.11.

29. *Against Marcion* 4.10.15–16.

30. E.g., Tertullian, *Against Marcion* 1.11, 14; 2.27; 4.26.1.

31. It is interesting to note that Christ *could* be incarnate without being born. Marcion may have assumed Jesus to have been human—body and all—but that the incarnation was simply Christ's way of communicating with every-body (pun intended).

Marcion's "-isms" #2: Gnosticism

The question of Marcion's docetism also raises the question, "Was Marcion a Gnostic?" Such a question, however, assumes there is a set definition of "Gnosticism." Like docetism, this problem will be discussed further in chapter 3. The debate related to Marcion, however, is one that plagues scholarship. The ancient orthodox opponents of Marcion portrayed him as just another evolution of Gnostic thinking. Thus, either he is a student of Cerdo or of Valentinus, or his students developed his thoughts further toward their inevitable and logical conclusion, full-blown Gnosticism, or both. This picture, however, is not compelling. Instead of the typical Gnostic mythologies with genealogies of aeons and emissions, which lead to the created realm, Marcion simply viewed God as a God of love and grace, not of law and judgment (as the Jews viewed God) *nor* as one of mythological fancy (as the Gnostics viewed him). Labeling Marcion a Gnostic is entirely unhelpful at this point, for one can no longer assume any of the other so-called Gnostic tenets.

from reading Mark's Gospel exclusively may be disconcerting to some readers, but it is worth pointing out because these ideas were more widely held in the first two centuries than the clean-cut categories of orthodox versus Marcionite would suggest.[32]

To recap, in accordance with Marcion's view that matter is not so much evil as a dead end, Marcion preached a gospel about an unborn but incarnate Christ. Christ died to free humans from the Creator-God's judgment, and Christ's spiritual resurrection is the hope for his followers' spiritual resurrection as well. In other words, the body—whether it be Jesus's or ours—is neither here nor there. The point is to save the soul. What, then, does that imply for Marcion's ethics? That is, what about what we do in our bodies?

What about Our Actions in Our Bodies (a.k.a. Ethics)?

Even though Marcion viewed creation and our created bodies as amoral—neither good nor bad—he still had clear teachings about what Christians should do in their bodies. Morality mattered to Marcion. The sources about his ethics are all negative; that is, they survive in the form of accusations

32. In a striking admission, Tertullian (*Against Marcion* 3.8) argues that Marcionism preceded Marcion in an earlier (much earlier) period: ". . . that Christ was a phantasm: except that this opinion too will have had other inventors, those so to speak premature and abortive Marcionites whom the apostle John pronounced antichrists."

against Marcionite practices. The two issues in particular that Marcion is attacked for are his views on marriage and his view of food. On both items, his opponents utilized the already-discussed accusation: Marcion hates the flesh.

One recurring accusation against Marcion is that he "hates" marriage. Even more interesting, Marcion's opponents claim that he teaches celibacy out of spite: if Marcionites refused to enter into the law of marriage and produce more earthly bodies, this would annoy the Creator-God, who established the laws of marriage and created their earthly bodies.[33] While some scholars accept the claim that Marcion rejected marriage out of a childish obstinacy, others find the claim to be another example of slander.[34] In Marcion's time, ascetic practices such as celibacy were highly regarded by many—if not most—Christians. The key question was whether Marcion *prohibited* marriage.[35]

The only sources attesting to Marcion's teaching on marriage claim he forbade it entirely. While it is tempting to side sympathetically with Marcion and dismiss this accusation as more character attack, it must be admitted that nothing in the sources calls this accusation into question. Many Christians from this period took Paul's (and Jesus's) preference for celibacy a step further and mandated celibacy. It is probable that Marcion did exactly that. This ban on marriage may have been motivated by a "hatred" of the flesh, as Marcion's opponents claimed, but the widespread practice among Christians who had no such disdain for the body allows us to assume Marcion held to celibacy as an important aspect of Christian bodily practice, without attributing an unorthodox motive.

The second of Marcion's teachings regarding the actions of the body is a strict view of fasting.[36] Just as many early Christians practiced celibacy, so also many (if not most) regularly fasted. Unlike his teaching on celibacy, this teaching of Marcion's is not said to have overstepped any direct commandment of Paul. Marcion "preaches" fasting.[37] So then, what is the big deal? Again, it has to do with his motivation: hatred for the Creator-God (if not the flesh

33. Clement of Alexandria, *Stromata* 3.3.12; Tertullian, *Against Marcion* 4.23.6; Hippolytus, *Refutation of All Heresies* 10.15.

34. Moll, *Arch-Heretic Marcion*, 133, accepts this motive. However, Andrew McGowan, "Marcion's Love of Creation," *JECS* 9, no. 3 (2001): 295–311, insists that the heresiologists misrepresent Marcion's ascetic practices as "hatred of creation/Creator," because Marcion wrote before a time when the doctrine of *creatio ex nihilo* had been unambiguously and unanimously defined. Moreover, McGowan insightfully notes that Marcionite "hatred" of the world, like Paul's attitude toward the world, was as much political as it was metaphysical.

35. Tertullian, *Against Marcion* 5.7.6: ". . . matrimony, which Marcion, of stronger character than the apostle, forbids."

36. Tertullian, *Against Marcion* 1.14.5; Hippolytus, *Refutation of All Heresies* 7.18.

37. Epiphanius, *Panarion* 42.3.3.

Marcion's "-isms" #3: Encratism

The heresy known as encratism taught a strict form of Christian living, and it rejected marriage. Encratism is a heresy because it contradicted Paul's clear teaching: marriage is permitted (1 Cor. 7:9), even if celibacy is preferred (1 Cor. 7:7–8). Paul's views, however, spread through multiple outlets in the second century, such as in the apocryphal *Acts of Paul and Thecla*, which was written in the decades following Marcion. In that story, Paul's enemies accuse him of destroying marriages, but Paul himself nowhere actually forbids anyone to marry in the text. The really tricky part is that Paul does sound like he destroys marriage: he tells married men to "have wives as not having them" (5)—and yes, that means exactly what you think it means. In this account Paul also says "virgins . . . should not marry but remain as they are" (11). While it is tempting to dismiss the apocryphal text as a misrepresentation of Paul, these two statements turn out to be almost verbatim quotes from Paul himself (see 1 Cor. 7:29 and 7:40, respectively). Whether or not the *Acts of Paul and Thecla* rightly interpreted and emphasized Paul's preference for celibacy is beyond the concern of our discussion. The relevant point here is that it illustrates how easily one could interpret Paul as advocating this teaching in the second century. To assume that the author of the *Acts* is a Marcionite, or responding to Marcion, is to accept the "orthodox" depiction of this teaching as unique to Marcion. Instead, the evidence strongly suggests that Marcion held to a common practice among first- and second-century Christians. See also 1 Corinthians 9:5, 15; Matthew 19:12 (cf. Tertullian, *Against Marcion* 4.11); Revelation 14:4; *2 Clement* 10.5; *Shepherd of Hermas* 2.4; 6.3; 29.6; 32.1–2, 38 as early examples.

made by him). One late account claims, "For fasting on the Sabbath he gives this reason: 'Since it is the rest of the God of the Jews who made the world and rested the seventh day, let us fast on this day, to do nothing appropriate to the God of the Jews.'"[38] This statement may even be a later Marcionite defense of the practice. Simply differentiating a Christian fast from a Jewish fast is not a "Marcionite" stance. Instead, differentiating Christian practices from Jewish ones seemed to be a common Christian trope.[39] While Marcion's opponents could interpret his strict teaching on fasting as malicious, this accusation more likely records just how much attention Marcion gave to the practices of the flesh.

38. Epiphanius, *Panarion* 42.3.4.
39. Cf. Matt. 6:2, 5, 16; *Didache* 8.1.

Aside from the attacks on Marcion for his view of marriage and meals, there is also the curious report about Marcionite martyrs that helps inform our understanding of Marcion's teachings about the flesh. The premise that Marcionites actually died for the faith is one that "orthodox" writers certainly would have contested, if they could have. Therefore, these reports are generally assumed to be historically reliable.[40] Two points can be drawn from these reports. Marcionites' sacrifice of their own bodies suggests that Marcion's teachings on the flesh did in fact take seriously one's actions and practices in the body.

Perhaps Marcion taught his followers to deny the flesh any gratification through marriage and meals, and perhaps he taught his followers to allow their flesh to be tortured because Marcion simply hated the flesh made by the Creator-God. On the other hand, given that so many, if not most, Christians valued celibacy over marriage, simplicity over indulgence, and martyrdom over apostasy makes it difficult to fault Marcion's motivation as heretical. Now that we have reviewed Marcion's teachings, at least as can be known by reading against the grain of his opponents' claims, let us attempt to encapsulate the orthodox response to Marcion and then draw some conclusions about this early Christian heresy.

The Orthodox Response

The "orthodox" response to Marcionism took many forms and was argued on many fronts. Here we will attempt to pull all of these threads together and provide a streamlined summary of the substance of "orthodoxy." The opposition to Marcionism arose primarily in regard to his view of Christ and secondarily regarding his use of Scripture. The primary concern had to do with the question "Who is Jesus?" The secondary was "How do we know who Jesus is?" Both are christological, but for those keeping track, the more exact categories of this christological "heresy" are the ontological and the epistemological. The ontological question has to do with "being," "nature," and "substance," signified by the "is" in the question "Who *is* Jesus?" The epistemological question has to do with knowledge and how knowledge is acquired, signified by the "know" in the question "How do we *know* who Jesus is?" The two are undoubtedly intertwined, but for the present purposes I will discuss each question in turn.

---

40. Tertullian, *Against Marcion* 1.24.4; Eusebius, *Ecclesiastical History* 5.16.21. However, see Justin, *1 Apology* 26.5: "But we do know that they [the Marcionites] are neither persecuted nor put to death by you, at least on account of their opinions."

The "orthodox" response to Marcion's "heresy" about who Jesus *is* can be summarized as follows: there is one God, Jesus. Even for Tertullian, when introducing Marcion's heresy as presenting "two Gods . . . the Creator . . . and his own," this is framed as a christological problem.[41] For Jesus is the "one Lord" by whom, in whom, and through whom all things are made (cf. John 1:3; Rom. 11:36; 1 Cor. 8:6; Col. 1:16; Heb. 2:10; Rev. 4:11). The God known in Jesus Christ is the same God seen in the Old Testament.[42] When the Old Testament God spoke, it was the preincarnate Word that was heard.

Marcion's primary error is to deny that Christ is the Creator. For example, the third-century writer Rhodo and the fourth-century writer Epiphanius explicitly denounce Marcion for separating the *Logos*, or Word, of the Lord from the *Archē*, who made the world (Gen. 1:1; John 1:1; 1 John 1:1).[43] Today, the Greek word *archē* is usually translated as "beginning," as in "In the beginning . . ." The term, however, could also mean "source" (*archē*) or "ruler" (*archōn*), and so many Christians from Marcion's era understood the Logos to be the very same being as the Archē.[44] Marcion and the orthodox party disagreed only as to the relationship between the Logos and the Archōn (now clearly meant as Ruler over creation). While the proper interpretation of John 1:1 is beside the point (for I doubt your biblical studies professor would approve of either interpretation), this example shows how Marcion's attempt to separate Christ the Word from the Creator-God/Archōn was rejected by the wider church.

The streamlined answer to Marcion given here, that Jesus is YHWH, is admittedly so nuanced in the orthodox texts that it is often difficult to see. For one thing, the orthodox would not have used the Hebraic name YHWH itself; rather, they would have used the Greek word that translates it, *Kyrios* ("Lord") or simply the term "God" without attempting to invoke God's proper name. For another thing, the full definition of the doctrine of the Trinity is yet to be forged against an array of heresies.[45] Nevertheless, the orthodox writers—unlike Marcion—clung to a strict monotheism and read the Old

---

41. See *Against Marcion* 1.2.
42. Tertullian, *Against Marcion* 2.27.
43. Eusebius, *Ecclesiastical History* 5.13.3–4; Epiphanius, *Panarion* 42.4.1.
44. See Joel C. Elowsky, ed., *John 1–10*, ACCS (Downers Grove, IL: InterVarsity, 2006), 3–7.
45. One concern about claiming "Jesus is YHWH" would be modalism, that is, that the Father and the Son (and the Spirit) are the same person, only appearing in different ways at different times (see chap. 4). Such a view is certainly not espoused by the early orthodox party's claim that Jesus is the Old Testament God known as YHWH. The only possible way to make such an accusation is to assume that the Old Testament God is the Father, and not the Son—an almost-unanimous assumption held by readers today, but one the early church did not share. Such a reading of the Old Testament is more Marcionite than it is orthodox.

Testament christocentrically, something they learned from the New Testament documents, where "Jesus is LORD," that is, the God of the Old Testament.[46]

This response about who Christ *is*, as we mentioned above, was coupled with debate about *how one knows* Christ. The orthodox response reaffirms—or perhaps, only after Marcion, fully recognizes—the importance of the Hebrew Scriptures even for the mission to the gentiles. The God known in Jesus Christ is the selfsame demiurge who created the world and the selfsame God who elected the descendants of Abraham.

Answering Marcion's use of Scripture was not a simple task, since there were many problems. The matter of which Scriptures were to be used and which could be rejected has already been discussed. Even if the traditional perspective is rejected and even if one were to accept that Marcion-like canons were common in the early second century, it is apparent that in response to Marcion, the progress of canonization comes into question. For one thing, the use of the four Gospels—all four and no more—will emerge after Marcion's time. Also, the collection of texts, such as Paul's letters, the "catholic" epistles, and so on will become more common after Marcion, resulting in whole books (or codices, a development from the use of scrolls). Then, aside from canonization, there remains the matter of how to use the Scriptures. Tertullian accused Marcion of reading the Scriptures selectively: "You take note of [God's] vengeance: think also of when he is indulgent."[47] Even in a sympathetic reading of Marcion as a product of his time, one can see that his reading of the two Testaments was simplistic. For one thing, the Old Testament repeatedly speaks of God as "merciful and gracious, slow to anger, and abounding in steadfast love" (Exod. 34:6; Ps. 103:8; etc.). It is, moreover, in the New Testament, even in Luke and Paul (Luke 22:7–20; Rom. 3:25; 1 Cor. 5:7; etc.), where God practices child sacrifice. The matter is more complex, of course, but that is exactly the point that Marcion ignored. The orthodox insisted that Jesus be understood as the God of the Old Testament, (perceived) warts and all.

By separating the substance of the orthodox argument ("Jesus is LORD") from the form of the orthodox response ("Marcion is an idiot"), the reader

---

46. Examples from Marcion's opponents include Justin Martyr, *Against Marcion* (cited in Irenaeus, *Against Heresies* 4.6.2); Irenaeus, *Against Heresies* 4.2, 9–10; 5.12.6; 5.17.1; 5.18.3; and Tertullian, *Against Marcion* 4.22.16. A very keen observation is made on this point by Epiphanius (*Panarion* 30.10.8). In the New Testament, the clearest claim that Jesus is YHWH is found in the "I AM" sayings of Jesus in John (8:24, 28, 58). But even Mark, with its allegedly low Christology, invokes this imagery (e.g., 1:3; 6:47–51). For Paul, see esp. his application of Isa. 45:23 to Jesus in Phil. 2:9–11. To be sure, the early Christians were not univocal in understanding Jesus as Lord to be YHWH, but such a formula represents a core conviction widely shared by the earliest believers (e.g., Jude 4–5).

47. *Against Marcion* 2.17.

can, I hope, use these abbreviations as mental flash cards to be compared with other Christologies discussed in the rest of this book and beyond.

At the beginning of this chapter, "Marcionism," or the gospel according to Marcion, is said to be the belief that Jesus is God 2.0. Of course, as with all oversimplifications, "God 2.0" poorly represents Marcion's thought. Marcion's "Marcionism" is his teaching that in Christ someone or something has surpassed and replaced the God who created the world and who called Israel. Marcion's "heresy" is supersessionism.

Supersessionism usually takes the form of church/Israel relations, especially in terms of a replacement. The church, so it is said, has replaced and surpassed Israel. The range of supersessionisms is too vast to cover presently, but in general the logic of replacement is the key issue. After the church is said to replace Israel, one can easily assert that the new covenant replaces the old covenant, baptism replaces circumcision, the Lord's Supper replaces sacrifice, Sunday replaces the Sabbath, and so on and so forth. These replacements are all allowed if, and only if, one accepts a theological supersessionism. If Christ supersedes and replaces YHWH of the Old Testament, then Christ can ignore Old Testament teachings and institutions. If not, but all of YHWH's commands are simply replaced, then God is fickle. For orthodoxy, however, one must reject Marcionism, and if one accepts that Jesus is YHWH incarnate, who fulfills the law both physically and spiritually, then one must embrace YHWH's word in the Old Testament as well.[48] How to do so, of course, is hotly debated.[49]

The early church generally looked to the spiritual meaning of the Old Testament. The sacrifices were never meant to be understood on a merely physical level; rather, God's people were to offer clean hands and a pure heart. Circumcision was always to be understood as indicating a circumcision of the heart. The whole nation of Israel itself was to be a kingdom of priests, for not all Israel according to the flesh is truly Israel.[50] The key in all

48. In this understanding, it must be clear that YHWH in the Old Testament is not God the Father, as is so often assumed in contemporary Christian readings. Rather, the Father is the one who sends his Son, but it is the Son who is manifested. Cf. John 5:46.

49. Daniel Boyarin, *Border Lines: The Partition of Judaeo-Christianity* (Philadelphia: University of Pennsylvania Press, 2004), is helpful on this point in that he accounts for Marcionism (see esp. p. 17).

50. E.g., *2 Clement* 14.2: "Moreover, the books and the apostles declare that the church not only exists now but has been in existence from the beginning. For she was spiritual." In other words, Israel is not replaced. The spiritual Israel is (and always was) the church, and vice versa. Those familiar with *Epistle of Barnabas* will recognize this pattern, although that author held to a curious view that the physical covenant was immediately and irrevocably broken at Sinai. Likewise, Justin Martyr, *Dialogue with Trypho*, and Irenaeus, *Against Heresies* 4.16, explain

of these interpretations is to listen to the Word of God, whether he spoke to the prophets of old or in the flesh. No supersessionistic reading is permissible in light of the belief that there is but one God, whose fullness is revealed in Christ. Tertullian insisted, "That man from Pontus has seen fit to invent a second god, while denying the first. . . . It ought to have been possible to confine my argument to this single theme, that the god brought in to supersede the Creator is no god at all."[51] Marcion's allowance for the Creator to be "superseded" by Christ results in a radical departure from what the majority of Christians had known in their faith and practice. In this light, Christology and Christianity as a religion can be rightly understood: Christianity is not merely a sect within Judaism, although according to a sociological model it was so; it is an affirmation of the God of Judaism, now said to be known in Christ. We will return to Christianity's relationship to Judaism in the next and final chapters of this work. For now, at the core of all his thoughts on the canon, the cosmos, and the flesh, Marcion's heresy is a christological one, a denial that Jesus is Lord.

Recommended Bibliography

Foster, Paul. "Marcion: His Life, Works, Beliefs, and Impact." *ExpTim* 121, no. 6 (2010): 269–80.

Frend, W. H. C. "Marcion." *ExpTim* 80, no. 11 (1969): 328–32.

Harnack, Adolf von. *Marcion: The Gospel of the Alien God.* Translated by John E. Steely and Lyle D. Bierma. Durham, NC: Labyrinth, 1990.

Knox, John. *Marcion and the New Testament: An Essay in the Early History of the Canon.* Chicago: University of Chicago Press, 1942.

Moll, Sebastian. *The Arch-Heretic Marcion.* Tübingen: Mohr Siebeck, 2010.

---

how this rationale is applied to all the law in its spiritual sense. The law is not superseded but is understood as it was always meant to be understood.

51. *Against Marcion* 2.1.

**Summary:
Ebionites**

Key Doctrine: Adoptionism
- My-Size Jesus
- Jesus is just a human, awarded by God

Key Dates
- 70: Destruction of the temple
- 135: Final expulsions of Jews from Palestine
- 190: The first mention of Ebionites

2

Ebion

Adoptionism

He will judge also the Ebionites; for how can they be saved unless it was God who wrought out their salvation upon earth?

—Irenaeus

. . . the Ebionites . . . who are poor in understanding (deriving their name from the poverty of their intellect—"Ebion" signifying "poor" in Hebrew).

—Origen

The ancients quite properly called these men Ebionites, because they held poor and mean opinions concerning Christ.

—Eusebius

Poor Ebion. No, really, his name means "poor one." What kind of parent does that to a kid? Whether he was poor financially cannot be known, but he was poor in intellect. Poor Ebion. His followers apparently were just as poorly endowed with rational skills, for they accepted his idiotic ideas.

Those followers, the Ebionites, believed that the Old Testament law remained in effect. At least, the parts that could be kept—animal sacrifice

41

could not be practiced after the destruction of the temple (70 CE). The other commandments, however, such as circumcision and Sabbath and kosher food laws, could still be practiced and should still be practiced.

Even worse than their ideas about the Mosaic laws was their understanding of Jesus. To the Ebionites, Jesus was a human. He had good human qualities: he was righteous, he was a great prophet, he was a great example. But beyond those human attributes, not much more can be said about Ebionite Christology. Jesus was certainly not divine in their view. Ebion's followers were strict Jewish monotheists, and to say that Jesus was God—alongside the heavenly Father-God Jesus prayed to—would be blasphemy in their eyes. Jesus was a godly prophet, so God *in a sense* adopted Jesus as a son. After Jesus was crucified, God raised him, carried him to heaven, and seated him in the seat of honor. But Jesus was not God. Ironically, even though the Ebionites differed drastically from Marcion by clinging to their Old Testament, they still made the same mistake as Marcion by saying that Jesus was not the Creator-God. Marcion thought the Creator was evil but that Jesus was a different God. The Ebionites believed that the Creator was good but that Jesus was merely a man.[1]

Thus believed Ebion and the Ebionites. At least, this is the gospel according to the Ebionites according to their opponents. To learn more about Ebion and the Ebionites we must look closely at the surviving records about them. These records are in fact reports coming from orthodox opponents alone, for none of the Ebionites' own writings survive, except for possible fragments of their gospel.

Seeing the Evidence

Have you ever seen one of those pictures made up of little dots that has a hidden image visible only when you stare at it long enough? They are called autostereograms. The Ebionite heresy is one of those images. In those pictures, you cannot really see the image itself. It is there, but only in a peripheral way. Only when you let your eyes lose focus on the actual dots in front of you does the image seem to emerge out of the background. If you try to focus your eyes directly on the image itself, it disappears.

The same thing happens with the Ebionites. We know of the Ebionites only by way of their opponents' statements about them, and the early Christian writers speak of the Ebionites only by way of comparing them with other

1. The technical term for teaching that Jesus was/is merely human is "psilanthropy."

heretics. The Ebionites are compared and contrasted with Jews in general and the Sadducees in particular, as well as Samaritans, and then with a whole host of other "heretics" such as Marcion, Apelles, Valentinus, Cerinthus, Carpocrates, the Nazarenes, and others. Only when this jumbled mix of different heresies is projected into a single constellation can we see the image that we call Ebionism.[2] The general contours of Ebionism are visible, but when we try to view it directly the ancient heresy retreats from our sight. In what follows we will revisit the ancient accounts of the Ebionites and try to discern hearsay from reliable data.

O Ebion, Where Art Thou?

The name Ebion is first recorded by the Latin writer Tertullian, and he is quick to point out the pun.[3] Ebion spoke Aramaic, and in Aramaic Ebion means "poor." Ebion is poor in IQ, according to Tertullian and all who rely on Tertullian's version of the origin of the Ebionites.

Ebion, however, never existed. The earliest source on the Ebionites, Irenaeus of Lyon, says nothing of an individual by this name. Neither do writers who were most likely to encounter the Ebionites in the flesh, such as Origen of Alexandria and Eusebius of Caesarea (see fig. 2.1). Those who do name Ebion (notably, the fourth-century writer Epiphanius of Salamis) probably do so on the assumption that every heresy derives from a founding heretic. But in this case, "Ebionites" probably just means "Poor Ones," not followers of (a person named) Ebion.

Why then would the Ebionites call themselves the "Poor Ones"? Jesus taught, "Blessed are you who are poor, for yours is the kingdom of God" (Luke 6:20; cf. Acts 4:32–35). Jesus's teaching on poverty was not new. It could be traced throughout the Old Testament, and into several diverse Jewish groups in the first century.[4] Perhaps the Ebionites took something akin to a vow of poverty. Perhaps they thought of themselves as "poor in spirit" (Matt. 5:3). None of our early sources clarifies.

2. This analogy is close to Epiphanius's description (*Panarion* 30.1.2–3).

3. Tertullian, *Prescript against Heretics* 10, 33; *On the Flesh of Christ* 14, 18, 24; *On the Veiling of Virgins* 6. See also Hippolytus, *Refutation of All Heresies* 7; Pseudo-Tertullian, *Against All Heresies* 3.3. Epiphanius, *Panarion* 30.1.5, also claims, "He is a Samaritan . . . while professing himself a Jew." Epiphanius's account, however, is late and problematic.

4. For example, the Qumran community who produced the Dead Sea Scrolls claimed that they were the *anawim*, the Poor Ones. See discussion in Sakari Häkkinen, "Ebionites," in *A Companion to Second-Century Christian "Heretics,"* ed. Antti Marjanen and Petri Luomanen (Leiden: Brill, 2005), 247.

Figure 2.1. Sources for the History of the Ebionites

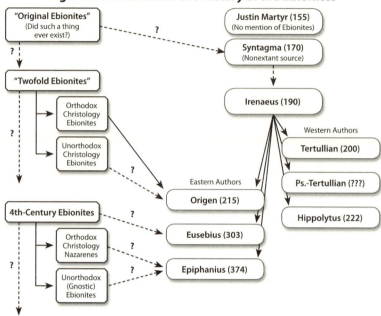

Epiphanius, writing very late (fourth century), claimed to know a group of Ebionites, and he also knew the earlier orthodox writers who discussed the Ebionites. So he harmonized everything he knew about them, claiming Ebion was the founder and the Ebionites were literally poor. In all likelihood Epiphanius had no firsthand account of a man named Ebion, but he instead did the best he could to reconcile the earlier writers whom he trusted with the current explanation of the name given by Jewish Christians he encountered.[5] With Ebion out of the picture, what, then, can we discover about the Ebionites?

Ebionite Beginnings

One characteristic trait orthodox writers use to describe the Ebionites is that they are Jewish. This trait, to be clear, is not meant as a compliment from

5. Epiphanius occasionally claims that you could "ask one of them," and then he reports what they "say" (e.g., *Panarion* 30.15.4; 30.18.7–9). His claim is problematic because of his assumption about who or what is an Ebionite; he seems to impose earlier writers' reports about Ebionites onto a group that somewhat fits those descriptions, even though it is in fact a different sect altogether (see more below).

Epiphanius of Salamis (ca. 315–403)

Epiphanius wrote the *Panarion*, or "Medicine Chest," in response to all of the heresies he understood to be plaguing the church. He was born in Palestine and trained in Egypt before later being appointed as bishop of Salamis in Cyprus. As someone who held to the Council of Nicaea's teachings (see chap. 5 concerning that council), Epiphanius lived during a time of great turmoil between the Nicene and anti-Nicene parties. As to the heresies he reports, Epiphanius relied heavily on previous sources. Often, however, he attempted to fill in the gaps in his sources. Therefore, his historical information is sometimes dubious.

Christians of the second, third, and fourth centuries. In the eyes of these gentile Christians, the Jews had rejected God by crucifying the Messiah, and so God condemned them as a people and destroyed their temple (in 70 CE). The Ebionites continued to keep the Mosaic law, and this was seen as a "curse" and a denial of grace (cf. Gal. 3:13).[6]

The Ebionites belonged to the ethnic heritage of Judaism. They continued to use Aramaic, and they centered in the region of Palestine.[7] According to one report, they were Christian in the sense that they accepted Jesus as the Messiah, but they believed Jesus was sent only to the nation of Israel.[8] According to another report, only their acceptance of Jesus as the Messiah distinguished them from other Jews: they even gathered as synagogues, not churches.[9]

The Ebionites were viewed as provincial and primitive by their orthodox opponents. Whereas early Christians exempted gentile converts from the law, later Christians would forbid Jewish Christians from keeping the law.[10]

The Jewishness of this group raises the question of how they began. If there was no founder named Ebion, and if the Ebionites' roots are in Judea,

6. On anti-Semitism in early Christian history, see John G. Gager, *The Origins of Anti-Semitism: Attitudes toward Judaism in Pagan and Christian Antiquity* (Oxford: Oxford University Press, 1985); and Marcel Simon, *"Verus Israel": A Study of the Relations between Christians and Jews in the Roman Empire (AD 135–425)*, 2nd ed., trans. H. McKeating (London: Valentine Mitchell, 1996).

7. Eusebius, *Onomasticon* 172.1–3, section 10 [Chi] on Genesis; cf. Epiphanius (*Panarion* 30.18.1), who claims Ebion preached in Rome and Asia Minor, while the sect is mostly found in Syria.

8. Origen, *On First Principles* 4.22; cf. Matt. 15:24.

9. Epiphanius, *Panarion* 30.18.2. Of course, *ekklēsia* and *synagōgē* are virtually synonymous. This may reflect a time when Jewish Christians continued to "congregate" loosely, before the emergence of the monepiscopate, or one bishop governing a community.

10. See, e.g., the infamous statements of John Chrysostom, and the Second Council of Nicaea (787), canon 8.

Keeping the Law

The relation of gentiles to the law proved to be one of the most controversial issues in the early Christian centuries. Several New Testament books address this issue, most notably Paul's letters. While Paul and others (see Acts 15) exempted gentiles from traditional Torah observances (circumcision, food laws, etc.), Paul and other Jewish Christians continued those practices.

After the New Testament period, when many gentiles joined the Christian movement, the allowance for Jewish Christians to keep the law was forgotten. Around 160 Justin Martyr authored *A Dialogue with Trypho*. In it, Justin debates Trypho, "a Jew," who does not accept Jesus's status as Messiah and Lord. Justin repeats many New Testament arguments about why gentiles keep the law spiritually and therefore are exempt from practicing the law "according to the flesh." He admits, however, that Christians disagree about this issue. Justin allows that Jewish Christians who practice the law will be "saved" (*Dialogue* 47), but only if they do not attempt to persuade gentiles to keep the law. Many later Christians forgot this allowance and saw any Torah observance as a heretical retreat from Christianity back into Judaism.

do they belong to the original Jerusalem community of Jesus followers? We know very little about the Jerusalem church after the temple was destroyed and the Jews were exiled from their holy city (70 CE). The sources indicate that the original Jesus community had continued under the leadership of Jesus's remaining relatives, such as James and Simeon, and that God commanded "the church in Jerusalem" to flee to Pella, a town across the Jordan River.[11] Later, the wider Christian communities were growing increasingly gentile in their membership. Could the Ebionites be the remnant of the original Jerusalem church, only they appear primitive and unorthodox to later gentile writers?

Some have understood the Ebionites as the last survivors of the original Christian community in Jerusalem.[12] According to this view, later Christians with no connection to Jerusalem or Judaism found these Jewish Christians unrecognizable, and so the "Poor Ones" became heretics. Such a view is admittedly attractive, for there is no denying the diversity of Christian groups in the early church, and these groups famously misunderstood one another.

11. See Eusebius, *Ecclesiastical History* 2.23; 3.20, 32; 4.8, 22.
12. See examples in Petri Luomanen, "Ebionites and Nazarenes," in *Jewish Christianity Reconsidered: Rethinking Ancient Groups and Texts*, ed. Matt Jackson-McCabe (Minneapolis: Fortress, 2007), 81–118.

Surely, Jewish Christianity could be reclaimed as one of the many diverse forms of Christianity, if not the original form.[13]

While such an understanding of the Ebionites is appealing, the major flaw lies in the notion of a single "Jewish Christianity." Christianity, arising from predominantly Jewish roots, resulted in innumerable forms of "Jewish Christianity" with no particular group under this label being uniquely tied to Jerusalem.[14] Jews lived throughout the region that became known as Palestine and even throughout the Persian and Roman empires. Alternatively, many other known forms of "Jewish Christianity" have ties to Jerusalem and yet were integrated with gentiles (e.g., the church in Antioch, Pauline churches, etc.).[15] Despite adamant attempts to connect Ebionites to the original Jerusalem church, no evidence survives that allows for such a simple and straightforward conclusion.[16]

Once we admit that no firm connection can be made between the Ebionites and the Jerusalem church, fixing a date for the beginning of the Ebionite movement becomes difficult. The first mention of them is made by Irenaeus around 190, but he is probably relying on a source dating back a generation before him.[17] Neither Justin nor Hegesippus mentions the Ebionites, despite explicit commentary on the various Jewish and Christian heresies. Although the Ebionites may very well have originated before the middle of the second century, and perhaps even in the first century, the lack of any source suggesting they did so makes it difficult to defend such an early dating. The next difficulty comes in specifying which group is referenced by the term "Ebionite." Different sources tell us different things.

13. Most famously argued by Walter Bauer, *Orthodoxy and Heresy in Earliest Christianity*, ed. Robert A. Kraft and Gerhard Kroedel (Philadelphia: Fortress, 1979); and James D. G. Dunn, *Unity and Diversity in the New Testament: An Inquiry into the Character of Earliest Christianity* (Philadelphia: Westminster, 1977), 244.

14. See bibliography and discussion in Matt Jackson-McCabe, "What's in a Name? The Problem of 'Jewish-Christianity,'" in *Jewish Christianity Reconsidered: Rethinking Ancient Groups and Texts*, ed. Matt Jackson-McCabe (Minneapolis: Fortress, 2007), 15–18; and Andrew S. Jacobs, "Jews and Christians," in *The Oxford Handbook of Early Christian Studies*, ed. Susan Ashbrook Harvey and David G. Hunter (Oxford: Oxford University Press, 2008), 169–85.

15. For example, the Nag Hammadi text *(Second) Apocalypse of James* has very little "Gnostic" material (see chap. 3), but claims a link to James and Jerusalem and so is often labeled a "Jewish-Christian" text.

16. Even Irenaeus's claim (*Against Heresies* 1.26.2) that they adored Jerusalem proves nothing, for many Christians in this era prayed toward the holy city. Epiphanius's connection of the Ebionites with Jerusalem (*Panarion* 29.7.7; 30.2.1) is clearly a harmonizing of Eusebius (*Ecclesiastical History* 3.5.3) and Irenaeus. These earlier sources knew of no direct link to Pella or Jerusalem. What is likely is that Epiphanius knew there were still "Jewish Christians" in the region, and he labels all such groups as "Ebionite."

17. Häkkinen, "Ebionites," 250–51, thinks Irenaeus relies on Justin's nonextant *Syntagma*, but it must have been expanded by someone after Justin.

Here an Ebionite, There an Ebionite, Everywhere an Ebionite

The earliest sources on the Ebionites speak of them as one sect, but a few generations later the church fathers begin to speak of different forms of Ebionism. Because of this development, it is common to subdivide this heresy into different groups:

1. The traditional Ebionites: These are probably the earliest, and they denied the divinity of Christ and continued to keep the Jewish law. Alternatively, some scholars are more inclined to think that they did affirm the divinity of Christ, but later retreated from the claim and returned to a more Jewish understanding of Jesus as merely a prophet.
2. The Nazarene Ebionites: These are either a separate sect altogether, known as Nazarenes, who never denied the divinity of Christ, or they are the ones who broke with the traditional Ebionites (or vice versa) because the traditional group tried to distance itself from the gentile church after the Bar Kochba revolt and denied the divinity of Christ.
3. The Gnostic Ebionites: These Ebionites, either a splinter group or a later development of the whole sect, incorporated a form of Gnosticism found in *The Book of Elchasai* into their beliefs.

These three kinds of Ebionites, however, are modern categories based on problematic sources. To go in reverse order, the so-called Gnostic Ebionites were known only to Epiphanius, but he more likely misidentified a Jewish Christian group with heretical beliefs as Ebionites simply because they were Jewish Christians.[18] The Nazarenes were likewise unheard of before Epiphanius, and later writers like Jerome used "Nazarene" as a synonym for "Ebionite" and applied it to all Jewish Christians.[19] The Nazarenes were probably considered separate by Epiphanius because Origen had earlier spoken of two kinds of Ebionites: christologically orthodox and christologically heretical.[20] What is more plausible than there having been two kinds of Ebionites is that Origen had read about the unorthodox Ebionites in Irenaeus but met some orthodox Jewish Christians. He, therefore, felt compelled to differentiate two kinds of Ebionites.

---

18. *Panarion* 30. They follow the *Book of Elchasai*, believe Christ and Adam were the same divine being, and believe that Christ and his female companion, the Holy Spirit, were ninety-six miles tall and invisible.

19. Epiphanius, *Panarion* 29. Luomanen, "Ebionites and Nazarenes," 83, believes Epiphanius "invented" the Nazarenes.

20. *Against Celsus* 5.61.

What's in a Name? Nazarenes, Nazirites, and Nazoreans

The Nazarenes are a sect described by Epiphanius as being similar to the Ebionites. The spelling of this group's name varies widely among scholars, because the spelling varies among the primary sources themselves. Further complication lies in the fact that the name reported by this group's opponents probably reflects an idea already common to Second Temple Judaism and/or early Christianity. For example, the Nazirite vow, taken by Samson (Judg. 13:5), Samuel (1 Sam. 1:11), and other Old Testament figures (Num. 6), seems to be reflected in New Testament figures such as John the Baptist (Luke 1:15). Some even think Jesus is called a "Nazarene" not because he was from Nazareth (the traditional view), but because he represents the ultimate embodiment of holiness, which is the aim of such a vow. A more likely connection is found in the traditional view that Jesus was from Nazareth (Matt. 2:23). His followers, therefore, will be called Nazarenes by their Jewish opponents (Acts 24:5), and those opponents may have linked this general title for Christians with their holiness (as in the rabbinic literature, where all Christians are *Nozrim*). No evidence exists, however, that shows a Christian group using this title for itself until Epiphanius's late attestation of this sect. Any direct historical link, therefore, between Epiphanius's Nazarenes and the original Jerusalem church is difficult to establish.

As for the so-called original Ebionites, known only to Irenaeus, even their Christology is uncertain, for he merely compares their view of Christ to that of Cerinthus and Carpocrates, which sounds suspiciously like guilt by association. Cerinthus and Carpocrates do not even have the same form of adoptionism: in one view the human Jesus is possessed by a heavenly being, in the other the human Jesus is merely human. Which is closer to *the* Ebionite Christology?

At this point, the heresy of the Ebionites has receded from our view entirely, and all we are left with are suggestions and possibilities—kind of like the image hidden in an autostereogram. Let us, then, take a step back from this array of heresy comparisons found in the early sources, and approach this heresy from another angle. Let us attempt to understand the Ebionites directly from their own scriptures.

Ebionite Scriptures

As with all we have said above about the Ebionites, the Ebionite scriptures do not survive but are known solely through reports about them from the orthodox writers. In the earliest mention of this heresy, Irenaeus merely states that the Ebionites "carefully" interpret the "prophets."[21] They also have a gospel as part of their scriptures, but which gospel is unclear. Irenaeus says they use only Matthew, but Eusebius will later say they use only the *Gospel according to the Hebrews*.[22] Once again the late fourth-century source on the Ebionites harmonizes these points: "They too accept the Gospel according to Matthew. . . . They call it, 'According to the Hebrews.'"[23] In order to sort the differing accounts of the Ebionites' gospel, scholars today often list three different texts.

1. *The Gospel according to the Hebrews*
   a. Alexandrian sources (Clement, Origen, and Didymus) report that this was once accepted as orthodox. While none of these writers mention the Ebionite use of this text, there are certain Semitisms, and so some scholars assume it was a Jewish Christian gospel.
   b. However, the logic of this assertion neglects to account for the fact that all early Christians and all early gospels were Jewish to some extent.

2. *The Gospel of the Ebionites*
   a. Known only from Epiphanius, this source omitted the birth narratives and genealogies, but harmonized other material from the Synoptics.[24]
   b. However, this title is a modern invention unknown to the ancient sources.[25] Also, since Epiphanius's Ebionites may be another group altogether (see previous section), this text may be irrelevant.

21. *Against Heresies* 1.26.2 (cf. the *ANF* translation). Cf. Tertullian, *Prescript against Heretics* 33.5; Hippolytus, *Refutation of All Heresies* 7.33; Origen, *Against Celsus* 5.61; Eusebius, *Ecclesiastical History* 3.27.2; Epiphanius, *Panarion* 30.33.4. Epiphanius, however, elsewhere (30.18.4) claims the Ebionites used only the patriarchs and Moses (i.e., the Pentateuch, not the Prophets and the later Writings).

22. Irenaeus, *Against Heresies* 1.26.2; Eusebius, *Ecclesiastical History* 3.27.4 (cf. 6.17).

23. Epiphanius, *Panarion* 30.3.7. On Matthew's Gospel as originally in Hebrew, see Papias (in Eusebius, *Ecclesiastical History* 3.39.16); Irenaeus, *Against Heresies* 3.1.1.

24. Interestingly, Tatian's *Diatessaron* reportedly began with the same omissions (Theodoret of Cyrrhus, *A Compendium of Heretical Mythification* 1.20). Epiphanius, *Panarion* 46.1.9, actually equates Tatian's *Diatessaron* with the *Gospel according to the Hebrews*—a point usually ignored by scholars: "It is said that the *Diatessaron*, which some call 'According to the Hebrews,' was written by him." Cf. Eusebius, *Ecclesiastical History* 4.29.6. Petri Luomanen, "Where Did Another Rich Man Come From? The Jewish-Christian Profile of the Story about a Rich Man in the 'Gospel of the Hebrews' (Origen, *Comm. in Matth.* 15.14)," *VC* 57, no. 3 (2003): 263, does not think the *Gospel of the Ebionites* and the *Diatessaron* were one and the same, but he does believe they were similar as mid-second-century Gospel harmonies. Yet beginning a gospel with Jesus's ministry does not necessarily imply heterodoxy (cf. the Gospels of Mark and John, as well as our understanding of Marcion's version of Luke [discussed in chap. 1]).

25. An instance such as "Gospel of the Ebionites" (Epiphanius, *Panarion* 30.13.6–8) is not a title at all; it is merely a stylistic shorthand for "*The Gospel according to the Hebrews*, which is used by the Ebionites" (cf. Jerome, *In Matthaeum* 12.13).

Four or One? Gospel Harmonies

In the late second century, when the four Gospels of Matthew, Mark, Luke, and John would come to be the norm for most churches, many Christians would begin to question the necessity of having four, and not one such gospel. Churches before this even varied as to whether to use only one as authoritative or whether to piece together Jesus's sayings and life from whatever sources they deemed reliable. Justin Martyr's quotes of the Gospels tend to synthesize material from the Synoptics, leading many scholars to believe he relied on a single text (or even that he had produced a single text) harmoniz-ing Matthew, Mark, and Luke. Justin's student, Tatian, famously produced the *Diatessaron*, which is a harmony of all four canonical Gospels. Some scholars have conjectured that there is a literary relationship between *The Gospel of the Ebionites*, known in Epiphanius, and these other Gospel harmonies. Both of these were known to have omitted the birth narratives, and Epiphanius (*Panarion* 46.1.9) even claims they were one and the same. While few scholars have been convinced by Epiphanius's claim, the similarities at least reflect a common tendency of mid- to late second-century Christians.

3. *The Gospel of the Nazareans*

   a. Jerome cites *The Gospel according to the Hebrews*, adding "which the Nazareans use," but this time the statement cited has material contradicting the description of Jesus's baptism known from the previous two texts.[26]

   b. However, this text, also unknown by this name in the ancient church, is known only in fragments, and the allegedly contradictory accounts of Jesus's baptism may be compatible.[27]

26. Differences in these gospels' accounts of Jesus's baptism include the following: in *Gospel according to the Hebrews*, the Spirit (the word for whom in Hebrew and Aramaic grammar is feminine) is Jesus's mother, and it is she who speaks to him, not the Voice from heaven (Jerome, *Commentary on Isaiah* 11.1–3 [text reproduced in Bart D. Ehrman and Zlatko Pleše, *The Apocryphal Gospels: Texts and Translations* (Oxford: Oxford University Press, 2011), 221]); in the *Gospel of the Nazareans*, Mary suggests Jesus be baptized, but Jesus questions the need for such an act since he is sinless (Jerome, *Against the Pelagians* 3.2 [text reproduced in Ehrman and Pleše, *Apocryphal Gospels*, 207]); in the *Gospel of the Ebionites* the quotation of Ps. 2:7 (found in the Synoptics) is completed with the psalmist's phrase "Today I have given you birth" (Epiphanius, *Panarion* 30.13.3–4). Perhaps Ebionites drew their adoptionistic view of Jesus from this text: Jesus was called God's Son, adopted, at his baptism. The problem with such a conclusion is that the (Gnostic?) Ebionites known to Epiphanius denied Christ's true humanity, saying he preexisted as an archangel (Epiphanius, *Panarion* 30.14.5 and 30.16.4–5).

27. Petri Luomanen, "'Let Him Who Seeks, Continue Seeking': The Relationship between the Jewish-Christian Gospels and the Gospel of Thomas," in *Thomasine Traditions in Antiquity:*

Identifying three different gospels also proves of little help in understanding the Ebionites. We seem to be left with little more than the probability that the (original?) Ebionites used a gospel text that was said to be of Hebrew (= Aramaic?) origin with close parallels to Matthew.

Nothing in our sources indicates that the Ebionites used any of the other writings that would later be included in our New Testament.[28] In fact, we are told that they explicitly rejected Paul.[29] If we have now established that the Ebionites insisted on keeping the law, and if we find them denouncing Paul, it would be tempting to identify them as the remnants of the so-called Judaizers, Paul's unnamed opponents in letters like Galatians. However, it is equally plausible that the orthodox opponents knew the Ebionites insisted on (converts?) keeping the law, and they deduced from this data that the Ebionites must have rejected Paul. Perhaps they simply did not know Paul.[30]

Once again the Ebionites themselves disappear when we attempt to look directly at their teachings and practice, for any claim about their use of other scriptures is unreliable, and nothing from their specific use of scriptures helps us get a clearer view of their teachings. It is tempting to supplement our understanding of the Ebionites by looking to other texts from this time with certain similarities, such as the *Didache* and Pseudo-Clementines. Such a move, however, would be to slip back into the stereotyping of all Jewish Christianity as looking alike. Therefore, let us set aside the Ebionite scriptures and try to understand the Ebionites' view of Christ.

Sonship, Adoption, and Possession

The Ebionites' Christology appeared too problematic for the orthodox writers, although their precise teachings about Christ are difficult to decipher from our sources. Once again we must differentiate earlier from later sources because there is such a gross discrepancy between the reports about their understanding of Jesus.

The Social and Cultural World of the Gospel of Thomas, ed. J. Ma. Asgeirsson, A. D. DeConick and R. Ero, NHMS 59 (Leiden: Brill, 2006), 119–53.

28. There is the possibility that the Ebionites knew of another work attributed to James, *Ascent of James*. In tandem was a work attributed to Peter, *Travels of Peter*, and possibly an *Acts of the Apostles* (not the canonical version) by an unknown author. The only source for Ebionite use of these texts, however, is Epiphanius, who is late and may be speaking of a different group.

29. Irenaeus, *Against Heresies* 1.26.2: "[The Ebionites] repudiate the Apostle Paul, maintaining that he was an apostate from the law." Also see Eusebius, *Ecclesiastical History* 3.27.4; Epiphanius, *Panarion* 30.16.8–9.

30. Cf. the *Didache*, which forbids meat offered to idols and has no literary allusions to Paul. This text need not be read as rejecting Paul, but only as ignorant of him and/or his teachings.

Editors or Inheritors of Their Gospel?

Did the Ebionites edit and modify the preexisting Gospels (which would later become canonical)? Or, is it possible that their gospel predates our canonical texts? Here it is tempting to question the accusation that the Ebionites edited and harmonized the Gospels. With Marcion (in chap. 1) such claims were said to be misunderstandings and misrepresentations, for his "canon" predated him. With the Ebionites, however, there is simply not enough evidence available. The earliest sources, like Irenaeus, that claim the Ebionites used Matthew have not actually seen the Ebionite gospel, or at least they do not comment on its specifics. If Irenaeus and Eusebius had not seen the gospel itself, they cannot inform our opinion as to what the Ebi-onites' supposed "Matthew" looked like. Was it exactly as our canonical form? Or was it already a harmony of previous gospels like the Ebionite version Epiphanius knows in the fourth century? Unfortunately, we cannot answer these questions with the limited information we have. The other possibility is that the Ebionite gospel is the original, Aramaic version of Matthew. While admittedly possible and certainly intriguing, such a conclusion is highly unlikely: the overwhelming majority of scholars have concluded that Matthew must have been written in Greek originally; and even the few scholars who think Matthew was originally written in Aramaic find that the Ebionite gospels must be derived from the later Greek version of Matthew.

Perhaps unexpectedly, the earliest reports about Ebionite theology begin by complimenting this heretical group. The Ebionites, unlike the Marcionites and Gnostics, rightly believe in one God, the God who made heaven and earth.[31] In this affirmation of their theology, the Ebionites are once again known only in comparison with other heretics. The same is true of their Christology, which is known only by way of comparison with two other heresies.

Irenaeus states that the Ebionites' understanding of Jesus was "similar" to that of Cerinthus and Carpocrates.[32] Carpocrates believed Jesus to be "just like other men," which finally sounds like a firm idea of adoptionism. However, it is not quite so clear-cut: Jesus's soul—like everyone's soul in Carpocrates's thinking—preexisted in the ethereal realm, but his soul did not forget his gnosis when the soul was trapped in flesh (= born). Because Jesus remained steadfast, God sent him a certain "Power" and enabled Jesus to disdain Jewish customs.[33] Cerinthus, similarly, held to a form of adoptionism

31. Irenaeus, *Against Heresies* 1.26.2; Hippolytus, *Refutation of All Heresies* 7.23.
32. *Against Heresies* 1.26.2.
33. Irenaeus's full treatment of Carpocrates is found in *Against Heresies* 1.25. As for saying that a "Power" adopted Jesus at baptism and then disowned him on the cross, see *Gospel*

according to which Christ was "not born of a virgin," but was simply the son of Joseph and Mary.[34] Then, at his baptism, Jesus received Christ (a different being/person) in the form of a dove, who later left him on the cross. This form of adoptionism is akin to what will be discussed in chapter 3: the docetic view of Christ, according to which Christ only appears to be human, is explained by saying that Christ is another being who descended on Jesus at baptism. If this is to be called adoptionism, then it must also be called "disownmentism": in the same way Jesus gets called "son" by God via Christ's possession/adoption of Jesus at his baptism, so Jesus gets abandoned on the cross when Christ is finished revealing secret gnosis and leaves him to suffer. The Ebionites, if they teach this, are still not depicting Jesus as being simply a human who was simply adopted as God's son. What is more, the exact teaching of the Ebionites has still not been clarified in contrast to Carpocrates and Cerinthus.

The later writer Epiphanius reports an encounter between the apostle John and Ebion. John, who for some reason never bathed, surprised his followers when he decided to go to the public baths. Once there, however, John found the heretic Ebion inside. "Let's get out of here in a hurry, brothers," John cried, "or the bath may fall and bury us along with the person who is inside in the bathing room, Ebion, because of his impiety."[35] This confrontation, while amusing, sounds suspect for various reasons. One problem is that the earlier version of this story, when Irenaeus tells it in the late second century, has John saying this about Cerinthus![36]

The confusion between Ebion and Cerinthus illustrates the problem in attempting to deduce Ebionite Christology. Just as we must question John's encounter with Ebion because it is a later confusion of two heretics, so we must question the later accounts of Ebionite Christology that are only based on a generic comparison with Carpocrates's and Cerinthus's heretical teachings.[37] Did the Ebionites teach a possessionistic form of adoptionism, through which the human being Jesus was inhabited by the heavenly spirit called Christ? Did this occur at baptism and end at the crucifixion? We simply have no reliable data with which to answer this question.

---

of Peter, where Jesus cries, "My Power, My Power, why have you forsaken me?" (trans. from Ehrman and Pleše, *Apocryphal Gospels*).

34. Irenaeus, *Against Heresies* 1.26.1. Probably dependent on Irenaeus, Tertullian also claims that Ebion's adoptionism entailed a heavenly "power" or "angel" descending on the human Jesus (*On the Flesh of Christ* 14.5).

35. Epiphanius, *Panarion* 30.24.5.

36. *Against Heresies* 3.3.4.

37. Pseudo-Tertullian, *Against All Heresies* 3.3, for example, mistakenly understands Irenaeus to say that Ebion was a disciple of Cerinthus.

Later writers who have no direct information on the Ebionites simply accept Irenaeus's statements: the Ebionites denied the virgin birth and thereby must have denied the divinity of Christ. Tertullian, for example, hears that Ebion denies the virgin birth (*On the Veiling of Virgins* 6.1) and so concludes that Ebion believes Jesus is "merely of the seed of David, and therefore not also the Son of God."[38] Similarly, Eusebius, who is clearly relying on Irenaeus for an Ebionite denial of the virgin birth, deduces that these heretics believed Jesus to be a "plain and common man."[39] These writers, however, clearly depend on Irenaeus, and yet they clearly go beyond Irenaeus's own statements. Are their interpretations reliable?

The notion of a strict adoptionism, according to which Jesus is *merely* a human who was called God's son, is far from verifiable. Irenaeus himself at least never claimed this for the Ebionites. Origen, who also knows Irenaeus's account, found some Ebionites who had an orthodox Christology. He is the first and only writer to speak of the "twofold" heresy of the Ebionites: the Ebionites who hold to the virgin birth (but keep the law) and those who deny the virgin birth (and keep the law).[40] It seems that Origen mistakenly took Irenaeus's comparison with Carpocrates and Cerinthus to mean that the Ebionites likewise denied the virgin birth and taught a possessionistic adoptionism. However, when Origen encountered other Jewish Christians who kept the law (his definition of an Ebionite), he was surprised to find them accepting the virgin birth. Thus, we do not have confirmation of Ebionite adoptionism, but evidence to the contrary.

Returning to Irenaeus, the bishop of Lyon does mention how the Ebionites claim Jesus was "begotten by Joseph."[41] So here is a clear indication that they denied the virgin birth. Or so it would seem. However, in this paragraph, Irenaeus is not addressing Christology, nor is he relying on firsthand or even secondhand information. Instead, he is discussing the reliability of the Septuagint (= pre-Christian Greek translation of the Old Testament), and Irenaeus deduces what readers of the Hebrew Scriptures stipulate about Jesus. Jewish opponents of Christianity insist that the word from Isaiah 7:14 is "young

---

38. Tertullian, *On the Flesh of Christ* 14; cf. *Prescript against Heretics* 33.11. Likewise, Hippolytus, *Refutation of All Heresies* 7.23.

39. Eusebius, *Ecclesiastical History* 3.27.2. For Eusebius's reliance on Irenaeus, see Eusebius, *Proof of the Gospel* 7.1, where the Ebionites translate Isa. 7:14 as "young woman" instead of "virgin." This information is known only from Irenaeus, *Against Heresies* 3.21.1 (see discussion below).

40. Origen in one instance speaks of Ebionites who think that Christ came only to carnal Israel (*On First Principles* 4.3.8), with no mention of heretical Christology. When he does mention "some" who deny the virgin birth (*Against Celsus* 5.61), he stipulates that the Ebionites are a "twofold sect."

41. Irenaeus, *Against Heresies* 3.21.1.

woman," not "virgin" as the Greek translates it. Irenaeus understands Ebionites to be "Jewish opponents of Christianity," and he knows they prefer the Hebrew (= Aramaic?) over the Greek Scriptures. Therefore—accepting an inductive reasoning—the Ebionites deny the virgin birth.[42] In truth, their Christology is not unearthed and revealed, but instead it has been assumed and stereotyped.

In light of the temptation to identify Ebionite Christology with Carpocratian adoptionism, it must also be remembered that Irenaeus likens Ebionite Christology to Cerinthus's thought as well. Cerinthus claimed that Jesus was the son of Joseph and Mary and distinct from the heavenly being named Christ who descended upon him at the baptism. Therefore, this is not the "low" Christology often implied in the term "adoptionism," according to which Jesus is merely a human called God's son. Instead, the human Jesus is adopted/possessed by the heavenly being Christ.

As mentioned above, Epiphanius reports that the Ebionites viewed Jesus as a preexistent angel.[43] This could be read as (a) a reliable account of Ebionite Christology that is similar to that of Carpocrates and Cerinthus; (b) an unreliable confusion of Ebionite Christology with that of Carpocrates and Cerinthus; or (c) a non-Ebionite Christology held by the Jewish Christian group known to Epiphanius that resembled the Ebionites of earlier reports. We simply have no firm or reliable information about the Ebionite understanding of Jesus.

In sum, the Ebionites may or may not have held to Jesus's preexistence. They may or may not have believed that a heavenly spirit, angel, or aeon (a concept usually associated with Gnosticism) named Christ adopted the earthly human named Jesus. They may or may not have claimed this adoption occurred at Jesus's baptism. They may or may not have taught a disownmentism according to which the heavenly Christ abandoned Jesus on the cross. All of these tenets are said to be taught by other heretics, and a comparison is made by some writers (but not others) with the Ebionites (but not all the Ebionites). With such uncertainty in the sources, how should we understand the Ebionite heresy?

The Orthodox Response

Whether or not the Ebionites ever existed (as a sect called Ebionites) is beyond the scope of what we can definitively argue presently. It may have been that

42. Using the same logic, Eusebius (*Ecclesiastical History* 6.17; cf. *Proof of the Gospel* 7.1) deemed Symmachus an Ebionite: Symmachus (in actuality a Jew) translated the disputed noun in Isa. 7:14 as "young woman" like the Ebionites (according to Eusebius's source, Irenaeus). Ergo, he must be an Ebionite. Today, scholars reject this fallacious reasoning for Symmachus, and the same should be acknowledged with the Ebionites.

43. *Panarion* 30.14.5 and 30.16.4–5.

there was a clearly defined sect who held strictly to the law, repudiated Paul, and held to some form of an adoptionist Christology. On the other hand, our sources equally attest to a wide diversity of groups that were "Jewish Christians" (in some ill-defined way) who may or may not have defined themselves as in solidarity with the "Poor," and these groups all looked alike to the later writers far removed from Christianity's Judean roots.

Regardless, the orthodox writers long remembered the Ebionites as quintessential examples of a *low* Christology—even though the attestation for low, rather than high, Christology is very late.[44] That is, the Ebionites held a view of Christ that denied his divine preexistence (high) and only affirmed his human birth (low). In this way, their adoptionism (imagined or otherwise) is most especially formative for the church's orthodoxy because it represents one extreme of a christological mistake (Christ is merely human) that would counterbalance the other extreme christological mistake said to be held by the Gnostics (Christ was merely divine; see chap. 3).

In the opposite direction, later thinkers like Paul of Samosata (bishop of Antioch ca. 260) would insist that Jesus was just a prophet adopted as "Son" by God, who placed his Word in him.[45] Such an "adoptionist" error would keep the heresy of "low Christology" alive in the memory of the orthodox party, even long after the so-called Ebionites were a direct threat to their communities. What, then, was seen to be such a threat from Ebionite Christology?

The orthodox writers found the Ebionites' low Christology to be problematic because of the implications for soteriology (= doctrine of salvation). The argument ran along two lines:

1. If Jesus became God's son by keeping the law, then none of us can be saved because we cannot fully keep the law.

2. If Jesus is not truly divine, then our salvation is only *from sin* and not *to God*.

44. For recent evidence that the earliest "Jewish Christians" held to a high Christology, see Daniel Boyarin, *The Jewish Gospels: The Story of the Jewish Christ* (New York: New Press, 2012). Boyarin insists, "It won't be possible any longer to think of some ethical religious teacher who was later promoted to divinity under the influence of alien Greek notions, with his so-called original message being distorted and lost; the idea of Jesus as divine-human Messiah goes back to the very beginning of the Christian movement, to Jesus himself, and even before that" (7).

45. Paul of Samosata's view of God, moreover, was probably modalistic (see chap. 4). The traditional portrayal of him, however, has been shown to be based on rhetorical caricature; see Virginia Burrus, "Rhetorical Stereotypes in the Portrait of Paul of Samosata," *VC* 43, no. 3 (1989): 215–25. The surviving evidence is simply too limited for any degree of certainty when it comes to Paul's teachings; see Frederick Norris, "Paul of Samosata: Procurator Ducenarius," *JTS* 35 (1984): 50–70.

Both of these arguments find Christology to be the central problem and salvation as a resulting symptom. Let us begin with the first argument, which involves the law.

According to the traditional understanding of the Ebionites, they taught that Jesus was adopted by God because he upheld the law in its entirety.[46] In our earlier discussion of the Ebionite scriptures, we noted that the Ebionites reportedly "rejected Paul." This positive view of the law's ability to save seems a perfect example of their disavowal of Pauline teaching (cf. Gal. 2:16; Rom. 3:20). Eusebius clearly thought that the Ebionites were rejecting Paul's notion of faith—not works—as the means of salvation: "For they considered him a plain and common man, who was justified only because of his superior virtue. . . . In their opinion the observance of the ceremonial law was altogether necessary, on the ground that they could not be saved by faith in Christ alone and by a corresponding life."[47] This statement reflects the central problem of low Christology and the resulting symptom of inadequate soteriology. If Christ is not God incarnate fulfilling the law, then we must save ourselves by the law (which is impossible according to Paul). The Ebionites (or groups of "Jewish Christians"), however, may not have consciously rejected Paul; they may simply have not known Paul. Perhaps their sole reliance on Matthew reflects a community who had not yet accepted a fourfold Gospel canon. Perhaps they simply have not been given Paul's letters, as he was the apostle to the gentiles and they (in some sense) are Jews. Regardless of the historical facts now clouded by our sources, the memory of the Ebionites in the minds of the orthodox writers is of a Christology and a soteriology that are insufficient because no one is saved by the law (cf. Acts 13:39; Heb. 7:19). We know and relate to God in Christ, not via the law.

The second line of argument against Ebionite Christology and soteriology has to do with reconciliation to God. If Jesus is merely a law keeper (rabbi, prophet, Nazirite, etc.), then we have not been reconciled to God in any real way. If Jesus is not Immanuel/God-with-us, then we have not known God. Irenaeus leads this kind of response by asking, "How can they [the Ebionites] be saved unless it was God who wrought out their salvation upon earth?"[48] Tertullian, similarly, will ask how Christ could really save us if he were anything other than God: a prophet or even an angel would still not restore us all the way to God, but would only reconcile us to the prophet or the angel.[49] The Ebionites theoretically could have responded that

46. Hippolytus, *Refutation of All Heresies* 7.23.
47. Eusebius, *Ecclesiastical History* 3.27.2.
48. *Against Heresies* 4.33.4.
49. *On the Flesh of Christ* 14 and 18.

salvation is more about entrance into heaven than about direct communion with God, but the orthodox writers would have found such a minimalistic understanding of salvation inadequate. Salvation is about nothing less than reconciliation to God.

What the Ebionites Remembered

The gospel according to the Ebionites (as remembered by orthodox opponents) is that we can become children of God if we keep the law, just like Jesus. Perhaps the Ebionites (or some Jewish Christian group/s) believed in Jesus and followed his teachings. They loved God and considered themselves followers of Jesus. It is hard to condemn such a group, especially if they championed Jesus's teachings about solidarity with the "poor" (e.g., Matt. 5:3; 6:1–3; 19:20–22; 25:31–46).

Today, we need not condemn them so much as evaluate their teachings' sufficiency. The heresy of this adoptionistic Christology lies in an inadequate understanding of who Jesus is and what Jesus does. With the luxury of a more complete collection of scriptures, and with the benefit of hindsight, later Christians realize that keeping the law and avoiding sin was never the aim of God's plan. Long before the law, humans stood in need of God, and long after Jesus's claim to fulfill the law, they stand in the same need. If Jesus is not God, our salvation cannot be complete in him.

Conclusion

I began this chapter by admitting that the Ebionite heresy is like an autostereogram image. Perhaps it would be better to conclude that the Ebionite heresy is more like a Rorschach test: the viewer decides which aspects to focus on in the inkblot that is our collective historical sources, deriving a corresponding image of the Ebionites. The Ebionites, like the butterfly seen in the Rorschach test, are still not visible. They are imagined, imaged in. I do not wish to suggest that, like a Rorschach test, one's perception of the Ebionites says more about one's psyche than about the Ebionites themselves (although this is always a possibility; witness the "quest" for the historical Jesus, wherein scholars were famously said to have looked down the long well of history only to find their own reflection staring back at them). Yet I do contend that one's perception of the Ebionites says more about one's historical theory and assumptions (e.g., about "Jewish Christianity") than about the Ebionites themselves. The Ebionites themselves remain beyond our scope.

What we can know about the Ebionites is the impression they left on the memory of the emerging orthodox church. Few, if any, of the church fathers had direct experience with a group self-entitled as Ebionites. The church fathers, however, record the legacy of a group who accepted Jesus as the Messiah while continuing to keep their Jewish customs. To some, this was benign, a relic of the past. To others, this was dangerous, a lukewarm position—being neither fully Christian nor fully Jewish—that misunderstood Jesus as one who earned his title by keeping the law. This adoptionistic Christology, real or rumored, had to be rejected for fear it would mislead unsuspecting converts with only half-truths. While Jesus does fulfill the law (Matt. 5:17), he is "more than" any mere prophet or earthly king (Matt. 12:41–42). The LORD himself promised to save us in person (e.g., Isa. 49:7–26), and Jesus saves because Jesus is Lord (Phil. 2:11).

Recommended Bibliography

Bauckham, Richard. "The Origin of the Ebionites." In *The Image of the Judaeo-Christians in Ancient Jewish and Christian Literature*, edited by P. J. Tomson and D. Lambers-Petry, 162–81. WUNT 158. Tübingen: Mohr Siebeck, 2003.

Häkkinen, Sakari. "Ebionites." In *A Companion to Second-Century Christian "Heretics,"* edited by Antti Marjanen and Petri Luomanen, 247–78. Leiden: Brill, 2005.

Klijn, A. F. J., and G. J. Reinink. *Patristic Evidence for Jewish-Christian Sects*. Leiden: E. J. Brill, 1973.

Luomanen, Petri. "Ebionites and Nazarenes." In *Jewish Christianity Reconsidered: Rethinking Ancient Groups and Texts*, edited by Matt Jackson-McCabe, 81–118. Minneapolis: Fortress, 2007.

Skarsaune, Oskar. "The Ebionites." In *Jewish Believers in Jesus*, edited by Oskar Skarsaune and Reidar Hvalvik, 419–62. Peabody, MA: Hendrickson, 2007.

Verheyden, Joseph. "Epiphanius on the Ebionites." In *The Image of the Judaeo-Christians in Ancient Jewish and Christian Literature*, edited by P. J. Tomson and D. Lambers-Petry, 182–208. WUNT 158. Tübingen: Mohr Siebeck, 2003.

**Summary:
Gnostics**

Key Doctrine: Docetism

- Looks-Can-Be-Deceiving Jesus
- Jesus is just a god, looking like a human

Key Date

- 130: Valentinus arrives in Rome

3

Gnostics

Docetism

A multitude of Gnostics have sprung up and have been manifested like mushrooms growing out of the ground.

—Irenaeus

It is as if one can identify various "spokes" of the Gnostic "wheel" but not the unifying "hub."

—Urban C. von Wahlde

In space, a birth of magnificent and magical proportions took place. But the birth was not finite, it was infinite. As the wombs numbered and the mitosis of the future began, it was perceived that this infamous moment in life is not temporal, it is eternal.

—Lady Gaga

The Gnostics exhibit all the classical traits of heresy.

First, they knew the truth, but turned to falsehood and intentionally misled their followers with foolish controversies and genealogies (cf.

Titus 3:9). On the other hand, they simply did not know how to read the Old Testament, and so they made every sort of ill-informed mistake.

In their arrogance they call themselves ones who have *gnōsis* (= "knowledge" in Greek). In reality these so-called Gnostics are ignorant: they do not truly know God. They do not even know the Scriptures, for they reject the right texts and accept false scriptures. They also read the right Scriptures the wrong way: they allegorize the Scriptures to make them say what they want them to say.

Their teachings are new and therefore blatantly false. Also, their teachings are old. They simply took the ideas of the pagan philosophers and baptized them with Christian terms. Their falsehood should be obvious because they do not follow Christ. Instead, they follow Basilides, Valentinus, Ptolemy— their teachers. Since they are Basilideans, Valentinians, or Ptolemeans, they are not Christian.

To add to their problems, they were lawless libertines, claiming that Paul said they were freed from the law, which allows them to sin as frequently and as grossly as they wish—just use your imagination here, and even then you probably will not be able to envision crimes as despicable as what these people do. At the same time, they think they're better than we are because they abstain from sex, marriage, meat, and any of the pleasures in life.

In short, the Gnostics are the quintessential heretics, making every mistake possible. They are so absurd no one would believe them. Yet they are so clever countless Christians have been misled by them.

They must be shunned and ignored; they must be engaged in order to disprove and defeat them.

Defining Gnosticism: Ancient Heresy or Modern Myth?

If the previous series of accusations looks to you like a dizzying display of doublespeak, you're not alone. The accusations against the Gnostics are all over the map, and students and historians alike shake their heads about what to believe and what not to believe. How can both sides in such an array of opposite claims be true? Perhaps our problem is with the category of Gnosticism.

Remember the famous story of the blind men describing an elephant? One feels the trunk and says an elephant is like a snake; one feels the leg and says the elephant is like a tree; one feels the side and says the elephant is like a wall; and so the story goes. The point is the blind men only get parts of the elephant right; they can't see the whole picture. Let us adopt that parable for the purpose of defining Gnosticism, only we will reverse the picture.

Key Terms of Gnosticism

aeons: A Latin word that, like the Greek *aiōn*, from which it derives, can be translated as "age" or "realm." The aeons in Gnostic thinking, however, are divine beings emanated from God.

cosmos: Usually translated as "world" but means specifically the created order.

demiurge: The name given to the creator of the cosmos. In Gnostic thinking the creator is not a good god but one of the lesser beings with evil intentions.

gnōsis: The Greek word for "knowledge." For Christians, this is especially the knowledge of God. For Gnostics, this is the secret knowledge unknown to other Christians.

plērōma: The Greek word for "fullness." For Gnostics, it is the heavenly realm where the divine aeons dwell.

phantasm: Literally, a spirit, but this term is used to describe Christ's appearance. In other words, Christ was not in the flesh, but only appeared so.

What if people with fully functioning eyes told the blind men what an elephant is like by describing each of the parts (which are like a snake, tree, wall, etc.). These blind men then go for a walk together. One finds a snake and says he has found an elephant's trunk, so he must have found an elephant. One finds a tree and says he has found an elephant's leg, so he must have found an elephant. One finds a wall and says he has found an elephant's side, and so on and so forth. In this retelling, the problem is that there is simply no elephant. There are only things that feel like parts of an elephant. What if, when it comes to Gnostics, there is simply no such thing as Gnosticism?

First, let us outline the traditional parts of Gnosticism—that is, the parts of the elephant in our analogy. The Gnostics generally held to the following teachings.

1. God reproduced himself. Initially, there was just God, but then something like God's Word and God's Spirit emanated from God. The process repeated itself with God's Truth, God's Wisdom, and all sorts of other aeons of God emanating from God. This view of God as a cosmic bubble machine results in some bubbles/emanations being smaller than others and some falling farther from God than others. In the end, some bubbles self-destruct, leaving a sticky residue.

2. The creation equals the fall. The sticky residue spoken of in the previous point is specifically Sophia (Greek for Wisdom herself; cf. Prov. 8), who

vainly sought to rise to God but instead was weighed down by Pride, which was born in her. Next, she bore Sorrow, Grief, and all sorts of other lower attributes (which in this telling are all aeons). These substances in effect become the material cosmos. In this telling, Sophia's Sorrow bore tears, which left eyecrust, and so began a whole series of material elements. Thus the cosmos was formed. This cosmos is different from the heavenly realm, where the higher aeons dwell, the realm called the *plērōma*. Therefore, the lower material cosmos with all of its mess is a far cry from God, who is perfect.

3. Human souls are pieces of God. Although some, or maybe all, souls preexisted in the heavenly realm, they fell into the cosmos and were trapped in their bodies. They now need to escape the world of flux and return to the stable world of perfect ideals, but since their bodies are made up of compound and confused substances, their bodies hinder their ascent back to God.

4. The creation was formed and shaped by the demiurge—not the first and highest God. The higher aeons made a maker, called the "demiurge," who would bring order to the cosmos, which was a "formless void" (cf. Gen. 1:2). Unfortunately, being himself oriented toward this lower order, this stupid demiurge never thought to look up to the *plērōma* and see the other divine beings above him. Thus, he *wrongly* claimed, "I am God, and there is no other god higher than I" (cf. Deut. 32:39).

5. The demiurge is evil. This creator-god exhibited ungodly qualities, such as jealousy (cf. Exod. 20:5). When the higher aeons slipped God's Spirit into the cosmos to help some of the trapped souls, the demiurge made arbitrary laws to prohibit their success. The first was forbidding souls to eat of the tree of gnosis, because this would make them like the gods. The dishonest demiurge even lied to the souls, bluffing that they would die if they ate of it (cf. Gen. 2:17).

6. The Savior came to rescue souls. First, the aeon named "Savior" appeared as a serpent and told the souls the truth about the fruit of gnosis (i.e., it would not kill them; cf. Gen. 3:4–5). Later, when the demiurge was persecuting souls with other plagues, the serpent was placed on a cross, and anyone who looked at it learned the secret to escape the pain and suffering of this world (cf. Num. 21:4–9; John 3:14). These kinds of secret messages were frequently sneaked into the demiurge's scriptures (a.k.a. the Old Testament).

7. The Savior fully appeared in order to reveal the secret gnosis. The Savior could not tell everyone the secret (cf. Mark 4:11), but some of his disciples

Nag Hammadi (1945)

In 1945 a pottery jar was reportedly discovered in a cave in central Egypt. Twelve leather-bound books, with pages made out of papyrus, were recovered, and additional pages found inside one of the books were collected as the thirteenth book. The texts consisted of Coptic translations of dozens of Gnostic texts. Although a few other Gnostic writings had survived, most had been eradicated by orthodox Christians, and so this discovery provided modern scholars with the opportunity to hear the Gnostics in their own words. The texts themselves turned out to be much more diverse than Gnostics were previously understood to be. Therefore, the Nag Hammadi texts allowed for a drastic revision to the historical understanding of the so-called Gnostics.

were ready. The spiritual ones, not the carnal (cf. 1 Cor. 3:1–8), received the Savior's secret teachings and then handed down the secret gnosis to their disciples. The majority of Christians do not have this gnosis. The secret is basically how to read the Scriptures to find the hidden meanings. The moral of the story is to resist the demiurge and escape this evil body and this evil world.

8. The Savior only appeared to have flesh. Since flesh is evil, the higher truth could not have truly become incarnate and experienced the lower passions. Instead, Christ only appeared to have flesh. In reality he was a hologram or ghost—the Gnostics' word for the Savior's appearance was "phantasm." Our word for this teaching is "docetism" (from the Greek *dokeō*, "to appear" or "to seem").

With these teachings so neatly outlined, it may seem like Gnosticism is easily understood and defined. The Gnostics, however, prove harder to nail down, for no single group of Gnostics taught all eight of the points outlined above. These teachings represent a scholarly stereotyping of Gnostic teachings. They are different parts of Gnosticism, but there is no Gnosticism.

When the Nag Hammadi texts were discovered in 1945, scholars were able to read what the Gnostics themselves said, as opposed to reading what the orthodox writers said about the Gnostics. The resulting picture that emerged was very different from the one painted by those orthodox heresiologists. The main difference was that the Gnostics, according to their own writings, were much more diverse than previously thought. Some believed in some of the teachings listed above; some did not; some believed in other teachings besides these. To return to our parable of the blind men feeling different things and thinking there was one elephant, it turns out something like that was happening with the traditional telling of "Gnosticism." They were in fact describing not parts of Gnosticism, but a variety of different sects.[1]

Blurred Lines: Gnosticisms and Orthodoxies

Once the concept of a single sect known as Gnosticism is expunged from our thinking, we can even return to the orthodox sources and see that they describe not Gnosticism,[2] but gnosticisms. Whereas one can speak more accurately about individual sects, such as Sethianism and Valentinianism (although even in these groups there is much more diversity than one might expect), there is no one thing called "Gnosticism."[3]

What about the people who called themselves "gnostics"? Can we not say that gnosticism consisted of such groups? There are two reasons why we cannot use the self-description "gnostic" as a criterion. First, the heretical groups attacked by the orthodox writers by and large did not call themselves "gnostics."[4] As Justin Martyr reports (ca. 160), despite his claim that these heretics are false Christs, "yet they style themselves Christians."[5] In other words, even if they did claim to follow the teachings of Valentinus or Ptolemy, they probably preferred simply to call themselves "Christians." Second, many Christians whom we would deem to be well within the bounds of orthodoxy called themselves "gnostic" or at least people who have true "gnosis"—the classic examples being the apostles Paul (e.g., 1 Cor. 8:7) and Peter (acc. to 2 Pet. 1:5–6; 3:18) and the second-century teacher Clement of Alexandria.[6] If not all gnostics called themselves that, and if some orthodox called themselves "gnostic," then the term itself is useless without further definition.

1. Marvin W. Meyer, *The Gnostic Discoveries: The Impact of the Nag Hammadi Library* (San Francisco: HarperSanFrancisco, 2005), 41, finds Irenaeus to be relatively fair in his presentation.
2. The capitalized term "Gnosticism" seems to imply a unified movement; but, as will be seen, we cannot clearly define any such movement. Hereafter, therefore, the term will be lowercased except when referring to the idea of a unified movement.
3. The view championed by Michael A. Williams, *Rethinking "Gnosticism": An Argument for Dismantling a Dubious Category* (Princeton: Princeton University Press, 1996). See also Karen King, *What Is Gnosticism?* (Cambridge, MA: Belknap Press of Harvard University Press, 2003); and Ismo Dunderberg, *Beyond Gnosticism: Myth, Lifestyle, and Society in the School of Valentinus* (New York: Columbia University Press, 2008).
4. *The Apocalypse of Peter* claims to be apostolic, as opposed to those (we would call orthodox) who "ruled heretically" (74). *The Testimony of Truth* attacks "heretics," like Valentinus and Basilides (56–58). Cf. *Concept of Our Great Power* 40, opposed to "evil heresies."
5. *Dialogue with Trypho* 35.
6. For Paul, see also *Hypostasis of the Archons* 86; see also Col. 1:13 and Eph. 6:12. For Clement, see his *Stromata*, esp. book 4.

Some recent scholars have tried to rescue the category of gnosticism.[7] If there is not an eight-point list accurately reflective of every gnostic and gnostic text, then such a list of characteristics at least helps us detect a kind of family resemblance among gnostics. If a specific gnostic or gnostic group fits some of these characteristics, they are gnostic. Such an approach, however, leaves much to be desired. After all, if it walks and talks like a duck *but does not look like a duck*, it is probably not a duck. It may be my six-year-old doing her most excellent duck impression! Other attempts that try to see gnosticism as a scholarly construct have their place, because we cannot remain speechless about such an important topic as gnosticism. Talking about "Gnosticism" (in this approach always written with quotes) or the heresy-formerly-known-as-Gnosticism (which always takes too long to say) is appropriate so long as the data is examined on a case-by-case basis. How does this particular group, writer, or text exhibit or not exhibit the traits we deem to be gnostic? Left only with this scholarly-construct understanding of gnosticism, we can proceed with our study, but simultaneously we must always aim for more precision.

One last point needs to be said about defining gnosticism in general. What was the origin of gnosticism? Again, the answer is simple, if you ask orthodox writers like Irenaeus.[8] Simon Magus (Acts 8:9–25) was jealous of the apostles and spread false teachings. His student, Menander, taught gnosticism to his own disciples, who kept adapting their teachings until you get to guys like Basilides, Valentinus, and Ptolemy. The orthodox account of the heretics' unbroken chain of anti-apostolic succession is convincing on the surface, but it lacks historical plausibility. Many of the so-called gnostic teachers and sects have little or no connection to other such groups. Irenaeus's description of these heretics as "mushrooms" that pop up everywhere yet out of nowhere seems more honest than his claim that there is a family tree of heretics.[9]

Today, in attempting to understand gnostic origins, scholars do not look for a succession of heretical teachers so much as they look for a background movement. While the various gnostic groups undoubtedly appropriated Platonistic philosophy (see esp. Plato's *Timaeus*), the claim that Greek philosophy

7. See Christoph Markschies, *Gnosis: An Introduction*, trans. John Bowden (London: T&T Clark, 2003); Antti Marjanen, "Gnosticism," in *The Oxford Handbook of Early Christian Studies*, ed. Susan Ashbrook Harvey and David G. Hunter (Oxford: Oxford University Press, 2008), 203–20; David Brakke, *The Gnostics: Myth, Ritual, and Diversity in Early Christianity* (Cambridge, MA: Harvard University Press, 2010). Less convincing is Birger Pearson, *Gnosticism and Christianity in Roman and Coptic Egypt* (New York: T&T Clark, 2004).

8. Unlike the thought of the Ebionites (see chap. 2), certain gnostics were read firsthand by Irenaeus (*Against Heresies* 1.pref.; 1.31.1; 3.11.9; 3.12.1–7; 3.13.2; cf. Clement of Alexandria, *Stromata* 4.12–13).

9. *Against Heresies* 1.29.1. Cf. Tertullian, *Against the Valentinians* 39.

is the intellectual ancestor for gnosticism is problematic for two reasons.[10] First, the tie to philosophy was used to dismiss these groups as heretics by some orthodox writers. Tertullian famously asked, "What has Athens to do with Jerusalem?"[11] This accusation, therefore, entails a polemic that tends to exaggerate the relationship with Greek philosophy.[12] Orthodox writers like Tertullian were themselves deeply indebted to Hellenistic thought, even when they distanced themselves from it. Second, not all of the so-called gnostics exhibit such blatant Greek thinking. There is much to suggest that Jewish esotericism (which predated Christianity) serves as the backdrop to many gnostic teachings.[13] Similarly, the mystery cults of the East help explain much of the material found in gnostic thinking.[14] We also must admit that the ancient world was much more complex than is often acknowledged: ancient thinkers did not need to choose between being Jewish and being Greek and being Eastern.[15] Therefore, any quest for the origin of gnosticism should probably look to all three of these backdrops, and such a quest should admit that there were likely origins (not origin—singular) of gnosticisms.

Another problem found in our either/or categories of gnostic and orthodox is that the sources display an overlap between the two. Even within orthodox Christianity, one can find gnostic tendencies. A few examples will suffice.

1. Although the idea of a chain of being (God as a cosmic bubble machine, mentioned earlier) is problematic and unscriptural, the orthodox Christians will use the same terminology (such as prolation and consubstantial) to argue for the doctrine of the Trinity (see chaps. 4 and 5).[16]

10. E.g., *Zostrianos*; cf. Porphyry, *Life of Plotinus* 16.

11. *Prescript against Heretics* 7. Cf. Justin Martyr, *Dialogue with Trypho* 35; Hippolytus, *Refutation of All Heresies*; Epiphanius, *Panarion* 26.9.3.

12. *Eugnostos the Blessed* begins by rejecting "all the philosophers."

13. *Eugnostos the Blessed, Thought of Norea,* and *Apocalypse of Adam* may be non-Christian texts. Much of their material comes from Jewish apocalyptic writings, and they contain no specifically Christian details. Similarly, in *On the Origin of the World* Jesus Christ is mentioned only once (105), as part of the heavenly court of Sabaoth. For Wisdom/Sophia in Jewish literature, see esp. Prov. 8; *1 Enoch* 42; Sirach 24; Wisdom of Solomon 7–8, and Philo. On the other hand, cf. Hippolytus, *Refutation of All Heresies* 6.29.

14. Hippolytus, *Refutation of All Heresies* 5.2; *Zostrianos*; Archelaus, *Acts of the Disputation with the Heresiarch Manes* 55.

15. Cf. *Exegesis of the Soul* and *Hypostasis of the Archons*, which seem reliant on Jewish wisdom literature, Hellenistic thought, and esoteric mythology. Similarly, see the syncretization of Pauline material (Gal. 1–2; 2 Cor. 12:2–4), Jewish apocalypticism (Dan. 7:13; *1 Enoch* 46–47), and Greek mythology (the Erinyes) in *Apocalypse of Paul*.

16. *Tripartite Tractate* 51 insists, "Yet [the Father] is not like a solitary individual. Otherwise, how could he be a father? For whenever there is a 'father,' the name 'son' follows. But the single one, who alone is the Father, is like a root with tree, branches and fruit" (cf. *Interpretation of*

2. Even though a wholesale revisionist reading of the Old Testament is rejected, mainstream Christians will embrace an allegorical reading of Scripture as the norm for Christian practice.[17] Even so, it should also be noted that many of the alleged gnostics read the Old Testament in the traditional, orthodox way.[18]

3. While the full-fledged gnostic dualism between body and soul (wherein body is bad and soul is good) is rejected by orthodox Christians, mainstream Christianity retained a body/soul distinction (wherein the soul is higher than the body, but the body is still good; cf. Matt. 26:41).[19]

4. As for secret gnosis, the secretiveness of Jesus's mission has always been accepted (see Mark 4:10–12), and Paul concedes that not everyone is ready for the "meat of the Word" (1 Cor. 3—also cited above).[20]

Knowledge 19). The exact same analogy is used by orthodox architects of the doctrine of the Trinity (e.g., Tertullian, *Against Praxeas* 8 and Hippolytus, *Against Noetus* 11.1; cf. Justin, *Dialogue with Trypho* 128.5), and will continue to be used as an analogy long into the trinitarian debates of the fourth century (e.g., Epiphanius, *Panarion* 62.1.5–9).

17. On Genesis, see *Hypostasis of the Archons*; *On the Origins of the World*; *Paraphrase of Shem*. See also sections of *Apocryphon of John*, *Testimony of Truth*, and *Tripartite Tractate*, wherein anyone resisting the Creator is praised.

18. E.g., the *Gospel of Philip* 74: "That one [the tree of knowledge] killed Adam, but here the tree of knowledge made men alive. . . . It became the beginning of death." This passage, however, represents an extreme denigration of the law—a point much debated in the early Christian centuries.

19. Concerns include the preexistence of souls, which is found in some gnostic texts (e.g., *Authoritative Teaching* 23; *Hypostasis of the Archons* 96; and *(First) Apocalypse of James* 35) and which was even entertained by Augustine until late in life (see *On Free Will* 3.20.56–57; *Retractions* 1.1.3). This view of bodies as a downfall of preexisting or eternal souls seems to require a negative view of creation, for the creation, in this view, *equals* the fall (e.g., *Tripartite Tractate* 115). Therefore, created bodies are necessarily deemed evil (e.g., *Apocryphon of John* 21; cf. Rom. 7:24). Similarly, the final salvation is offered only for the soul and not for the body in some texts (e.g., *Paraphrase of Shem* 34; *(First) Apocalypse of James* 27). Irenaeus and those who follow his line of thinking insist that proper protology (created bodies are good) and proper eschatology (bodies will ultimately be redeemed) necessarily correspond with proper Christology (God incarnate). However, rejection of "fleshly" weakness (e.g., *Second Treatise of the Great Seth* 70) could be a rejection of sinful flesh (cf. Rom. 7:5, 18, 25).

20. Basilides cited Eph. 3:3–5 and 2 Cor. 12:4 to show that Paul reserved some teachings for the elect (according to Hippolytus, *Refutation of All Heresies* 7.14). However, texts like *Apocryphon of James* and *Book of Thomas the Contender* are labeled gnostic solely on the basis of the notion of "secret knowledge" (see the opening line of each), even though nothing in the content of the books is necessarily heretical. Alternatively, *Gospel of Truth*, which is generally understood to be more strictly gnostic, says this secret is meant to be shared with all, but sin blocks most people from seeking it: "Speak of the truth with those who search for it and of knowledge to those who have committed sin in their error" (32). The same occurs at the end of *Apocryphon of John*; after John is told to share the gnosis "secretly," the text ends, "And he went to his fellow disciples and related to them what the savior had told him" (31–32), implying that the secret is told to any who follow Christ. To be sure, some texts certainly claim this secret

Cosmogony

"Cosmogony," which is derived from the Greek words *kosmos* (= the world/universe) and *gignomai* (= come into being), is the term used to describe one's belief about the origin of the universe. Early Christians debated how to interpret the scriptural teaching on creation. Based on the wording in Genesis 1:2, many ancient Hebrews understood the material earth to be coeternal with God (as did virtually all ancient Near Eastern religions). God created—or "constructed" or formed—the earth into an ordered world, but from a "formless void" and a chaotic "deep" that already existed. Many early Christians, however, often understood God as the creator of "all things" (John 1:3; Acts 4:24 with reference to Exod. 20:11 [cf. Ps. 146:6; Neh. 9:6]; Rom. 11:36; 1 Cor. 8:6; 11:12; Eph. 3:9; Col. 1:16; Heb. 11:3; Rev. 4:11; also see Eccles. 11:5; Isa. 6:62). Therefore, *all things* must have been created from *no*-thing (hence the theological phrase *ex nihilo*; see *Shepherd of Hermas* 26.1 for an early expression of this thinking, and cf. Rom. 4:17 and 1 Cor. 1:28).

Another prominent cosmogony from the ancient world is found in Plato's *Ti-maeus*. There the cosmos of temporal and changeable matter came into being by a god, called the "demiurge" (artisan or maker). Later Platonists would debate (a) whether the world truly had a beginning or was coeternal with the realm of forms, and (b) whether the demiurge and his world were good or flawed/evil. The gnostics (like Marcion; chap. 1), were accused of holding to option (b). Many gnostics also syncretized this understanding of the world's origin with the common notion in ancient Mediterranean and Eastern cosmogonies wherein all things, including the demiurge himself, somehow emanated from the original god(s). In other words, all the heavenly and the material elements somehow emanated from the divine reality, perhaps in a chain of being. Or, at least that's how they were heard by their orthodox opponents.

Irenaeus distinguished the orthodox cosmogony and that of the gnostic view by rejecting any form of pantheism or panentheism. Because God is the maker of "all things," and because God calls his creation "good" (Gen. 1:4, 9, 12, 18, 21, 25, 31), two things must be confessed. God creates; everything else is created.

Therefore, not all Christians have obtained or are ready to obtain the higher gnosis. Since many of the so-called gnostic sources even exhibit more orthodox versions of these different tenets, it must be admitted that gnostic tendencies fit within the bounds of Christianity.[21] The question about whether

gnosis more strictly (e.g., *Apocalypse of Peter* 73); nevertheless, such an array of options belies the idea that gnostics (all of them and only them) held to secret knowledge.

21. For example, the *Teachings of Silvanus* affirms Christ as the Creator and creation as good (see esp. 100 and 113).

a specific teaching has crossed the bounds of acceptable orthodoxy must be assessed on an individual basis.

Some different cases, therefore, will be outlined briefly to illustrate the different groups and expressions of gnostic thinking. After that historical review, we will more closely examine the problematic theology in general and unorthodox Christology in particular.

Gnostic Factions: Every One of You Saith, I Am of Paul, and I of . . .

How did gnosticism begin and multiply so quickly? One of our earliest sources on the subject tells us about the origin and propagation of the gnostic heresy. The general outline of gnostic sects is usually as follows: (a) Simon Magus, the father of heresy, taught several students who established their own sects; (b) the Sethian branch of gnosticism stemmed from these early groups, and they were more akin to Eastern mystery cults; and (c) the Valentinian school, which was more Greek and philosophical, spawned many teachers who kept changing Valentinus's doctrines. This threefold schema, while oversimplified, is a common understanding of the major branches of gnosticism. We now need to review each branch in order to see how reliable our information is about each group and to see what parts of gnosticism each represents.

Simon Magus

Irenaeus claims that the mention of "what is falsely called knowledge" in 1 Timothy (6:20) was directed against Simon the Magician (Acts 8:9–25). Simon and his student Menander reportedly taught a form of cosmogony wherein God had Ennoea (from a Greek word for an idea in the mind) spring from his head. In turn, Ennoea herself bore more divine beings, which were the angels and archangels who created the world. One of Simon and Menander's students, Saturninus, modified the teachings about creation only slightly, adding more detail about the salvation of souls, but Basilides elaborated a great deal (see fig. 3.1). Other groups also allegedly spring from this early line, but the evidence is shaky at best.

Sethians

Groups like the Barbeloites, Ophites, and Sethites differ a great deal from the heretical teachers named in connection to Simon. Like Basilides, this

Figure 3.1. The Cosmology of Basilides

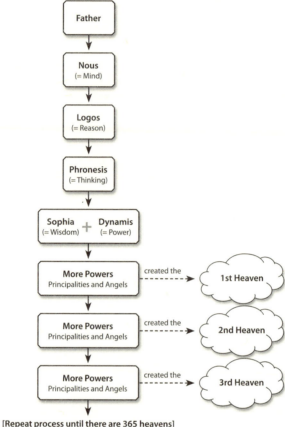

[Repeat process until there are 365 heavens]

group claimed that a whole series of aeons emanated from God. While their family tree of aeons will not be recounted in full, it is important to see their radically different view of Christ. The Barbeloites, for example, spoke of a being called Light and named him Anointed (i.e., Christ) but distinguished him from Logos, Truth, Wisdom, Savior, and a whole host of other aeons.

Also in this branch is included the Ophites, whose name derives from the Greek word for serpent. They read the Old Testament in such a way that any enemy of the demiurge is a friend of the Savior.[22] Sources are unclear as to whether the Ophites, Sethites, Cainites, and other sects are somehow

---

22. In so doing, they separated most attributes and names of God into different aeons: e.g., "Iao," as in *YHWH*; "Sabaoth" (cf. Isa. 6:3); "Adoneus," as in *Adonai*; "Eloeus," as in *Elohim*; etc.; see Irenaeus, *Against Heresies* 1.29–30.

Valentinus

Little is known of this teacher from Egypt, who worked for a time in Alexandria. According to Clement of Alexandria (*Stromata* 7.17), his followers claimed he learned from an otherwise unknown Theudas, who himself learned from the apostle Paul. According to Irenaeus, he came to Rome around 136 to 140, but after around fifteen years of teaching he left the church of Rome. Tertullian says this was due to jealousy: Valentinus was overlooked as a candidate for bishop of Rome (*Against the Valentinians* 4; cf. *Prescript against Heretics* 30.2). While such a report is today dismissed as slander, it may betray the fact that the church in Rome did not expel Valentinus. The reasons could be: (1) Valentinus began to teach heresy only out of spite and only after this event—an unlikely explanation; (2) Valentinus developed his system of heretical cosmology only later—also implausible given the alleged connections with Alexandrian forms of gnosticism; (3) Valentinus's heresy simply had not been exposed yet—a possible scenario; (4) Valentinus taught in one of many schools and/or house churches yet to be organized in Rome at this time—the most likely possibility. So many of Valentinus's "disciples" reportedly founded their own schools or sects that scholars conclude he must have been a very influential individual. The details of this influence, unfortunately, are obscure.

connected or even the same form of Christianity. These groups offered an elaborative rereading of the Scriptures, one that reimagined the entire world and its relation to the heavenly realm.[23] While all of these elements look dubious at best, the problem again becomes especially clear in their Christology: Jesus, who is possessed by Christ and Wisdom, is crucified and left to die by these aeons, who cannot be harmed. On a more positive note, Christ-Sophia did return to Jesus's body after three days and raise his soul (not his fleshly, created parts). The problems in these teachings, such as polytheism, apparently even concerned some of the thinkers from within these sects. Valentinus reportedly amended these forms of gnosticism.

---

23. In his debate with Celsus, an anti-Christian writer, Origen describes the diagram made by the Ophites, said to be a gnostic sect (*Against Celsus* 6.24–38). While Origen's description is incomplete, many have attempted to reconstruct the diagram. Three such attempts are the following: Jacques Matter, *Histoire critique du gnosticisme* (Paris: F. G. Levrault, 1828), 3:105; Andrew J. Welburn, "Reconstructing the Ophite Diagram," *NovT* 23, no. 3 (1981): 283; and Alistair H. B. Logan, *The Gnostics: Identifying an Early Christian Cult* (London: T&T Clark, 2006), 42. (Logan's work has been made available online at http://www.gnosis.org/library /ophite.htm.)

Valentinians

Valentinus allegedly founded a heretical "school."[24] Irenaeus's claim that
the Valentinians emerged from the Ophite form of gnosticism looks compelling because Valentinus's system mirrors much of what was seen in it. One
difference seems to be that Valentinus dropped the Hebraisms and utilized
more strictly Greek terminology. Also, Irenaeus's account of Valentinus's cosmogony provides one of the more complete pictures of how Christ emerged
as born of light but the demiurge was weighed down by the material order.
While this sounds like outright polytheism, Valentinus's student Marcus apparently explained this with an elaborate theory of how numbers contain other
numbers, and so there can be a plurality within a unity—something that will
be important in later debates about the doctrine of the Trinity.[25] Marcus even
applies this method to the Savior, so that names like Christ, Son, and others
can be understood as a unity.[26] While uncompelling to most later Christians,
this view can be sympathetically understood as an attempt to confess that the
"*plērōma*/fullness of Deity" (Col. 2:9) revealed in Christ includes all God's
aspects, attributes, and eternal nature; in short, Christ is the "aeon of aeons."
The especially problematic aspect of the Christology becomes apparent when
seen in light of Christ's work. Was God in Jesus Christ saving the world? For
gnostics, the answer is no; it only seemed so.

In order to see how salvation worked in Christ, it will help to turn to
another one of Valentinus's students, Ptolemy. Having explained that the
divine reality emanates forth as a *plērōma* of aeons, Ptolemy teaches about
Jesus's nature. Ptolemy affirms Marcus's way of thinking, according to
which Christ is somehow the unity of all the aeons of God, and yet there
is still a glaring problem: placing the Savior himself into a material body.
That material body would trap him just as the other souls' material bodies
had trapped them, or at least it would contaminate him with the same disease. The solution: the Savior joins himself to the soul called Christ (≠ the
heavenly aeon of this name). Christ's soul, then, "with unspeakable skill,"

24. Tertullian, *Against the Valentinians* 39, claims Valentinus preceded all other gnostics.
This claim, however, seems to derive from his reading of Irenaeus's logical, not chronological,
ordering (*Against Heresies* 1.11.1: ". . . those heretics . . . The first of them, Valentinus . . .";
also cf. *Against Heresies* 3.2.1).
25. See Hippolytus, *Refutation of All Heresies* 6.29, for Pythagoras's influence. Cf. *Gospel
of Truth* 23, 51, 52; *Gospel of Philip* 53–54, 76; *Valentinian Exposition* 22; and *Teachings of
Silvanus* 96, which insists, "For he who says, 'I have many gods,' is godless" (96).
26. *Gospel of Philip* 56: "Jesus's is a hidden name, 'Christ' is a revealed name. . . . Christ
has everything in himself, whether man or angel or mystery, and the father." Cf. *Apocryphon
of John* 2; *(First) Apocalypse of James* 26; and *Tripartite Tractate* 62–63: "He is the Son, who
is full, complete and faultless."

Ptolemy

A certain gnostic teacher named Ptolemy was thriving in the mid-second century. Irenaeus says he was a student of Valentinus. A later church father, Epiphanius, records a previously unknown letter of Ptolemy to a woman named Flora. Flora's question reflects a perspective much like Marcion's: How could the good God known in Christ have inspired the law (i.e., our Old Testament)? Ptolemy's answer is more nuanced than Marcion's: rather than rejecting the Old Testament God as evil and the Christ-God as good, Ptolemy believes that there are three sources to the law. Some parts of the law are in fact good and divine, while others are traditions of elders and need to be abolished, while still others were given by Moses himself but were to be amended. An earlier writer, Justin Martyr (ca. 155), mentions a Christian teacher named Ptolemy who died as a martyr. Traditionally, however, this has been deemed a different Ptolemy, for surely Justin would not have used a heretic for an example of Christian devotion. On the other hand, it may be anachronistic to think that Ptolemy would have been recognized as a heretic by all Christians in his own time. In the end, it must be admitted that there is too little information on which to base any firm decision, for Ptolemy would have been a relatively common name (e.g., *The Acts of Peter* also mentions a certain Ptolemy).

is given visible and tangible qualities.[27] Valentinus himself reportedly had taught that Jesus's heavenly body was in fact so pure that he did not even poop.[28] (That's right, I said "poop." Talk about a whole new meaning to the term "impassible." No such thing as "Holy crap"? . . .) This soul-body is a quasi-material body, which can suffer and die.[29] Or at least, so it would seem.[30] Ptolemy claims the Savior aeon is not joined to Jesus's soul-body until his baptism in the Jordan River. At that point, Jesus is adopted by the Savior, who is *a* holy spirit in the form of a dove. This union, however, is

27. Irenaeus, *Against Heresies* 1.6.1. Basilides allegedly taught that Jesus's soul-body was created "at the time of the generation of the stars" (Hippolytus, *Refutation of All Heresies* 7.15).

28. See Clement of Alexandria, *Stromata* 3.7.59.

29. Cf. *Tripartite Tractate* 114, where some are said to believe that the Savior's flesh was created before the cosmos. Valentinus himself is reported to have taught, "A body, therefore, was spun for him out of invisible psychic substance, and arrived in the world of sense with power from a divine preparation" (*Extracts from Theodotus* 59, cited in Daniel R. Streett, *They Went Out from Us: The Identity of the Opponents in First John* [Berlin: de Gruyter, 2011], 46).

30. This understanding of Christ's body is sometimes called "ouranosarkic"—literally "heavenly" (*ouranos* = Greek for "heaven") + "flesh" (*sarx* in Greek). An ouranosarkic view of Christ sees his flesh as superhuman, and therefore not really capable of suffering. It merely appears to suffer and die.

Were Gnostics Feminists?

In a chapter entitled "God the Father/ God the Mother," Elaine Pagels outlines a pattern in second-century sources (in *The Gnostic Gospels* [1979]). Heretical texts like those found in Nag Hammadi viewed God as both male and female, and they permitted women to have equal roles with men. Orthodox texts, however, describe God exclusively in male terms and "accept the domination of men over women." Pagels acknowledges that there is diversity on both sides, and even gnostic texts (e.g., *Gospel of Thomas* 114; *Eugnostos the Blessed* 85/*Sophia the Blessed* 107; *The Second Treatise of the Great Seth*) can be decidedly chauvinistic. On the other hand, Pagels cites an exception to the orthodox pattern, Clement of Alexandria, who has remarkably egalitarian remarks to make about women's status. Like much of what scholars see in "Gnosticism," the discussion of this issue will best be served by rejecting an either/or view of gnosticism versus orthodoxy, and instead allowing the sources themselves to be represented in their full diversity.

temporary, for the heavenly aeon(s) forsake(s) Jesus before his crucifixion (cf. Mark 15:34//Matt. 27:46).

In short, it was Jesus—and not God in any sense—suffering and dying on the cross. This self-sacrificial act was symbolic and meant to rescue souls, not bodies. As one text has it: "The Lord said, 'Brother Matthew, you will not be able to see it as long as you are carrying flesh around.'"[31] While many of the so-called gnostics have been misrepresented in their teachings, and while many gnostic doctrines may in fact be problematic, the various problems intersect in the gospel itself. Who is saving us and how? The teaching known as docetism, according to which Christ seems to be incarnate so as to suffer and die for us, needs to be discussed now at greater length.

Early Docetists

There is more to Jesus than meets the eye. This claim is central to all Christian thinking. Jesus has a mysterious side to him—one could say a secret side. When this claim is interpreted in too gnostic a direction, however, orthodox writers become nervous. While there is more to Jesus than meets the eye, the more is still harmonious with and not in opposition to that which the eye can

31. *Dialogue of the Savior* 132.28.

see. Gnostics, according to their orthodox opponents, fail to hold on to the visible because they stress the invisible.[32]

The gnostic teaching about Christ, docetism, makes God's salvific work only an appearance. God was in Christ saving the world, or so it seemed. The Logos took on flesh and dwelt among us (John 1:14); or, maybe he merely appeared to do so. To place this in context, we should admit that docetic teaching was held very early. Even within the New Testament texts, scholars detect a concern with docetic Christology (2 John 7; cf. 1 John 4:2–3). The implication is that someone is claiming a nonfleshly appearance of Christ. Who was teaching this and why remain unanswered questions, but we know that other early Christians were concerned about any denial of Christ's real flesh.[33]

It is tempting to accept Hippolytus's claim (ca. 225) and think of a sect of Christians who "styled themselves Docetae" or Docetists.[34] The existence, however, of such a distinct group has been seriously questioned. Clement of Alexandria (ca. 200) knows of "docetists," but they are not a separate form of gnosticism for Clement—he calls anyone who teaches that procreation is evil a docetist.[35] As with our discussion of "Gnosticism" earlier, we must avoid making docetism into a fixed thing.[36] Instead, we will need to speak of a spectrum of docetic thinking among early Christians.

Irenaeus warns that there are some, whom he unfortunately does not name, who believe the virgin Mary remained a virgin even after giving birth to Christ, because Jesus's soul-body simply passed through Mary "like water through a tube," leaving Mary's body completely intact.[37] Even orthodox writers, however, can teach something along these lines, for later tradition will affirm that Christ's birth was miraculous and left Mary's hymen intact. In the *Proto-Gospel of James*, which was widely accepted as orthodox, the emphasis falls on Christ's divinity and miraculous birth. When a midwife arrives and doubts the virginal state of Mary, she checks the hymen and is shocked to find it intact. The midwife is even more shocked when her hand catches on fire. The midwife's prior statement, "If I do not insert my finger and examine her condition, I will not believe," probably echoes the statement of Thomas made after the resurrection in the Gospel of John (20:25). This apocryphal version,

32. E.g., *Book of Thomas the Contender* 138 (but cf. John 3:11–12).
33. E.g., Ignatius, *To the Smyrnaeans* 5; *To the Trallians* 10; Polycarp, *To the Philippians* 7.1–2.
34. *Refutation of All Heresies* 8.1–4.
35. *Stromata* 3.17.102.
36. Ronnie Goldstein and Gedaliahu A. G. Stroumsa, in "The Greek and Jewish Origins of Docetism: A New Proposal," *ZAC* 10, no. 3 (2006): 423, extend Williams's approach to "Gnosticism" (*Rethinking "Gnosticism"*) for the study of "Docetism."
37. Irenaeus, *Against Heresies* 1.7.2. This teaching is probably implied by *Testimony of Truth* 45. Tertullian (*On the Flesh of Christ*) counters such an argument in lurid detail.

however, seems naively to subvert the scene in John, wherein Jesus's materiality is confirmed. If Jesus's infant body did not rupture Mary's virginal state, how could it be truly flesh?[38] Clearly, "gnosticism" is not in view in this story, but the *Proto-Gospel* does illustrate how easily early Christian devotion could be drawn to an overly exalted and thereby docetic view of Christ's flesh.[39] On the other hand, we must also admit that many of the so-called gnostic texts in fact do affirm a real flesh of Christ that suffered and died.[40]

Scholars usually list three forms of this teaching in order to capture more of the diversity in the sources.

1. *Phantasmal docetism*, in which Christ appeared to be flesh, but in reality was only a spirit. This form is very rare in the sources.[41]

2. *Possessionistic docetism*, in which Christ appears to be in flesh but in reality has attached himself to Jesus the human—much as a demon possesses a person. This form is found frequently in the sources.[42] Also, there is virtually no difference between this form and some kinds of adoptionism discussed in chapter 2.

3. *Replacementist docetism*, in which Christ appears to be crucified, but in reality Simon of Cyrene took his place. This form of docetism, too, is very rarely found in the sources.[43]

In any of these forms of docetism, Christ the heavenly being was not really incarnate and did not really die on the cross.

In sum, there are texts that have been categorized as orthodox that lend themselves to docetic thinking, while many gnostic texts oppose docetism. With the diverse expressions of docetism and with the overlap between heretical and orthodox texts about the nature of Christ, it is easy to see why gnosticism and the docetists have been so difficult to define.

38. A question asked by Tertullian, *On the Flesh of Christ*. Tertullian comes to the opposite conclusion: Mary lost her virginal state in the birth of Christ, because Christ's flesh was material.

39. For more overtly docetic overtones, see *Acts of John* 88–93, 98, 101–3.

40. E.g., *Apocryphon of James* 5; *Gospel of Truth* 18, 26 (cf. 31); *Letter of Peter to Philip* 133, 136, 138–39; *Melchizedek* 5; *Tripartite Tractate* 115 (cf. 125; and Irenaeus, *Against Heresies* 1.6.1).

41. Perhaps the *Gospel of Peter* 10 (cf. Eusebius, *Ecclesiastical History* 3.3.2; 3.25.6); however, cf. section 19, which suggests a possessionistic docetism. Similarly, *Trimorphic Protennoia* 47 suggests the flesh of Christ is merely a costume or "tent"; however, cf. section 50: the fact remains that Christ does put on the garment of human flesh (cf. John 1:14), and so this is not a strict phantasmal docetism.

42. E.g., *Gospel of the Egyptians* 64 seems to teach a possessionistic Christology, referring to "Jesus the living one, even he whom the great Seth has put on."

43. *Second Treatise of the Great Seth* 51–52, 56. Cf. Irenaeus, *Against Heresies* 1.24.4; Pseudo-Tertullian, *Against All Heresies* 1.5.

Gnostic Writings

Most heretics have no voice of their own. Once they were declared heretics, they were excommunicated and their books were burned. With the gnostic writings, however, a surprising number have survived. The most important discovery is the Nag Hammadi texts (discussed above), but many other writings have survived through various means. Since defining gnosticism has proved problematic in recent decades, defining which texts were "gnostic" has also become more difficult than one might imagine. While a complete list of texts suspected of gnosticism cannot be listed here, some key works have been preserved in quotes from church fathers and even in manuscripts discovered in modern times: *Excerpts from Theodotus*; *Letter to Flora*; *Pistis Sophia*; *The Book of the Great Initiatory Discourse* and the *Untitled Treatise*; *The Gospel of Mary* (also in Nag Hammadi); *The Apocry-*phon of John*; *Sophia of Jesus Christ* (also in Nag Hammadi).

The most important discovery is the Nag Hammadi texts (discussed above). These codices contain forty-six different works, which range widely in date with the *Gospel of Thomas* likely containing material from the first century but most dating to the third century and some to the fourth. Moreover, not all of these texts are gnostic, even though scholars initially classified them as such (e.g., *Gospel of Thomas*). For that matter, they are not even all Christian (e.g., Plato's *Republic* and *The Sentences of Sextus*). *The Thought of Norea* may be exclusively Jewish. Therefore, scholars are unsure even as to what kind of person or group would have collected such a diverse display of writings. Was the person or community who placed all of these texts in a jar and hid them gnostic? Probably, but it depends on what you mean by "gnostic."

Today, historians can read the so-called gnostics sympathetically to see them as honest believers honestly struggling to articulate their belief that there is more to Jesus than meets the eye. This is not the traditional understanding of heresy as deviation from a clearly formulated truth. In the second and third centuries, however, orthodox writers dismissed all forms of erroneous docetism together as a dangerous heresy, and the picture that emerges in the rearview mirror of history is that all of these docetists were one group known as gnostics. Now, even with our more nuanced understanding of how widespread and diverse docetism was in the early centuries, we still need to listen to the orthodox response, which admittedly oversimplifies and even misrepresents gnostic docetism. The orthodox response should be heard because in listening to it we can better understand what was seen to be at stake in the incarnation.

The Orthodox Response

The orthodox writers thought the full incarnation of Christ was essential to a true Christian understanding of God and how God works to save us. Take the most common form of docetism, possessionistic docetism: if the Word of God, or the heavenly Savior, simply indwells the human Jesus (even if this is a very special human), then all sorts of problems arise. Who do we claim is our Messiah, Savior, and Lord? Whom do we praise in our worship? Also, this looks like the heavenly aeon made someone else do the dirty work and then abandoned him when the work got the dirtiest.

Taking the other form of docetism, phantasmal docetism, we still have equally problematic questions.[44] What exactly was accomplished in Christ's death on the cross, if it was merely a vision? Is communication of information enough when it comes to salvation, or do we need something with more substance to be done for us?[45] Also, doesn't this approach make Christ dishonest, only pretending that he is in a body? The same problem is heightened with the third form, replacementist docetism!

Alternatively, the orthodox party insists that the real and complete incarnation of God is the whole of Christian faith. First, creation, even fallen, is not repugnant to God; God is the creator who called creation "good." Nor can creation, even fallen, be harmful to God; God is almighty and interacts with this world. Also, God chose to save us himself, not by sending someone else, but by "pitching his tent" in our midst (John 1:14). Moreover, if God chose to save us in person in our midst, and we are enfleshed persons, then God must have decided to become enfleshed entirely—not only in appearances. Finally, if God chose to save us completely, then God must save us body and soul—not just soul.[46] God did not appear to us merely as a visible soul but appeared completely manifest, body and soul. Anything short of this understanding of the incarnation results in a stunted view of God and God's work in Christ.[47]

44. For the sake of simplicity, I discuss only the two main forms of docetism. For fuller treatment of all three, which distinguishes the theory that Simon the Cyrene replaced Jesus (see Irenaeus, *Against Heresies* 1.24.4, cited above), see Georg Strecker, *The Johannine Letters: A Commentary on 1, 2, and 3 John*, ed. Harold Attridge (Minneapolis: Fortress, 1996), 69–76. For more recent discussion that follows the same outline, see Streett, *They Went Out from Us*, 38–48.

45. However, the implication may be stronger than simply mental cognizance: in *Sophia of Jesus Christ* 107, the Savior says, "I came from the places above. . . . I have wakened that drop that was sent from Sophia." The information imparted by Christ's revelation, then, is actually a reminder to the elect that they are part of God and they should return to God.

46. In his works *On the Flesh of Christ* and *On the Resurrection of the Flesh*, Tertullian gives the most sustained response to the teaching that Christians will rise with a "spiritual body."

47. For discussion of who was saved/elect, see Perkins, *Gnostic Dialogue*, 183, who believes that gnostics were originally universalists. It was only after polemic encounters that gnostics began differentiating which human souls were truly spiritual and which were not.

Incarnation and Sacrament: That Which We Have Seen and Touched

Beyond the importance of Christ's material body for the Christian witness (1 John 1:1), orthodox writers also saw docetism as a threat to Christian practice. Irenaeus takes the incarnation so seriously that he emphasizes how we participate in Christ through physical means (e.g., the Eucharist/Lord's Supper). His emphasis that God works through these physical means (i.e., sacramentalism) simultaneously assumes that God creates matter and that he re-creates it for our salvation. The alternative is to so overemphasize the soul over the body (Platonic dualism) that what happens in the body almost does not matter. Ignatius of Antioch, after denouncing docetic Christology, accuses his opponents of rejecting the sacramentality of the Christian faith (*To the Smyrnaeans* 5–6). Many orthodox writers assumed that a rejection of Christ's material body resulted in a rejection of the church's sacraments.

The actual beliefs of docetic thinkers, however, prove to be more complicated, for some did practice baptism, communion, and other physical acts of worship. Rather than simplifying the choices into docetic/nonsacramentalism and orthodox/sacramentalism, we should see the sources themselves along a spectrum of views.

The concern for how docetic thinking affects the worship and sacramentalism of the faith is a long-lasting theme among the orthodox writers. In fact, the theme can be reversed so that any questioning of the sacramentality and tangibility of the faith will be heard as an implicit form of docetism. For example, in iconoclast controversies of the seventh and eighth centuries, anyone who rejects icons and relics will be deemed a heretic, for to do so is to deny God incarnate, God made visible, and God made tangible (see chap. 9, "Iconoclasts").

To be sure, the gnostic heresy, in the eyes of the orthodox writers, included many problematic teachings, beyond the Christology highlighted here—as mentioned above. The common gnostic idea of creation (= protology) resulting from a series of emanations from God was often bookended with an idea that all things should be absorbed back into the One (= eschatology).[48] Between this "Once upon a time" and "The End" stood a radically different climax to history: instead of God incarnate saving us, a quasi-divine emissary tells us the secret to escape this fallen world. All this is to say that when a gnostic pulls one doctrinal thread, the whole theological fabric begins to unravel.

The central concern with Christology underscored in this chapter does not take away from the importance of any other doctrines contested between

48. E.g., *Gospel of Philip* 53; *Gospel of Mary* 7; cf. Eph. 1:10.

orthodox and gnostic writers. The Christology is central in the sense that Christology serves a central role in relating the many other doctrines for both the orthodox and the gnostic views. While those other doctrines have not been given the attention they deserve for a sustained discussion of gnostic theology, the focus on Christology has enabled us to succinctly address the reasons that gnostic thinking proved untenable for most Christians.

The Gospel according to Gnostics

The docetic emphasis from some early Christian circles may not be convincing or adequate for our theology today, but we can nonetheless appreciate the convictions the so-called gnostic groups were attempting to defend. The gospel according to gnostic teaching is that we can know the perfect God in spite of an imperfect world.[49]

God, according to Christian thinking, is so perfect that God transcends all ambiguity. Whether God foreknows or foreordains, whether God is just or merciful, whether God existed before all things, outside all things, and permeates all things, and whether all things will be summed up in or by God are all irrational questions for gnostics. God is neither male nor female, neither tall nor short, neither yin nor yang. God is "great," and by that Christians must confess that God is greater than any possible limitation on God's God-ness.[50] Once the Christian has confessed God to be wholly other than this chaotic world of flux, then the problem arises as to how the transcendent God could relate to and interact immanently with this world. Admittedly, this is more of a problem for ancient Christians steeped in the philosophical thinking of Plato, but the truth is that anyone who looks at this matter long enough will begin to ask the same question (cf. Ps. 8:3–4). Although the gnostic attempt to create a chain of being between the perfect God and the imperfect cosmos is problematic and unworkable for the whole of Christian teaching, the gnostics are to be lauded for their attempt to proclaim God's utter and absolute goodness.

49. One often-overlooked element in their teachings is the social outcry against the "world" (i.e., the political realm). Elaine Pagels has championed this understanding of gnostics in many of her works. More recently, see Dunderberg, *Beyond Gnosticism*; Michael A. Williams, "Life and Happiness in the 'Platonic Underworld,'" in *Gnosticism, Platonism, and the Late Ancient World: Essays in Honour of John D. Turner*, ed. Kevin Corrigan and Tuomas Rasimus (Leiden: Brill, 2013), 497–523; Williams, "A Life Full of Meaning and Purpose: Demiurgical Myths and Social Implications," in *Beyond the Gnostic Gospels: Studies Building on the Work of Elaine Pagels*, ed. Eduard Iricinschi, Lance Jenott, Nicola Denzey Lewis, and Philippa Townsend, Studies and Texts in Antiquity and Christianity (Tübingen: Mohr Siebeck, 2013), 19–59.

50. Pseudo-Dionysius's *Mystical Theology* is the most acute example of such thinking for later orthodoxy.

In one of the books of the Writings, Job has come to realize that his world is not so just. He has lost his earthly goods, his children, and even his bodily health, which convinces Job that God should be put on trial (Job 19:6–21), even if he must escape the flesh to see such a courtroom (Job 19:25–27). God, however, does not make Job wait for an out-of-body experience to "see" such divine justice. Instead, God answers Job out of the most chaotic image (Job 38:1), the "storm" (NIV) or "whirlwind" (NRSV). God's answer, moreover, sets Job back in his place by reminding him of his finitude in comparison with God's transcendence: "Where were you when I laid the foundation of the earth? Tell me, if you have understanding. Who determined its measurements—surely you know! Or who stretched the line upon it?" (38:4–5). Despite any temptation to distance God from this chaotic cosmos, God—who indeed transcends these horizons—chooses to be revealed through the material order. The biblical view of God, therefore, while drawing a distinction between Creator and creation, need not draw any distance between this world and the God who is greater than the world.

Similarly, Jesus, according to Christian thinking, is unique. While at first glance Jesus looks like a prophet or an aspiring king, Christians confess that Jesus is "greater than" our categories for him (cf. Luke 11:29–32). He is greater than a prophet, greater than a priest, greater than a king. Once the Christian has claimed this notion of "greater than" for Jesus, it is hard to know where to stop: Jesus ultimately is said to participate in the same greater-than nature as God.[51] While gnostics may mistakenly deduce from Jesus's divine status that Jesus must transcend all the pains of this world, the gnostics are to be lauded for their attempt to confess Christ as more than meets the eye.[52]

In the Gospel according to Matthew, Peter was the first to realize Jesus was "greater than" (Matt. 16:13–16). Like the gnostics, however, Peter could immediately make the wrong deduction from Christ's "of God" status. Jesus's "secret gnosis" that he revealed to his disciples includes the part about suffering, but Peter rebukes Jesus because one who is greater-than and of-God must be incapable of conquest, weakness, pain, and death (Matt. 16:21–23). Jesus responds with his own rebuke of Peter's thinking: he calls it diabolical, of Satan. The real secret or mystery about Jesus is that Jesus is greater-than because he is of-God *and* he chooses to suffer and die.[53]

---

51. *Apocryphon of John* 2: "He is the invisible of whom it is not right to think of him as a god, or something similar. For he is more than a god, since there is nothing above him."

52. For the value of gnostic Christology in terms of the historical Jesus, see Riemer Roukema, *Jesus, Gnosis and Dogma* (London: T&T Clark, 2010).

53. James is said to make the same mistaken assumption about Jesus's suffering and death in *Apocryphon of James* 5–6. Despite this text being labeled "gnostic," Jesus corrects James

While God is greater than *and* other than our categories, this statement must be nuanced when we talk about God in Christ. While Christ is greater than and other than our categories in a certain sense (because he preexisted with God and as God; John 1:1–3), he is also not other than us in another sense (because the Word became flesh; John 1:14). Although the Son of God, as the "reflection of God's glory and the exact imprint of God's very being" (Heb. 1:3), transcends all, there is also a sense in which the Son of God was "made lower" (Heb. 2:9):

> Since, therefore, the children share flesh and blood, he himself likewise shared the same things, so that through death he might destroy the one who has the power of death, that is, the devil, and free those who all their lives were held in slavery by the fear of death. For it is clear that he took not on him the nature of angels; but he took on him the seed of Abraham. Therefore he had to become like his brothers and sisters in every respect, so that he might be a merciful and faithful high priest in the service of God, to make a sacrifice of atonement for the sins of the people. Because he himself was tested by what he suffered, he is able to help those who are being tested. (Heb. 2:14–18)[54]

It is true: there is more to Jesus than meets the eye. The problem arises when gnostics so emphasize this fact that they end up saying that there is *less* to Jesus than meets the eye. If our concern to make Jesus more than human results in portraying Jesus as unhuman, then our picture of Jesus becomes distorted.

Where Do We Go from Here?

With Christ's divine nature now decisively declared (contra adoptionism) and with Christ's human nature now conclusively claimed (contra docetism), orthodox writers have the two ingredients essential for a full and robust Christology, only the particulars of which need to be ironed out (see chaps. 5–9). Before proceeding directly to these debates, however, we must first address a larger question that has arisen. How does Jesus relate to the Father (and the Spirit)? This question was most clearly addressed in the controversial trinitarian scheme known as modalism, to which we may now turn (chap. 4).

---

on this point: "But I [James] answered and said to him, 'Lord, do not mention to us the cross and death, for they are far from you.' He answered and said, 'Verily I say unto you, none will be saved unless they believe in my cross.'"

54. I have supplemented the NRSV's "helped the angels . . . the descendants of Abraham" with the KJV's more literal "he took not on him the nature of angels; but he took on him the seed of Abraham."

Recommended Bibliography

Lewis, Nicola Denzey. *Introduction to "Gnosticism": Ancient Voices, Christian Worlds.* Oxford: Oxford University Press, 2013.

Logan, Alastair H. B. *The Gnostics: Identifying an Early Christian Cult.* London: T&T Clark, 2006.

Markschies, Christoph. *Gnosis: An Introduction.* Translated by John Bowden. London: T&T Clark, 2003.

Pearson, Birger A. *Ancient Gnosticism: Traditions and Literature.* Minneapolis: Fortress, 2007.

Roukema, Riemer. *Jesus, Gnosis and Dogma.* London: T&T Clark, 2010.

Scholer, David M. *Nag Hammadi Bibliography 1970–1994.* Leiden: Brill, 1997. See also the supplemental bibliographies of Scholer published annually in the journal *Novum Testamentum*.

**Summary:
Sabellians**

Key Doctrine: Modalism
- The Clark Kent Theory of Jesus
- The Father, Son, and Spirit are just different costumes or "modes" of God

Key Date
- ca. 220: Sabellius is condemned in Rome

4

Sabellius

Modalism

And we have now shaken this sect off, and trampled it in its turn by the power of the Holy Trinity, like a libys or molurus or elops, or one of those snakes which look very alarming but can do no harm with their bites.

—Epiphanius

The Sabellians, they say, spring from the Noetus I mentioned already, for, according to some, Sabellius was also a disciple of his. But why Epiphanius counts them as two heresies I do not know.

—Augustine

"Do the math!"[1] That's the simple point made by Sabellius when it comes to God. Doing the "math" looks something like the following line of logic:

1. I am indebted to my colleague Robert Creech for this phrase as a way of summarizing the debate.

Q: Is the Father God?

A: Yes [this one's a no-brainer].

Q: Is the Son God?

A: Yes [see chap. 2].

Q: Is there more than one God?

A: No [see chap. 1; better yet, see Exod. 20:1–4; Deut. 4:35; 6:4; Isa. 44:5–6; 1 Cor. 8:4, etc.].

Q: So is the "Son" simply the Father incarnate?

A: Umm . . . I don't think so.

This kind of mathematical reasoning typifies Sabellius's view of God. The answers represent the common response of his opponents. The orthodox by and large agreed with the first three answers, and yet when it came to identifying the Father as the Son, the orthodox party balked—uncertain at first as to how to get out of this theological corner into which Sabellius's math had painted them.

Before we can see exactly how Sabellius's argument works, we need to define some terms. First, who was Sabellius, and what is Sabellianism?

Sabellius, Sabellians, and Sabellianism

Sabellius is a shadowy figure in the history of early Christianity. Little is known about his life, and yet he is remembered as the "arch-heretic" of the Sabellian sect. Because of references to his time in Rome, he is believed to have been a priest in the capital city, while later writers claim he was from Pentapolis in Africa.[2] The writers who report Sabellius's teaching hear him saying Christ was the Father incarnate.[3]

The sources about Sabellius are also scant. None of his own writings survive, and so all information is secondhand (at best!). The third-century writers, such as Hippolytus and Novatian, tell us little about Sabellius, but simply assume him to be heretical and compare the teaching of other heretics to his.

2. See the references in Hippolytus below for Rome. Basil of Caesarea, *Letter* 125, calls Sabellius a "Libyan" (a common label among Greek writers for all Africans). For Pentapolis, see Eusebius, *Ecclesiastical History* 7.6.

3. E.g., Novatian, *On the Trinity* 12. Later in the same work (26), Novatian explains the Sabellianist math: "If it is asserted that God is one, and Christ is God, then say they, 'If the Father and Christ be one God, Christ will be called the Father.' . . . For they are not willing that He should be the second person after the Father, but the Father Himself." Also see Epiphanius, *Panarion* 62.1.4 for a summary.

Bishops of Rome

The bishop of Rome, known today as the pope (Latin = *papa*), most certainly did not function as the head of the whole church in the earliest times. However one interprets the keys given to Peter (Matt. 16:19), the earliest office of bishop in Rome appears much less authoritative than one might expect. The current view of many scholars is that Rome did not even have one single bishop who presided over a diocese (as bishops would later), but instead there was a loose band of house churches. Sooner or later (a point of much debate), these churches organized themselves under one bishop. It is likely that this began to happen in the late first or early second century when the overseer/bishop (Greek *episkopos*) was placed in charge of the common funds of the Roman congregation. In the latter decades of the second century the bishop's responsibilities and authority expanded.

The first list of Roman bishops is found in Irenaeus (*Against Heresies* 3.3.3). While it is unlikely that Irenaeus invented this information, scholars often doubt the list's reliability. It is convenient that Irenaeus lives during the administration of the twelfth bishop of Rome, given that Irenaeus's argument centers on the succession of authority from the twelve apostles. More remarkable is that the sixth bishop of Rome after Peter happened to be named "Sixtus" (Latin for "sixth"). Perhaps Irenaeus found this list in Rome but did not realize that it was incomplete (the "sixth one's" name was not known), with the result that the list

was largely anachronistic. Clement is listed as third after Peter and as the author of *1 Clement* (usually dated ca. 96). This letter, however, does not name an individual author, and it gives the impression that there is no single bishop of Rome or of Corinth in its time. All this is to say that the data from before Irenaeus gives the impression that the bishop of Rome was an office still in development (a point that is acknowledged today by most Roman Catholic historians and that does not pose any problem to their view of the papacy; the Spirit, after all, leads the church into all truth [John 16:13]). The earliest bishop of Rome whose date and authority can be secured with some sense of certainty is Victor I, but even the extent to which he can be understood as the single bishop presiding over the diocese of Rome, not to mention the church universal, is debated. For the convenience of the reader, the following list of traditional dates is provided for the bishops of Rome covering the time of the modalist controversy. Their names and order are not in dispute, only their precise dates and the nature of their authority.

Bishop	Dates of Service
Soter	ca. 166–ca. 175
Eleutherus	ca. 175–89
Victor	189–98
Zephyrinus	198–217
Callistus	217–22
Urban	222–30
Pontian	230–35
Anterus	235–36
Fabian	236–50

Hippolytus

The early Christian writings attributed to Hippolytus have raised numerous problems for historians. The traditional version goes as follows. Little is known about the life of Hippolytus (ca. 170–235), but he became a presbyter, or elder, in Rome sometime in the 190s. Hippolytus then came into conflict with the bishop of Rome, Zephyrinus (bishop ca. 198–217), and his successors Callistus I, Urban I, and Pontian. The exact details of the controversy are unclear, but Hippolytus attacked his opponents for laxity and modalism.

Hippolytus is said to have then been elected as an antipope, or rival bishop in Rome (cf. Eusebius, *Ecclesiastical History* 6.20.2–3), but before his death in exile Hippolytus allegedly encouraged his followers to reconcile with the rightful bishop and so was considered a martyr of the church.

The most recent scholarly consensus has rejected all of the above information. Problems especially arise in at- tributing certain works to Hippolytus (e.g., *The Apostolic Tradition*). At the heart of the issue is a statue discovered in Rome in 1551. Under what is as- sumed to be the figure of Hippolytus himself, the statue has a seat with the titles of various writings inscribed on the side—writings presumably written by Hippolytus himself. Such a presump- tion, however, may not be safe, for the statue turns out to have originally been of a woman (perhaps a personi- fied virtue, such as Wisdom herself). The writings, then, may represent those collected by the owner of the statue, or of the house church that met in the house where the statue resided. The Hippolytus known from commentar- ies and who is commonly believed to have written *The Refutation of All Heresies* is either a representative of one house church in Rome (i.e., not someone claiming to be *the* bishop over the whole diocese) or an otherwise un- known Eastern bishop.

Fourth-century writers, such as Athanasius and Epiphanius, have no firsthand knowledge and rely on earlier reports. This allows little more than the safe assumption that Sabellius was rejected in Rome before about 220.[4] Assump- tions about Sabellius's teaching, however, remain unverifiable. Instead, we must look to the other "Sabellianists," as they were later labeled, in order to understand the kinds of teaching associated with this heretic.

Sources familiar with Roman Christianity mention Sabellius only in com- parison with other "Sabellianists," some of whom even predate Sabellius! We can deduce from these sources that Sabellianism, or whatever we call it, was frequently taught by some in or around Rome. For example, a certain teacher named Noetus came from Smyrna to Rome around 190, teaching a strict

4. Based on the information related to Bishop Callistus (see below).

monotheism wherein Christ is worshiped as God.[5] Noetus could be viewed sympathetically as striving to avoid Marcion's mistake in affirming two gods. He reportedly taught, "One and the same God is the Creator [*demiourgos* in Greek—i.e., demiurge] and Father of all things; and . . . when it pleased Him, He nevertheless appeared [i.e., in Christ]."[6] Noetus's concern, therefore, is to avoid any ditheism, or separation of God and Christ into two gods.

As with so many heretics, sorting out Noetus's teachings from later Noetians and from opponents' caricatures is not easy.[7] Noetus allegedly converted Zephyrinus and Callistus, two bishops of Rome, to his heresy.[8] In their defense, bishops of Rome for ages past had staunchly insisted on the oneness of God against dangerous thinkers like Marcion.[9] Without the aid of later ecumenical councils to explain and fully articulate the doctrine of the Trinity, Christians could have easily slipped into a naive kind of monotheism.[10]

Another example of a proto-Sabellian is Praxeas. Nothing is known of this person outside of Tertullian's attack against him in his work *Against Praxeas* (ca. 210). Whoever he was (Praxeas may even be a pseudonym), he allegedly persuaded the bishop of Rome at the time to teach Sabellianism—that is, that the Father and the Son were the same person, so that the Father suffered on the cross.[11]

5. Hippolytus, *Against Noetus* 1.6–7: "Glory to Christ . . . [the] one God." For the debate about the authorship of works attributed to Hippolytus, see Ronald E. Heine, "Hippolytus, Ps.-Hippolytus and the Early Canons," in *The Cambridge History of Early Christian Literature*, ed. Frances M. Young, Lewis Ayres, and Andrew Louth (Cambridge: Cambridge University Press, 2006), 140–51. Since it does not significantly affect our understanding of modalism, I will refer to Hippolytus as the author of both works. It should also be noted that Hippolytus's *Refutation* has a numbering system in *ANF* different from the critical editions of his Greek text. I will follow the English translation's numbering for the convenience of the reader, unless otherwise noted.

6. Hippolytus, *Refutation of All Heresies* 9.5. See also the assertion that the preincarnate Jesus, "the Word," was the one heard in the Law and the Prophets (*Against Noetus* 11.4–12.1).

7. Josef Vogt Hermann, "Noet von Smyrna und Heraklit: Bemerkungen zur Darstellung ihrer Lehren durch Hippolyt," *ZAC* 6, no. 1 (2002): 59–80. For a source in English, a brief statement to this affect can be found in John Behr, *The Way to Nicaea*, vol. 1 of *Formation of Christian Theology* (Crestwood, NY: St. Vladimir's Seminary Press, 2001), 147n15.

8. Hippolytus, *Refutation of All Heresies* 9.6–7.

9. Hippolytus, *Refutation of All Heresies* 9.7: "'For,' says Callistus, 'I will not profess belief in two Gods, Father and Son, but in one.'"

10. Callistus, however, did claim to avoid such a naive view: "Callistus contends that the Father suffered along with the Son; for he does not wish to assert that the Father suffered, and is one Person" (Hippolytus, *Refutation of All Heresies* 9.6). Ronald E. Heine, "The Christology of Callistus," *JTS*, n.s., 49 (1998): 58–60, finds Callistus to represent the "Roman school" of thought, which differed from Noetus and Sabellius by defending monarchianism while attempting to avoid the kind of patripassianism that "crucifies the Father." Cf. Tertullian, *Against Praxeas* 27 (discussed below).

11. Tertullian, *Against Praxeas* 1. However, cf. sections 27–29 of the same work, where the accusation changes.

Modalism in Smyrna and Asia Minor

Several sources mention a connection between modalism and Asia Minor (Tertullian, *Against Praxeas* 1), and the city of Smyrna in particular (Hippolytus, *Against Noetus* 1). While there is no firsthand evidence to support this claim, there is an interesting comparison in the letters of Ignatius of Antioch. Ignatius writes to one of the churches of Asia Minor, commending them for taking "on new life through the blood of God" (*To the Ephesians* 1). Such a statement sounds so much like patripassianism that in the later versions of Ignatius's letters someone amended the phrase to say "the blood of Christ." To be clear, while Ignatius uses modalist-sounding language, Ignatius himself is not therefore a modalist. At numerous times he differentiates the person of the Father from the persons of the Son and the Spirit. Instead, Ignatius's language simply reflects (1) someone who has a high Christology—Jesus is God; and (2) someone embroiled in the docetist controversy—God became flesh, and his flesh and "blood" were real, not phantasmal. Therefore, while Ignatius himself was not a modalist, his language illustrates how easily second-century Christians could slip into modalist-sounding speech and thought.

Several people taught Sabellianism in Rome, but the direct link to Sabellius himself is dubious. Therefore, we need to differentiate the heresy itself from the heretic. To describe this teaching, theologians use a number of terms other than Sabellianism, including "monarchianism," "modalism," and "patripassianism." Let us define each in turn.

"Monarchianism" is a name given to this teaching—probably by the so-called heretics themselves—because it focuses on the one (i.e., "mono") *archē* (= "origin" in Greek), which of course is God. To simplify, the teaching strongly emphasizes monotheism. Confusion arises, however, from the fact that scholars use forms of this name to describe two heresies: dynamic monarchianism and modalistic monarchianism. The dynamic kind protects the oneness of God by claiming that Jesus was simply called God and thus became the Son of God. In other words, dynamic monarchianism is the same as adoptionism (see chap. 2). This chapter will focus on the modalistic kind. "Modalistic monarchianism" is the most precise label. "Modalism" is the most concise one. Under either name, this is the belief in God as one person who changes "modes of being," roles, or merely costumes.

The modalists start with the first "mode" in which God was known: a father figure (Creator, Shepherd, King, etc.). Next, God was known to us in

Figure 4.1. The Trinity according to Modalism

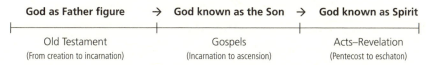

God as Father figure	→	God known as the Son	→	God known as Spirit
Old Testament		Gospels		Acts–Revelation
(From creation to incarnation)		(Incarnation to ascension)		(Pentecost to eschaton)

Christ as a "Son"; he was born of Mary. However, this is not *another* God, like Marcion and the gnostics would claim (see chaps. 1 and 3). Instead, the modalists insist on strict monotheism and stress that Jesus is Immanuel, the same God, now "with us."[12] God has been born in the flesh—put on another costume, as it were. Third and finally, Christ our Lord ascended back to heaven and so is no longer present with us physically, but he is present to us spiritually, that is, as Spirit. And so we have our one God (monarchianism), known in three different ways of being (modalism).

Modalism is here caricatured as God changing costumes. Kind of like Clark Kent and Superman: ever notice how those two are never seen in the same room at the same time? That's because they're the *same person*, only wearing different outfits. This caricature, while helpful for remembering and understanding this heresy, needs to be dissected in order to attempt to hear the modalists' rationale for describing God in this way. We will return to this task in a moment, but for now let us define the last significant term used to describe Sabellius's heresy.

In addition to "modalism" and "monarchianism," this same teaching also can be found under the label of "patripassianism." This is the term used by this teaching's most ardent opponents in the West.[13] They claimed that the logical conclusion of the modalist heresy is that God the Father (Latin: *pater*) is the one who suffered (Latin: *passio*) on the cross. The modalists are said to "have crucified the Father!"[14] This claim is immediately compelling, because anyone who is familiar with the Gospels will see it is not the Father on the cross. It is the Son, and he even cries out to the Father from the cross (Luke 23:34, 46).

Since these different labels appear in different sources, great confusion can arise about which heretics and what heresies are in view in any given text. The confusion continues for some time, for Sabellianism in some form will still haunt the debates of later generations of Christians.

12. For modalism as inherently born out of Christology, see Brian E. Daley, "'One Thing and Another': The Persons in God and the Person of Christ in Patristic Theology," *ProEccl* 15, no. 1 (2006): 17–46.
13. E.g., Cyprian, *Letter* 73.4.2.
14. Tertullian, *Against Praxeas* 1.

What about the Spirit?

So far, the focus has been on how the modalists failed to distinguish the Son from the Father. What about the Spirit? Most of the texts from this controversy mention the Holy Spirit only as an afterthought (see Hippolytus, *Against Noetus* 8.1; 14.2; *Refutation of All Heresies* 9.7; Tertullian, *Against Praxeas* 9.1–4). An explanation of the Spirit as distinct from the Son will come only as an addendum to the central argument that the Son is distinct from the Father. Even Tertullian makes the distinction in this way in a work famous for its alleged "Montanism" or emphasis on the ongoing work of the Spirit (*Against Praxeas*).

This likely means that the Spirit was not the central point of discussion for the modalists themselves, and the orthodox writers had to address the issue of most concern to the modalists, that is, Christology. On the other hand, it must be admitted that the Pneumatology (doctrine of the Holy Spirit) of the first two Christian centuries was underdeveloped for many Christ followers. Many were more binitarian than trinitarian. They had a clear picture of Jesus as distinct from the Father and yet "one" with the Father. The Holy Spirit is simply less understood. As Origen says (in the third century!), "Then, thirdly, the apostles related that the Holy Spirit was associated in honour and dignity with the Father and the Son. But in His case it is not clearly distinguished whether He is to be regarded as born or innate, or also as a Son of God or not: for these are points which have to be inquired into out of sacred Scripture according to the best of our ability, and which demand careful investigation" (*On First Principles* pref.4). Similarly, Novatian famously wrote a work entitled *On the Trinity*, but he offers little commentary on the Holy Spirit, except for mention of a liturgical formula such as is used in baptism. Once Jesus's full divinity is firmly established against Arianism (see chap. 5), it is not long before the same will be affirmed of the Spirit against Macedonianism. In 381 the Council of Constantinople amended the Nicene Creed to affirm the Spirit as "co-worshiped and co-glorified with the Father and the Son." Before this time, many Christians—orthodox and modalist alike—struggled to appreciate and articulate the full personhood and divinity of the Holy Spirit.

Latter-Day Sabellianists and the Trinity

The difficulties inherent in speaking about the oneness of God while simultaneously speaking about a divine Father, Son, and Spirit bring our discussion to the doctrine of the Trinity. Before this doctrine can be completely articulated, the heresy known as Arianism needs to be explained (see chap. 5), and so we cannot give this subject a complete treatment at this time.

Full-fledged trinitarianism aside, it still needs to be made clear how much the fear of Sabellianism affected later thinkers embroiled in the fourth-century battles about the Trinity. The fourth-century Nicene party that history will deem orthodox will be accused of modalism, and some in that party may in fact have held to a crypto-modalistic way of thinking of God. At least in one case, even those from within that school of thought found one of their own to have slipped into a modalistic way of speaking about God.

In the late fourth century Marcellus of Ancyra was a staunch defender of the Nicene position regarding the full divinity of Christ. Adherents of this orthodoxy, as will be discussed in full in chapter 5, understood the Father and the Son and the Spirit to be one in essence, that is, in their "being" or "is-ness."[15] Opponents of Nicaea, however, heard this emphasis on oneness as a revival of Sabellianism: if the Father's "is-ness" is the same as the Son's "is-ness," then the Father *is* the Son. Writers like Athanasius had to distance their view from modalism, but Marcellus seems to have actually held to a form of modalism in his explanation of this Nicene way to speak about the oneness of God, asserting that the Father and the Son are the same in essence and the same *person*.[16]

Born around 280, Marcellus became a bishop by 314. After attending the Council of Nicaea (325), Marcellus worked tirelessly to oppose Arian theology. Arius said the Son is not the same as the Father in terms of "being." Marcellus's opposition, in response, seems to have swung the doctrinal pendulum so far in the opposite direction that his own allies felt forced to denounce him.[17] Basil of Caesarea wrote to Athanasius—both of them were enormously influential bishops at the time—and complained, "Marcellus . . . exhibited an impiety diametrically opposed to that of Arius."[18] The diametric opposition

15. The Greek word is *ousia*.

16. Pseudo-Athanasius, *Orations against the Arians IV* 3.23.4. On these discourses and the denial of Athanasian authorship of the fourth oration, see David M. Gwynn, *Athanasius of Alexandria: Bishop, Theologian, Ascetic, Father* (Oxford: Oxford University Press, 2012), 10. The fact that Athanasius himself did not write this work does not alter the point made here: the Athanasian party needed to distance itself from Sabellianism. An earlier but more antagonistic source for Marcellus is Eusebius of Caesarea's *Against Marcellus* and his *Ecclesiastical Theology* (which, unfortunately for the nonspecialist, are not available in an English translation). For Marcellus's early career and fight with the anti-Nicene parties, see Joseph T. Lienhard, "Basil of Caesarea, Marcellus of Ancyra, and 'Sabellius,'" *CH* 58 (1989): 157–58.

17. Whether Athanasius himself denounced Marcellus is debatable, according to Joseph T. Lienhard, "Did Athanasius Reject Marcellus?," in *Arianism after Arius: Essays on the Development of the Fourth-Century Trinitarian Conflicts*, ed. Michel R. Barnes and Daniel H. Williams (Edinburgh: T&T Clark, 1993), 65–80. Christopher A. Beeley, *The Unity of Christ: Continuity and Conflict in Patristic Tradition* (New Haven: Yale University Press, 2012), 139–61, underscores Athanasius's indebtedness to Marcellus, even though Athanasius certainly disagreed with Marcellus's modalism.

18. *Letter* 69.2.

mentioned refers to Marcellus's attempt to counter Arius's view of Christ as a *deuteros theos* (= second god who is a different "being"). Alternatively, Marcellus insisted that God was one in essence and nature. These exact terms in Greek (*ousia* and *hypostasis*, respectively) were not well defined in his day, and so were open to misunderstanding. If the Greek term *hypostasis* is translated as "nature" (as given here), then Marcellus remains in the orthodox/ Nicene camp.[19] On the other hand, if the Greek term *hypostasis* is translated as "person" (as it will be in the late fourth century), then to say God is one *hypostasis*/person is inescapably modalistic.[20]

Marcellus seems to have offered a unique explanation of how God is eternally one person who is manifest in Christ.[21] Marcellus understood the Word (and Spirit) of God to be essentially the same as God—an aspect of God's Godness, as it were. This Word aspect of God became uniquely manifest in Christ, and even then, only for a time. The Word of God (and the same goes for the Spirit aspect of God) was revealed in history in order for time-bound humans to know and understand God. The Word (and Spirit) of God, however, ultimately will be reabsorbed in/into God (cf. 1 Cor. 15:24–28).

While Marcellus seems to make the Word a distinct person from the Father at least for a time, this sounded to his opponents much the same as modalism. After all, God has simply put on this costume called the Son (and Spirit), but God will change back out of this costume eventually. God is ultimately one.

As with so many other heretics, scholars today question this caricature of Marcellus's thought. Perhaps the extension and contraction of God's Word is a misrepresentation of Marcellus (evidenced only in citations of him from his opponents), but his refusal to speak of three *hypostaseis* drew the ire even of his friends.

19. The term *hypostasis* is used in the New Testament in this way (see 2 Cor. 9:4; 11:17; Heb. 1:3; 3:14; 11:1). Western representatives at the Council of Sardica (343) spoke of God as "one *hypostasis*," because they thought the term was the equivalent of "essence" (*ousia*). For the differing understandings of these terms in the East and West, and for their relevance for more recent theologians, see Paul M. Collins, *Trinitarian Theology, West and East: Karl Barth, the Cappadocian Fathers, and John Zizioulas* (Oxford: Oxford University Press, 2001), 116–17, 134–37.

20. The terms are still ill defined, even for Basil; see Stephen M. Hildebrand, *The Trinitarian Theology of Basil of Caesarea: A Synthesis of Greek Thought and Biblical Truth* (Washington, DC: Catholic University of America Press, 2007), 64–65.

21. Marcellus's party, of course, tells a different story, claiming that he was misrepresented by the Arians. Marcellus's own works are mostly lost to us, but see his letter (in Epiphanius, *Panarion* 72) to Pope Julius (r. 337–52), as well as fragments of his teachings cited by his opponents. For other works attributed to Marcellus, see Joseph T. Lienhard, "Marcellus of Ancyra in Modern Research," *TS* 43 (1982): 486–503.

Although Marcellus's form of modalism differs from Sabellius's, he is accused of Sabellianism and denounced as a heretic.[22] The heresy, therefore, would more accurately be labeled modalism (not Sabellianism), but only if it is acknowledged that modalism itself can be expressed in diverse forms.

Monarchianism(s): Diverse Christian Monotheisms

Modalism was a diverse phenomenon. We would do better to speak of the various attempts to defend the oneness of God. The various attempts, then, would be seen to fall across a spectrum of "monarchianisms" (see fig. 4.2). At the far right end of the spectrum lies modalistic monarchianism. This is the patripassianist teaching according to which the One Divine Person was first known as a Father, but then became known as a Son. On the other end of the spectrum is dynamic monarchianism. This is the adoptionistic or docetic form of speaking about the incarnation, because the One Divine Father then chose to be revealed through a human being or through human flesh. As was seen in earlier modalist teachers, some heretics may have vacillated between these two extremes in an attempt to explain God's oneness and still speak with scriptural language about the Son (and Spirit). Another reason the options cannot be limited to a simple either/or is that some thinkers like Marcellus can offer a modified form of modalistic monarchianism that should not be placed to the extreme right side of the spectrum. Instead, Marcellus allegedly differentiated the person of the Father from the Son *for a time* but held that God's oneness is ultimately going to be the essence of God for all eternity.

Figure 4.2. The Spectrum of Monarchianisms

Dynamic Monarchianism	Orthodox Monarchianism	Modalistic Monarchianism
One Divine Father and an adopted Son	One Divine Being eternally existing as three persons	One Divine Person known in different modes

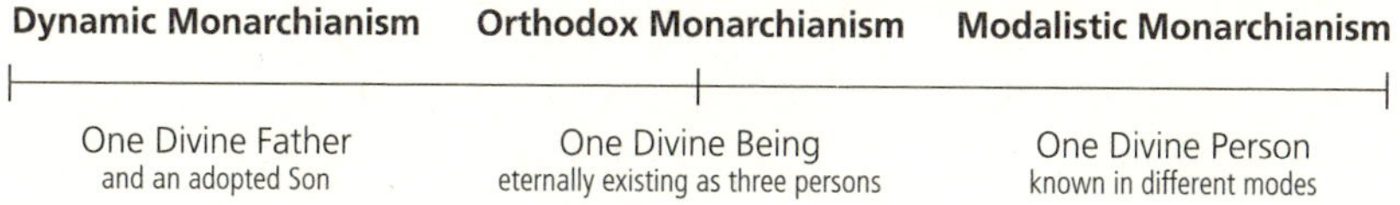

There is another benefit to seeing monarchianism as encompassing a spectrum of views. With this way of thinking, we can also see the orthodox teaching about God's oneness as lying along this spectrum. It is not altogether and categorically different from the heresy of monarchianism. Orthodox writers also claim to be monarchian. Only they claim to hold in tension what the heretical forms of monarchianism lost through an oversimplified view of God.

22. Marcellus dies in 374, and the "Marcellians" are condemned at the Council of Constantinople (381). See Epiphanius, *Panarion* 72; Socrates, *Ecclesiastical History* 1.36; and Sozomen, *Ecclesiastical History* 2.32.

In order to better see the orthodox monarchian view of God, let us review the orthodox response to "Sabellianism."

The Orthodox Response

Given the sympathetic approach used here, it is easy to reconsider the responses of some Christians to modalism. Perhaps Zephyrinus and Callistus were not themselves "Noetians" or "Sabellians," but perhaps they simply struggled to articulate God's oneness. Their attempt to hold to the monarchy of God could easily be deemed heretical by later standards of orthodoxy. In their own time, however, the answer was not so clear.

In this way we can see the "orthodox" answer as itself initially diverse and not without its own difficulties.[23] Nevertheless, even using the standards of later trinitarianism, some of the earliest responses to modalistic thinking offer surprisingly helpful and insightful critiques. Many of the early orthodox opponents of modalism shared common concerns. These concerns, for the sake of convenience, can be listed under the two categories of reason and Scripture.

Under the category of reason, the opponents challenged the modalist view of God: it is simply unreasonable, or better, irrational, because it is inconsistent with itself. The derogatory tone was unmistakable in these writers, for the modalists are "simpletons."[24] Later writers, like Epiphanius, attack even more aggressively: the Sabellians were persuaded "due to some sort of stupidity," for the error is pure "idiocy."[25] Tertullian could not help but mock even how the modalists pronounce the word *monarchia*: "Even Latins so expressively frame the sound, and in so masterly a fashion, that you would think they understood monarchy as well as they pronounce it."[26] Even worse than their lack of enunciation, for Tertullian, is their lack of comprehension.

The modalist explanation of the *monarchia* of God is simplistic because modalists see a monarchy as something held by one person (e.g., a king). Tertullian, however, claims that he too holds to God's monarchy, but a monarchy can be shared by more than one person.[27] For example, in Tertullian's day, the emperor, Septimius Severus, declared his sons, Geta and Caracalla,

23. For a fuller treatment of the terms and development in these writers, see Aloys Grillmeier, *Christ in Christian Tradition*, vol. 1, *From the Apostolic Age to Chalcedon (451)*, trans. J. S. Bowden (London: Mowbray, 1965), 132–57.

24. Tertullian, *Against Praxeas*. The Latin term *simplici* is translated by Evans as "simple minded."

25. Epiphanius, *Panarion* 62.1.1; 62.2.6; 62.8.4.

26. Tertullian, *Against Praxeas* 3.

27. Tertullian, *Against Praxeas* 3.

to be coemperors with him.[28] No doubt, the father in this triad had priority, but the other two persons nevertheless shared in the one rule. So with God, argued Tertullian: the Father has a logical priority, but the Father shares his monarchy with the Son and the Spirit.

The explanation for the apparent discrepancy between God's oneness and the diversity within God is found in another word: "economy." This word should not be understood in its current sense of an economic or monetary system. Instead, the word *oikonomia/oeconomia* (first in Greek, and then borrowed by Latin writers) implies an ordering within a single system.[29] Take, for example, light: (1) the source of light can be distinguished from (2) the ray of light and from (3) the point illuminated by it. Are there three "lights"? No, only one light with a diverse "economy." Take, for another example, water: (1) the spring of water can be distinguished from (2) the stream flowing from that source and (3) the pool of the water gathered below. Are there three "waters"? No, only one water with a diverse economy. And so, the analogy goes, the same can be said of God: (1) the Father can be distinguished from (2) the Son and (3) the Spirit. Are there three "gods"? No, only a diverse economy within God. Tertullian's formula that God is *una substantia, tres personae* will become the norm for trinitarian orthodoxy. God is one essence in three persons. Therefore, the oneness/*monarchia* and the threeness/*economia* are held together in tension.[30]

The crux of this argument lies in the concept of the Logos or Word (cf. John 1:1–18). Justin Martyr had earlier used this concept to explain how Jesus both was born at a certain point in time and preexisted with/as God. Since Jesus is identified as the Word of God, Justin simply asks when God's Logos (logic, reason, order, etc.) began to exist. Was God ever without Logos? Of course not! answered Justin.[31] Later antimodalist writers used this same concept to

28. Tertullian may in fact have this analogy in mind when he writes *Against Praxeas* in 210. Severus had appointed his sons as coemperors in 209. Also, see the allusion to this royal triad in his work *On the Pallium* 2.7: "the triple virtue [or power] of the current government . . . God favors so many Augusti."

29. The Greek word, *oikonomia*, derives from the words *oikos* (household) and *nomos* (law). In this way, the "laws of the household" or "household management" was applied to the wider administration of government. Cf. Hippolytus, *Against Noetus* 3.4.

30. The use of these examples can be found in Tertullian, *Against Praxeas* 8. For the analogy of the sun with rays (and a point of light), see *Epistle of Barnabas* 5; Justin Martyr, *Dialogue with Trypho* 128; Irenaeus, *Against Heresies* 2.13.5; Hippolytus, *Against Noetus* 11.1; Origen, *On First Principles* 4.28.

31. Justin borrows this approach from the Jewish writer Philo of Alexandria (around 20 BCE–50 CE) as well as the Greek philosophical tradition available to Justin and Philo. For ancient sources and exposition, see G. L. Prestige, *God in Patristic Thought* (London: SPCK, 1956), 97–128.

explain how God and God's Word are united ("one") and also distinct (i.e., the economy of God).[32]

To be sure, the idea of economy raises the potential for more problems: isn't the source of light greater than the ray of light? Early writers like Justin and Tertullian may be in danger of answering this in a way that would be deemed heretical in later generations (i.e., the heresy of subordinationism; see chap. 5).[33] This danger is important to keep in mind since the modalists are attempting to protect their theology from this sort of error. Nevertheless, even allowing that the modalists were trying to avoid their own error, the orthodox answers provide the ability to hold the paradoxical beliefs about God in tension in ways that the modalist options do not. God is one and yet God is three. When we "do the math," as the modalists ask, we are forced to choose either one or three. When God is one *in a certain way*, as the orthodox party will contend, there is room to still confess a distinction of persons within God's one *monarchia*.

Why must we confess one God? Why must we also believe in a distinction of persons? The orthodox will answer that the Scriptures teach both of these truths, which brings us to the other category used to answer the modalists.

In addition to reason, the orthodox insisted that Christian teachings fit with what is revealed in Scripture.[34] Separating Scripture from reason as we have done is unfair to the ancient writers, for they did not see reason as prior to or in authority over Scripture.[35] However, the debate revolved around how to interpret Scripture, and so the argument (but not the content of the argument) was metabiblical. Once the terms "monarchy" and "economy" were better defined, then the argument could return to the Scriptures to see how best to interpret them.

The Scriptures most relevant and most debated came from the Gospel of John. Therein, the modalists hear Jesus say, "the Father and I are one" (John 10:30), and "Whoever has seen me has seen the Father" (John 14:9).[36] These

32. See *Against Noetus* 10.1–11.1; cf. Justin, *Dialogue with Trypho* 128.4–5.

33. Although even staunch Nicenes like Athanasius can condone such analogies (see Athanasius, *Defense of the Nicene Definition* 25).

34. Hippolytus, *Against Noetus* 2.4: "This is not the way in which the Scriptures explain the matter"; and 3.3, "It is the Scriptures that speak correctly, whatever other notions even Noetus might think up."

35. Hippolytus, *Against Noetus* 9.1: "There is one God, and we acquire knowledge of him from no other source, brethren, than the Holy Scriptures"; and 9.3: "Not in accordance with private choice, nor private interpretation, nor by doing violence to the things that God has given—but rather let us look at things in the way God himself resolved to reveal them through the Holy Scriptures."

36. Novatian, *On the Trinity* 27; Athanasius, *On the Opinion of Dionysius* 26.

verses, according to the modalists, prove that Jesus and the Father are the same person. Beyond the Gospel of John, this idea fits within the overarching concerns of Scripture, which is strictly monotheistic. The orthodox party, however, will have a different reading.

Jesus's statement that he and the Father "are one" must be read alongside other statements of Jesus, even statements Jesus makes within the same Gospel. The twelve (or more) disciples should be "one." In fact, they should be "one" in the same way God is, for Jesus prays to the Father on the disciples' behalf: "so that they may be one, as we are one" (John 17:11). So are there twelve disciples, or are the twelve disciples "one"? Turns out it's not so easy to "do the math" when it comes to Christian doctrine.

Returning to the term "Logos," discussed above, the Son (esp. John 1:18), who is God's Logos, both is "God" and also is "with God" (John 1:1). The philosophically abstract term can simultaneously be used to identify the Son with the Father and to differentiate the Son from the Father. On a less philosophical and more practical level, we could simply ask, "To whom does Jesus pray?" (in John 17, for example). The fact that Jesus relates to God the Father implies a relationship with God the Father, and this is a Father/Son relationship. Jesus claims to be the "I Am" of the Jewish Scriptures (throughout John), and this is certainly from within a monotheistic framework. We must then conclude that the Scriptures both teach monotheism (*monarchia*) and reveal distinctions within God (*economia*).

In the eyes of their opponents, the modalists' dismissal of one part of the scriptural teaching (i.e., three divine persons) makes them heretical and invalidates their understanding of the other part of scriptural teaching. Not only are they irrational; they are unbiblical.

Let us take the example of Jesus's baptism as a test case.[37] Jesus is in the water. The Voice speaks about this Son from heaven. The Spirit descends from heaven onto the Son in the form of a dove. Assuming all who wrote and read this scene were Jewish monotheists, we must prohibit any attempt to make the three distinct persons mentioned here (the Father, Son, and Spirit) into three gods. Instead, the one God is simultaneously present as three persons. The Clark Kent theory of Jesus simply cannot explain scriptural passages like this one.

Before leaving this discussion, let us define one more term that was central to the orthodox version of God's monarchy. The term "person" meant something different in the early Christian centuries than it does today. Today, we tend to think of an independent self—a Descartian ego, in philosophical

---

37. Matt. 3:13–17//Mark 1:9–11//Luke 3:21–22 and John 1:32–34. The scene is used as a test case by Epiphanius, *Panarion* 62.5.4–62.6.5.

terms. However, if this meaning is used of the three divine persons, then we inevitably end up as tritheists rather than monotheists, for three persons in this sense would entail three independent beings.

The early church fiercely clung to the monotheism of its Jewish ancestry, and insisted that God is one Being.[38] The alternative and more ancient definition of person (Greek = *prosōpon*; Latin = *persona*) is a "face" or "mask." In an ancient play an actor could enter the scene wearing a smiley-face *persona*. That same actor could then switch *persona* and play the antagonist, wearing a frowning-face mask. With this image in mind, we can see how easy it would have been to slip into a modalistic way of thinking about God's personalities: God the Father simply changed masks, roles, and costumes in Christ and in the Spirit.[39] The analogy of an actor's mask, however, must not override how Scripture speaks of God in scenes like Christ's baptism. Rather than one *persona* after another (like Clark Kent and Superman), God simultaneously exists as three persons. To use the Greek term *prosōpon*, the Sabellianists were not just monotheistic; they were monoprosopistic in their understanding of God. Alternatively, Scripture, according to orthodox thinkers, revealed God to be triprosopistic—one Being in three *prosōpa*, or persons. The technical terminology used in this debate will be vital for understanding the debates of later centuries. Many so-called heretics will misapply, misunderstand, or be misunderstood in their use of concepts like *person* when speaking of Christ. Before turning to those later debates, however, we can now revisit the modalist understanding of God and the gospel.

What Sabellius Remembered

The modalists may have been clinging to the simple and ancient truth that there is one God. This was not simply a stubborn affront to polytheism, paganism,

38. Tertullian's Latin phrase *una substantia* will become the *homoousios* clause of the Nicene Creed (see chap. 5).

39. See Hippolytus, *Against Noetus* 14.2: "While I will not say that there are two gods—but rather one—I will say there are two persons [*prosōpa*]." Also, see where Hippolytus (*Refutation of All Heresies* 9.5) is concerned with Noetus's one-person conception of God. Noetus believed, said Hippolytus, "that this person suffered by being fastened to the tree, and that He commended His spirit unto Himself, having died to appearance, and not being (in reality) dead. And He raised Himself up the third day, after having been interred in a sepulchre, and wounded with a spear, and perforated with nails." (Note that Hippolytus does not use the Greek term *prosōpon* here.) Both Hippolytus (*Against Noetus* 7.1) and Tertullian (*Against Praxeas* 22 and 26) invoked the grammatical distinction between the personal and impersonal pronouns found in Scripture, the personal being used for speaking about the persons of God, and the impersonal for God's essence.

or even Marcionism. Noetus, Praxeas, and Sabellius may have been attempting to emphasize an important insight of the Christian tradition: the one God who made and rules the world (note the "monarchy" in this premise) is the same God who saves and restores the world.[40] They accused their opponents, namely, the orthodox, of losing the essential unity of God and Christ, and in the centuries that followed many who thought themselves orthodox made this exact mistake (see chap. 5).[41] The gospel according to ancient modalists is that God himself has come to save us. God did not send an emissary to do the dirty work of redemption. Jesus is Immanuel, God-with-us.

The orthodox view of God eventually comes to affirm this same connection between God's oneness and God's salvific work just as staunchly.[42] The only difference will lie in *how* God is understood to be revealed. Because the modalistic reduction of God into one person cannot explain what is revealed about God's work in Christ (e.g., in the baptism of Christ), the orthodox party will more carefully nuance how Jesus is God and yet *with* God. God the Father is distinct from the Son and the Spirit. The Son prayed to the Father (not to himself). The Son died on the cross (not the Father himself). Such distinctions are the only way to make sense of the message Christians have always confessed (cf. Acts 2:37–39; Rom. 10:9).

Now that the Marcionites have demonstrated the inadequacy of separating the Creator and Christ as different Gods, and now that the Sabellianists have demonstrated the inadequacy of equating the Father and the Son as the same person, the orthodox party will have clearly defined boundary markers for a sound and nuanced confession of who God is in Christ. The only remaining theological question has to do with the relationship between the Father and Son. This question, and the insufficient answer given by the Arians, can now be explored (see chap. 5).

Recommended Bibliography

Brent, Allen. *Hippolytus and the Roman Church in the Third Century*. Leiden: Brill, 1995.

40. A point argued strenuously in some of the most celebrated texts of orthodoxy: e.g., Justin, *Dialogue with Trypho*; Irenaeus, *Against Heresy*; and Athanasius, *On the Incarnation*.
41. Hippolytus, *Refutation of All Heresies* 9.6: "Zephyrinus . . . called us worshippers of two gods"; Tertullian, *Against Praxeas* 3: "And so [modalists] put it about that by us two or even three gods are preached."
42. Basil Studer, *Trinity and Incarnation: The Faith of the Early Church*, ed. Andrew Louth, trans. Matthias Westerhoff (Edinburgh: T&T Clark, 1993), 65–76.

Dünzl, Franz. *A Brief History of the Doctrine of the Trinity in the Early Church*. Translated by John Bowden. London: T&T Clark, 2007.

Heine, Ronald E. "Hippolytus, Ps.-Hippolytus and the Early Canons." In *The Cambridge History of Early Christian Literature*. Edited by Frances M. Young, Lewis Ayres, and Andrew Louth, 140–51. Cambridge: Cambridge University Press, 2006.

McGowan, Andrew. "Tertullian and the 'Heretical' Origins of the 'Orthodox' Trinity." *JECS* 14 (2006): 437–57.

Williams, Daniel H. "Monarchianism and Photinus of Sirmium as the Persistent Heretical Face of the Fourth Century." *HTR* 99, no. 2 (2006): 187–206.

Summary: Arians

Key Doctrine: Subordinationism

- Jesus the Second-Best God
- Jesus is almost, but not quite, God

Key Dates

- 325: Arius is condemned at Nicaea
- 381: The Second Ecumenical Council affirms full trinitarianism

5

Arius

Subordinationism

The Arians . . . like a swarm of gnats, they are droning about us.

—Athanasius

Arius . . . no small fire was lit from him, and it caught on nearly the whole Roman realm, especially the east.

—Epiphanius

Once upon a time (ca. 320), in Alexandria, Egypt . . .

"Excuse me, ma'am," Arius said to a woman in the market. "This infant you're carrying, did this child exist before you conceived it and gave birth to it?"

"No. Of course not! What kind of absurd question is this?"

"How about the Son of God? Did he exist before the Father begot him?"

"Hmm. I guess that's also absurd."

"Great answer. I wrote a song about it. Want to hear it? It goes like this:

> *The one without beginning established the Son as the begin-*
>   *ning of all creatures,*
> *And, having fathered such a one, he bore him as a son for*
>   *himself.*
> *He [the Son] possesses nothing proper to God, in the real*
>   *sense of propriety,*
> *For he is not equal to God, nor yet is he of the same substance.*[1]

Pretty catchy tune, huh? Join in, everybody!"

The previous scene is reported to have been a common occurrence. Athanasius, the famous opponent of Arianism, claimed that Arius would hassle "silly women" with such questions and convert the simpleminded and the unsuspecting.[2] Arius also wrote pop songs called the *Thalia* to influence the unlearned masses.[3] Since this Arian debate marks one of the most significant moments in the history of Christianity, we will try to hear both sides of the debate between orthodoxy and Arianism.[4] In doing so, we will discover that the options were not so simple in the fourth century. Let us begin with what we know of Arius.

Arius and His Background

Little is known of Arius's early life or background, for all report him as an "old man" when the controversy begins in the 320s. Some say he was from Libya. If correct, this would help explain his teachings, since the Sabellians allegedly

1. Translation from Rowan Williams, *Arius: Heresy and Tradition*, rev. ed. (Grand Rapids: Eerdmans, 2002), 102.
2. E.g., *Orations against the Arians* 1.7.22. Earlier, Alexander claimed Arius tried to "contaminate the ears of the simple" (according to Socrates, *Ecclesiastical History* 1.6).
3. The debate over the *Thalia* is complex. Arius probably wrote some verses, but there are lines in the *Thalia* that contradict early statements made by Arius. Some verses, therefore, are likely from a later Arian, and not from Arius himself.
4. Fragments of Arius's teachings are preserved in citations by his opponents. These have been collected by scholars, but unfortunately for the nonspecialist, no such work exists in English. See Hanns Christof Brennecke, Uta Heil, Annette von Stockhausen, and Angelika Wintjes, eds., *Athanasius Werke, 3.1: Dokumente zur Geschichte des arianischen Streites* (Berlin: de Gruyter, 2007); cf. H.-G. Opitz, *Athanasius Werke, 3.1, Lieferung* (Berlin and Leipzig: de Gruyter, 1934). For discussion and bibliography, see Williams, *Arius*, 48–81 (= part 1, chapter B, "The Nicene Crisis: Documents and Dating"); R. P. C. Hanson, *The Search for the Christian Doctrine of God: The Arian Controversy, 318–381* (Grand Rapids: Baker Academic, 2005), 3–18; and J. Rebecca Lyman, "Arius and Arians," in *The Oxford Handbook of Early Christian Studies*, ed. Susan Ashbrook Harvey and David G. Hunter (Oxford: Oxford University Press, 2008), 254.

Athanasius

Athanasius, born around 295, soon came into the good graces of the bishop of Alexandria, named (conveniently) Alexander. After Alexander died (328), and at the time that Eusebius of Nicomedia was seen to be reviving Arianism, the people of Alexandria elected Athanasius as their new bishop. As someone who remembered Arius from his days as a priest in Alexandria, Athanasius took center stage in the immediate debates over Arianism and defended the Council of Nicaea (325).

Athanasius had a variety of enemies. He was put on trial in 335 at the Council of Tyre and was exiled numerous times throughout his career (hence the proverbial phrase *Athanasius contra mundum*, "Athanasius against the world"). His staunch defense of Nicaea would eventually win out at the Second Ecumenical Council, Constantinople (381)—even though Athanasius himself died in 373. For his lifetime of tenacious teaching, one source called him "the father of orthodoxy" (Epiphanius, *Panarion* 69.2.3).

More recent scholarship has questioned Athanasius's version of the story and even Athanasius's character. Athanasius utilized every political maneuver available to him to counter his many enemies—as did all parties in his day. Some now see Athanasius as inventing Arianism by shifting the debate away from strict ecclesiology (who's in charge?) to strict theology (who's a heretic?). Others find Athanasius as simply less influential than previously thought in terms of the final theology formulated against the "Arians" at the Second Ecumenical Council. While this debate is ongoing among scholars, Athanasius will long be remembered as a saint and defender of truth by Christians who hold to orthodoxy.

were popular in that region, and one of the Arian party's primary concerns was to avoid modalism.[5] Also, Arius was tall, a fact mentioned immediately before the tale of Arius's seduction of seventy virgins, seven presbyters, and twelve deacons[6]—Arius's own unholy "calling" of the twelve, the seventy, and the seven, as it were.[7]

More reliable information arises about Arius's work in Alexandria.[8] There is a report that Arius, or at least *an* Arius, took sides in the dispute known as

5. For modalism, see chap. 4. For Arius as Libyan, see Epiphanius, *Panarion* 69.1.2; cf. 69.3.2. Also, see the claim that Arius has the support of "the whole of Egypt and Libya" (Eusebius, *Life of Constantine* 2.61, and again in 2.62). Cf. Dionysius of Rome in Athanasius, *Defense of the Nicene Definition* 26.

6. Epiphanius, *Panarion* 69.3.1–2.

7. Cf. Mark 6:7//Matt. 10:1//Luke 9:1; Luke 10:1; and Acts 6:3.

8. Even this information, however, comes from late and secondhand sources. See Winrich A. Löhr, "Arius Reconsidered: Part 1," *ZAC* 9, no. 3 (2005): 543. What follows is the general consensus of scholarly reconstructions today.

Church Offices

The exact hierarchy of offices in the earliest Christian communities is not entirely clear to historians. Significant positions, however, did develop within Christian churches over time. In the *Didache*, only bishops and deacons are mentioned, although "apostles and prophets" who traveled from church to church may have been seen as an essential part of the church's structure and life. Other early texts will only mention "elders" (e.g., *Letter of Polycarp*), while other early texts will speak of "elders" or "priests" (Greek = *presbyteroi*) as synonymous with "bishops" (e.g., *1 Clement*). Ignatius of Antioch is the first to insist on the threefold office of bishop, priest/elder, and deacon.

The early *episkopos* (Greek for "supervisor") of the house church eventually developed into the sole authority in a diocese (known as the monepiscopate), that is, the "bishop" as we think of today. As church networks expanded and became more structured, the bishop of a major city also functioned as an overseer of other bishops in the region; thus the office known as metropolitan (similar to an archbishop) emerged. Eventually, this role developed further in the most prestigious of Christian cities, such as Alexandria and Antioch, where the bishop of that city was also the patriarch over the whole region. Once this structure became normative and widely recognized, the various regions simply had to negotiate borders (e.g., canon 6 of the Council of Nicaea [325]) and how to settle interregional disputes (e.g., canon 5 of the Council of Nicaea [325]).

the Melitian schism.[9] Such reports of Arius's involvement, however, may be the work of later opponents wishing to discredit Arius.

The real conflict began in 318 when Arius objected to one of Bishop Alexander's sermons. Alexander had taught on the subject of God's oneness and God's threeness, and even sympathizers of Alexander admitted that the bishop used terminology that was "too philosophical."[10] Arius heard the bishop's explanation as a thinly veiled return to gnosticism, or some other form of heresy in which God changes and gives birth.[11] If Alexander was not saying this, then he must be making the opposite error, Sabellian patripassianism, and so Arius publicly accused the bishop of heresy.

Arius's accusations must have been somewhat plausible, for his view spread rapidly throughout the region.[12] Alexander responded by summoning

9. On the identity of this Arius, see Williams, *Arius*, 32–41, 251–52.
10. Socrates, *Ecclesiastical History* 1.5.
11. See Epiphanius, *Panarion* 69.6.4 and 69.7.6.
12. Eusebius, *Life of Constantine* 2.61; Socrates, *Ecclesiastical History* 1.5.

Constantine "the Great" (ca. 272–337)

Constantine was the first Christian emperor of Rome. His ascent to power culminated in a battle in which he drove Maxentius and his army into the Tiber River. This victory was seen as a miracle. Constantine had allegedly converted to Christianity after having a vision of Christ (Lactantius, *On the Death of the Persecutors* 44). Constantine was commanded to emblazon the first two Greek letters of the name Christ, *X* (chi) and *P* (rho), on his soldiers' shields: ☧. According to Eusebius, Christ told Constantine, *In hoc signo, vinces*—"In this sign, conquer!" (*Life of Constantine* 1.28).

Constantine's "conversion," however, has often been interpreted more as a politically expedient alignment with the popular new religion than as a true change of heart. He was not baptized until on his deathbed, and by the "Arian" bishop, Eusebius of Nicomedia.

Also, he continued to function as the "pagan" *pontifex maximus* and offer sacrifices to the Roman gods. On the other hand, one cannot be too dismissive about the state of Constantine's soul, for many Christians at this time preferred to delay baptism, and every emperor was expected to oversee all aspects of the empire, including the religious ceremonies. A Christian emperor was an entirely new phenomenon for the Roman Empire.

Constantine did bring sweeping changes to Christianity. What is remembered as the Edict of Milan (313), issued by Constantine and Licinius (emperor of the eastern empire), permitted Christians to worship freely, officially ending persecution. Constantine himself supported the building of churches, and he promoted Christianity in various ways, including summoning church councils to decide on matters of orthodoxy.

a regional synod of around one hundred bishops. Those gathered excommunicated Arius and his supporters. The controversy, however, quickly expanded beyond Alexandria and Egypt.

A bishop named Eusebius in Nicomedia befriended Arius, and Eusebius's alliance proved to be an important one for Arius. The bishop had connections with Emperor Constantine. Thus, the rejection of Arius in Alexandria and the acceptance of him in Nicomedia resulted in a pan-Mediterranean dispute. To settle it, Constantine organized what would become known as the First Ecumenical Council, Nicaea 325, or Nicaea I. In order to appreciate the decisions of this council, we must first review Arius's teachings.[13]

13. Dissecting Arius's teaching from that of Arius's followers or even that of those labeled Arians has proved difficult but important and helpful for historians (see David M. Gwynn, *The Eusebians: The Polemic of Athanasius of Alexandria and the Construction of the "Arian Controversy"* [Oxford: Oxford University Press, 2006], 169–244).

Arius and His Teaching

Arius taught subordinationism.[14] He subordinated the Son to the Father. His understanding of Christ at first glance looks very close to the orthodox understanding. For Arius, Jesus of Nazareth, the Messiah prophesied of old, preexisted as the Son of God. The Son of God, however, is not fully God for Arius.

The Son is a little less than the Father, as with any parent/child relationship. The Son—while firstborn of all creation (Col. 1:15) and so very old!—is still not as old as the Father, who is eternal.[15] Since the Son is younger, the Son is subordinate to his elder Father—thus the description of Arius's heretical teaching as "subordinationism."

How did Arius justify this view? Let us attempt to outline his rationale. The primary concern for Arius, or the starting point for his thinking, is much debated by scholars. Perhaps his concern was to avoid the Sabellian heresy (see chap. 4), and so he erred in the opposite direction. Another possibility— one more attested in the sources—is that Arius began with a philosophical concern about God's nature.[16]

What does it mean for God to be God? According to Arius, the answer is simple: God is simple. By simple, he means what Plato, Aristotle, and many of the Greek philosophers meant: God is simply God, no parts (e.g., arms, legs), and nothing else is greater (i.e., bigger, stronger, etc.).

Once God's divine nature is defined in such a way, Arius has to decide whether Jesus is God. His answer: Jesus is *sort of* God. He is divine, for his preincarnate divine nature did not have parts (e.g., arms, legs), and as cocreator with the Father, the Son of God had divine attributes (i.e., omnipresence, omnipotence, etc.).

The orthodox opponents of Arius by and large agree with this line of thinking. One key problem, however, is the idea that nothing is greater (bigger, stronger, etc.) than God when applied to the Son. Is the Father greater than the Son? Arius says yes, for the Son is "begotten of the Father," so the Father is older/eternal while the Son had a point when he began to exist.

---

14. "Subordinationism" is meant to replace "Arianism," which is too generalized and ill defined and which was not invoked until much later by Athanasius. Even "subordinationism," it must be admitted, is still problematic and does not account for the role of Origen's teachings, which were influential to most of the thinkers involved in the Arian controversy, only in different ways.

15. Epiphanius, *Panarion* 69.6.3. Cf. Epiphanius, *Panarion* 69.6.1–7; Socrates, *Ecclesiastical History* 1.5; Sozomen, *Ecclesiastical History* 1.15.

16. See G. Christopher Stead, *Doctrine and Philosophy in Early Christianity: Arius, Athanasius, Augustine* (Aldershot, UK: Ashgate, 2000).

Subordinationism: Less than God

Arius's teaching, that the Son is less divine than the Father, is a form of subordinationism. That is, the Son is subordinate to or lesser than the Father. This form is specifically an ontological subordination because the Son's essence or being (*ontos*) is the aspect of the Son that has been subordinated (see fig. 5.1).

Figure 5.1. Ontological Subordinationism

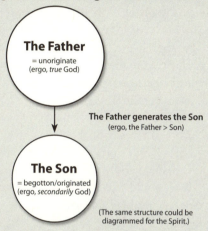

The Father
= unoriginate
(ergo, *true* God)

The Father generates the Son
(ergo, the Father > Son)

The Son
= begotton/originated
(ergo, *secondarily* God)

(The same structure could be diagrammed for the Spirit.)

Arius's teaching could also be understood in terms of time: chronological subordination. For the Son is later than the Father. The Father is eternal, but the Son had a "birth" and so is merely everlasting. This seems inevitably to result in a corresponding ontological subordination, but the two kinds of subordination can be distinguished (see fig. 5.2).

Figure 5.2. Chronological Subordinationism
Timeline

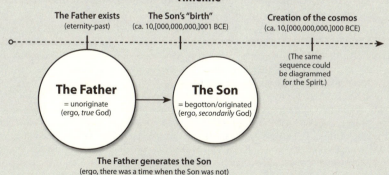

The Father exists
(eternity-past)

The Son's "birth"
(ca. 10,[000,000,000,]001 BCE)

Creation of the cosmos
(ca. 10,[000,000,000,]000 BCE)

(The same sequence could be diagrammed for the Spirit.)

The Father
= unoriginate
(ergo, *true* God)

The Son
= begotton/originated
(ergo, *secondarily* God)

The Father generates the Son
(ergo, there was a time when the Son was not)

Arius, like many Christian thinkers, drew a sharp distinction between created and uncreated. Only God is uncreated. The only question remaining is where that leaves Jesus, and this is where Arius's dividing line between uncreated and created not only separates God from creation but separates the Father from the Son.

Since the Son was "begotten" (= *gennētos* in Greek) of the Father, and since we know that this term is metaphorical—God does not really have reproductive organs or "parts" (see above), then the Son of God must have been "created" (= *genētos* in Greek).[17] If the distinction between the Greek terms *gennētos* and *genētos* is unclear to you, then you are not alone; even in Arius's day, especially when heard aloud, the two concepts sounded synonymous. This lack of clarity caused much trouble in the Arian debates, but Arians found the lack of distinction to prove their point.[18] Saying the Son was "begotten" is the same as saying the Son "originated." To be God, however, is to be unoriginate (= *anarchos* in Greek).[19] Is the Son "God"? No, not in this way of speaking. But, in a certain way of speaking, yes.

To have divine attributes is not quite the same as being fully divine. For example, many humans display godly attributes: justice, mercy, goodness, and so on. Those who do so would typically be said to share in these qualities by grace (very Protestant terminology), or to participate in the divine nature (the terminology of the early church; see 2 Pet. 1:4). Just, merciful, and good humans would not be divine in their own nature.

So it is with the Son. The Son displays many godly attributes: not just the ones listed above like justice and mercy, but the big ones like omnipotence and omniscience.[20] Arius, however, insists that the Son displays these divine attributes in the same way that we share in those moral attributes: by grace or participation.[21] God the Father shares his divine power with his Son.

While God shares most of his attributes with the Son, such as love, goodness, omnipotence, omnipresence, there is one attribute that cannot be shared:

17. See Arius's argument in Epiphanius, *Panarion* 69.8.4. Arius's early statement against understanding the Son as somehow emanating from the Father is directed against any description of God (the Father) in material terms (see Arius's statement in Epiphanius, *Panarion* 69.6.4; 69.7.6), which is a misunderstanding. The Nicene party also denounced such a view (e.g., Athanasius, *Defense of the Nicene Definition* 2).

18. Hanson, *Search for the Christian Doctrine of God*, 202–7.

19. Athanasius, *Orations against the Arians* 3.26.28.

20. Those familiar with the systematic distinction of divine and moral attributes will notice a collapsing of these categories. Theologians had not so clearly distinguished them in Arius's day, which enabled his argument. For Basil's influential contribution to this issue, see Mark DelCogliano and Andrew Radde-Gallwitz, eds. and trans., *St. Basil of Caesarea: Against Eunomius* (Washington, DC: Catholic University of America Press, 2011), 46–55.

21. See Löhr, "Arius Reconsidered: Part 1," 550, for examples.

eternality. The Son had a beginning. To be sure, this was before *the* beginning (Gen. 1:1), for the Son helped create the world (John 1:1–3). Nevertheless, before *the* beginning of the cosmos, the Father begot the Son.[22] If the Son had a beginning, then—as Arius's infamous axiom states—"there was a time when the Son was not."[23]

If there was a time when the Son did not exist, then the Son is not divine, or at least not "fully" divine, or "truly" divine. Instead, Arius borrows a term from the Jewish writer Philo of Alexandria and calls the Son a *deuteros theos*, a "second god." With this phrase, the monotheistic warning lights all begin to blink furiously for the orthodox party. How can there be two gods?

Arius's response to those who claimed true monotheism is two-sided. In the technical rhetorical device known as "I'm rubber; you're glue," Arius returns the charge of heresy onto his opponents: his view looks like polytheism to his enemies because his enemies teach modalism.[24] If they say that Jesus is God (contra the Ebionites) and there is only one God (contra the Marcionites and gnostics), then modalism seems to be the only plausible explanation of their position.

Arius's other way of responding is a more nuanced explanation of his view of the Son as a *deuteros theos*. God is the only "true God," but one could—as Christ himself did—refer to other gods without denying the monotheistic faith. "Jesus answered, 'Is it not written in your law, "I said, you are gods"'?" (John 10:34; cf. Ps. 82:6). This passage from the monotheistic Jewish scriptures could not be interpreted in a way that detracts from the *monarchia* of the one true God (see chap. 4). Nevertheless, we can say that Christ followers are "divine" in a certain sense: they are God-like, or God-ly; they are good, just, and so on. At the same time, however, these whom Jesus called "gods" are not God by nature. So it is with the Son of God: the Son is godly, godlike, divine. *Another divine being.*[25] The Son is much more divine than Christ followers, but not as divine as the Father. Attributing "divine" status to the Son does not detract from the monotheistic faith in the Father.

22. See Arius's statement in Epiphanius, *Panarion* 69.7.3.

23. Socrates, *Ecclesiastical History* 1.5; also see the anathemas in the Creed of Nicaea.

24. Disclaimer: "I'm rubber; you're glue" is not actually a technical rhetorical device. However, see J. Rebecca Lyman, "A Topography of Heresy: Mapping the Rhetorical Creation of Arianism," in *Arianism after Arius: Essays on the Development of the Fourth-Century Trinitarian Conflicts*, ed. Michel R. Barnes and Daniel H. Williams (Edinburgh: T&T Clark, 1993), 45–62.

25. This idea will be the central point debated at the Council of Nicaea in 325, where the council defines the Son as *homoousios* with the Father.

Arius and His Literal Reading of Scripture

One more aspect of Arius's teaching should be discussed. In attempting to defend their own positions, both sides turned to Scripture. Both sides, however, found support for their own view there, and so part of the debate entailed how to read the Scriptures when different parties interpret them in different ways.[26]

Arius claimed that his opponents allegorized the Scriptures and thereby twisted the plain meaning into something foreign to the Scriptures themselves. He found passages to speak of how God "made" Christ or how the Son was "firstborn."[27] Perhaps Arius is twisting the Scripture away from its context in these passages because they speak more to Christ's earthly ministry than to his preexistence. Nonetheless, Arius used these verses to support his own viewpoint.

One last example deals with how early Christians read the Old Testament. In the book of Proverbs (and elsewhere in the Writings of Jewish scriptures), "Wisdom" herself speaks. Today, most commentators apply literary theory to say that this is personification (or in classical Greek rhetoric, *prosōpopoeia*), a literary device whereby a personal address is spoken by an impersonal thing or concept. However, in Second Temple Judaism, "Sophia" (= "wisdom" in Greek) took on a life of her own, and so by the time Christians read Proverbs, they see the preincarnate Logos and Wisdom as one and the same.

Once again the debate, too large to recount here, revolves around whether preincarnate Wisdom was "created" (8:22) or "brought forth/born" (8:25).[28] Wisdom's birth, for Arius, is again metaphorical and interpreted in light of the previous verse, where Wisdom is said to be created.[29] Arius's opponents, of course, argued in the opposite direction: the so-called creation of Wisdom (in 8:22) is ambiguous at best and so should be interpreted by the later verse, which calls Wisdom's beginning a "birth" (8:25).[30] The difference for the orthodox party at Nicaea between "birth" and "creation" is enormous, and

26. See Sara Parvis, "Christology in the Early Arian Controversy: The Exegetical War," in *Christology and Scripture: Interdisciplinary Perspectives*, ed. Angus Paddison and Andrew T. Lincoln (London: T&T Clark, 2007), 120–37.

27. E.g., Acts 2:36; Rom. 8:29; Col. 1:15.

28. For discussion, see Frances Young, "Exegetical Method and Scriptural Proof," in *Studia Patristica* 19, ed. Elizabeth A. Livingstone (Leuven: Peeters, 1989), 291–304 (esp. 300). For a more recent bibliography on this debate, see Mark DelCogliano, "Basil of Caesarea on Proverbs 8.22 and the Sources of Pro-Nicene Theology," *JTS* 59, no. 1 (2008): 183–90.

29. If not Arius himself, Arius's supporters made this argument (see Eusebius of Nicomedia's remarks in Theodoret, *Ecclesiastical History* 1.5).

30. For pre-Arian interpretations, see Manlio Simonetti, *Studi sull' Arianesimo* (Rome: Editrice Studium, 1965), 1–85.

John 1: "The *Logos* Was *Theos*"

Why not refute Arius with one single prooftext? John 1:1 says, "The Word was God." Case closed.

While this verse does conclude the matter and deny subordination-ism for most Christians today, it was not so straightforward to Arius. The key question is how to interpret the closing phrase of the verse, "the Word [*Logos*] was God [*Theos*]."

Arius heard the emphasis as one that rejects modalism, for the next verse says, again, that the Word was *with* God. Arius's interpretation depends on what can best be seen when dia-gramming the sentence—your middle-school English teacher would be so proud! Clearly the *Logos* is the subject, and the form of "to be" is the verb. What part of the sentence is "God"?

If the Greek word *Theos* functions as a predicate nominative, as it does in our English translations, then Arius is wrong: the Word was God. If, however, *Theos* functions as a predicate adjec-tive, then Arius might be right.

Let's give a parallel example. In the sentence, "David is a man," the word "man" is a predicate nominative. If we changed the sentence to say, "David is," as I'd like to think, "manly," then this last word is now a predicate adjec-tive. The Greek word *Theos* in John 1:1 could function as either, which allows Arius to read the term to say the Word means "*godly*," or divine. The only question remaining is, just *how* divine is the Word? Is the Word *fully/truly* God? Which becomes a theological question bigger than one prooftext.

we can now turn to that council to see the debate and to see how different these concepts proved to be.

The Council of Nicaea (325)

In the town of Nicaea (modern Iznik, Turkey) 318 bishops from the *oikoumenē*, the inhabited earth, convened to address, among other things, the Arian con-troversy.[31] We do know the participants were almost exclusively Eastern, since the primary dispute was between the bishops of Nicomedia and Alexandria. Nevertheless, in a representative way (counting Rome's representatives) and in the sense that the worldwide church (i.e., both East and West) eventually accepted this council as authoritative, Nicaea became the first "ecumenical council."

Constantine, who summoned the bishops and opened the proceedings, accepted the advice of Eusebius of Nicomedia and assumed that Arius's view

31. 318 is probably a symbolic number; see Gen. 14:14 and *Epistle of Barnabas* 9.7.

represented the correct teachings shared by the worldwide church. To his credit, after Constantine convened the council, he deferred to the bishops themselves and allowed them to proceed largely without his interference.[32] It must have been surprising to the Arian party, who had Constantine's support going into the council, when Constantine allowed the anti-Arian party to win the debate.

During the proceedings, some requested that a creed be formulated using only words and phrases found in Scripture. However, as mentioned above, most of the language found there (such as John 1:1) could still be affirmed by Arians, only with a subordinationist interpretation. As Athanasius put it, the Arians were "whispering to each other and winking with their eyes," because they knew that strictly scriptural language could not exclude their view.[33] Several statements of faith were offered, but the one glaring omission in the pre-Nicene formulae was a clear rejection of subordinationist Christology.

Note how credible Arius's claim to orthodoxy was in his own day. If no pre-Nicene anti-Arian creed can be procured, then who is to say that Arius is the heretic? He seems to teach what the church has taught since apostolic times—or at least he does not teach something contrary.[34]

With both sides at an impasse, the Western representatives requested an audience with Constantine and his advisors. In effect, they pointed out how Tertullian had resolved this issue generations ago against the modalists.[35] God is *una substantia, tres personae*—"one substance, three persons." Constantine's advisors were convinced, and so the motion went before the council: All in favor, say "Aye." All opposed . . . shall be exiled. . . .[36] Not surprisingly, the motion passed with an overwhelming majority.

32. The popular view that Constantine is responsible for enforcing Christian trinitarian orthodoxy is rightly corrected by Charles Freeman, *A.D. 381: Heretics, Pagans, and the Dawn of the Monotheistic State* (Woodstock, NY: Overlook Press, 2009). Theodosius is the first emperor to enforce widely and actively what we call orthodoxy. Freeman, however, is too one-sided in his criticism of Theodosius. The Arian emperors who preceded him were equally eager to coerce. Few, if any, were playing nice at this time. For an introduction to this phenomenon, see Philip Jenkins, *Jesus Wars: How Four Patriarchs, Three Queens, and Two Emperors Decided What Christians Would Believe for the Next 1,500 Years* (New York: HarperOne, 2010); for a more technical and theological introduction, see Daniel H. Williams, "Constantine, Nicaea and the 'Fall' of the Church," in *Christian Origins: Theology, Rhetoric and Community*, ed. L. Ayres and G. Jones (London: Routledge, 1998), 117–36.

33. *Defense of the Nicene Definition* 20; cf. Athanasius, *To the Bishops of Africa* 5.

34. On the other hand, the same could be said for the anti-Arian view, as was evidenced at the council.

35. Adolf von Harnack, *History of Dogma*, trans. Neil Buchanan (Boston: Little, Brown, 1905), 2:257, comments, "[This formula] was worked out by Tertullian with admirable clearness."

36. This exaggerated simplicity should not be taken to mean that Constantine allowed no debate on the matter; see Athanasius's own account and Hanson's discussion in *Search for the Christian Doctrine of God*, 162.

Just what exactly did the creed of Nicaea teach? In order to explain this definition of orthodox faith, it is worth quoting the creed in part. Then, some of the key statements can be analyzed.

> We believe . . . in one Lord Jesus Christ, the Son of God, the Only-begotten, begotten from the Father, that is from the substance of the Father, God from God, light from light, true God from true God, begotten not made, consubstantial [*homoousios*] with the Father, through whom all things came to be, both those in heaven and those in earth. . . .
>
> And those who say "there once was a time when he was not," and "before he was begotten he was not," and that he came to be from things that were not, or from another hypostasis or substance, affirming that the Son of God is subject to change or alteration—these the catholic and apostolic church anathematizes.[37]

The Creed of Nicaea (325): "Anathematizes"

The final paragraph is what most obviously (1) refutes Arianism and (2) distinguished the creed formulated at Nicaea from the "Nicene Creed," which was a later revision of Nicaea's original statement made at the Council of Constantinople (381) and which has been confessed by churches up to the present. All of the wrong teachings (= subordinationism) are clearly articulated so that the right teaching (= orthodoxy) is unmistakable. The council *is not* teaching one doctrine in order to confess another. Herein lies a key insight into how "orthodoxy" functions. Orthodox teaching is a negative statement: do *not* teach [*insert heresy here*]. The proper understanding is far from explained, but instead is simply confessed as a mystery:

Jesus is "God."

How can this be?

It is a mystery.

The church's confession appears to be a contradiction:

$$1 \text{ "God, the Father almighty"}$$
$$+ 1 \text{ "Jesus Christ . . . true God"}$$
$$\overline{\qquad\qquad\qquad\qquad}$$
$$\neq 2 \text{ Gods}$$

---

37. Although the records of the council itself have not survived, many contemporary sources attest to the creed itself. The version most often cited is that read and reaffirmed at the Council of Ephesus (431).

Instead, these two paradoxical truths are held together in tension and confessed boldly.

The bishops at the council focused on finding a concise way to confess what the whole of the Scriptures revealed: Jesus is fully God (i.e., *not* subordinationism), and yet he is distinct from the Father (i.e., *not* modalism). A concise statement like this, it had to be admitted, was not found in Scripture, and so the solution came from a postapostolic phrase. The word "consubstantial" purports to be more of a clarification of what the church has always confessed, and less an explanation of how this confession can be true.

The Creed of Nicaea (325): "Consubstantial"

The Greek word *homoousios*, translated here as "consubstantial," is a technical term that will be seen by many after Nicaea as problematic. We will first sympathetically attempt to understand how the word was used at the council before returning to a more critical evaluation of the term in light of the so-called heretics' objections to it.

The term captures the idea from Tertullian's Latin statement about God as *una substantia*. The idea of substance in English implies material substance, but this was not necessarily true for ancient Latin or for the equivalent Greek term, *ousia*. The terms could also be translated as "essence," for the Greek term is simply a form of the verb "to be."

Something's "being" or "essence" has to do with what something really "is." What is an "apple"? It would be tempting to answer this by describing specific parts or aspects of an apple: a kind of fruit, something red, a core and a stem and seeds and skin, and so on. Such an answer, however, would never be precise enough: there are many fruits; not all apples are red; the parts could be describing a pear; and so on. Ancient thinkers, like Plato, attempted to see past these parts and aspects of things to the "essence" of something. The essence of an apple is not the parts of the apple, it is its apple-ness, its apple-icity. Notice that we are not talking about the material substance that makes up any given apple. Instead, we are talking about the "substance" or "essence" of what makes the apple an apple. Today, we can speak about the "substance" of the argument or the "essence" of the story line in a play. This is closer to how the concept worked at Nicaea:

> Is Jesus divine?
> In *essence*, yes.

The bishops at Nicaea believed Christ was not less than divine, but truly divine or "true God." How could this be, since there is only one God?

The idea of consubstantiality can be understood as describing the process of birthing a child. Jesus is "begotten from the Father." What does this mean? Surely it does not mean that God has a womb or "parts" (see above). Equally problematic would be to claim that it implies creation, for then the Son would not be a Son but a creature, according to Alexander's party at Nicaea. Instead, the concept of being begotten implies (1) a kind of relationship and (2) something about the Son's nature.

"The apple doesn't fall far from the tree." This saying assumes that apple trees bear or "beget" only apples (cf. Gen. 1:11–12). Likewise, when humans beget offspring, they share a "kindred," or they are of "like kind." Even beyond the specific questions of genes and DNA, the simple observation can be universally made that humans give birth only to other humans (*not* dogs, cats, etc.).

My son is begotten of me (even though his mother did most of the work), and therefore he is as human as I am. What nature or "essence" did my son inherit? The same essence, humanity. The same can be said of God. God's Son, begotten of the Father, is as divine as the Father is.[38] What is the Father's nature or "essence"? God-ness/divinity—God is simply God. What nature or "essence" did the Son inherit? The same essence, divinity. Nevertheless, we must still ask, how are they "one" and not two gods?

The answer to this question requires analogies. With humans, each human being has a human nature. One aspect of that human nature is to be finite. With God, each divine person has a divine nature. One aspect of divine nature is to be infinite. We humans, however, bound by our finite nature, cannot truly comprehend infinity. Instead, we symbolize it (∞) and define what it is not (infinite = *not* finite). Therefore, we must rely on symbols and analogies to give us a way to imagine what is beyond our horizon.

Analogy #1: Imagine you wanted to make a clay vase. First, you would need to take the "substance" of clay, and then mold it into the particular shape of the vase. In our analogy, this first vase is the Father. Now, imagine you wanted to make a second clay vase that is *homoousios* with the first vase. To do so, you would *not* go get another lump of clay. Instead, you would take the exact same clay used to make the first vase, and then shape it into the second vase. The clay used to make vase 1 is the "substance" (*ousia, substantia*), and so for vase 2 to be "consubstantial" (*homoousios/una substantia*), you must use the exact same substance. At this point, there is an obvious objection: with

---

38. Athanasius, *Defense of the Nicene Definition* 10.

vases, you would have to destroy vase 1 to change it into vase 2, and with God this would be the heresy of modalism (see chap. 4). With vases, this objection would be valid. With God, however . . . all things are possible.

The analogy fails when we think of God in terms of material substance. Instead, think of God's own nature. God the Father's nature/being is shared by God the Son, who is begotten of the Father. Remember, this nature/being or essence is immaterial and infinite. The Father and the Son are two distinct persons (i.e., *not* modalism), but one in terms of their "essence"; God is One-Being (i.e., *not* polytheism).

Analogy #2: If the analogy of clay proves problematic, let us try the analogy of fire. Whenever God's people have attempted to envision the invisible God, fire has offered useful imagery (e.g., burning bush, pillar of smoke/fire, etc.). After all, fire is a mysterious "substance." Imagine a flame. In order not to get burned, I must hold a torch, but I am interested in the flame, not the torch I'm holding. Now imagine I wish to make a second flame from this first flame. To do so, I must hold a second torch, but remember I care about the flame on the torch, not the torch itself. I would then touch the second torch to the first flame and draw from it a second flame. Now, we could ask, when did this second flame begin to exist? If we simply allowed the imagery of the flames to guide our answer, we would have to admit that the second flame always already existed within and wholly as the first flame. So with God: the Second Person of God always already existed within and wholly as the substance of the First Person of God. The Son is, like the flame brought forth from the first flame, "light from light," "God from God."

Today, modern thinkers like us, who have had Chemistry 101, know that there is no such "substance" as "flame." Instead, what we are seeing is actually heat and light being given off from the chemical breakdown of the fuel (i.e., the torch) in the reaction known as fire, but . . . you have to forget all of that and simply see the image for what it is supposed to be in this analogy: a mysterious substance!

Now that we have avoided ontological subordination, we have to guard against one more error in our thinking. For the analogies given here to work, we must not apply the same timetable to God as we do to vases and torches (chronological subordination). Also, rather than thinking of God modalistically—as being first a Father(-figure), and then born as a Son, and later known Spiritually, or as Holy Spirit—the Nicene bishops understood God to be eternally three persons. At least as far back as Origen (ca. 230), some Christians have understood the act of the Father begetting the Son as an act that did not so much "occur" (in the past) but that is an eternal relationship, what is known as the "eternal generation" of the Son by the Father.[39] By stating that the Father begot the Son "in eternity" (notice the past tense does not quite fit here), the orthodox party avoids the subordinationist Christology of Arius. The Father is not older than the Son. While there is a logical priority of the Father over the Son ("The Father is greater than I," John 14:28), the two are equal in their "is-ness" or "being" ("The Father and I *are* one," John 10:30). This logical priority is neither chronological nor ontological, for the Father and the Son are coeternal and consubstantial—a point that will be discussed again in the conclusion.

Now that we have fully explained and even defended the term *homoousios*, we need to see why so many found it controversial. After Nicaea, the Arian party did not simply concede, and the Nicene party did not simply hold sway over the whole church. The fault lines of these parties will be mapped below, but first let us see the initial objections to the idea of the Son as consubstantial with the Father.

After Nicaea: In Search of Orthodoxy

After the council, many criticized the term *homoousios*. The reasons for doing so can be summarized in five points.

1. It is unknown to Scripture and the early apostolic tradition, which makes it novel.[40]
2. It is a technical term, borrowed from philosophy.
3. It implies a materialistic understanding of God's nature.
4. It was used by the gnostics to speak of the many emanations from God.
5. It was used by the Sabellianists to explain how the *personae* of the Father, Son, and Spirit were actually "One-Being."[41]

39. Against the common view of Origen as a subordinationist, see Christopher A. Beeley, *The Unity of Christ: Continuity and Conflict in Patristic Tradition* (New Haven: Yale University Press, 2012), 17–31. To be sure, there is enough material in Origen for Arius/Arians to claim him too, but his view of eternal generation will be appropriated by the Nicenes and ultimately will become the norm after Constantinople.

40. Sozomen, *Ecclesiastical History* 4.12.

41. The term was actually condemned at the Council of Antioch in 286, a point apparently overlooked by the bishops at Nicaea. One solution to this problem by Eastern bishops who supported *homoousios* was to insist also that God be understood as three *hypostaseis*, not just *prosōpa*, for *hypostaseis*/"entities" was a stronger word than *prosōpa*/"faces" and implied true distinctness of the Father, Son, and Spirit. Illustrating how easily the Nicenes could be interpreted as modalists, Athanasius refused to affirm a tri-hypostatic view of God until his *Tome to the People of Antioch* 5–6 (ca. 362). The Sabellianists had (allegedly) affirmed that

Given all of these serious objections to the term *homoousios*, it is no surprise that many resisted the term and looked for alternative ways of articulating the underlying concept.

The either/or labels of orthodoxy versus heresy fail to capture the various responses to Nicaea. Historians instead have attempted to map out these complex reactions with more nuanced categories.

In order to understand the counterarguments against Nicaea, we will briefly trace the aftermath of the council in terms of the key figures involved. If Nicaea stands as one landmark for the Arian controversy, then the next ecumenical council, Constantinople 381, certainly represents a bookend. Although Arianism did not disappear after this later council (and so "bookend" is too strong of a concept), 381 certainly marked a decisive blow for subordinationist teaching. Therefore, the following comments on individuals' roles highlight the trajectory from Nicaea to Constantinople, even if this is a luxury that individuals at that time could not have foreseen. In order to help organize who teaches what view, let us first provide some categories for the various positions.

Many objected to the Council of Nicaea and were therefore "anti-Nicene," and yet many of these same objectors were equally unhappy with Arius's teaching. In the immediate aftermath, there was not simply a "Nicene party" and an "Arian party"—although the "Nicene party" claimed the choice was that simple.[42] Instead, the Nicene party was flanked by several groups.[43]

> Option #1: *Homoousians, or Nicenes.* Believed that the Father and the Son are the *same substance*. This party will be led by Athanasius but supported by Rome and most of the West, and then later will be joined by the Cappadocian Fathers.

> Option #2: *Anomaeans, or Arians.* Believed that the Father and the Son *are not* the same substance (Greek *an* + *homoios* means "not like").

God changed "faces," and so did confess three divine *prosōpa*, but not three distinct entities/*hypostaseis*. For the Sabellianist views, including Marcellus of Ancyra and his role in fostering further suspicion about the Nicene party, see chap. 4.

42. Largely due to Athanasius's description of Arianism (which included Eusebius of Nicomedia et al.) in his *Orations* (penned while in exile in ca. 339 in order to gain Rome's support) and the argument of reductio ad absurdum in Athanasius's *On the Councils* (359).

43. See Williams, *Arius*; Hanson, *Search for the Christian Doctrine of God*. Even a reference to the four "parties" outlined here can be misleading; see Winrich A. Löhr, "A Sense of Tradition: The Homoiousian Church Party," in *Arianism after Arius: Essays on the Development of the Fourth-Century Trinitarian Conflicts*, ed. Michel R. Barnes and Daniel H. Williams (Edinburgh: T&T Clark, 1993), 81–100. Moreover, the notion of a single "original Nicene theology" has been replaced with a "pro-Nicene culture" by Lewis Ayres, *Nicaea and Its Legacy: An Approach to Fourth-Century Trinitarian Theology* (Oxford: Oxford University Press, 2004), 236–40.

Arius himself, of course, is included in this party, but this party drew on other sources than Arius.[44]

Option #3: *Homoiousians, or Semi-Arians*. Believed that the Father and the Son are of *similar substance*. This party rejects Arian subordinationism but also fears that the Nicenes hold to a form of modalism.

Option #4: *Homoeans*. Believed that the Father and the Son are "like in representation" (Greek = *homoios kata tas graphas*). This formula is admittedly the least committed, as it was meant to be a compromise between the Nicenes and the Homoiousians.[45]

With these four parties outlined, it becomes readily apparent that "orthodoxy" was far from obvious in the fourth century. This can be further seen in a survey of the major figures involved in the aftermath of Nicaea.

Arius: Traditionally said to have been exiled at the council, and Constantine ordered all his books burned.[46] He was later rehabilitated by sympathizers at the Synod of Tyre (335). He died, allegedly from a most violent case of diarrhea, the next year, before Constantine could reinstate him as presbyter in Alexandria.[47]

Alexander: Bishop of Alexandria whose views won approval over Arius's at the Council of Nicaea. After his death in 328, his successor Athanasius championed his insistence on the eternality of the Son.

Eusebius (of Nicomedia): Exiled soon after Nicaea for continued support of Arius.[48] Earned reinstatement in 329 by arguing that Arius's views

44. See details in Michael Butler, "Neo-Arianism: Its Antecedents and Tenets," *SVTQ* 36, no. 4 (1992): 355–71.

45. See the confession of faith in Athanasius, *On the Councils* 8, which seems remarkably Nicene, only sans any term for essence: "We believe in . . . one Only-begotten Son of God, who, before all ages, and before all origin, and before all conceivable time, and before all comprehensible essence, was begotten impassibly from God. . . . God from God, like to the Father who begat him" (*NPNF*[2] 4:454). Athanasius's vehement rejection of this "dishonesty" (*On the Councils* 9) illustrates how entrenched the Nicenes had become.

46. See the instruction of Constantine's *Epistle* (in Socrates, *Ecclesiastical History* 1.9).

47. The traditional dates from the early sources have been followed here (mainly Athanasius himself; for a vivid exaggeration of Arius's unseemly death, see Socrates, *Ecclesiastical History* 1.38). See discussion in Timothy David Barnes, "The Exile and Recalls of Arius," *JTS* 60 (2009): 109–29; and Hanns Christof Brennecke, "Die letzten Jahre des Arius," in *Von Arius zum Athanasianum*, ed. Annette von Stockhausen and Hanns Christof Brennecke (Berlin: de Gruyter, 2010), 63–83.

48. Some early sources claim Eusebius of Nicomedia and Theognis of Nicaea were exiled at the Council of 325 (Socrates, *Ecclesiastical History* 1.14; Sozomen, *Ecclesiastical History* 2.16), but more recent scholarship has shown this as a misunderstanding. The bishops were in fact Secundus and Theonas, both from Libya (see Socrates, *Ecclesiastical History* 1.9).

do not necessarily contradict Nicaea.[49] After several influential Nicene bishops were removed, he was installed as the patriarch of Constantinople. Another example of Eusebius's influence was that he baptized Constantine on the emperor's deathbed (337). Eusebius himself then died in 341.

Athanasius: Exiled on five occasions. During one he went to Rome and gained the favor of Pope Julius. The Western bishops supported Athanasius and defended Nicaea. Thanks to the Rome/Alexandria alliance, Nicene orthodoxy held its ground until Constantius's reign ended. Athanasius died in 373.

Constantius II[50]: Became emperor of the East upon Constantine's death, and eventually ruled over the whole empire. He summoned several anti-Nicene councils. Constantius died of a fever in 361.

Julian: Julian's soldiers declared him the sole emperor soon after the death of Constantius II, and he announced his allegiance to the old gods of Rome. Although Christians, for this reason, dubbed him "Julian the Apostate," his ascension to power initially helped the Nicene party, for he allowed bishops like Athanasius to return from exile.[51] His reign, however, was short-lived; he died in battle in 363, and the emperors that immediately followed were less engaged in the church disputes.

Theodosius I: Reigned from 379 to 395, and his long tenure enabled the Nicene party to regain and hold key positions in the church. Theodosius summoned another council, which would later be deemed ecumenical, the First Council of Constantinople (381).

The Cappadocians Fathers: Influential thinkers and bishops whose support of Nicaea ensured its victory at the First Council of Constantinople (381): Basil of Caesarea (330–79), Gregory of Nazianzus (329–90), and Basil's younger brother, Gregory of Nyssa (ca. 331–ca. 395), all served in the region of Cappadocia.

All of these people and events culminated in the First Council of Constantinople (381). Even here no Western bishops were present, but the council did reaffirm Nicaea. Gregory of Nazianzus presided originally at its head, and Emperor Theodosius supported the decision. The Creed of Nicaea was

---

49. Socrates, *Ecclesiastical History* 1.14.

50. 317–61; r. 337–61. See Ammianus Marcellinus, *Roman History*; Athanasius, *History of the Arians*.

51. Athanasius, however, soon criticized Julian's apostasy, and so Julian had Athanasius exiled again.

What about the Spirit? Pneumatomachianism

Although the focus during the Arian controversy fell directly on the Second Person of the Trinity, the debate certainly affects one's view of the Third Divine Person, the Holy Spirit. Arius himself believed in "a Father, a Son, and a Holy Spirit" (in Epiphanius, *Panarion* 69.8.1), but he immediately describes the Son in subordinationist terms, with no mention of the Spirit.

Later, Constantius appointed an anti-Nicene patriarch of Constantinople named Macedonius. As part of the Homoiousian party, Macedonius subordinated the Spirit to the Son by declaring that the Spirit was a created being. Basil wrote *On the Holy Spirit* in response, which is the most complete and clear defense of the full divinity of the Spirit in its time. Basil and the other Cappadocians labeled Macedonius's view "pneumatomachianism," or "fighting the Spirit." The "Macedonians" were condemned at Constantinople (381), and even though the council could not be persuaded to add the *homoousios* to the creed for the Spirit, the Spirit is affirmed as "co-worshiped and co-glorified with the Father and the Son," which implies full divinity.

reaffirmed (albeit revised), and the term *homoousios* was decreed to be official orthodox teaching. Even the Spirit was said to be equal with the Father at this council. In this way, all forms of theological subordinationism were condemned outright. The persons of the Son and the Spirit were definitively declared to be fully divine: as fully God as the Father is God. And with this victory, the anti-Nicene parties, or "Arianism," went into steep decline.

Many Arians did continue to teach subordinationism, and this form of Christianity especially thrived outside of the empire's control. The so-called barbaric tribes, like the Goths and the Vandals, were evangelized by Arian missionaries. Regardless, where Christianity survived in the West, the Nicene Creed would be upheld.

Arianism: Partial Orthodoxy

Few have stepped forward to defend Arius and claim that his view of the Son was either misrepresented or was in fact a valid doctrine.[52] Instead, the revisionist

52. Colin Gunton's claim that twentieth-century theologians' "favorite heresy" was Arianism is of course a caricature ("And in One Lord Jesus Christ . . . Begotten, Not Made," in *Nicene Christianity: The Future for a New Ecumenism*, ed. Christopher R. Seitz [Grand Rapids: Brazos, 2001], 35). Similarly, Maurice Wiles, *Archetypal Heresy: Arianism through the Centuries* (Oxford: Oxford University Press, 1996), defends "Arianism," by which he means a nondivine

focus has been on the category of "Arianism" as a distinct heresy deviating from a clearly defined orthodoxy. Contrary to the traditional view, many scholars now sympathize with the so-called Arians and Semi-Arians who suspected Nicaea to be a Trojan horse for modalism and yet struggled to articulate their own orthodoxy without slipping into an outright Anomaean subordinationism.[53] Perhaps we should exposit what is considered today the orthodox view as articulated by the Cappadocian father Gregory of Nyssa in order to see just how razor-thin the line is between orthodoxy and subordinationism.[54]

Gregory is asked by a friend named Ablabius (which is Greek for "Oblivious") a simple question, "Why not say 'three gods'?"[55] Ablabius's rationale is straightforward: Peter, James, and John are three distinct persons who all share the same human nature. We call them "three men." So with God: the Father, the Son, and the Holy Spirit are three distinct persons who all share the same divine nature. Why not say "three gods"?

Gregory's answer is multifaceted so as to cover all of the bases. For example, one answer given is that we are not pagan polytheists—which only begs the question, why not? More substantially, he insists that while Ablabius's analogy is correct, the premise is flawed. In common parlance, people may call Peter, James, and John "three men," but this is incorrect!

Peter, James, and John are one "man" for Gregory, which sounds bizarre, except that Gregory's Greek allows the abstract noun to slip into the even more abstract category of "man," or, as we prefer today, "humanity." (Think back to the apple's essence: apple-icity). There are not multiple humani-*ties*.[56] It must be affirmed that there is one humankind, even though everyday language ignores this truth. So with God: there is one divinity or Godhead, even though we know three divine persons.

In regard to Ablabius's analogy, there is a difference for Gregory. Unlike Peter, James, and John, the Father, Son, and Spirit's one nature entails one activity (or "one energy") and one will. Gregory goes so far in celebrating the

---

Jesus. The closest to a defense of Arius would be G. Christopher Stead's statement: "Arius, of course, was not wholly free from blame. Yet the Christian Church has much to deplore in its treatment of him" ("The Word 'from Nothing,'" *JTS* 49 [1998]: 684).

53. Löhr, "Sense of Tradition," 81–100.

54. Constantine (as cited in Eusebius, *Life of Constantine* 2.68) sees little to no difference between Alexander and Arius: "And yet, having made a careful enquiry into the origin and foundation of these differences, I find the cause to be of a truly insignificant character, and quite unworthy of such fierce contention." Both sides, of course, disagreed with his conclusion.

55. The following discussion echoes Ayres, *Nicaea and Its Legacy*, 345–63. For the development of trinitarian thinking before and against Arius, see Declan Marmion and Rik Van Nieuwenhove, *An Introduction to the Trinity* (Cambridge: Cambridge University Press, 2011), 29–62.

56. A truth that the twentieth century had to come to terms with after the Nazi ideology took "race" to its logical conclusion.

unity that he almost slips into an outright modalism wherein no distinction of persons can be found. Nevertheless he does avoid modalism, and he does so by pointing out the one thing that differentiates the persons: their "mode of existence" (*tropos hyparxeōs*, a technical phrase roughly equivalent to "person" for the Cappadocians).

What is this idea that differentiates one divine person from another? Cause. The Father is the cause of the Son and the Spirit, because the Father begets the Son and breathes forth the Spirit. These relationships cannot be reversed—the Son does not beget the Father—which creates a hierarchy in God. Subordinationism? Not exactly.

The monarchy of the Father is said to be different from Arius's subordinationism. First, Arius has a chronological subordination—the Father is older than the Son. While we finite humans experience cause sequentially, God—according to orthodox thinking—transcends space and time. Therefore, the Son is "eternally begotten" (i.e., not temporally or sequentially), and there is no chronological subordination.[57]

Next, Arians and Semi-Arians are heard as teaching (and the Anomaeans certainly did teach) an ontological subordination. Ontology, or the study of "being" (Greek = *ontos* [participle form] or *ousia* [substantive/noun form]), has to do with something's essence or substance. The Son, for the Nicenes, is *homoousios* with the Father. The Son *is* as fully divine as the Father *is*: "God from God, light from light, *homoousios* with the Father . . ." Therefore, there is no ontological subordination.

Although we have ruled out chronological and ontological subordination, there is still a logical hierarchy within the Godhead. The Father is the Father, and the Son is the Son—the order cannot be reversed to say the Son begets the Father. This implies that there is a causalogical hierarchy. While modern thinkers such as Jürgen Moltmann fear that this inevitably results in subordinationism, the fourth-century Nicenes believed that the doctrine of the monarchy of the Father remained faithful to Scripture (e.g., John 14:28).[58] Scripture always speaks of God in hierarchical terms, and here is where we can at least sympathize with Arius for wishing to preserve the Father's unique role as the Archē, or source of all being (1 Cor. 8:6a)—as did Gregory of Nyssa and the rest of the Nicenes.

57. Gregory learned this point from Basil (see *Against Eunomius* 2.11–14).

58. See Jürgen Moltmann, *The Trinity and the Kingdom of God* (San Francisco: Harper & Row, 1981). What I find even more problematic for Moltmann's version of the social analogy for the Trinity is the fact that once the hierarchical metaphors are removed from God's eternal reality, the person formerly known as Father recedes entirely from view. What is known as unique about the "Father" apart from the Son and/or the Spirit? All unique descriptions of the Father in Scripture are in a hierarchical relation to the Son and/or Spirit. If this relationship is removed, then what is known about the "Father"?

Whereas Arius could avidly defend God's monarchy, he could not simultaneously articulate why we also worship the Son. Thinkers like Gregory confessed that the Son is both distinct from the Father and yet one in essence with the Father (1 Cor. 8:6b). Nicaeno-Constantinopolitan orthodoxy (a.k.a. trinitarianism) offers a way to express belief in both aspects of the divine mystery as it has been revealed in Scripture.[59]

One last point needs to be restated before we leave Arianism. Athanasius led the charge against the Arians by arguing along several lines. Subordinationism, for example, leaves Christians with (at least) two gods and thereby abandons the monotheistic heritage and embraces polytheism. On another front, Athanasius argued even more intently that Arius's view of Christ as a created being makes salvation impossible.[60] If the goal of salvation is to reconcile us fully to God (see 2 Cor. 5:16–21), then Arius's Christ does not accomplish our salvation. Instead of Immanuel, God-with-us, we have the highest creature from God with us. Arius's god has sent an emissary to do his dirty work. Athanasius's God, however, came in the flesh for our salvation.

Where does all this leave orthodoxy? Now that we have established Christ as fully God (against Arius), we need to ask how the incarnation can be expressed. The primary answer is that God came "in the flesh," but as we will see in the next chapter (against Apollinaris), this could easily be misunderstood.

Recommended Bibliography

Ayres, Lewis. *Nicaea and Its Legacy: An Approach to Fourth-Century Trinitarian Theology*. Oxford: Oxford University Press, 2004.

Hanson, R. P. C. *The Search for the Christian Doctrine of God: The Arian Controversy, 318–381*. Grand Rapids: Baker Academic, 2005.

Löhr, Winrich A. "Arius Reconsidered: Part 1." *ZAC* 9, no. 3 (2005): 524–60.

———. "Arius Reconsidered: Part 2." *ZAC* 10, no. 1 (2006): 121–57.

Lyman, J. Rebecca. "Arius and Arians." In *The Oxford Handbook of Early Christian Studies*, edited by Susan Ashbrook Harvey and David G. Hunter, 237–57. Oxford: Oxford University Press, 2008.

Stead, G. Christopher. "Arius in Modern Research." *JTS* 45, no. 1 (1994): 24–36.

Williams, Rowan. *Arius: Heresy and Tradition*. Rev. ed. Grand Rapids: Eerdmans, 2002.

59. On Scripture, see Ayres, *Nicaea and Its Legacy*, 31–40. On appropriation of trinitarianism in contemporary thought and practice, see Marmion and Van Nieuwenhove, *Introduction to the Trinity*, esp. 62–78 on Arius's contribution to this doctrine.

60. Arius's soteriology is seen as insufficient by Williams, *Arius*, 239–45, 256–59. Athanasius's reaction to Arius assumed the "coherence" of creation-incarnation-salvation; see Khaled Anatolios, *Athanasius* (New York: Routledge, 2004), 39–86; Anatolios, *Athanasius: The Coherence of His Thought* (New York: Routledge, 2005).

**Summary:
Apollinarians**

**Key Doctrine: Apollinarianism
or Subhumanism**

- God-in-a-Bottle Jesus
- Christ has a human body, but is
  a divine soul or mind

Key Dates

- 360: Apollinaris becomes bishop
  of Laodicea
- 381: Apollinarianism condemned at the Council of
  Constantinople

6

Apollinaris

Subhumanism

And to the angel of the church in Laodicea write: The words of the Amen,
the faithful and true witness, the origin of God's creation: I know your
works; you are neither cold nor hot. I wish that you were either cold or
hot. So, because you are lukewarm, and neither cold nor hot, I am about
to spit you out of my mouth.

—Revelation 3:14–16

Who would not feel pity upon the man of this melancholy?

—Gregory of Nyssa

Young Apollinaris loved to hear great orators. For going to a recitation
by one of these pagans, his bishop excommunicated him for supporting
unchristian events. Apollinaris decided right then and there to try to
"greatly injure the Church" by inventing a heresy about Jesus that would lead
people astray. At least, that is the version of the story told by his opponents.[1]

1. Sozomen, *Ecclesiastical History* 6.25.

129

What was this heresy he allegedly invented? Apollinaris claimed the Son of God was incarnate, that is, enfleshed or, better, "*in* flesh." Why is this so harmful or even heretical? Because Apollinaris's explanation of the incarnation is incomplete: he explained Christ's body to be a tent, an earth-suite, in which the Logos resided (see John 1:14, "the Word . . . tabernacled among us" [my literal translation]).

Why was this a problem? His opponents heard him to say that Christ was not fully human. The logic stems from the way one understands human nature. Humans consist of two basic "parts": a body and a soul. Apollinaris, it was said, understood the incarnation in terms of the body or "flesh" (cf. *caro/carnis* in Latin, hence the term "in-*carn*-ation").[2] That is, the Word of God put on the outer flesh, and he resided where a human soul normally resides within the body.

Still not seeing the problem? The incarnation, for Apollinaris's opponents, is not simply about placing a genie in a bottle. Christ cannot be understood as "appearing" to be human (see chap. 3). Instead, Jesus must be fully human. To hear Apollinaris tell it, Christ has a human body, but not a human soul, and therefore is not *fully* human. After the battle with Arianism (see chap. 5), the Nicene party had secured Christ's status as fully divine, but Apollinaris risks achieving that status by sacrificing a belief in Christ's humanity.

In order to understand Apollinaris's teaching more fully and with a sympathetic reading, we will first review Apollinaris's life and the controversies in which he was embroiled.

Apollinaris: Like Papa, like Son

Historians remember Apollinaris as "of Laodicea" in order to distinguish him from the other men from antiquity with the same name. He was born in Laodicea (the modern city of Latakia in Syria), and he eventually became the bishop there. Even though he is remembered as "Apollinaris the Syrian," Apollinaris's heritage stems from Alexandria.[3] His father, Apollinaris the elder, came from Alexandria to teach rhetoric and grammar, and he then became a priest in the Laodicean church.[4] The ties to Alexandria apparently remained, for when Athanasius passed through Laodicea on his return from

2. The Greek term is *ensarkos*. See Apollinaris (Pseudo-Gregory the Wonder-worker), *Exposition of the Faith* 16: "For God, having been incarnated [*sarkōtheis*] in the flesh of man . . .."
3. Gregory of Nyssa, *Antirrheticus adversus Apolinarium* 2.
4. Socrates, *Ecclesiastical History* 2.46.

a second exile (346), Apollinaris Sr. and Jr. hosted him.[5] This act of allegiance to Athanasius meant an open declaration for Nicene Christology. Apollinaris's bishop, George, however, was an Arian/anti-Nicene/Homoiousian (see chap. 5; for simplicity, I will use "Arian" throughout this chapter), and so he excommunicated both Apollinaris the elder and the younger.[6]

Perhaps the problem began earlier. There is another report—mentioned in this chapter's opening—about how both Apollinaris the elder and the younger were previously warned by their bishop, Theodotus, not to attend lectures by a famous non-Christian Sophist in town. When George succeeded Theodotus as Laodicea's bishop, he warned the father and son again. They did not comply, and so he excommunicated them.[7] Such a report, of course, sounds like slander to many modern scholars: it may be an attempt to depict Apollinaris as a troublemaker from a young age.

Apollinaris did serve in the church as a lector or reader—an official office by that time—and when his bishop, George, died (360), the Arian party installed a certain Pelagius as the new bishop in order to advance their party's teaching.[8] In response, the Nicene party appointed Apollinaris as bishop of Laodicea, and so he led a rival congregation in that city.[9]

Up to this point in his story Apollinaris belongs to the orthodox party that will eventually win the debate against Arianism. He is such a staunch defender of Nicaea that he will break fellowship from the church in Laodicea and its bishop.[10] Against the Arians, Apollinaris defends Christ's status as fully divine.[11] His problem arises when he turns his attention to the incarnation, for he allegedly does not profess that Christ is fully human.

5. For the wider and more complex ties between the churches of Laodicea and Alexandria, see Mark DelCogliano, "The Eusebian Alliance: The Case of Theodotus of Laodicea," ZAC 12, no. 2 (2008): 250–66.

6. Sozomen, *Ecclesiastical History* 6.25.

7. Socrates, *Ecclesiastical History* 2.46. However, Sozomen, *Ecclesiastical History* 6.25 (cited in the previous paragraph), says that Theodotus corrected them and that the Apollinarii were then repentant and remained in the church until George excommunicated them for their association with Athanasius.

8. Socrates, *Ecclesiastical History* 2.46.

9. The traditional chronology used here is debatable: Apollinaris may have preceded Pelagius (I am indebted to Kelley McCarthey Spoerl for sharing her as-yet-unpublished paper on this subject entitled "The Circumstances of Apollinarius's Election in Laodicea"; see also her helpful essay "Apollinarius and the First Nicene Generation," in *Tradition and the Rule of Faith in the Early Church: Essays in Honor of Joseph T. Lienhard, SJ*, ed. Ronnie J. Rombs and Alexander Y. Hwang [Washington, DC: Catholic University of America Press, 2010], 109–27).

10. Something Cyprian (*On the Unity of the Church* [ca. 250]) had earlier forbidden.

11. Apollinaris and the orthodox party agree on this point: the Logos is the "Demiurge"/Creator of Genesis (e.g., Athanasius, *Letter to the Africans* 4; Pseudo-Athanasius, *Against Apollinaris* 1.8, 14).

Excursus: Fully Human *and* Impassible

According to classical Christian theology, God's attributes include immutability (does not change) and impassibility (does not suffer). While many modern theologians often reject both of these attributes and claim that the postapostolic church adopted these from Greek philosophy, many church historians find that this modern accusation is unfounded. While there is undoubtedly a certain amount of borrowing from Greek philosophical terminology, the question is whether the early church adopted philosophical commitments. For example, Plato claimed that God is immutable and impassible, so God does not love (a view often called strong impassibility). Early Christians, however, insisted that God loves even though they would use the same terms to describe God (a view often called weak impassibility).

The early Christian commitment to these concepts comes more from the view of God as creator of "all things" (Eccles. 11:5; Rev. 4:11). If God is "before time" and "outside the cosmos"—concepts that stretch finite language beyond its capacity—then God must be atemporal (= eternal) and aspatial (a.k.a. omnipres-

ent). This view of the transcendent and infinite God also requires that God is not material or physical in any way, for God creates the material world. God as non-physical/nonmaterial is therefore unharmable, unconquerable—cannot suffer. Is this an "apathetic" God? While this may be how modern English speakers hear the term "impassible" (cf. the Greek term *apathē*), this would be a misreading of the early Christian writers. For them, God certainly cares, loves, creates, redeems, and so on—all while remaining nonphysical/immaterial and therefore unconquerable/unharmable. It would be equally unfair to interpret the modern belief in a passible God as a claim that God is "pathetic" (cf. the Greek term *pathētos*)!

When it comes to the incarnation, Christ is said to be *both* passible and impassible. Contradiction? Nope: paradox. Christ is passible in his human nature, for his flesh is finite, harmable, and so on. This human nature, however, has not replaced the divine nature of the Word of God. Instead, the Word assumed/took up/joined himself to human nature while remaining divine (and therefore infinite, immutable, impassible, etc.).

Apollinarianism

Apollinaris, with other Apollinarians like Vitalis, so emphasized Christ's divinity that he allegedly lost sight of Christ's humanity.[12] His Christology, and especially his view of the incarnation of Christ, is best seen in light of

12. For Vitalis, see Gregory of Nazianzus, *Letter* 102; Epiphanius, *Panarion* 77.20.1–77.24.5. Also see H. Lietzmann, *Apollinaris von Laodicea und seine Schule: Texte und Untersuchungen* (Tübingen: Mohr/Siebeck, 1904), 273–76.

An early expression of this is found in Ignatius of Antioch (early second century). In his letter *To the Ephesians*, Ignatius confesses Christ "is both flesh [*sarkikos*] and spirit, made and not made, God in man [*en anthrōpō theos*] . . . of Mary and of God, first passible [*pathētos*] and then impassible [*apathēs*]" (7.3 [my trans.]). Ignatius is not emphasizing how Christ is simultaneously passible and impassible. In Ignatius's telling of the gospel, Christ first experiences suffering and death on Good Friday, but then rises on Easter Sunday unconquerable/unharmable and immortal (cf. Heb. 2:10). On the other hand, Ignatius certainly believes that Jesus was fully God prior to Easter: he speaks of the "blood of God" shed on Good Friday (*To the Ephesians* 1.1). The point is to see how Ignatius so easily speaks of Christ as both human ("flesh . . . made . . . of Mary") and divine ("spirit . . . not made . . . of God"). These two natures are joined together, since Christ is "God in man."

This twofold way of talking about Christ will continue into Apollinaris's time. In response to Apollinaris's view of God "in flesh," other writers will insist that Christ is fully and completely human (flesh and soul/mind) while also remaining fully and completely divine (immutable, impassible, etc.). One antiheretical writer will counter Apollinaris by saying, "It is remarkable that we confess that he truly suffered and yet is truly impassible. For because of its changelessness, impassibility and co-essentiality with the Father, his divine nature did not suffer; his flesh suffered, and yet the divine nature was not separate from the human nature in its suffering" (Epiphanius, *Panarion* 77.32.6). A later example comes from a work once thought to have been written by Athanasius: "Christ is one, the self-same, both God and Man . . . a convincing proof alike of the Passion and the impassibility. . . . Therefore, it is He who suffered and who did not suffer; being impassible and unchangeable and unalterable in the Divine nature, but having suffered in flesh" (Pseudo-Athanasius, *Against Apollinaris* 1.10–11). These later writers are important for understanding what is at stake. Christ must be affirmed as fully divine (against Arius), but this cannot come at the expense of him being fully human (against Apollinaris). Once both the humanity and the divinity are fully affirmed, then Christian theologians will move to the next logical question of how these two aspects of Christ are united (see chaps. 7 and 8).

the controversies that preceded him. We have already mentioned the Arian controversy, which Apollinaris so vigorously opposed. In addition, Apollinaris was concerned to avoid what he saw as an alternative heresy, the monarchianism of Paul of Samosata, allegedly being revived by Marcellus of Ancyra and others (see chaps. 2 and 4).

Whereas Arius permitted the Word of God to be passible by making the Word a created being, Paul of Samosata had earlier protected God's impassibility by differentiating Jesus Christ from the Word of God, who descended on Christ at his baptism. Against Arius, Apollinaris insisted that the Word of God was uncreated and therefore impassible.[13] Against Paul, Apollinaris insisted that the Word of God was one and the same as Jesus of Nazareth. How then could the impassible Word suffer?

Apollinaris found the answer to this dilemma in a biblical phrase: the Son of God suffered "in the flesh" (1 Pet. 4:1). How did he do so? Via the incarnation, the Logos "gave himself over to the flesh . . . [and] was brought into conjunction with the flesh after the similitude of man; so that the flesh was made one with the divinity."[14] The point is that Jesus of Nazareth was none other than the Word of God "in the flesh." In his technical terminology, Christ is one "principle" (= *hegemonikon* in Greek), not two "persons" (i.e., the Word and Jesus).[15] If this sounds orthodox, that is because it is—so far. Early in Apollinaris's career, he voiced this view and was well received.[16] Trouble arose for Apollinaris on two fronts: first, another controversy arose in Antioch that split the Nicene party, and second, in this period many technical terms were ill defined. Let us address each in turn.

During the Melitian schism in Antioch, Apollinaris turned powerful allies into enemies by choosing sides. Leading anti-Arians like the Cappadocian Fathers now saw Apollinaris as heretical. In all likelihood the ambiguity in Apollinaris's technical terms was interpreted critically so as to have him teach a deficient Christology.

One technical term that would prove especially difficult for christological debate was *hypostasis*. This Greek word has the sense of "existence." The question is whether it implies something's *inner* being (i.e., essence) or whether it refers to a *specific* being (i.e., individual or entity). If it means "inner being,"

13. Some sources suggest that Apollinaris's Christology is in fact borrowed from Arius (e.g., Epiphanius, *Panarion* 69.19.7; Pseudo-Athanasius, *Against Apollinaris* 1.15; 2.3). Apollinaris, it is argued, conceded Arius's view of the incarnation in order to champion an anti-Arian view of the preincarnate Logos. These sources should not be entirely dismissed, but they are suspect. While it is likely that Arians (i.e., Anomaeans; see chap. 5) held to this view of the incarnation, we have no reliable data to suggest that Arius himself did. Moreover, since the time of Justin Martyr, church fathers rarely articulated Christ's human nature in terms of a human soul. Therefore, if Arius spoke of the Logos "in the flesh" without mention of a human soul, he was in good company (see discussion in William P. Haugaard, "Arius: Twice a Heretic? Arius and the Human Soul of Jesus Christ," *CH* 29, no. 3 [1960]: 251–63). Silence about Christ's human soul does not necessarily imply a denial of Christ's human soul.

14. Apollinaris (Pseudo-Gregory the Wonder-worker), *Exposition of the Faith* 2 (cf. 6).

15. Aloys Grillmeier, *Christ in Christian Tradition*, vol. 1, *From the Apostolic Age to Chalcedon (451)*, trans. J. S. Bowden (London: Mowbray, 1965), 227.

16. See Gregory of Nazianzus, *Letter* 101. Athanasius once articulated an Apollinarian-sounding Christology (e.g., *On the Incarnation* 44, written early in Athanasius's career). However, Athanasius later affirmed a human soul in Christ (see *Tome to the People of Antioch* 7 [ca. 362]). Scholars are divided on whether Athanasius held to an Apollinarian view, and the difficulty may lie in the nature of the evidence—Athanasius is not answering Apollinaris's question.

Melitian Schism of Antioch

In 360 Melitius of Antioch (not the Melitius of Lycopolis, responsible for the Melitian schism mentioned in the last chapter) supported Nicaea. When the emperor Constantius II discovered this, he replaced him with an Arian bishop. In 362 the emperor Julian permitted Melitius's return, but the restored bishop would be exiled twice more under the next Arian emperor, Valens. Finally, Melitius was reinstated for his defense of Nicaea and given the honor of presiding during some of the sessions of the Council of Constantinople (381, the same year Melitius died).

The schism occurred during his first exile, but Antioch already had two parties pitted against each other even before Melitius became bishop. Much earlier, one of Melitius's predecessors had been Eustathius, who was staunchly Nicene and opposed any compromise with the Homoiousian party. In 326 a synod had met and found Eustathius to be guilty of Sabellianism—no surprise,

since the synod consisted of "Arian" members. The congregation in Antioch now had factions both for and against Eustathius.

When Paulinus was appointed as the bishop of Antioch as a replacement for Melitius, the Antiochene parties became entrenched. The Eustathian party supported Paulinus, and the new Melitian party claimed it was the truly orthodox/Nicene church. The difficulty for those outside of Antioch was that both Paulinus and Melitius were Nicene. Athanasius came to Antioch during this time, but eventually supported Paulinus. Other Nicenes, however, such as Basil of Caesarea, continued to support Melitius. Apollinaris sided with neither, but appointed Vitalis as bishop around 376. Because Apollinaris rejected Basil's candidate, Basil now turned against Apollinaris and attacked his view of the incarnation (see Basil, *Letter* 263), even though he had earlier been allies with Apollinaris in supporting Nicaea.

then it would be synonymous with "essence" or even "nature," and then God the Father and the Son are one *hypostasis*/Being (as said in the original Creed of Nicaea [325]). On the other hand, if it implies an individual, then God the Father and the Son are two different *hypostaseis*, or (we would say) persons.

As noted in the previous two chapters, this term proved difficult for those wishing to avoid modalism on the one hand and subordinationism on the other. Apollinaris sides with the Nicene view that ultimately succeeded at Constantinople (381) in terms of trinitarianism: *hypostasis* should be seen as synonymous with the Greek term *prosōpon* and the Latin term *persona*, and so there are three *hypostaseis*/persons in God (thus avoiding Sabellius's modalism).[17] Because of this definition, he insisted that the Word of God

17. See Joseph T. Lienhard, "Two Friends of Athanasius: Marcellus of Ancyra and Apollinaris of Laodicea," *ZAC* 10, no. 1 (2006): 56–66.

Apollinaris in His Own Words

What did Apollinaris write? According to Basil, who is not happy about it, Apollinaris "filled the world with his works" (*Letter* 263.4). Basil's comment, of course, is hyperbole, but it does contain a kernel of truth. Apollinaris was widely respected for his intellectual acumen, and he did write a number of works. Unfortunately, most of his works have suffered the same fate as most heretical tomes and no longer survive.

There are a number of fragments from Apollinaris. Most of them are citations of him by his opponents and so are somewhat suspect (see especially Gregory of Nyssa, *Antirrheticus adversus Apolinarium* [ca. 382]). A number of Apollinaris's statements, however, have been preserved more positively in medieval *catenae* (collections of comments on Scripture from the church fathers). Jerome especially appreciated Apollinaris's insights and cited him frequently in his own exegetical works.

A few Apollinarian works survive largely by accidents of history. A work formerly attributed to Gregory Thaumaturgus (= "the Wonder-worker") entitled *An Exposition of the Faith* (*Kata meros pistis*) has now been accepted as written by Apollinaris himself. Also, some works formerly attributed to Athanasius have been thought by some to be Apollinarian, such as *On the Incarnation of the Word of God*, *Against the Sabellians*, and *That Christ Is One*. Basil of Caesarea wrote the work entitled *Against Eunomius*, but now the last two of the five books in this work are, ironically, suspected to be from the hand of Apollinaris. Likewise, two of Basil's letters and three of John Chrysostom's sermons are suspected of being written by this so-called heretic, but all survive because of the false attribution to an orthodox author.

incarnate is one *hypostasis*, not two (thus avoiding Paul of Samosata's heresy).[18] Some of his opponents, however, could hear this statement on the incarnation as reverting to the earlier meaning of *hypostasis* as nature, as in the Word incarnate's one nature.[19]

Why is a one-nature incarnate Word a problem? For Apollinaris's enemies, this idea has several possible implications. One is that Christ has a divine nature (clearly Apollinaris is not Arian), and therefore Christ's one nature/*hypostasis* is not human.[20] How then can Christ suffer and die, when divine

18. For Apollinaris's reaction to Paul of Samosata, see Gregory of Nyssa, *Antirrheticus adversus Apolinarium* 7 and 10. As with the last point, however, Apollinaris is not always consistent in his terminology. Few were in this period.

19. Kenneth Paul Wesche, "The Union of God and Man in Jesus Christ in the Thought of Gregory of Nazianzus," *SVTQ* 28, no. 2 (1984): 83–98, explains how the Stoic link between nature (*physis*), *hypostasis*, and *prosōpon* contributed to Apollinaris's unique formulation.

20. See Gregory of Nazianzus, *Letter* 202; Gregory of Nyssa, *Antirrheticus adversus Apolinarium*. See also Sozomen, *Ecclesiastical History* 6.27, where Apollinaris is accused of claiming

nature is impassible and immortal? Another option is that Christ simply appeared to have a human nature. This is the docetic heresy of the gnostics (see chap. 3).[21] Surely, this is not Apollinaris's aim. Another possibility is that the Word's divine nature "mixed" with a human nature.[22] This possibility is more of an accusation stemming from later debates, and so it will be dealt with more fully in chapter 8. For now, suffice it to say that such a "mixed" nature would be neither human nor divine, but some mutant.

How did Apollinaris defend himself against these accusations? His answer—as heard by his opponents—avoided all of these pitfalls, and yet in doing so he was heard to have invented another "novel teaching" (i.e., heresy).[23] Apollinaris insisted that the Word incarnate is one *hypostasis*/person and therefore can suffer "in the flesh."[24]

If the flesh is the outer person, then the Word's outer expression, or body, can suffer and be crucified. Whereas the inner person is normally identified as the soul, Apollinaris simply taught that the Word was Christ's inner person. By using the term "soul" to express his idea, however, Apollinaris raised a number of problems.

The Greek word for "soul," *psychē*, not only implied the inner person that animates the flesh (cf. the Latin *anima* = soul, or animator of flesh); the concept

---

that even Christ's flesh descended from heaven (cf. John 3:13). Apollinaris likely did use this verse to emphasize how Jesus is the same *hypostasis*-person as the Word of God, but probably not the same *hypostasis*-nature appearing on earth with the same nature he had prior to his earthly birth. For discussion and a different conclusion, see Stephen H. Webb, *Jesus Christ, Eternal God: Heavenly Flesh and the Metaphysics of Matter* (Oxford: Oxford University Press, 2011), 112–18. Webb's desire to reclaim an eternal flesh for Christ has biased his reading of the evidence for Apollinaris. Frances Young notes two studies refuting this reading of Apollinaris in *From Nicaea to Chalcedon: A Guide to the Literature and Its Background*, 2nd ed. (Grand Rapids: Baker Academic, 2010), 250; see also the argument made by Rowan A. Greer, "The Man from Heaven: Paul's Last Adam and Apollinaris' Christ," in *Paul and the Legacies of Paul*, ed. William S. Babcock (Dallas: Southern Methodist University Press, 1990), 165–82.

21. Gregory of Nazianzus, *Letter* 102: "At another time they bring in His flesh as a phantom rather than a reality . . . some delusive phantom and appearance."

22. Gregory of Nazianzus, *Letter* 102: "And so they declare that the Perfect Man is not He who was in all points tempted like as we are yet without sin; but the mixture of God and Flesh." Similarly, Gregory of Nyssa, *Antirrheticus adversus Apolinarium* 51, compares Apollinaris's Christ to the fawns of Greek myth. These seem to be *reductio ad absurdum* caricatures. Gregory of Nazianzus (in Sozomen, *Ecclesiastical History* 6.27) accuses Apollinaris of claiming that the Word of God suffered. However, this seems to be another caricature (in light of Gregory of Nyssa, *Antirrheticus adversus Apolinarium* 58).

23. Gregory of Nazianzus, *Letter* 101.

24. Wesche, "Union of God and Man," 85, uses Apollinaris's own logic (as expressed in *Exposition of the Faith*—formerly attributed to Gregory the Wonder-worker) to find that two natures would inevitably lead to two *hypostaseis*/persons. This logic enabled Apollinaris to avoid Sabellianism in trinitarian theology, but it forced him into a monophysite Christology (see further discussion in chap. 8).

Excursus: Early Christian Anthropology

Against Apollinaris, many argued that Christ must be fully human. The Council of Nicaea, they argued (e.g., Pseudo-Athanasius, *Against Apollinaris* 1.2), had already affirmed this. The Creed of Nicaea (325) states, "The Son of God . . . for us humans [Greek: *tous anthrōpous*; Latin: *homines*] and for our salvation . . . came down and became incarnate [*sarkōthenta/incarnates est*], became human [*enanthrōpēsanta/homo factus est*]." Notice that to be "flesh" (*sarx/carne*) is the same as to be "human" (*anthrōpos/homo*). Therefore, if Apollinaris wishes to be faithful to Nicaea, then he must affirm the Word of God incarnate as human, not just in a human body.

What does it mean to be fully human? "Man," or *adam* in the Hebrew, became a living soul (*nefesh*) when given the "breath of life" (Gen. 2:7). Humans in the Old Testament do not so much "have" souls—they are souls (in Ezek. 18:4, cf. RSV, "All souls are mine"; NRSV, "All lives are mine"). This monistic anthropology of the Hebrew language can be contrasted with the dualistic anthropology of classical Greek thought. For most ancient Greeks, the body and the soul are distinct and largely independent: the body dies, but the soul lives on, immortal. In the New Testament, this Greek vocabulary is certainly present (Rev. 20:4), but in an accommodated form (Matt. 10:28). Also, sometimes the body/soul dichotomy is synonymous with the flesh/spirit distinction (e.g., Matt. 26:41), while other times the soul (*psychē*) is distinct from the spirit (*pneuma*); see Hebrews 4:12.

Therefore, what does it mean to be fully human in the New Testament? Paul is an interesting case, for he can sometimes use bipartite language, while at other times he can speak of humans as tripartite (1 Thess. 5:23). Suffice it to say that New Testament scholars have reached no consensus on what Paul meant by these terms, for he offers no clear definitions. What can be clarified is Paul's distinction between body (*sōma*) and flesh (*sarx*): Paul tends to use the term "flesh" to mean "sinful flesh," which is thereby antithetical to the spirit (*pneuma*)—see especially Galatians 5:16–17. Paul certainly affirms the body (*sōma*) as good, but this body has become contaminated by sin (Rom. 7:17) and so is fleshly. On a similar note, the material body characterized by the soul (*sōma psychikon*) is contrasted with the body of the resurrected state, a body characterized by the spirit (*sōma pneumatikon*)—see 1 Corinthians 15:42–49. In this sense, the spirit is the highest attainable state for a human, while the flesh and even the soul represent something less than ideal. Similar language can be found in other New Testament writers, for God is spirit (John 4:24), and so anyone "of God" must be "of the spirit" as well, not merely of the flesh (John 3:6). These passages are arrayed by anti-Apollinarian writers (e.g., Gregory of Nyssa, *Letter* 101) to justify reading John 1:14 to say "the Word became human" (not just "flesh," for flesh in John is contrasted with the divine nature, or "Spirit," and so must imply human nature).

It can be conceded that the Bible has no single anthropology; instead, various Scripture passages speak of humans in various ways. While this may seem to allow thinkers like Apollinaris to define humanity to suit their own needs, other early Christian writers agreed on a central principle. God made humans good and whole. The classic Greek dualism was rejected by thinkers like Justin Martyr, who insisted that body and soul began as a united entity, "man"/a human being (*Dialogue with Trypho* 5). Sin and death ruptured this union, and God *by grace* keeps humans from total annihilation after bodily death.

This fracturing of the body/soul is not the natural state, however, and the soul is not naturally immortal. From this view of the creation of humanity, Irenaeus insists that a soul of a human is not a human, but only a part. Neither is the body the whole of humanity, but only a part (*Against Heresies* 5.6.1). This view, sometimes called integrative holism, implies that for Jesus to be human, he must consist of all the "parts" of being human, including the body and the soul—making Apollinaris's teaching heretical. This raises one last question for early Christian anthropology.

How many parts are there to a human? The early Christian councils and creeds never offered a final answer to this question. By the seventh century, some (the monergists and monophysites; see chap. 8) are still debating what it takes to understand Jesus as fully human, and they find within the human many "parts": the body and soul are distinct, and within the soul there is not only the human mind, but also human energy and will. What is a human "energy"? John of Damascus admits there may not be any such thing as energy within humans (*An Exact Exposition of the Orthodox Faith* 3.15, citing Gregory of Nazianzus)! However, John insists that *if* humans have a part called "energy," *then* Christ must have a human energy—for Christ must be fully human.

This late example helps illustrate how the early christological debates were concerned more about Christ than about philosophically dissecting humans. Nonetheless, however one decides to demarcate what it means to be human, one must then affirm the same about the incarnate Word, for he had to be made "fully human in every way" (Heb. 2:17 [NIV]), except for sin (Heb. 4:15)—and sin, it should be stated, is only part of fallen human nature. Christ enters into the world and "tabernacles" among us (John 1:14) with more than a soulless or mindless body; the Word took up a fully human nature (cf. Heb. 2:16 as used by Athanasius [cited in Epiphanius, *Panarion* 77.7.1]).

of the *psyche* includes much of the human nature, such as human emotions and human reason. If Christ does not have a human *psyche*, then Apollinaris has still not avoided docetism: Christ appears to be tempted, to mourn, and to suffer psychologically (in his *psyche*), but in reality these were all merely outward acts.

We can be fairly certain that Apollinaris did not mean to deny the human *psyche* of Jesus, for there is a report that Apollinaris changed his terminology. Instead of saying Christ had no human soul, he said that the Logos of God took on human flesh and a human soul. The only stipulation, of course, is to avoid Paul of Samosata's adoptionism/possessionism and stipulate that this soul of Jesus is not a different *persona* from the Word.[25] Now, Apollinaris simply needs to explain how the person of the Word was "in" flesh.

Since the highest aspect of the human soul (according to ancient thinking) is the reason or logical mind (= *nous* in Greek), and since the Logos of God is God's reason or logic, then the Word of God simply replaced what is normally the *nous* or mind in the soul of Christ.[26] This solution was especially appealing since early Christians thought of the image of God in humanity as the reason itself, or the rational mind.[27]

While certain aspects of this teaching were appealing, many still found Apollinaris's view problematic. After all . . .

a. if the criterion is now to have Christ fully human, and

b. if to be fully human is to have a body and soul, and

c. if a soul includes a human mind,

d. then Apollinaris still depicts Christ in such a way that is not fully human.[28]

e. In sum: belief in a mindless soul = belief in an incomplete human soul = subhumanism.

Apollinaris may not have a mind, his opponents quipped, but Jesus certainly did.[29] While Apollinaris likely did not see Jesus as less than human, his teachings were heard as inevitably leading to this heresy.[30]

---

25. Apollinaris (Pseudo-Gregory the Wonder-worker), *Exposition of the Faith* 15 and 19.

26. Gregory of Nazianzus, *Letter* 202: "He assumes that that Man who came down from above is without a mind." Rufinus, *Ecclesiastical History* 2.20, says Apollinaris originally denied that Christ had a human soul, but then retracted and denied that Christ had a human *nous*.

27. Our bodies, after all, don't "look like" or "reflect" God; our soul is the "image." See Vitalis's explanation of an Apollinarian Christ as "perfect man" (in Epiphanius, *Panarion* 77.23.2).

28. Epiphanius, *Panarion* 77.1.4.

29. Paraphrase of a point found in several early writers, e.g., Gregory of Nazianzus, *Letter* 101: "If anyone has put his trust in Him as a Man without a human mind, he is really bereft of mind, and quite unworthy of salvation."

30. Gregory of Nazianzus, *Letter* 101: "But if He has a soul, and yet is without a mind, how is He man, for man is not a mindless animal? And this would necessarily involve that while His

Apollinarianism—but not Apollinaris!—was condemned at the Second Ecumenical Council, Constantinople, in 381 (see canon 1 of the council). Whether the finer nuances of his teaching were missed, or even if his teachings were maliciously misrepresented, the heresy known as Apollinarianism became an influential benchmark in orthodox thinking. It is, therefore, worthwhile to listen to the orthodox response to Apollinarianism in order to hear what concerns drove the alternative understanding of Christ.

The Gospel according to Apollinaris

Christ Jesus frees us from the bondage of the flesh, according to Apollinaris, by taking up our flesh, healing it from the disease of sin, and making it godly (*theosis*).[31] In this expression of the gospel, Apollinaris especially echoes Paul's teaching on salvation. Our minds are trapped in this bondage of sinful flesh (Rom. 7:5), and so we still do what we know we should not do (Rom. 7:14–15). To save us from "this body of death" (Rom. 7:24 ESV) the Logos of God entered into our same situation (Rom. 7:25). Did Jesus become human to do so? Apollinaris does not seem to make that question the priority. Instead of focusing on humans, who are of "the first man"/Adam, Apollinaris focuses on "the second man [who] is from heaven" (1 Cor. 15:47).[32]

Back to our question, did Jesus become human according to Apollinaris? To answer this question, Apollinaris shifts from Paul to John: "The Word became flesh and tabernacled among us" (1:14, my literal translation). Is this enough? Perhaps Pauline and Johannine thought can be more completely integrated.

It is true that Apollinaris avoids strict docetism because his Christ has real flesh, not just the appearance of flesh. The flesh of Apollinaris's Christ, however,

---

form and tabernacle was human, His soul should be that of a horse or an ox, or some other of the brute creation."

31. For Apollinaris's adherence to Pauline anthropology, see Young, *From Nicaea to Chalcedon*, 249–50. The following paragraph follows the explanation given by Wesche, "Union of God and Man," 88–89; although along with the insights of Christopher A. Beeley, "The Early Christological Controversy: Apollinarius, Diodore, and Gregory Nazianzen," *VC* 65, no. 4 (2011): 376–407.

32. While Gregory of Nazianzus and Gregory of Nyssa are usually portrayed as countering Apollinaris because of his deficient soteriology, it is now admitted that Apollinaris's view of Christ was in fact deeply concerned with salvation, only he used a different framework to understand Christ's means of saving; see Brian E. Daley, "'Heavenly Man' and 'Eternal Christ': Apollinarius and Gregory of Nyssa on the Personal Identity of the Savior," *JECS* 10, no. 4 (2002): 469–88; and Kelley McCarthy Spoerl, "The Liturgical Argument in Apollinarius: Help and Hindrance on the Way to Orthodoxy," *HTR* 91, no. 2 (1998): 127–52.

is just a "mask."[33] Christ is still putting on an act, seeming to be human. Docetism! Or, at least, neo-docetism. When Jesus underwent psychological duress, as in the wilderness temptations, was he just pretending? Similarly, when Christ mentally deliberates as in the garden of Gethsemane, is it just an act?

An axiom previously used against the gnostics—*Quod non assumptum, non sanatum*—becomes the norm for Christology in response to Apollinaris: "For that which He has not assumed He has not healed; but that which is united to His Godhead is also saved."[34] If the gnostic Christ did not assume a human body, then the human body is not healed/saved. Likewise, if the Apollinarian Christ did not assume a human mind, then the human mind is not healed/saved. In fact, this way of thinking assumes the human mind did not need saving, which makes God the "God only of the flesh, and not of souls."[35] Apollinaris himself began with Christ's divinity (contra Arius), and found a logically sound way to get Christ into human "flesh." His orthodox trinitarian theology, however, was not enough. His one-sided Christology left him marked as a heretic.

The Orthodox Response: Heresy?

Of the major heresies treated in this book, Apollinaris's teaching is the last eventually abandoned by all as untenable.[36] Even the later Alexandrian tradition, which wished to stress the oneness and the divinity of Christ in the flesh, would reject Apollinarianism because it makes Jesus's human experience a farce. The alternatives to Apollinarianism, however, have their own problems, or at least they will prove less than persuasive. What we will see, therefore, is that none of the post-Apollinarian options can claim absolute victory. The Nestorian option (chap. 7) will be denounced by the Christian empire, but the so-called Nestorian church, the Church of the East—as it calls itself—will thrive for generations even until the present. The monophysite option (chap. 8) will likewise continue in sectors outside of Byzantine control, such as Egypt's

---

33. The following response to Apollinaris is that of Gregory of Nazianzus, *Letters* 101 and 102.

34. Gregory of Nazianzus, *Letter* 101.

35. Gregory of Nazianzus, *Letter* 101. Augustine is often credited with (or blamed for!) inventing the doctrine of original sin. It would be more accurate to say Augustine was the first to insist on original guilt applied to all, even infants. Earlier writers, however, were equally aware of the totally depraved state of humans: that is, every part of humanity is fallen and in need of divine healing.

36. See Charles E. Raven, *Apollinarianism: An Essay on the Christology of the Church* (Cambridge: Cambridge University Press, 1923), who admits having once accepted Apollinarianism. However, after his thorough study of the Apollinarian controversy, he conceded that this Christology is inadequate and indefensible.

Coptic Church, which is still active today. The Chalcedonian option, known to Eastern Orthodox, Roman Catholic, and Protestant Christians simply as orthodoxy (see conclusion), will claim a clear majority, but it cannot claim to be unrivaled or the only tenable option. Apollinarianism's condemnation marks the end of an era.

What was the immediate response to Apollinarianism? The reaction to Apollinaris resulted in an emphasis on the full humanity of Christ—so far, so good. The Word must assume a fully human nature, must be a full human being. Still good? Perhaps.

When anti-Apollinarians so emphasized Jesus as a complete human being—body and soul—then the tendency to speak of both the divine Logos and the human Jesus became problematic.[37] The thinkers who emphasized the two natures of Christ, such as Diodore of Tarsus, would be remembered by historians as the Antiochene school. The most (in)famous representative of the Antiochene school, Nestorius, will be condemned for this emphasis, which brings us to our next chapter.

Rather than a true conclusion to this chapter, we should end with "To be continued . . ." The reason for such a cliff-hanger is that Apollinarianism never really goes away; instead, the (over-)reaction to Apollinarianism results in its own alleged heresy, Nestorianism (see chap. 7). In turn, the response to the Nestorian heresy seems to revert to a form of the Apollinarian heresy, monophysitism (see chap. 8). Were these heresies really so vicious and destructive to Christianity? Is there an orthodoxy that can avoid both of these pitfalls? Let us turn to each and see.

Recommended Bibliography

Daley, Brian E. "'Heavenly Man' and 'Eternal Christ': Apollinarius and Gregory of Nyssa on the Personal Identity of the Savior." *JECS* 10, no. 4 (2002): 469–88.

Gemeinhardt, Peter. "Apollinaris of Laodicea: A Neglected Link of Trinitarian Theology Between East and West?" *ZAC* 10, no. 2 (2006): 286–301.

Lienhard, Joseph T. "Two Friends of Athanasius: Marcellus of Ancyra and Apollinaris of Laodicea." *ZAC* 10, no. 1 (2006): 56–66.

Raven, Charles E. *Apollinarianism: An Essay on the Christology of the Early Church.* Cambridge: Cambridge University Press, 1923.

Teal, Andrew. "Athanasius and Apollinarius: Who Was the Chicken and Who Was the Egg?" *StPatr* 46, no. 3 (2010): 281–88.

37. Basil Studer, *Trinity and Incarnation: The Faith of the Early Church*, ed. Andrew Louth, trans. Matthias Westerhoff (Edinburgh: T&T Clark, 1993), 194–97.

**Summary:
Nestorians**

Key Doctrine: Dyoprosopitism
- Occupy Jesus
- The Son of God is a different person who inhabits Jesus the human

Key Dates
- 431: Council of Ephesus
- 433: Formula of Reunion

7

Nestorius

Dyoprosopitism

"The *Lord* has done this for me," [Elizabeth] said. . . . But why am I so favored, that the *mother of my Lord* should come to me?" . . . And Mary said, "My soul glorifies the *Lord*, and my spirit rejoices in God my Savior."

—Luke 1:25, 43, 46; emphasis added

Christ . . . had, beyond all others, in Himself that pre-eminent birth which is from the Most High Father, and also experienced that pre-eminent generation which is from the Virgin, the divine Scriptures do in both respects testify of Him.

—Irenaeus, *Against Heresies* (ca. 190)

Nestorius . . . he confuses everything.

—Cyril

There's something about Mary.

Nestorius—that troublemaking, heretical blasphemer—will go so far as to venerate her, but he refuses to call Mary by her rightful name:

145

Mother of God. She is the Mother of Christ, he says, but not the Mother of God.[1]

Or, at least that is Nestorius's problem according to Nestorius's opponents. All the Protestants in the audience may already be applauding Nestorius for his anti-Catholic courage.[2] But before we go crowning Nestorius as the proto-Reformer of the fifth century, we must clarify the problem.

Is Jesus God? Obviously by now (see previous chapters), the answer is yes. Next question: is Mary Jesus's mother? Again, this is painfully obvious, and no one has ever questioned this one (except maybe Marcion; see chap. 1). So then, to take score of what we have briefly said thus far:

> Premise (a):   Jesus is God.
> + Premise (b):   Mary is Jesus's mother.
> _____
> = Conclusion: Mary is the Mother of God.

What could be more obvious?[3] Nestorius thinks the logic is not so simple.

Nestorius is remembered as denying this conclusion because he disputes premise (a), Jesus is God. Instead, he says that Jesus is human, on whom the Word of God rested. Ebionite adoptionism? Gnostic possessionism? Not exactly. Nestorius's position differs from the earlier heresies. The way in which it differs can best be seen as a reaction against Apollinaris (see chap. 6).[4] We will, therefore, first discuss the alleged heretical teaching before turning to Nestorius's own life and thought.

Nestorianism: (Over-)Correction of Heresy

If Apollinaris's mistake was to see Christ's body as a mere earth-suite for the Logos, then Nestorius must correct this view by taking seriously Jesus's human *nature* (key term). Jesus's humanity is complete. He is fully human. One could go so far as to say that Jesus is a complete human *being* (key term). How could this human being, Jesus, also be God? How could the infinite, immutable, impassible, immortal God be present in a finite body, change/

---

1. Nestorius, *First Sermon against the Theotokos* (in Richard A. Norris Jr., ed., *The Christological Controversy* [Philadelphia: Fortress, 1980], 123–31).

2. As did Martin Luther; see Carl E. Braaten, "Modern Interpretations of Nestorius," *CH* 32 (1963): 252–53.

3. The basic argument of Cyril's *Second Letter to Nestorius* (= *Letter* 4).

4. The Apollinarians thought the orthodox were Nestorian in this sense: "You [Apollinarians] calumniously say, that we [orthodox] say there are two Sons, and call us 'man-worshippers'" (Pseudo-Athanasius, *Against Apollinaris* 1.21).

Cyril of Alexandria

Cyril became bishop of Alexandria in 412 after the death of Theophilus, the previous patriarch and Cyril's uncle. Cyril had watched his uncle rule Alexandrian Christians with a heavy hand. Theophilus even orchestrated the trial and condemnation of John Chrysostom, then patriarch of Constantinople. When Nestorius gave audience to a group of Alexandrians who took issue with Cyril, Cyril in turn made Nestorius the target of an investigation and council, which resulted in Nestorius being declared a heretic.

Because of his tactics against Jews, various heretics, and especially Nestorius, modern historians have questioned Cyril's moral character. Edward Gibbon famously dubbed him "the episcopal warrior" (*Decline and Fall of the Roman Empire* [orig. 1781], 2:185). In a recent trend among scholars, a new consensus has emerged in which Gibbon's verdict has been dismissed as too one-sided. No one "played nice" in Cyril's day, not even Nestorius, who utilized similar tactics against heretical groups under his jurisdiction in Constantinople. Also, the evidence of Cyril's draconian methods is less than one might think after hearing modern portrayals. Of course, official Catholic and Orthodox tradition has declared Cyril to be a saint, and so there have always been voices defending him.

grow, suffer, and die? Since we must avoid the Apollinarian heresy, it cannot just be the outer flesh that experiences these things. Nestorius provides an answer that utilizes that first key term we mentioned: Christ has two *natures*.

As an analogy to Nestorius's bi-nature doctrine, let us take someone who is bilingual. If someone is truly fluent in both English and Spanish, that person is fluent in the vocabulary, grammar, and even the cultures represented by each language. He or she can wake up and speak Spanish in the home, then go out for breakfast and order food in English. No confusion, no psychological split, no personality disorder. The person simply has two languages/cultures.

So with Christ: he can speak human and divine. To be sure, Christ doesn't have a native language in addition to which he adopted a second. Christ has two natures from the time of his conception and birth, kind of like someone born into a bilingual household—and with this point Nestorius has avoided any form of adoptionism/possessionism.[5] Christ can simply utilize his two different natures:

- Christ, in his human nature, can truly/naturally get sleepy, *and* . . . Christ, in his divine nature, can truly/naturally calm the wind and the waves (Matt. 8:23–27//Mark 4:35–41//Luke 8:22–25).

5. Nestorius, *Bazaar of Heracleides* 1.1.71.

- Christ, in his human nature, can truly/naturally get hungry, *and . . .* Christ, in his divine nature, can truly/naturally multiply the fish and loaves (Matt. 14:13–21//Mark 6:30–44//Luke 9:10–17//John 6:1–14).
- Christ, in his human nature, can truly/naturally weep, *and . . .* Christ, in his divine nature, can truly/naturally raise his friend back to life (John 11:35–44).

We could do this all day (John 21:25).

So far, so good. Nestorius clearly means to protect Christ's divine attributes (immutability, impassibility, etc.); the only question is how to do so. Even Cyril of Alexandria, Nestorius's primary opponent, agrees. The defense of Christ's immutability and impassibility is articulated in Cyril's important "Dogmatic Letter" (= *Letter* 4, esp. sect. 5), which was accepted at three ecumenical councils as the standard of orthodoxy against Nestorianism. Nestorius, however, was not so sure, for Cyril's language sounded as if God the Word changed and suffered.[6] It must be admitted that at times Cyril sounds as if he believes in the mutability of the Word.[7] Cyril, however, does not deny the Word's immutability; he elsewhere clarifies,

> We must follow these words and teachings, keeping in mind what having been made flesh means; and that it makes clear that the Logos from God became man. We do not say that the nature of the Word was altered when he became flesh. Neither do we say that the Word was changed into a complete man of soul and body.[8]

Cyril confesses Christ incarnate as retaining a fully divine/impassible nature, but he simultaneously wishes to confess Christ's suffering and work as something undertaken and experienced by none other than God the Son.[9] Nestorius differs in how to confess Christ's experience of suffering.

---

6. See his response to Cyril (= Cyril, *Letter* 53): "You thought that they had said that the Word, who is coeternal with the Father, is able to suffer."

7. In *Letter* 1.17, after citing Heb. 2:17, where Christ is said to have been "made like his brethren in all things," Cyril insists, "For something said to have been made like something else must necessarily pass from a state of non-resemblance to resemblance."

8. *Letter* 4.3. Similarly, he states (*Letter* 39.6) that Christ "has been called the Son of Man after remaining what he was, this is God, immutable and inalterable according to nature. . . . For he remains what he is always, and he is not changed, but instead never would be changed and will not be capable of alteration. Everyone of us confesses that the Word of God is, moreover, impassible" (cf. *Letter* 53). John A. McGuckin, *St. Cyril of Alexandria: The Christological Controversy; Its History, Theology, and Texts*, rev. ed. (Crestwood, NY: St. Vladimir's Seminary Press, 2004), 191, argues that Cyril's language of God-suffering or God-changing was always emphatically speaking of God in the flesh and never negates the impassible, immutable divine nature.

9. For discussion of how Cyril can speak of Christ's "suffering impassibly" (*apathōs epathen*), see Paul L. Gavrilyuk, *The Suffering of the Impassible God: The Dialectics of Patristic*

For Nestorius, Christ's human nature suffers while Christ's divine nature remains impassible. The problem arises when Nestorius so distinctly divides these two *natures* that he begins to speak about two *persons*: Jesus the human suffers while God the Son does not.

To return to Mary, Nestorius allegedly said that he could not worship a newborn baby as the God who made the universe.[10] Such a statement is likely Nestorius's way of distinguishing Christ's two natures: Mary bore Jesus's fleshly/human nature; she did not generate the Son's divine nature. So far, so good.

Nestorius made this division so sharply, however, that he began to speak not only of two natures but of two persons: the baby born of Mary is Jesus the human; the Logos who made the universe is the Son of God. Mary is the mother of Jesus. God is the Father of the Son. These two are united at Jesus's conception, but they remain two distinct *prosōpa*, or persons.[11] This two-person Christology, or dyoprosopitism, is Nestorius's great heresy.

In order to try to hear Nestorius in his own words, let us turn to the history of Nestorius's life and the controversies in which he was involved.

The "Bazaar" Life of Nestorius

Nestorius was born around 381. We know little of his background and upbringing, but he was certainly formed by his experiences in Antioch.[12] He probably studied with Theodore of Mopsuestia, which is significant since many would attribute Nestorius's heresy to Theodore's misleading.[13] He became a monk and a priest, and then in 428 he rose to the rank of patriarch of Constantinople.

Thought (Oxford: Oxford University Press, 2004), 135–71, in his chapter entitled "Nestorianism Countered: Cyril's Theology of the Divine Kenosis"; and Christopher A. Beeley, *The Unity of Christ: Continuity and Conflict in Patristic Tradition* (New Haven: Yale University Press, 2012), 268–70.

10. In Cyril, *Letter* 23.2.

11. At least, that is how Cyril portrays Nestorius (*Letter* 1.22; *Letter* 2.1). However, Cyril admits that the question is not about the "person" of the Word, but about the divine nature: "But perhaps you will say this, 'Tell me, then, is the Virgin the mother of divinity?'" (*Letter* 1.19). Later, the Council of Ephesus (431) denounces Nestorius for saying "Jesus is not God" (Cyril, *Letter* 23.4); i.e., he is a different person from the Son of God. For Nestorius's defense against this charge, see *Bazaar of Heracleides* 1.1.54–72.

12. The common view of the Antiochene and Alexandrian "schools" being at odds with each other has been heavily criticized; see Gavrilyuk, *Suffering of the Impassible God*, 137–39.

13. See John Behr, *The Case against Diodore and Theodore: Texts and their Contexts* (Oxford: Oxford University Press, 2011); and Frederick G. McLeod, *Theodore of Mopsuestia* (New York: Routledge, 2009).

Constantinople had been elevated to the status of "New Rome," first politically by Constantine himself and then religiously at the Council of Constantinople (381). This move had famously irritated the Alexandrians, whose city had always claimed to be "second only to Rome" in the empire. It probably even worried the church in Rome, whose claim to "primacy" was a growing emphasis at this time. While we might like to think that the church fathers were above such political machinations and petty disputes about rank (see Matt. 20:16), the records from the time give historians the opposite impression.

One leader in particular would capitalize on the dispute with Nestorius: Cyril, the patriarch of Alexandria. Nestorius's Christology came to Cyril's attention in a secondary manner. Before Nestorius even arrived in Constantinople, a christological debate was already under way.[14] A number of Christians insisted on calling Mary *Theotokos* (= "Mother of God" or "God-birther"). Others, however, believed that this title misrepresented the incarnation, for Mary gave birth only to Jesus's humanity while God eternally begot his divinity. This second faction insisted on the title *Anthropotokos* (= "Mother of Man," or "Man-birther"). Nestorius certainly sympathized with the latter group, for his Antiochene heritage had tended to stress the difference between the divine and human aspects of the incarnation. Nevertheless, he offered what he thought was a mediating position: he called Mary *Christotokos*. By the time Cyril came into conflict with Nestorius, Nestorius used this previous debate to turn the tables on Cyril, but Cyril's contact with Nestorius arose from a different matter altogether.

When four Alexandrians arrived in Constantinople reporting Cyril's abusive tactics, Cyril was none too pleased with Nestorius's willingness to give the disgruntled Alexandrians an audience. Like his uncle Theophilus had done to John Chrysostom a generation earlier, Cyril offered a countercharge against Nestorius. Cyril claimed that Nestorius's *Christotokos* compromise was a thinly veiled heresy.[15] By inquiring into Nestorius's Christology, Cyril made Nestorius's theological integrity the focal point, and he persisted until the matter had to be decided by a council.

First, Cyril set the chessboard against Nestorius through a series of letters. Cyril requested that Nestorius explain his Christology, to which Nestorius consented. Nestorius's explanation, not surprisingly, did not satisfy Cyril, and so he forwarded Nestorius's letter to Pope Celestine in Rome. Cyril argued in

14. Susan Wessel, *Cyril of Alexandria and the Nestorian Controversy: The Making of a Saint and of a Heretic* (Oxford: Oxford University Press, 2004), 84–87.

15. Cyril, *Letter* 1.5, admitted that the term *Theotokos* was not used by the apostles but maintained that they did teach this belief.

his own letter that Nestorius's views were sinister and heretical, and Celestine concurred with Cyril.

Nestorius in response appealed to the emperor, Theodosius II. The emperor, an ally of Nestorius, agreed that a council was needed to settle the matter, but things did not turn out the way either intended. Cyril successfully deposed Nestorius at the Council of Ephesus (431) by using forceful tactics in the synod itself.

The sequence of events for this council is somewhat stupefying. For the sake of succinctness, they will be laid out chronologically:

November 19, 430: The emperor invites leading bishops to Ephesus.[16]

June 7, 431: The date set for the council to begin. The council is delayed as it waits for bishops from the West and from Syria. The most notably late is John, patriarch of Antioch.

June 22, 431: With 154 bishops present, Cyril begins the council, even though the absent bishops of the West and of Syria have still not arrived.

- Candidian, the official representative of Emperor Theodosius II, objects to Cyril's actions.
- Nestorius refuses to acknowledge the validity of the council and does not attend the council.
- Cyril has Nestorius deposed in absentia. Cyril's formula, that Christ is one *hypostasis*, is accepted (without definition, which will be important for later debates; see below and chap. 8).

June 26, 431: John of Antioch arrives but refuses to recognize the council.

- John summons his own council, with fifty bishops and with Candidian's support, denouncing Cyril.

July 9, 431: Representatives of Rome arrive, supporting Cyril.

Early August: The new representative of the emperor, John, then arrests Cyril, Nestorius, and the bishop of Ephesus, sending the other bishops home.

September 11: Cyril persuades the emperor (allegedly by bribes), and Nestorius is deposed.[17] Nestorius returns in shame to Antioch to be a monk. Cyril returns, without permission, to Alexandria.

These basic events more or less summarize the Council of Ephesus (431). Cyril's Council of Ephesus would be remembered as the Third Ecumenical

16. Mostly from eastern provinces, but others were also invited. Also of interest, the council met "in the great church dedicated to Mary" (Cyril, *Letter* 23.4), which must have made for a formidable space in which to deny the title "Mother of God."

17. For the charge of bribes, see Nestorius, *Bazaar of Heracleides* 1.3 (127); cf. Cyril, *Letter* 96.

Nestorianism: Political vs. Theological

Political Battle Lines		Theological Battle Lines	
Nestorius vs.	Cyril		Cyril
John vs.	Celestine		John
Theodoret vs.	Memnon	Nestorius vs.	Celestine
			Memnon
			Theodoret (?)

Council for most of the church, but Nestorius and his followers would always remember it as Cyril's false synod.

John of Antioch's alternative council did affirm Nestorius, but with the emperor backing Cyril and exiling Nestorius, John would later reconcile with Cyril (433). Was this a compromise, a flip-flop? Perhaps. Alternatively, it could be argued that both John and Cyril agreed theologically on the fact that Nestorian dyoprosopitism is heresy; the only questions were how to articulate the orthodox alternative and whether Nestorius should really be condemned without a chance to explain his views.[18] Although John and many Antiochenes originally formed a party contrary to Cyril and his political maneuvering, the two sides did come to see the common ground they shared in their view of the incarnation.

Nestorius would later (435) be exiled to Petra, in Idumea, and then again to the Great Oasis in Upper Egypt, where he died. Before he died, however, Nestorius told his side of the story.

Nestorius in His Own Words

In previous chapters we have bemoaned the fact that most heretics cannot speak for themselves because, as heretics, their books were burned.[19] To be sure, the majority of Nestorius's prolific writing career is lost to us, but history has allowed him a few exceptions.[20] For centuries, we had to rely on scraps of his statements, mostly quoted by his enemies who were refuting him

18. As argued by Donald M. Fairbairn, "Allies or Mere Friends? John of Antioch and Nestorius in the Christological Controversy," *JEH* 58, no. 3 (2007), 398; the "Political vs. Theological" table is taken from Fairbairn.
19. *Theodosian Code* 16.5.66.
20. Jerome, *On Illustrious Men* 104, says he wrote "innumerable" works.

Nestorius's Works

In 1889 a Syriac translation of what was originally a Greek text was discovered, entitled *The Bazaar of Heracleides*. This text had actually been mentioned by writers from Nestorius's era, and some of them believed the text was written by Nestorius himself. The title is mistaken, for the word "Bazaar" or "commerce" (*tegurta*) is a mistranslation into Syriac of the Greek word for "treatise" (*pragmateia*). The name Heracleides in the title is inexplicable.

Scholars debate whether the text is truly reliable. The final form of the text certainly appears later than Nestorius, but this could be explained as scribal additions. The options are (a) Nestorius himself wrote the text; (b) a later Nestorian wrote the text; or (c) original works of Nestorius were compiled into this text, either by Nestorius himself or by a later Nestorian. Scholars have yet to reach a complete consensus on this issue, but most believe Nestorius is the author, at least in part.

There is also a series of sermons and a small collection of letters, originally attributed to other writers like John Chrysostom, that are now thought to have been written by Nestorius himself. Just how certainly these texts can be attributed to Nestorius is still up for debate, and whether they could revise our understanding of Nestorius's Christology is even less clear.

(and thus poorly represented him).[21] In modern scholarship, however, some of Nestorius's texts have come to light.

Nestorius tells his side of the story in a work known as *The Bazaar of Heracleides*. This lengthy work is not without problems: many passages look like later additions meant to vindicate Nestorius. Given some of these uncertainties, historians today generally accept one of the following three options.

Option 1: Nothing changes. The fragments previously known from Nestorius were his true teachings; this later work, if it is even reliable, represents later attempts to express his theology in a way that would appease the orthodox party. These attempts, however, are too little and too late.

Option 2: Everything changes. The fragments are misrepresentations of Nestorius's views. His opponents painted him in the worst possible light. The *Bazaar*, which is mostly reliable, represents Nestorius's real Christology. We should no longer call him a heretic. He was simply misunderstood.

21. Collected in Friedrich Loofs, *Nestoriana: Die Fragmente des Nestorius* (Halle: Niemeyer, 1905).

Option 3: Modest change in Nestorius's status. Instead of a malicious instigator of heresy, Nestorius is sympathetically seen as in a no-win situation. This ambiguous third option could tilt more toward a defense of Nestorius, wherein he was simply misunderstood, or this option could retain a criticism of Nestorius as offering at best a confusing and incoherent view of Christ. Nestorius himself, we already knew, was not given a fair hearing, and therefore he did not have the opportunity to work out his view of Christ in a public exchange of ideas.[22] His teachings, as they are recorded, may still be deemed heretical, but it must be emphasized such a demarcation is using a later standard of orthodoxy than was available to Nestorius.

Because the first two options are difficult to substantiate—the evidence for or against Nestorius is mixed—the third option offers the most promise in a revised understanding of this controversial figure. This obviously is a debate that we cannot begin to resolve in this present work. We should, however, at least turn to some of Nestorius's statements about Christ in this work and attempt to hear Nestorius in his own words.

Nestorius's First Objection: Order. Nestorius's first complaint about his christological debate with Cyril addresses the political tactics used by Cyril.[23] Nestorius claims he was never given a fair hearing, and Cyril used brute force to ensure that Nestorius was found guilty of heresy. On these points, scholars generally agree with Nestorius. Cyril began the council without waiting for the other bishops to arrive, and he carried out the council in direct opposition to the emperor's directives. The whole affair is out of order.

In Cyril's defense, John of Antioch likely stalled intentionally because he hoped to derail Cyril.[24] Also, Cyril had the support of the bishop of Rome, and historically the Rome-Alexandria alliance was enough to sway the worldwide church—witness Athanasius's *Contra Mundum* in the fourth century.[25]

22. As did Cyril, for example, in the Formula of Reunion, which can be found in Cyril, *Letter* 39; text and translation are available in Jaroslav Pelikan and Valerie Hotchkiss, eds., *Creeds and Confessions of Faith in the Christian Tradition* (New Haven: Yale University Press, 2003), 1:168–71. See discussion in McGuckin, *St. Cyril of Alexandria*, 114–16. Cyril and the Antiochenes likely interpreted the Formula in different ways, esp. the phrase "for a union of two natures took place." For a helpful review of Cyril's thought, see Beeley, *Unity of Christ*, 259–72. Perhaps the disagreement was more about semantics than Christology (see McGuckin, *St. Cyril of Alexandria*, 143).

23. See Nestorius, *Bazaar of Heracleides* 1.3.

24. Although John claims he made all haste (see Cyril, *Letter* 22), Cyril claims the whole council believed John to be stalling intentionally (Cyril, *Letter* 23.3).

25. Cyril's greatest rhetorical achievement was his ability to cast himself in the role of Athanasius; see Wessel, *Cyril of Alexandria*, 296–302.

Nevertheless, even if Cyril is not the villain, Nestorius cannot be blamed for wanting a chance to defend himself and articulate his Christology before a truly ecumenical council.

Is there any basis to Nestorius's claim? What if Nestorius had been given a fair hearing? To look to Cyril's example, it seems that extended opportunity for debate in fact helped develop his thinking. At one point Cyril refused to say "two natures" in fear that the phrase led to Nestorian dyoprosopitism. Cyril, however, continued in communion with others who disagreed. After some time—and, yes, with some imperial pressure—Cyril and John of Antioch both signed the Formula of Reunion (433), which affirmed the "two natures" of Christ.[26] What would the outcome have been if Nestorius had been given such a chance? Such a hypothetical question cannot be answered, but it is interesting to note that John of Antioch believed that all would have been resolved if such a situation had unfolded. Before the Council of Ephesus, John wrote a letter to Nestorius (430) saying, "For certainly, if many genuine colleagues were to have the freedom to examine this question freely, we should easily come to one accord, and what seems to be gloomy would become joyful."[27] Either Nestorius stubbornly refused to enter into such an open discussion (as he is accused of doing in his own time) or the deck was stacked against him from the beginning (as historians today often assume). Either way, we are left with highly biased sources, and we must set ourselves to the task of attempting to reinterpret the teachings of both sides.

Nestorius's Second Objection: Doctrine. Nestorius's second complaint is a counterpunch. Nestorius sounds like a heretic to Cyril. Why? Because Cyril himself is a heretic, and orthodoxy sounds like heresy to heretics.

Cyril accuses Nestorius of heretical Christology: Nestorius is reviving Paul of Samosata's possessionistic adoptionism (see chap. 2). In response, Nestorius charges Cyril with holding heretical Christology: Cyril is rehashing Apollinaris's God-in-a-bod view of the incarnation (see chap. 6).[28] Since Cyril denies a fully human Jesus, Cyril's dislike of Nestorius's emphasis on the human nature of Jesus serves as further evidence of Cyril's own flawed teachings. Who is right in this he-said/he-said argument?

In the end, we may find that both Nestorius and Cyril were so emphasizing a particular point that they each slipped into problematic teachings of their

26. See Cyril, *Letter* 39.3: ". . . as pertaining to one person, . . . as pertaining to two natures . . ."
27. Cited/translated in Fairbairn, "Allies or Mere Friends?," 388.
28. Nestorius, *Bazaar of Heracleides* 1.1.82, 92. Cyril, therefore, must adamantly distance himself from Apollinaris: "For we do not subscribe to the teachings of that crazy Apollinaris. But since we uphold the truth, we anathematize Apollinaris" (*Letter* 31.2).

own. At least, this is the conclusion one could draw about Nestorius, given how his own peers and friends heard his teaching in his own day, and about Cyril, given how his followers (the so-called monophysites; see chap. 8) heard him in later generations.

Nestorius vs. Cyril: In Their Own Terms. To sum up the christological tradition received by both Nestorius and Cyril, the church has insisted on speaking about Jesus as fully God (contra Arius) and fully human (contra Apollinaris). The question now is how Christ's full divinity relates to Christ's full humanity. Nestorius and Cyril approach this question from opposite directions.

Nestorius wishes to speak of Jesus as a complete human being, not just flesh. This emphasis logically requires a clear distinction between Christ's humanity and divinity (for the two are very different—compare the divine attributes discussed at the beginning of the chapter).

Cyril wishes to speak of Christ as fully God, especially given the legacy in Alexandria of combating Arianism.[29] Even in the incarnation, Christ's full divinity is stressed. This, as we will see more fully in the next chapter, could lead to an eclipse of Christ's humanity, even though this is clearly not Cyril's aim.[30]

To Nestorius, Cyril sounds like an Apollinarian (Christ only has human flesh) or an Arian (the Word is less than divine and changed into a human). To Cyril, Nestorius sounds like an adoptionist who so emphasizes the human Jesus, he makes him a different person from God the Son.

In truth, Nestorius is simply trying to protect the full divinity and immutability of the Son, while Cyril is merely trying to emphasize the full divinity of the Son incarnate. Although they both share common doctrinal ground (Christ's divinity), they each defend opposite ends of the field.

Time for some definitions. The terms used by these two patriarchs differ significantly.[31] Nestorius wishes to speak of Christ's two natures. When doing so, he can use the term adapted as orthodox by later Christians, *physis*, or he can use the term *hypostasis*, which was earlier a synonym of *physis*. In the Arian controversy *hypostasis* originally meant nature (as in the Creed of Nicaea [325]), but the various anti-Nicene parties were finally convinced that Nicaea was not modalistic precisely because its supporters began using *hypostasis* as a stronger term than *persona*. Christian theologians today commonly think of *hypostasis*

29. Athanasius's influence has been unquestioned. However, for Cyril's unique amalgamation of Athanasius with other sources, like Gregory (if not the priority of these other sources in his thought), see Christopher A. Beeley, "Cyril of Alexandria and Gregory Nazianzen: Tradition and Complexity in Patristic Christology," *JECS* 17, no. 3 (2009): 381–419.

30. See Hans van Loon, *The Dyophysite Christology of Cyril of Alexandria* (Leiden: Brill, 2009).

31. See Nestorius, *Bazaar of Heracleides* 2.1.

as a synonym of *persona*, but this meaning was still unclear in Nestorius's day. When Nestorius affirmed Christ's two natures by saying Christ had two *hypostaseis*, Cyril's party heard Nestorius to teach that Christ was two persons.[32]

To add to the confusion, Nestorius would even go so far as to speak of Christ's two *prosōpa*, or persons, in his works.[33] This would confirm his opponents' suspicion that Nestorius thought of Jesus and the Logos as two different persons. Even here, however, Nestorius's use of *prosōpon* suggests that he is invoking a more archaic meaning.

Nestorius's use of the term *prosōpon* proves to be one of the most difficult parts of his teachings to understand, explain, and/or defend. Early in the debate, Nestorius was heard as teaching that two *prosōpa* were "joined together" (*synapheia*) in Christ.[34] Cyril's party, however, wanted to stress the total union (*henōsis*), or oneness, of Christ. Cyrilian minds wanted to know: Does Nestorius mean that two persons (*prosōpa*) fellowshiped (*synapheia*) together in Christ's body? He certainly sounded this way to Cyril, and so Nestorius was denounced for teaching possessionistic adoptionism: the Son of God inhabited Jesus the human.

Later, in the *Bazaar*, Nestorius claims that the two *prosōpa* were united by becoming one *prosōpon*. Whatever Nestorius means by this term, he most likely did not have the same concept in mind as the orthodox party did when it defined *prosōpon* as representing a distinct entity. For example, Scripture can speak of a man and a woman becoming "one" in terms of a shared life. This does not mean, however, that the two persons become one person. They become one "flesh," or embodied life together. For another example, trinitarians will speak of three distinct *prosōpa* in God, even though God is "one." This does not mean, however, that the three divine persons become or are one person. Instead, they are one in nature and being. How could Nestorius speak of two such "persons" becoming one "person," without destroying the distinctness of the two? Nestorius must be using this term with a different understanding.

Perhaps Nestorius's understanding of *prosōpon* was not so individualistic. Perhaps he spoke of two *prosōpa* like we would speak of an outward

---

32. Cyril, *Letter* 17.9, 13; 50.20, 28; and more extensively in *That Christ Is One*. To add to the confusion, Cyril could say that Christ is "one *physis*" (e.g., *Letter* 45.6; cf. 46.6; and *Scholia on the Incarnation* 11 [trans. in McGuckin, *St. Cyril of Alexandria*, 303]), a formula that gives rise to the monophysites (see chap. 8) but that is understood by scholars today (at least Orthodox, Catholic, and Protestant scholars) to be Cyril's idiosyncratic use of the term.

33. Most scholars since J. F. Bethune-Baker (*Nestorius and His Teaching: A Fresh Examination of the Evidence* [Cambridge: Cambridge University Press, 1908], esp. 82–100) read Nestorius as using *prosōpon* in two different ways: outward manifestation and person.

34. E.g., Cyril, *Letter* 5.6; 17.10; Nestorius, *Bazaar of Heracleides* 1.1.57, 61, 70–71.

"character" or "manifestation."[35] If so, then one could sympathize with his view of Christ as having two natures (*physeis/hypostaseis*), each of which included outward aspects (*prosōpa*). Christ's human aspect/character/*prosōpon* would have included all human traits (eyes, ears, nose, mind, etc.).

In fact, this link between nature and *prosōpon*/outward aspects was the exact same logic Apollinaris employed to affirm Christ as one *prosōpon*, only he could not articulate Christ's fully human nature—Christ had one nature for Apollinaris because Christ was one *prosōpon*, only the divine that was "in flesh."[36] Nestorius simply corrected Apollinaris's mistake: Christ had a fully human nature, which necessarily includes a human *prosōpon*, and Christ's divine aspect/character/*prosōpon* would have included all divine traits (all-seeing, all-hearing, all-knowing, etc.). Because Nestorius aims to speak of the union of these two character traits, we can sympathetically assume that he never intended to speak of two "persons" the way his opponents caricatured him as speaking (God the Son + Jesus the human). Instead, he simply wished to stress the difference between the two natures of the one Christ (thus, Mary gave birth to Christ in terms of humanity). This more archaic meaning of the term *prosōpon* allows for a rereading of Nestorius's teaching.

Rehabilitating Nestorius?

Understanding Nestorius in this way allows us to draw a different conclusion about his Christology than his opponents did in the fifth century. Whereas they heard his dyoprosopitism as two persons, today we can hear him speaking of Christ with two faces ("face" being the original meaning of *prosōpon* in Greek).[37] Instead of the Son of God being conjoined to Jesus the human, like we think of conjoined twins, Nestorius spoke of Christ like we speak of Frank and Louie. You've not met Frank and Louie? Allow me to introduce you.

Frank and Louie is (not are) a Janus cat.[38] One cat with two faces. "FrankenLouie," as he is often called (I'm not making this up, I promise), made the *Guinness Book of World Records* for being the longest-living Janus cat, and while he sounds like a monstrosity, his outgoing personality (singular)

35. Roberta C. Chestnut, "Two Prosopa in Nestorius' Bazaar of Heracleides," *JTS* 29, no. 2 (1978): 398–409.

36. Kenneth Paul Wesche, "The Union of God and Man in Jesus Christ in the Thought of Gregory of Nazianzus," *SVTQ* 28, no. 2 (1984): 85–87.

37. On the theological background to *prosōpon* as "face," see Paul B. Clayton Jr., *The Christology of Theodoret of Cyrus: Antiochene Christology from the Council of Ephesus (431) to the Council of Chalcedon (451)* (Oxford: Oxford University Press, 2007), 56–74.

38. Eric Skarda, "Two-Faced Cat Defies Science, Sets Guinness World Record," *Time*, September 30, 2011, http://newsfeed.time.com/2011/09/30/two-faced-cat-defies-science-sets-guinness-world-record/.

Contested Terms

The key theological terms used in the fourth and fifth centuries were not clearly defined at the beginning of the debates. Different writers used the same terms in different ways. To add to the confusion, sometimes the same writers would use the same term in different ways at different times. The following chart provides examples of key terms. The question marks indicate that later readers debate how a certain writer or writers defined the given term.

		Nestorius	Cyril	Ephesus (431)
Ousia	=	Essence	Essence	Essence
Physis	=	Nature	Manifestation of essence?	Nature?
Hypostasis	=	Nature	Manifestation of nature?	Person?
Prosōpon	=	Manifestation of nature?	Person	Person

has won a significant following. FrankenLouie eats out of both mouths and looks in two directions at once, but the two *prosōpa* are united in one cat, always working in harmony.

Similarly, Nestorius's Christ has two faces, or manifestations. The key difference from FrankenLouie is that Christ's human face is visible, while Christ's divine *prosōpon* is invisible (John 1:18)—FrankenLouie's *prosōpa* were both visible. When Nestorius looks at the face of the human Jesus, by faith he sees the Son of God looking back at him: "They are indeed two, but it is one and the same appearance."[39]

This sympathetic reading risks giving Nestorius too much credit.[40] The main justification of our sympathetic reading of Nestorius is that Nestorius's own followers read him in a similar way. Nestorianism, in a sense, never went away. Instead, Nestorius's legacy continued in the Far East. The so-called Nestorian Church, or the Church of the East, continued to thrive outside of the reach of the empire. These "Nestorians" will be discussed further below, but for now it is worth noting that they deny being heretics, defend Nestorius as misrepresented, and reject dyoprosopite Christology.

One other point that helps to rehabilitate Nestorius is that his formula "two natures" actually became the norm in later orthodoxy. Pope Leo the Great

39. Nestorius, *Bazaar of Heracleides* 1.1.72. Also see Brian E. Daley, "Christ and Christologies," in *The Oxford Handbook of Early Christian Studies*, ed. Susan Ashbrook Harvey and David G. Hunter (Oxford: Oxford University Press, 2008), 895, with citations of other passages of the *Bazaar of Heracleides*.
40. Nestorius never mentioned a Janus cat, and the Roman god "Janus" who had two faces often suggested the negative connotation of being "two-faced."

Diagramming Divine Sentences

In the fourth-century debates over Arianism, a consensus emerged in which God was spoken of as three persons (*hypostaseis, prosōpa*). For the present purposes, we could say there are three "subjects" in God. That is, if one were to diagram sentences, any one of the three persons of God could be the subject of a given sentence.

Diagram	(Subject)	(Verb)	(Object)
Sample sentence #1:	"God the Father . . .	loves . . .	us."
Sample sentence #2:	"God the Son . . .	redeems . . .	us."
Sample sentence #3:	"God the Spirit . . .	sanctifies . . .	us."

Even more specific verbs could be attributed to specific persons of God in certain instances: the Father begot the Son; the Son became flesh; the Spirit descended at Pentecost; and so on. In every instance, however, the subject of each sentence performed the action itself inseparably from the other two subjects. When the Son became flesh, he did not do so apart from or independent of the Father and the Spirit—such a statement would be tritheistic, not trinitarian. Instead, the three persons of God always cooperate in every action, according to classical Christian theology. Gregory of Nyssa famously argued for this understanding of their unity (in *To Ablabius*), so as to say that the Father judges, the Son judges, and the Spirit judges, but there *are not* three divine judges. Instead, the three persons are united in their act of judging. The Father, Son, and Spirit always *co-operate* or *collaborate*. In other words, while there are three subjects in God, there is only one agency in God. All

would write his *Tome*, which was read and affirmed at the next ecumenical council (Chalcedon 451), and therein he freely spoke of Christ's "two natures." Leo could even speak of Christ's two natures "in such a way that they appear at times to be independently acting subjects."[41] For example, when referring to the resurrection and ascension, Leo maintains that "it was the assumed nature not the Assuming nature which was raised."[42] When Leo's *Tome* and two-nature Christology were canonized at Chalcedon (451), Nestorius and his supporters believed their Christology had won the day. The anti-Nestorians, however, disagreed.[43] It is important, therefore, to turn back to the orthodox

41. Beeley, *Unity of Christ*, 273.

42. Leo, *Letter* 35.2. Note how generous the translator is to Leo, ensuring that he is read in an orthodox framework.

43. Aloys Grillmeier, *Christ in Christian Tradition*, vol. 1, *From the Apostolic Age to Chalcedon (451)*, trans. J. S. Bowden (London: Mowbray, 1965), 433.

three subjects are always cooperating in the verb.

In the fifth-century debates over Nestorianism, a new consensus emerges in which Christ incarnate is said to have two natures (*physeis*). For the present purposes, we could say that there is only one "subject" in Christ. That is, if one were to diagram sentences, only the person of Christ could be the subject of the given sentence, but—and here's a key distinction between Christology/incarnation and theology/Trinity—there would always be two verbs, even when only one is explicit while the other is merely implicit.

Diagram	(Subject)	(Verb) [Implied Verb]	(Modifying Prepositional Phrase) [Implied Modifying Prepositional Phrase]
Sample sentence #1:	"Christ . . .	suffers . . .	in his human nature."
		[*is impassible . . .*	*in his divine nature.*]
Sample sentence #2:	"Christ . . .	changes . . .	in his human nature."
		[*is immutable . . .*	*in his divine nature.*]
Sample sentence #3:	"Christ . . .	dies . . .	in his human nature."
		[*is immortal . . .*	*in his divine nature.*]

In sum, while the trinitarian debates had to clarify that God is three subjects but one agency (three colaborers), the christological debates conclude that Christ is one subject with two agencies (one multitasker). That is, Jesus and God the Son are "one and the same" person, but the divine and human natures are distinct so as to keep both divine and human actions present.

stance at Ephesus (431) and Chalcedon in order to hear why Nestorianism was seen as such a threat.

The Orthodox Definition: The Hypostatic Union

The one aspect of orthodox thinking and of Chalcedonian Christology that is difficult to find in Nestorius is Leo's counteremphasis to the two natures of Christ: while the two are distinct natures, these two are "one and the same" person.[44] This is known as the hypostatic union: Christ's two natures are united

44. Certainly the emphasis of Cyril throughout his *That Christ Is One* (see other examples in Brian E. Daley, "'One Thing and Another': The Persons in God and the Person of Christ in Patristic Theology," *ProEccl* 15, no. 1 [2006]: 40). Cyril's phrase "out of two natures" (*ek dyo physeōn*) is even stronger than Leo's "in two natures" (*en dyo physesi*); see van Loon, *Dyophysite*

in one *hypostasis*, one person. In other words, the Son of God was the same person born of Mary, and so Mary is the Mother of God (the Son). Whether Nestorius ever expressed the unity of Christ so strongly remains unclear.[45]

Nestorius's overemphasis on Christ's two natures allegedly results in two subjects. The Son of God performs divine actions (creation, miracles, etc.), while Jesus the human performs all of the earthly actions (eats, sleeps, suffers, dies, etc.). The orthodox party, on the other hand, can speak of one subject performing both actions: Jesus Christ is Lord of heaven and earth, and "the one and the same" (*hena kai ton auton*) Son of God suffered and died.[46]

The technical phrase for this is *communicatio idiomatum*, or the "communication of properties." Things pertaining to Jesus's human nature can also, via the incarnation, be spoken about "God" and vice versa.[47] While God the Son is eternal, immutable, impassible, and immortal, he (not another subject or person) assumed human nature and aged, changed, suffered, and died in that human nature (though not in the divine).[48] This two-nature Christology requires a rigid distinction between nature (*physis*) and person (*hypostasis/prosōpon*). Christian practice, however, has not always been so rigid when speaking about "God."

The Orthodox Clarification: *Communicatio Idiomatum*

Until somewhat recently, Christians would speak of "man" in a double-sense: *a* human being and humanity. This was a practice made very convenient in

---

Christology, 24–29, for secondary sources, and 554–56 for the primary. Leo, perhaps due to an inadequate understanding of Nestorius, will not stress the unity enough for later Cyrilians. After Chalcedon (451) Leo will have to emphasize that "one and the same" is intended to affirm one divine person in Christ (see Bernard Green, *The Soteriology of Leo the Great* [Oxford: Oxford University Press, 2008], 28–35, 230–47).

45. His strongest statement does seem to account for a true unity (*Bazaar of Heracleides* 1.1.59). In other passages, however, Nestorius offers a weaker statement of unity, leaving suspicion about his view of the incarnation. For example, Nestorius affirms not a "hypostatic union" but a "nominal union" (see Nestorius's reply to Cyril [= Cyril, *Letter* 5.4] and discussion in Fairbairn, "Allies or Mere Friends?," 395). That is, some names (e.g., Christ and Son) apply to both Jesus and the Word, and so the two can be spoken of as one. Likewise, Theodoret (counterstatement 2) thinks the hypostatic union "is superfluous," but he cannot offer an alternative explanation: "It is quite sufficient to mention the union" (trans. *NPNF*[2] 3:27). No further discussion is given, which seems to result in two subjects, the God/Logos who assumes and the man/Jesus who is assumed (counterstatement 3).

46. Cyril, *Letter* 4.6.

47. A point Nestorius rejected (Cyril, *Letter* 5.7–8).

48. As Cyril says (*Letter* 55.33), "We stoutly maintain, following the plans of the Incarnation, that who is God was beyond suffering [*ton epekeina tou pathein hōs theon*], suffered in his own flesh as a human being [*tē idia pathein anthrōpinōs*]." In his *Twelve Anathemas*, however, Cyril was not so clear (see Theodoret's counterstatement 1).

Chalcedonian Definition and the Hypostatic Union

The Council of Chalcedon could not issue a new creed, because the Third Ecumenical Council (Ephesus 431) outlawed any new creeds. "But," according to a statement issued by the council, "there are those who are trying to ruin the proclamation of the truth, and through their private heresies they have spawned novel formulas." Nestorius is named as one of these heretics, and against his alleged belief in "a duality of sons" the council gave the following "definition": "We all with one voice teach the confession of one and the same Son, our Lord Jesus Christ: the same perfect in divinity and perfect in humanity, the same truly God and truly man . . . one and the same Christ, Son, Lord, only-begotten, acknowledged in two natures [*en dyo physesin*]."

biblical thinking since the first human's/man's name meant "human"/"man." The same has been true with language about "God": this could refer to *the* God, or to the divine nature—"divinity." For example, when speaking about the attributes of "God," most Christian textbooks do not clarify which person (*hypostasis/prosōpon*) is in view. Instead, it is simply said that "God" is almighty, all-knowing, and so on, and the reader learns that this applies to all three divine persons, so that the Son of God is almighty, all-knowing, and so on. Is this true, however, once God is incarnate?

Yes, in a sense. After all, we cannot say that the Son "changed." Why not? Two reasons: first, the classical Christian view of God is that God is immutable, but that only begs the question. The second and more important reason is that we do not wish to speak of the Son changing into something else: as if the Son *was* divine, but now *has become* human.[49] If so, then has "God" really come to save us? The church fathers spoke of Christ as retaining his fully divine nature, but also "assuming" or taking up (Heb. 2:16–17) a human nature. Therefore, in one sense Christ as "God," or in his "divine nature," does not change, but simultaneously "God" (the Son) does change *in his human nature.*

Surely we do not want to say that God the Son was omnipresent and infinite, and then at the first Christmas God the Son was present only in Bethlehem. Would God's Logos/Reason/Word then be absent in Jerusalem and Rome? Of course not. Instead of saying Christ's divine nature shrunk down from

49. The Greek word for "become" in John 1:14 does not require the idea of change. Instead, it is a narratival description, meaning "it came to pass" or "it happened." Thus, Heb. 2:16–17 must supplement John 1:14 for our understanding of the incarnation.

infinite omnipresence into the size of a Christmas present (i.e., a genie in a bottle—Apollinarianism), we believe Christ's divine nature remained infinite and omnipresent. How can this be?

Remembering *the* divine nature and *a* divine person, we can admit the distinction and simultaneously permit the word "God" to mean both. In so doing, Chalcedonian two-nature thinkers will affirm the following sorts of statements.

Theologically speaking . . .	Can God die? No. God is immortal.
Christologically speaking . . .	*Did* God die? *Yes!*
Theologically speaking . . .	Can God change? No. God is immutable.
Christologically speaking . . .	*Did* God change? *Yes!*
Theologically speaking . . .	Can God be tempted? No. God is impeccable.
Christologically speaking . . .	*Did* God experience temptation? *Yes!*
Theologically speaking . . .	Does God have a mom? Not eternally.
Christologically speaking . . .	*Did* Mary become God's mother? *Yes!*

Is this contradictory doublespeak? *No.* It is the paradox and mystery of the incarnation. It is an expression of faith in the one person, "one and the same Son, our Lord Jesus Christ" (i.e., the *hypostatic* union). It was none other than God who was born, suffered, died, and rose.

Without allowing our speech to use the device of *communicatio idiomatum* we inevitably slip into a form of Nestorianism (even if Nestorius himself did not, or did not intentionally, do so). We would have to speak of Jesus, but not the Son, being born of Mary. Jesus, but not the Son of God, who suffered and died. If we speak like this, why do we credit God with our salvation? And why do we worship Jesus, who is merely human?[50] Our Christian language is ripped apart at the seams.[51] On the other hand, if we embrace *communicatio idiomatum*, we can easily answer the question: How can we justify speaking in this way of an impassible God suffering? Answer: Because of the hypostatic union—the divine and the human are united in the selfsame person/*hypostasis* of Christ.

---

50. Cyril accuses Nestorius of *anthrōpolatria*, human-worship (e.g., *Letter* 46.10), or worshiping *anthrōpos theophoros*, a man bearing God (see *Against the Blasphemies of Nestorius*). For Nestorius's defense against such a charge, see the fragment read at Ephesus 431 (trans. in McGuckin, *St. Cyril of Alexandria*, 371).

51. Some have called for a reconsideration of this Christology, such as Charles M. Stang, "The Two 'I's of Christ: Revisiting the Christological Controversy," *AThR* 94, no. 3 (2012): 529–47. This approach seems inherent in modern theologians such as Paul Tillich who clearly identify both the agency and the subjectivity of Jesus as altogether different from the eternal Word. Whether such an approach can adequately answer the traditional questions and concerns voiced here remains to be seen.

This critique of Nestorianism—or now we should say, dyoprosopitism, since Nestorius himself probably did not teach it—is not meant to claim that the opposing viewpoint was not without its own problems. Cyril's most loyal followers will in turn be accused of the opposite heresy, monophysitism (see chap. 8). In order to see the full extent of the debate about Nestorianism in particular, we will briefly outline the lingering debates about this issue after the Council of Ephesus (431).

Later Nestorian Controversies

After the Council of Ephesus (431) many others were accused of Nestorianism. Many supporters of Nestorius attacked Cyril, and several of the so-called Antiochene school will therefore become suspect. In particular Theodore of Mopsuestia, Theodoret of Cyrus, and Ibas of Edessa will be condemned for alleged Nestorianism.

To say these three were "Nestorian" is even more problematic and unfounded than saying Nestorius was "Nestorian." Ibas successfully persuaded Cyril to sign a statement affirming Christ's "two natures."[52] Even with this ecumenical feat, Ibas will be remembered for criticizing Cyril, and therefore he will still be suspected of Nestorianism.

All three of these writers—known to history as the Three Chapters—will be accused of Nestorianism in future councils. At the "Robber Synod" of Ephesus (449; see chap. 8), they will be condemned. At the next ecumenical council, the Council of Chalcedon (451), Theodore's memory—for he had died by that time—would be left unmolested, even if suspect. Theodoret and Ibas were both reinstated at Chalcedon, but only after explicitly denouncing Nestorius and dyoprosopitism. Despite receiving this sanction from an ecumenical council, these three thinkers would be distrusted for generations by many who were loyal to Cyril's memory.

A century later, in an attempt to placate the Cyrilian party, the emperor Justinian (r. 527–65) will condemn the memory of Theodore, Theodoret, and Ibas as Nestorian. Justinian will also summon the next ecumenical council, Constantinople II (553), which will confirm this postmortem anathema of the Three Chapters. The decision will prove so controversial that the pope at the time, Vigilius, who is summoned to Constantinople, will refuse to

---

52. John, patriarch of Antioch, under much political pressure, had already agreed to denounce Nestorius (in Cyril, *Letter* 35). This statement, which John also signed, ensured that Nestorius would not be rehabilitated, for it agrees to call Mary the Mother of God, and it embraces *communicatio idiomatum* as the proper way to speak about Christ's two natures.

attend the council and will sign a statement denouncing the Three Chapters only after a six-month imprisonment. Many in the West, especially in North Africa, will condemn both Justinian and then Vigilius for troubling the dead and for overturning Chalcedon: these saints were approved at the previous ecumenical council and were not alive to defend themselves.

Despite years of imperial heavy-handedness against the Nestorian party, dyophysites prevailed in most of Christianity. The Council of Chalcedon had formally canonized two-nature Christology, even as it emphasized the hypostatic union. Nevertheless, because many followers of Cyril perceived Chalcedon as conceding too much to Nestorianism, this party perennially called for Nestorians to be denounced. Attempts to appease this party, like Justinian's attack on the Three Chapters, only further entrenched the opposing party, the Church of the East.

Further east and out of the reach of Byzantine emperors, many so-called Nestorians continued to stress the distinction between Christ's divine and human natures.[53] The school of Edessa, mentioned above as led by Ibas, had for some time supplied Syria and Persia with educated clergy. When Emperor Zeno closed the school for its Nestorianism (489), it was largely relocated further east to Nisibis (in what is today the southeast of Turkey). The churches connected with this center of thinking and learning spread further east and were welcomed and at times supported by the Persian Empire. A synod of 486 would establish an Antiochene Creed. Also, in response to Justinian's Three Chapters controversy, a synod of 585 would formally approve Theodore of Mopsuestia's writings.

The so-called Nestorian Church would thrive during the Mongol period and only begin to decline in the later Middle Ages when a constellation of sociopolitical forces aligned against it.[54] Of course, these Christians do not accept the title "Nestorian," which was meant to be pejorative. Instead, they refer to themselves as the Assyrian Church of the East. This church still exists in many parts of the world today, and it defends Nestorius as its theological patron who was maligned in the fifth century.

Today, the Assyrian Church and other Christians have officially recognized each other and no longer deem one another heretics. In 1994, Pope John Paul II met with the Catholicos-Patriarch Mar Dinkha IV, and they issued a joint statement declaring that the past controversy was "due in large part to

53. See Louise Abramowski and Alan E. Goodman, ed. and trans., *A Nestorian Collection of Christological Texts*, 2 vols. (Cambridge: Cambridge University Press, 1972).

54. Several splinter groups emerge from this movement, some still surviving to this day in regions as diverse as Iraq to India; see Mark Dickens, "The Church of the East: The Rest of the Story," *FH* 32, no. 2 (2000): 107–25; and Wilhelm Baum and Dietmar W. Winkler, *The Church of the East: A Concise History* (London: Routledge, 2010).

misunderstandings."[55] Both churches acknowledge each other as sharing a common faith in Christ, whose "divinity and his humanity are united in one person."[56] The two "sister Churches" still have questions to resolve, and so they are not in "full and entire communion."[57] Whether the current debates can be resolved, and if so, how, is of course beyond the scope of this present chapter. In summary, we need to restate the Nestorian debate from the fifth century and see how this has resituated the state of Christology for the debates that follow.

The Gospel according to Nestorius

If Nestorius says what he allegedly said, then Nestorius has placed man (i.e., Jesus) in communion with God (i.e., the Son). This is good news, according to Nestorius: if the Word can do this with Jesus, there is hope for all of us![58] Since Jesus was united completely with God the Son and since his will was completely subjected to God's will, Jesus becomes our primary example to follow.[59] "For Nestorius, salvation is a human task of ascending toward a perfect age, what Nestorius's teacher Theodore has called the 'second katastasis,' an ascent that we accomplish as we follow the graced man Jesus who led the way for us."[60] The "ascent" mentioned here refers to our salvation: just as Christ descended and ascended (Phil. 2:6–11), so can we by being like-minded with Jesus (Phil. 2:5).

This emphasis on Christ's human suffering is in fact shared by Nestorius's opponent. Christ "emptied himself" (Phil. 2:7), or poured himself out in the most humiliating, painful, and terminal way.[61] What is more, God in that act

55. John Paul II and Mar Dinkha IV, *Common Christological Declaration or The Joint Declaration from John Paul II, and Mar Dinkha IV,* http://www.vatican.va/holy_father/john_paul_ii /speeches/1994/november/documents/hf_jp-ii_spe_19941111_dichiarazione-cristologica_en.html.

56. Even the title "Mother of Christ our God and Saviour" is affirmed.

57. However, see the Pontifical Council for Promoting Christian Unity's statement that permits admission to communion in certain circumstances, "Guidelines for Admission to the Eucharist between the Chaldean Church [which is in the Roman Catholic communion] and the Assyrian Church of the East," http://www.vatican.va/roman_curia/pontifical_councils/chrstuni /documents/rc_pc_chrstuni_doc_20011025_chiesa-caldea-assira_en.html.

58. Nestorius, *Bazaar of Heracleides* 1.1.59.

59. Nestorius, *Bazaar of Heracleides* 1.1.77; 1.1.85–86. Thus, John Cassian, *On the Incarnation of the Lord* 3, dubbed Nestorius a Pelagian (Pelagius was a heretic who allegedly taught works righteousness and who was also condemned at Ephesus 431). However, see also Nestorius, *Bazaar of Heracleides* 1.1.80, for alternative models of soteriology in his thought.

60. Fairbairn, "Allies or Mere Friends?," 392.

61. Which is still different from modern understandings of *kenōsis* (Phil. 2:7), wherein the Logos "empties" himself of divine attributes.

conquered humiliation, pain, and death. This means that other humiliated, suffering, and dying humans can follow Christ down the same path, trusting that God will also raise them.[62]

Nestorius and his opponents disagree about whether this human suffering was undertaken by a human bearing God or by God "in human form" (Phil. 2:8). Because God the Son is "one and the same" person as Jesus who suffered and died, the followers of Jesus can worship him and follow him, knowing that they have been reconciled to none other than God. Did Nestorius teach otherwise? Did he believe in a two-subject, dyoprosopite Christology, according to which the Word of God occupied Jesus? If so, then it is difficult to see how his "gospel" is in keeping with the good news proclaimed by the apostolic community.

On the other hand, because Nestorius's opponents will emphasize that in Christ *God* was at work, many of their followers will make an equal and opposite mistake by losing sight of Christ's *humanity*. After all, how can both natures of Christ be protected without retreating back to a Nestorian dyoprosopitism? The answer to that question will require more than two hundred years of intense debate.

Recommended Bibliography

Chadwick, Henry. *The Church in Ancient Society: From Galilee to Gregory the Great.* Oxford: Oxford University Press, 2001. See especially chapter 51, "The Christological Debate, I: To the First Council of Ephesus (431)."

Chestnut, Roberta C. "Two Prosopa in Nestorius' *Bazaar of Heracleides.*" *JTS* 29, no. 2 (1978): 392–409.

McGuckin, John A. "The Christology of Nestorius of Constantinople." *PBR* 7, nos. 2–3 (1988): 93–129.

Wessel, Susan. *Cyril of Alexandria and the Nestorian Controversy: The Making of a Saint and of a Heretic.* Oxford: Oxford University Press, 2004.

62. J. Warren Smith, "Suffering Impassibly: Christ's Passion in Cyril of Alexandria's Soteriology," *ProEccl* 11 (2002): 463–83.

Summary:
Monophysites

Key Doctrine: Monophysitism
- Mutant Jesus
- Jesus is 50 percent divine and 50 percent human

Key Dates
- ca. 380–456: Eutyches
- 451: Council of Chalcedon (Eutyches is condemned)
- 553: Council of Constantinople II (attempt to placate monophysites)
- 680–81: Council of Constantinople III (monophysites and monothelites condemned)

8

Eutyches

Monophysitism

Go to the most devout presbyter and archimandrite Eutyches and read to him the indictment brought against him, and bid him appear before this holy synod and defend himself, since the accusation is not a trivial one.

—Flavian, patriarch of Constantinople

Nor have they recorded in these minutes what I said.

—Eutyches

Hercules is not exactly human. He's part human and part not human. He's part divine. Like any other demigod (= *half*-god), Hercules has divine strength but human characteristics. There's pretty much nothing Hercules can't do when he sets his mind to it, but you wouldn't know that from looking at him because Hercules looks like any other human. He has the strength of a god and the likeness (*homoiōma*) of a human.

This is what Eutyches said about Christ. The Word was "born in human likeness" (Phil. 2:7).

Also . . .

169

Zeus is not really human. Sometimes he appears human, or in human form, but he's divine through and through. Sometimes Zeus metamorphosizes into a bull or a swan so as to take young maidens unawares. The change in *morphē*, or "form" (i.e., meta-*morph*-osis), however, is simply for the sake of appearances. Zeus always remains divine. He never actually takes on the limitations of humans or swans.

This is what Eutyches said about Christ. The Logos appeared "in human form [*morphēn*]" (Phil. 2:7).

Rules of Engagement: Eutyches, Monophysites, and Miaphysites

The problem with the above caricature is twofold. First, Eutyches did not teach that Christ metamorphosed from divinity into humanity, and neither did he claim Christ was half man and half god. These are (mutually exclusive!) depictions of Eutyches's thinking, taken to its (allegedly) logical conclusion.

The second problem with such caricatures is that they will be applied to all "monophysites," but the so-called heretics labeled "monophysites" will not all teach the same thing. Like so many heresies we have reviewed thus far, monophysitism is a misleading and unreliable category. Instead, we will find a whole range of views collected under this umbrella of a term, and these various monophysitisms in fact describe Christ in very different ways. The term "monophysite" means "one who holds to one [*mono-*] nature [*physis*]." Often the "monophysites" are more concerned to *deny* two natures than they are concerned to define Christ as one-natured.

These problems require that the following discussion will have to aim in two directions. First, we will begin very narrowly, zooming in on the person and teaching of Eutyches. He is the main villain, according to those who wish to confess Christ has two natures (dyophysites). Second, we will survey very broadly, widening the lens to take in the larger monophysite controversy. This controversy stems back at least as far as Apollinaris (see chap. 6) and then continues to be an unresolved matter that continues into the present day by way of the Oriental Orthodox Christians.

This chapter will attempt to accomplish both of these tasks while upholding two concerns. First, because the chapter must focus (briefly) on Eutyches and then review (broadly) the ongoing monophysite controversy, the discussion will have to cover more material than previous chapters. This will allow less time to fully represent Eutyches's and the monophysites' own version of things in a sympathetic reading, as we have striven to do in previous chapters.

The Oriental Orthodox Churches

The schisms that will result after the Council of Chalcedon will produce what are today often called the Oriental Orthodox family of churches. Because these churches do not recognize Chalcedon's "two-nature" formula, they are often called monophysites. They reject this label, however, since it is too broad and includes Apollinaris and Eutyches. The Oriental Orthodox do hold to a belief in "one nature" (*mia physis*), and they do so largely because Cyril affirmed this formula. The various branches of these churches still exist today in places like Egypt, Ethiopia, and Syria. When the Byzantine Empire lost territories to the spreading Muslim armies, these traditions became minorities and developed largely independently from ot of Christianity.

Why are they called Oriental Orthodox? This title can be somewhat confusing because "Oriental" means "Eastern," but these churches are not part of "Eastern" Orthodoxy, which is Chalcedonian. The problem lies in the relative nature of this adjective: "Eastern" means "more east than us," and thus "Eastern Orthodox" are called that only by Westerners (like Roman Catholics and Protestants; those who are called "Eastern Orthodox" prefer the title "Orthodox Catholic Church"). Likewise, the various Oriental traditions refer to themselves, using various titles such as "apostolic" and "catholic," simply as "orthodox."

The concern to represent these so-called heretics fairly does drive the following presentation of material, but the presentation will have to be concise. The second concern mirrors the first in that we wish to represent fairly the monophysite side of the story, but more specifically we wish to do so out of a concern to be charitable about a Christian tradition that our brothers and sisters in many parts of the world still cherish as "Orthodoxy."[1] The Oriental Orthodox churches do not call themselves "monophysites" (preferring instead "miaphysites"), and they sincerely believe—with good reason—that their predecessors have been misrepresented and maligned. We would hope that if anyone from these traditions reads the following chapter, they will feel that the material was presented fairly and respectfully. This chapter will cover more centuries and more viewpoints than previous chapters, and so due to constraints of space and time these two concerns will have to be more implicit than explicit. If any section fails to address either of these concerns, the author

1. For sources and discussion on both the fifth-century debates and the contemporary ecumenical dialogues, see Hans van Loon, *The Dyophysite Christology of Cyril of Alexandria* (Leiden: Brill, 2009), esp. 43–60.

egs the reader's forgiveness, patience, and leniency—graces that, ironically, were not granted to most of the characters in our story, such as Eutyches.

Eutyches's Life and Teaching

When Eutyches enters our story (440s), he is an influential spiritual leader in Constantinople. As the supervisor of an important monastery, or archimandrite, he held the respect and reverence of many in the church. Eutyches also held considerable political influence: his godson was the chamberlain of Emperor Theodosius II, which sounds inglorious today, but at the time these eunuchs served as powerful advisors to the emperors. These connections would enable Eutyches to establish himself at the heart of the christological debates.

Eutyches emerged from his life of seclusion in the wake of the christological controversies between the Apollinarians, the Nestorians, and the Cyrilians. Eutyches believed that Nestorianism still haunted the halls of the church, and so he attempted to further establish Cyril's teaching as normative.[2] By emphasizing Cyril's thoughts on the oneness of Christ, he seems to have slipped into a form of monophysitism that denies the twoness of Christ. Monophysitism is the teaching that Christ had only one nature. Just how Eutyches envisioned Christ's one nature is at best unclear and at worst heretical.

Earlier, Nestorius had claimed that his own teaching sounded heretical (dyoprosopite) to heretics (Cyril and the monophysites) because they denied Christ's two natures (divinity and humanity). Eutyches is remembered as an instance in which this truly happened: he heard orthodox explanations of Christ's two natures (dyophysitism) as heresy *precisely because* Eutyches himself held to a heretical view of Christ's one incarnate nature (monophysitism).[3] Let us try to unravel Eutyches's own statements from the accusations made against him.

Eutyches wants to avoid Nestorius's mistake of speaking about Jesus the human as a different person than God the Son. In order to avoid this, Eutyches speaks of "God suffering," and "God dying," and so forth. So far, so good, if he is utilizing the method of *communicatio idiomatum* (see chap. 7). When he is asked, however, about Christ's natures, Eutyches's answer is convoluted. Many after the Formula of Reunion spoke of Christ's two natures: Christ

2. In 448 Eutyches claimed to be a follower of Cyril's teachings: "For I have held the same as my forefathers" (Leo, *Letter* 21.3 from Eutyches to Leo).

3. This is the response of Leo: "What advantage is it to that most unwise old man under the name of the Nestorian heresy to mangle the belief of those, whose most devout faith he cannot tear to pieces" (Leo, *Letter* 35.1).

must be confessed as *both* fully divine *and* fully human. Eutyches, we can generously assume, did not wish to deny either Christ's divinity or his humanity, for he believes Jesus to be God incarnate. Eutyches will not, however, state that Christ had two natures when incarnate. Instead, Eutyches simply speaks of Christ's oneness: Jesus the human and God the Son are one person *with one nature.*[4]

This last statement raised eyebrows.

What kind of nature does Christ have? Is Christ's nature divine, and therefore *not* human?[5] Eutyches's first response was to restate that Jesus is God incarnate, or "in the flesh." God the Son, therefore, had human flesh.

This statement only raises additional problems. Does Christ have human flesh but not a complete human nature, with a human soul and human mind? Is this a return to Apollinarianism?[6] In order to defend himself against this charge, Eutyches anathematizes Apollinaris.[7] Also, Eutyches unequivocally states that Christ is fully human, or "perfect man":

> For He who is the Word of GOD came down from heaven without flesh and was made flesh in the holy Virgin's womb unchangeably and unalterably as He Himself knew and willed. And He who was always perfect GOD before the ages, was also made perfect man in the end of the days for us and for our salvation.[8]

Eutyches here unequivocally affirms Christ's humanity. The way in which Christ is human may be the problem.

If Christ is not in two natures, did he change from a divine nature to a human nature? If Eutyches were to say yes, he would be denying that Christ was and is fully divine. God's immutability is unquestioned at this time, and to say God the Son changed into a human nature in the incarnation would be to say the Son was not so immutable and divine from the start.[9] Instead,

4. A concept he learned from Cyril's phrase "one incarnate nature of the Word of God" (*mian physin tou theou logou sesarkōmenēn*), who learned it from Gregory of Nyssa (see Christopher A. Beeley, "Cyril of Alexandria and Gregory Nazianzen: Tradition and Complexity in Patristic Christology," *JECS* 17, no. 3 [2009]: 403, for sources).

5. Also see Leo's accusation of docetism in *Letters* 31.1; 35.1; 59.1 (where it is called Manichaeanism); 109.3; 124.2 (where it is called Manichaean and Marcionite).

6. Eutyches is labeled by Flavian as teaching "the heresy of Apollinaris" (in Leo, *Letter* 26.1, Flavian to Leo).

7. Leo, *Letter* 21.3 (Eutyches to Leo). Leo is not convinced, and so he accuses Eutyches of crypto-Apollinarianism: "He who denies the true Manhood of Jesus Christ, must needs be filled with many blasphemies, being claimed by Apollinaris as his own" (*Letter* 35.1; cf. *Letters* 109.3; 124.2).

8. Leo, *Letter* 21.3 (Eutyches to Leo).

9. At one point (*Letter* 119.2), Leo claims Eutyches thought the Word changed into mutable/passible flesh, so all of Christ's actions were really done by his divine nature (i.e., it only

Eutyches asserts that the Word was made flesh from the Virgin "unchangeably and unalterably."[10] That is, the Word remained what he always was: fully divine.

If Eutyches teaches that Christ always was and always remained fully divine, and if Eutyches claims that God—incarnate unalterably—became fully human or a "perfect/complete man," then why not say Christ has two natures? Also, what does it even mean to say the Word "immutably changed"? Eutyches, it seems, will not answer the first question and say that Christ has two natures because he fears the two natures will inevitably retreat into two persons—in other words, Nestorianism. Eutyches, it seems, cannot answer the second question because Eutyches simply has no good answer.[11]

If Christ remained divine and yet became human in Eutyches's view, then the only alternative left to explain Eutyches's Christology is to see Christ's two natures as "mixing" together. The patriarch of Constantinople at the time, Flavian, accused Eutyches of saying, "Our Lord Jesus Christ ought not to be understood by us as having two natures after His incarnation."[12] For those who heard this accusation, like Pope Leo in Rome, Eutyches must be saying, "Before the Incarnation indeed, our Saviour Jesus Christ had two natures, divinity and humanity: but . . . after the union they became one nature."[13]

What kind of nature is this new, united nature? Eutyches, it seems, cannot say. Then again, he may not have been given an opportunity to provide an answer. Eutyches's self-defense (in writing as well as in person) was ignored. Flavian refused to hear him, and demanded that Eutyches affirm "two natures" in Christ.[14] Flavian, on the other hand, denied that Eutyches ever offered any such statements.[15] Leo was convinced by Flavian when he received the proceedings of the 448 synod.[16] Whether or not Eutyches had the opportunity do so, he never answered the question about what kind of nature Christ had.

Perhaps this question should not or could not be answered. Perhaps one must appeal to mystery—an option that we will revisit at the end of this

---

appeared to be a human nature). This certainly misrepresents Eutyches, but Leo thinks this is the logical conclusion of his teaching.

10. Theodoret, *Compendium of Heretical Mythification* 13: "He asserted that the God-Word . . . was immutably changed and became flesh (I have used his own ridiculous language)."

11. Although, even if he does not have a good answer, he is in good company: Cyril affirmed almost identical statements about the incarnation (see chap. 7).

12. Flavian (in Leo, *Letter* 22 [Flavian to Leo]); cf. Leo, *Letter* 26 (Flavian to Leo).

13. Flavian (in Leo, *Letter* 26.1 [Flavian to Leo]); cf. Leo, *Tome* 6 (= *Letter* 28.6). I have altered the translation from "Godhead and manhood" to "divinity and humanity."

14. See Leo, *Letter* 21.1 (Eutyches to Leo).

15. Leo, *Letter* 26.3 (Flavian to Leo).

16. Leo, *Letter* 34.1.

chapter. On the other hand, Eutyches's opponents will fill in the blanks for Eutyches. And they do not give him the benefit of the doubt when doing so.

Since Eutyches claims the human and divine natures united to form one nature in Christ, this new nature must be a mixture of human and divine. The analogy here would be a hybrid. A dog and a wolf combine to make *neither* a dog *nor* a wolf, but a new thing altogether. A horse and a donkey combine to make *neither* a horse *nor* a donkey, but a mutant, a mule.[17] These hybrids result in a *tertium quid*, a "third thing." Today, an analogy could be found in a science laboratory: take one beaker filled with blue liquid; then take another beaker filled with red liquid.[18] Pour them together so that they mix in a third beaker, and what do you have? (If you said purple, then you're missing the point of this exercise.) The correct answer is *neither* red *nor* blue, but a "third thing"! So it is with Eutyches's model of Christology: take human nature and divine nature and mix them together. What results? A Christ who is *neither* human *nor* divine, but some *tertium quid*.

To be sure, Eutyches most certainly did not teach that Christ was neither divine nor human.[19] He, however, did not clarify what he taught. Even Pope Leo, in his famous *Tome* written against Eutyches, paints the picture of a Eutyches who could not even understand his own convoluted teaching. Leo portrays Eutyches, not so much as heretical, but as "stupid."[20] The orthodox response to Eutyches admittedly caricatures Eutyches's teaching so as to

17. For Apollinaris's alleged use of this analogy, see Aloys Grillmeier, *Christ in Christian Tradition*, vol. 1, *From the Apostolic Age to Chalcedon (451)*, trans. J. S. Bowden (London: Mowbray, 1965), 224 (but cf. 225n1).

18. The Eutychians allegedly used the chemical analogies of gold and silver or lead and tin. Theodoret, *Eranistes* 2 (trans. Gérard H. Ettlinger, *Theodoret of Cyrus: Eranistes* [Washington, DC: Catholic University of America Press, 2003], 112), acknowledges, however, that later Eutychians denied using such analogies. Instead of "mixing," the Eutychians would have preferred to say the human nature was "swallowed up" or absorbed by the divine nature, "in the same way the sea absorbs a drop of honey" (Ettlinger, 123). Thus, "out of two natures" there resulted "one nature." This is still, however, a mixing in the dyophysites' eyes—or worse, an annihilation of the human nature: is Christ no longer human in the temptation, crucifixion, resurrection, and ascension?

19. Compare the earlier writers (e.g., Gregory of Nazianzus, *Letter* 101; and *Oration* 38.13). If there is a difference between these earlier writers and Eutyches, it is that earlier writers attempted to speak of immaterial aspects of the human nature, such as spirit, soul, or mind, mixing with the divine nature, which is by definition immaterial (John 3:6; 4:24; a tradition stemming back at least to Origen [see, e.g., *Against Celsus* 3.41]). Instead of "mixing" as a material analogy for two immaterial substances, Eutyches allegedly mixed a material nature (humanity) with an immaterial nature (divinity). It is noteworthy that Cyril, in *On the Unity of Christ* 736A (trans. John Anthony McGuckin, *On the Unity of Christ* [Crestwood, NY: St. Vladimir's Seminary Press, 2000], 77), clarified that the human and divine "came together . . . without mixing."

20. See Leo, *Tome* 5–6.

show where Eutyches's Christology leads when taken to its (extreme) logical conclusion.[21]

Eutyches refused to admit that his form of monophysitism led to such a conclusion, and so he appealed to a higher authority: the emperor. In 448 Flavian convened a council in Constantinople that found Eutyches guilty of heresy. Eutyches, however, called on his friends in high places and won an appeal with Theodosius II. A new council would be convened, much like the one that condemned Nestorius, that is, the previous ecumenical council, Ephesus (431).

This new council would also meet in Ephesus, and the hope was clearly to ensure the same results: the dyophysites would be condemned. Also as in Ephesus, the patriarch of Alexandria would preside.

The Council of Ephesus (449)

If you thought the previous Council of Ephesus (431) was chaotic (see the time line in chap. 7), then you are going to love what we have in store here. Theodosius II puts his full support behind Eutyches, requesting that bishops from all over the empire attend. Pope Leo in Rome, however, cannot leave the city at that time, due to the Vandal invasion.[22] He does, however, send his representatives to read his *Tome* against Eutyches. The pope's important letter, however, is not granted a reading.

Dioscorus, the patriarch of Alexandria and successor of Cyril, has already decided in favor of Eutyches. He refuses, therefore, to acknowledge the pope's representatives or his directives. Next, Dioscorus declares Flavian, patriarch of Constantinople, who has denounced Eutyches, to be the true heretic: Flavian is declared a Nestorian. Dioscorus has brought his band of monks with him from Egypt, and they seize the patriarch of Constantinople by force and threaten any who oppose Dioscorus. Their handling of Flavian is so brutal that the patriarch dies en route to his exile. After that, Dioscorus anathematizes other "Nestorians," like Theodoret of Cyrus and Ibas of Edessa, for confessing Christ's two natures. While the monophysites claim the council to be an ecumenical victory over dyophysitism, other influential

---

21. Christopher A. Beeley, *The Unity of Christ: Continuity and Conflict in Patristic Tradition* (New Haven: Yale University Press, 2012), 275, summarizes the problem well: "Even if Eutyches's preference for a single-nature Christology is supported by the similar custom of both Gregory and Cyril, he has obviously adopted a novel, extreme position by refusing to confess that there is also an orthodox sense in which Christ now exists in two natures, as Gregory and Cyril happily conceded."

22. Leo, *Letter* 31.4.

leaders disagree. Thus the council turns out not to be so ecumenical and not at all well received.

Pope Leo, a dyophysite, hears of Dioscorus's actions and condemns the council. The pope calls Ephesus (449) a *Latrocinium*, a "Robber Council."[23] Emperor Theodosius ignores Leo's call for a new council, and the patriarch of Alexandria responds by excommunicating the pope.

When Dioscorus dismissed the council, monophysitism appeared to be the orthodox Christology of the church, for it had the political enforcement of the emperor's support. At least, this was true for two years. The tables were turned when Theodosius died suddenly (July 28, 450), after being thrown from a horse and breaking his spine. The new emperor, Marcian, had been a general and became emperor by agreeing to marry Theodosius's sister Pulcheria (while still respecting her vow of celibacy!). Pulcheria had dyophysite sympathies, and so it was probably at her behest that Marcian allowed for a new council, Chalcedon (451), which would overturn Dioscorus's actions at Ephesus (449) and support Rome's stance on Christ's two natures.

Dioscorus's actions at Ephesus were remembered in ill terms. The letter of the Council of Chalcedon reporting its decisions to Leo describes the decisions at Ephesus (449) as accomplished by "terror-won votes."[24] Leo himself describes Dioscorus at this council as follows: "A worthy preacher of the devil's errors has been found in this Egyptian plunderer, who, like the cruelest tyrant the Church has had, forced his villainous blasphemies on the reverend brethren through the violence of riotous mobs and the blood-stained hands of soldiers."[25] Similarly, Theodoret of Cyrus, who had been condemned as a Nestorian under Dioscorus, complains,

> For the most righteous prelate of Alexandria was not satisfied with the illegal and most unrighteous deposition of the Lord's most holy and God-loving bishop of Constantinople, Flavian, nor was his wrath appeased by the slaughter of the other bishops likewise. But me, too, he murdered with his pen in my absence, without calling me to judgment, without passing judgment on me in person, without questioning me on what I hold about the Incarnation of our God and Saviour.[26]

On the other hand, Dioscorus is remembered by his own party as simply upholding the anti-Nestorian teachings of Cyril. It seems that he also

23. Leo, *Letter* 95.2 (cf. Matt. 21:13).
24. Leo, *Letter* 98.2.
25. *Letter* 120.3.
26. In Leo, *Letter* 52.3.

carried out the same tactics as Cyril, only he was even more forceful. Most find Dioscorus to have overreached in doing so, and the tactical error not only resulted in his council being overturned; it also entrenched two camps against each other in such a way as to allow little to no chance of reconciliation.

The Council of Chalcedon (451)

Just across the Bosphorus Strait from Constantinople, under the watchful eye of the capital, the neighborhood of Chalcedon provided an apt place for the next ecumenical council. Marcian summoned the council, and installed Rome (via Leo's representatives) as head of the council.[27] This council certainly had more credibility as to its ecumenical status: in attendance were the patriarchs of Constantinople, Antioch, Jerusalem, and Alexandria—to name but a few.

Several actions were taken at the council. The Nicene Creed, Cyril's second letter to Nestorius, the Formula of Reunion, and Pope Leo's *Tome* were all read and declared orthodox Christology. Dioscorus was removed from his patriarchate and exiled. Likewise, Eutyches's teaching was condemned, for he was not in attendance, and Eutyches himself was exiled.[28] Alternatively, Flavian, who had died at the hand of Dioscorus's monks, was declared orthodox. Theodoret of Cyrus and Ibas of Edessa were also reinstated as orthodox: their dyophysitism, it was decided, was not the same as Nestorius's, for Nestorius had also held to dyoprosopitism. Instead of teaching two persons, the council affirmed those who confessed two natures in the one person of Christ.[29] This dyophysite-yet-monoprosopite Christology would need much explanation and defining.

At the fifth session, the council formulated a *Symbolum*, or creed-like statement. The new patriarch of Constantinople called the statement "a definition of the right Faith," and so it became known to later Christians as the Chalcedonian Definition.[30] The key phrase against Eutyches emphasized that Christ's two natures undergo "no confusion, no change [Greek:

27. See Leo, *Letter* 93.1.
28. The letter from the Council of Chalcedon reports that Eutyches refused to attend, "shirking the trial" (Leo, *Letter* 98.3).
29. See Leo, *Letter* 93.3: "Let the decrees specially directed against Nestorius of the former Synod of Ephesus, at which bishop Cyril of holy memory presided, still retain their force, lest the heresy then condemned flatter itself in aught because Eutyches is visited with condign execration."
30. Leo, *Letter* 101.3.

Chalcedon, Canon 28: Old Rome and New Rome

At the last session of the Council of Chalcedon, a debate ensued over "canon 28." This ruling stated that "Constantinople New Rome" rules with "equal privileges" to Old Rome. The reason given is that, like Old Rome, Constantinople is "honoured with the imperial government and the senate."

The Roman representatives, speaking through a translator, objected that this canon had been decreed in an unofficial meeting, but the Easterners responded that the meeting was public knowledge and accused the Romans of avoiding the meeting intentionally. One hundred eighty-two bishops signed the canon, and numerous bishops testified in this last session that they had done so freely, not under duress as one representative of Rome had claimed.

After the council ended, Leo's approval of Chalcedon was slow in coming. Eventually, Leo did approve Chalcedon's proceedings but rejected the last canon (*Letter* 98.4). The Eastern and Western traditions would simply disagree on this point.

asygchytōs, atreptōs; Latin: *inconfuse, immutabiliter*]."[31] The Definition was laid on the altar of St. Euphemia—where a miraculous flow of blood was famously known to manifest itself—so as to receive the martyr's blessing and heaven's approval.

Eutyches himself, we should note, was not only absent at Chalcedon; he was nowhere to be found. To recap, he had been found guilty of heresy in a local synod of Constantinople (448) under Flavian, then acquitted at Ephesus (449) under Dioscorus, and then again found guilty in absentia at Chalcedon (451). After his acquittal at Ephesus, the emperor arrested him because of Leo's appeal. At that point, Eutyches simply "vanishes from history," and Eutychianism will be from then on condemned.[32]

After Chalcedon: Schisms

Like the so-called Robber Synod (Ephesus 449), the Council of Chalcedon was not received well by all. Cyril (at times) had clearly rejected "two natures in Christ," and the anti-Chalcedonians, while allowing "out of two

---

31. The natures also were confessed to be without "division" or "separation" in order to protect against Nestorianism.

32. Richard Price, "The Council of Chalcedon (451): A Narrative," in *Chalcedon in Context: Church Councils 400–700,* ed. Richard Price and Mary Whitby (Liverpool: Liverpool University Press, 2009), 72.

The Coptic Church

Christians in Egypt by and large rejected the Council of Chalcedon. The church in Egypt comes to be known as the Coptic Church, named so because of the Coptic language spoken there. To this day, the Coptic Church, although a minority in Egypt, continues to practice Christianity, using the ancient Egyptian language in their liturgy and Scriptures. The Egyptian Christian tradition has developed largely independently from Chalcedonian forms of Christianity, a process amplified by the spread of Islam into Egypt.

natures," will vehemently reject this council's "in two natures" formula as crypto-Nestorian.

Egypt

The news of Patriarch Dioscorus's removal from office and exile enraged the Christians in Egypt. When Proterius, the new patriarch, was appointed, the Alexandrians revolted. A riot broke out and overpowered the imperial soldiers, who retreated to the Temple of Serapis. Unable to gain an entrance, the mob burned the temple to the ground with the soldiers inside. Further reinforcements from Marcian held back the monophysite mob for a time, but after the emperor's death (457) another riot erupted. The Alexandrians demanded a new monophysite patriarch, and they appointed "the Weasel" Timothy—so nicknamed because of his scrawny face. The Chalcedonian sources report that the same mob murdered Proterius, but the monophysites claim one of the soldiers actually killed him.[33]

Palestine

Monophysite sympathies were also present in Palestine, where monks around Jerusalem resisted Chalcedon's teachings. Although he had originally sided with Dioscorus, Juvenal, the patriarch of Jerusalem, "broke his promises" and supported the council.[34] In response to the unrest in this region, Pope Leo in Rome recognized that his *Tome* had deficiencies and needed to be distanced

33. See Evagrius, *Ecclesiastical History* 2.8, for the gruesome details of the murder, which allegedly include cannibalism. Cf. the "monophysite" John Rufus, *Life of Peter the Iberian* 95, who refuses to recount the "inappropriate" events.

34. According to the monophysite account of (Pseudo-)Zachariah the Rhetor, *Ecclesiastical History* 3.3; cf. the Chalcedonian account in Evagrius, *Ecclesiastical History* 2.5. For full discussion, see Ernest Honigmann, "Juvenal of Jerusalem," *DOP* 30, no. 5 (1950): 209–75.

from Nestorianism, and so he wrote to the monks and attempted to persuade them to accept Chalcedonian Christology with more robust emphasis on the oneness of Christ's *persona*.[35] Many monks were not convinced. Palestinian and Egyptian monophysites then were able to garner more support in the following years, and a monophysite/anti-Chalcedonian party would soon emerge and divide many parts of the empire.

Constantinople

After a few years the new emperor, Zeno, attempted to reconcile the two parties.[36] His edict, the *Henoticon* (482), excommunicated both Nestorius and Eutyches, the one an extreme form of dyophysitism and the other an extreme form of monophysitism. By this time, both parties agreed on these actions: even monophysites anathematized Eutyches's form of monophysitism, just as the dyophysites had rejected Nestorius's dyoprosopitism. Zeno's *Henoticon*, however, made no mention of Chalcedon or of Christ's nature(s). Instead, the debate over "nature" was avoided altogether. Instead, the emphasis on Christ's divine birth from the Father and his human birth by Mary was embraced, while emphasizing that Christ is "one and not two [*hena . . . kai ou dyo*]."[37] This verbiage only begs more questions: "one" what, nature? person? "not two" what, persons? natures? Zeno provided no answer, and so neither party was fully satisfied.

Rome

The monophysites certainly appreciated the *Henoticon*'s emphasis on "one and not two." Evagrius prematurely concluded, "When this was read, all those in the city of Alexandria were united with the holy universal and apostolic Church."[38] Pope Felix in Rome, however, viewed Zeno's statement as a rejection of Chalcedon, and he demanded that Acacius, the patriarch of Constantinople who had advised Zeno, come to Rome to explain his actions. Acacius responded by coercing Felix's emissaries to receive communion in an explicitly monophysite service. Felix excommunicated these emissaries,

35. Leo, *Letter* 124. Cf. Bernard Green, *The Soteriology of Leo the Great* (Oxford: Oxford University Press, 2008), 188, 230–47.
36. See W. H. C. Frend, *The Rise of the Monophysite Movement: Chapters in the History of the Church in the Fifth and Sixth Centuries* (Cambridge: Cambridge University Press, 1972), 143–83.
37. The *Henoticon* is recorded in Pseudo-Zachariah, *Ecclesiastical History* 5.8; Evagrius, *Ecclesiastical History* 3.14.
38. Evagrius, *Ecclesiastical History* 3.14.

the patriarch of Constantinople, and the patriarchs in communion with him in Antioch and Alexandria. The patriarchs returned the favor and excommunicated the pope.

Closer to Compromise: The Fifth Ecumenical Council

The West under "Old Rome" and the East under "New Rome" would not be able to recognize each other's orthodoxy until 519, when Emperor Justin I demanded the parties reconcile.[39] He did this by siding with the pope on the issue of Rome's primacy (a controversy stemming back at least to the Twenty-Eighth Canon of Chalcedon). In truth, the East was not so united as it appeared, and so this did not resolve the christological debate. Initially, Peter "the Stammerer," the patriarch of Alexandria (473–81), had interpreted the *Henoticon* as a rejection of Leo's *Tome* and the Chalcedonian Definition, and so he supported the statement.[40] Signing the statement, however, further exacerbated the problem. The dyophysite patriarch of Antioch, Calandion, had also supported the statement, and so many of Peter's flock in Egypt mistrusted the document and him for supporting it. A generation later, when Justin formally reunited the East and West by recognizing Rome's seniority, many in Constantinople remained monophysite in their Christology, and so the controversy festered. One monophysite sympathizer was Theodora, who married Justin's nephew and adopted son, Justinian, and who used her influence to aid the monophysite cause.[41] This time of schism was not formally between dyophysites and monophysites; instead it was between dyophysites and those who did not say "nature" at all. Monophysitism, however, was spreading throughout the East, especially in Syria.

A Syrian monk named Jacob had been living in Constantinople, and he was sent in 542 as the monophysite bishop of Edessa. Edessa has already been mentioned as a center for Nestorianism (see chap. 7), but now the imperial pressure was turning it into a monophysite stronghold. Jacob would appoint bishops throughout Asia Minor and Syria, mostly using "orthodox" monks (i.e., monophysites) from the region around Palestine who

---

39. Despite the unyielding demands of Pope Hormisdas (the correspondence, unfortunately, is not available in English, but can be found in CSEL 35.2).

40. Peter's ordination was also seen to be unlawful by his opponents because there were not three or more bishops present (see Nicaea I, canon 4). In Egypt, however, the process of laying the deceased patriarch's hand on the new successor was said to be an ancient and sufficient ritual. See the sources in Henry Chadwick, *The Church in Ancient Society: From Galilee to Gregory the Great* (Oxford: Oxford University Press, 2001), 595.

41. Made infamous by Procopius's *Secret History*.

had resisted "the Chalcedonians."[42] Jacob even went so far as to appoint a monophysite patriarch in Antioch. Thus the "Jacobite" church became a hierarchy separate from any Nestorians still in the region and even from the Chalcedonians.[43] When the christological mood changed in Constantinople and monophysitism was suppressed, Jacob had to travel incognito in order to avoid capture. He would be remembered as Jacob Baradaeus, or Jacob "the Beggar," for the ragged cloak he wore—a pitiful disguise according to Chalcedonians. Alternatively, the Syrian church would remember his garb as a pious display of humility.[44]

Although Empress Theodora sympathized with monophysitism, the emperor Justinian sought above all a united church for his empire. He had little patience, therefore, with strict partisans. His attempts to appease the monophysites by denouncing the Three Chapters as Nestorians has already been recounted (chap. 7). The Council of Constantinople (553) would even acquiesce and allow both "one nature" and "two natures" to be used so long as they were interpreted in an orthodox way, since Cyril had done so.[45] Justinian, however, refused to equate Leo's form of dyophysitism with Nestorianism. Therefore, he still failed to appease many, if not most, monophysites.

Justinian attempted to impose his neo-Chalcedonian orthodoxy by establishing and supporting bishops and churches loyal to his theological agenda. The monophysites would call those so-called orthodox churches "Melkites," that is, those in communion with "the King" (from the Syriac word *malkaya*).

It is worth restating that monophysitism was a diverse phenomenon. Most but not all monophysites rejected Eutyches's alleged view according to which the two natures are "mixed" into one, but many if not most monophysites held fiercely to Cyril's teaching that "out of" the two natures of divinity and humanity Christ had "one nature."[46] The reason is that any division between the two natures seemed to inevitably lead back to Nestorius's dyoprosopitism. On the other hand, the emphasis on the one nature itself seemed to lead toward extreme views, such as that of Julian of Halicarnassus.

Julian taught that Christ's flesh was incorruptible. This radical form of monophysitism was easily attacked as docetist, and therefore could be used by the dyophysites as proof that monophysitism (caricatured as a monolithic

---

42. Pseudo-John of Ephesus, *Life of James* 229.

43. The Jacobites claimed the name derived from James/Jacob the brother of Christ, the first bishop of Jerusalem, whose faith is still held in Syria (Pseudo-John of Ephesus, *Life of James* 256).

44. Pseudo-John of Ephesus, *Life of James* 234–35.

45. Constantinople II, anathema 8.

46. Even Dioscorus conceded that Eutyches's form of monophysitism "deserves not only punishment but hell fire" (trans. Richard Price and Michael Gaddis, *The Acts of the Council of Chalcedon* [Liverpool: Liverpool University Press, 2007], 1:159).

sect) denied the truly human nature of Christ.[47] Other anti-Chalcedonians had to distance themselves from the different forms of monophysitism (Apollinarian, Eutychian, Julian, etc.). This party has been described as a "fissiparous Monophysite community."[48] It is probably better to see monophysitism not as a party at all, but a shared concern of numerous Christians to defend the divinity of Jesus Christ.

The countercharge to this shared concern is that monophysites deny the humanity of Jesus, and so are a vicious, heretical sect.[49] Clearly, the vast majority of Christians labeled monophysites taught nothing close to this. Instead, they feared a revival of Nestorianism in which Jesus the human does all the work, while God the Son is a different person who merely spectates. Each party had misunderstood and/or misrepresented the other, and so the two parties largely remained at an impasse for the following generations.[50] The next viable attempt to pacify both sides would not arrive until Sergius I, patriarch of Constantinople (610–38), attempted to shift the discussion into new categories.

Monophysitism, Take 2 (and 3): Monoenergism (and Monothelitism)

How many "energies" did Christ have? No one was sure in the seventh century, for neither Chalcedon nor Cyril had tried to answer this question. Sergius shifted the debate from nature to energy in order to break the impasse between the two camps. In his view, the concept provided neutral ground on which both sides could agree: Christ had one "energy."

The Greek word *energeia* had been used of the triune God's united "action," "work," and "power." This one divine energy was said to be shared by all three persons of the Godhead, and it was united in Christ to the human nature. In other words, any "operation" of Christ was seen to be divine.[51] This sounded plausible enough for Sergius to convince Byzantine emperor Heraclius, and Heraclius in turn appointed monoenergists as patriarchs of

---

47. The technical term is "aphthardocetism," from the Greek *aphthartos*, meaning "incorruptible." Justinian allegedly endorsed this view in his last days (Evagrius, *Ecclesiastical History* 4.39). Perhaps the view espouses Christ's sinlessness, and so his flesh's un-corrupt-ed-ness (not uncorrupt-*ability*).

48. Chadwick, *Church in Ancient Society*, 627.

49. See Gelasius, *On the Two Natures*.

50. The underlying difference between the two parties is recognized by Boethius, *Against Eutyches and Nestorius*.

51. Pope Vigilius had stated the same in a letter read at Constantinople II (553) (seventh session; Price, *Acts of the Council of Constantinople 553*, 2:80), but later church leaders would claim this was a corrupted text and not Vigilius's original teaching.

Antioch and Alexandria. Even the pope in Rome favored the one-energy view.[52] One voice, however, dissented: Sophronius, the new patriarch of Jerusalem, saw monoenergism as simply monophysitism in disguise.[53]

Sophronius argued that two "energies" or "operations" were at work in Christ. On the one hand, Christ "operated" in human "power" or capacity, such as when he would sleep. On the other hand, Christ "operated" in divine "power" or capacity, such as when he calmed the wind and the waves. All of this was covered, according to the dyophysites, in earlier debates: Christ's two natures entailed two energies. Sergius of Constantinople and Heraclius admitted defeat on this front and so revised their view: instead of debating "energies," they turned to Christ's will.[54]

How many wills are there in Christ? Monothelitism, the teaching that there is one (*mono*) will (Greek *thelēma*), promises a way to account for both the one-energy and the two-energy concerns. On the one hand, Christ is tacitly admitted to have two natures, for he is fully human and fully divine (two natures), and he performs human and divine operations (two energies).[55] On the other hand, Christ is adamantly professed to have united these two natures via one will. This one will in Christ prevented the two natures from splitting back into some sort of Nestorian dyoprosopitism.

Monothelitism quickly gained support. Not only did the emperor and the patriarch of Constantinople accept it, but those formerly in support of monoenergism in Antioch and Alexandria sided with this stance. Even more important for the movement was the fact that Pope Honorius in Rome supported this teaching. Especially devastating for the dyothelite cause, Sophronius of Jerusalem died (638), and he did so without a successor. Jerusalem was by this time under Muslim rule, and the Christian community would not have a clearly established patriarch there for some decades. It appeared that none was left to oppose monothelitism. One dissenting voice, however, remained to confess something different.

52. For further discussion and possible defense of Pope Honorius, see Gerald O'Collins, *Christology: A Biblical, Historical, and Systematic Study of Jesus* (Oxford: Oxford University Press, 2009), 200. Also, it should be admitted that the seventh-century thinkers had no consistent tradition on which to rely. Previous church fathers used these terms in various and inconsistent ways (see Cyril Hovorun, *Will, Action and Freedom: Christological Controversies in the Seventh Century* [Leiden: Brill, 2008], 163).

53. See his *Synodical Letter*.

54. Several of the primary texts for the monoenergists are available in English in Pauline Allen, *Sophronius of Jerusalem and Seventh-Century Heresy* (Oxford: Oxford University Press, 2009), 160–217 (= part 3, "A Monoenergist Dossier").

55. Even Sergius admitted this in 638 in a statement he issued with Emperor Heraclius called the *Ekthesis*.

Maximus the Confessor had been a student of Sophronius in Jerusalem, and he claimed to speak on behalf of the Chalcedonian party from Jerusalem and elsewhere when he rejected the monothelite view.[56] Just as monoenergism represented monophysitism in disguise, so monothelitism simply expressed the monophysite heresy in different terms, according to Maximus.

While it may at first sound counterintuitive to claim that Christ had two wills, Maximus and his dyothelite supporters were able to array logical arguments and scriptural proofs. The dyothelite Christology starts with a monothelite theology: that is, Maximus and others claimed the common Christian belief stemming back to the Cappadocian Fathers that there was only one divine will in the triune God. The persons of the Trinity never "willed" different things from one another. The divine persons are always united in will/purpose (as they are united in energy/action). In Christ, therefore, this one divine will was present.

In addition, Christ clearly had the capacity/nature to will human things, the most famous example of which is his prayer in the garden of Gethsemane (Luke 22:42): it is only *natural* for a human to *will* to survive, to live, and to avoid suffering.[57] Against the objection that these two wills in Christ must lead inevitably to a splitting of Christ into two persons (Nestorianism), the orthodox party insisted that the two wills were in fact united in one person (i.e., the hypostatic union of Chalcedon). It was Christ who willed divine things, and "one and the same" Christ willed human things.[58] There is no division in these two wills, for Christ submitted his human will to the divine will at all times—a model for all Christians to follow.

During the political unrest of both Muslim and Persian victories in the eastern parts of the Byzantine Empire, Maximus had fled to Carthage in the West. Because of alleged scandal against the emperor, Patriarch Pyrrhus of Constantinople was exiled to Carthage. In 645 Pyrrhus and Maximus agreed to hold public debates on the issue, and Pyrrhus dramatically conceded that monothelitism was a heresy.[59]

---

56. For Maximus's terms and primary texts, see Beeley, *Unity of Christ*, 294–302; and more extensively, Demetrios Bathrellos, *The Byzantine Christ: Person, Nature and Will in the Christology of Saint Maximus the Confessor* (Oxford: Oxford University Press, 2005).

57. For the sake of space, I have left the question of whether Christ had a "deliberative will" (*gnōmē*) in addition to a "natural will" (*thelēma physikē*) unaddressed. For this issue, see Paul M. Blowers, "Maximus the Confessor and John of Damascus on Gnomic Will (*gnōmē*) in Christ: Clarity and Ambiguity," *USQR* 63, nos. 3–4 (2012): 44–50.

58. A reverse analogy can be found in humans who have two wills due to *sin* (Rom. 7:15–20). Christ conversely took up a second will in the incarnation in order to redeem sinners.

59. Maximus's *Dialogue with Pyrrhus* is likely more of a caricature of their debate than a fair representation of monothelite objections.

Two popes in Rome, Severinus and John IV, had already succeeded Pope Honorius, but unlike their monothelite predecessor, they denounced Emperor Heraclius's *Ekthesis*. By the time of Maximus's success, the new Roman pope, Theodore, also rejected monothelitism and petitioned to have Pyrrhus, now a dyothelite, reinstated in Constantinople. The request was refused in the imperial city, and so Theodore excommunicated Paul, the current patriarch of Constantinople, who quickly responded in kind.

Another important change in the politics of the day occurred when Emperor Heraclius died (641). His grandson and eventual successor, Constans II, attempted to uphold Heraclius's *Ekthesis* and its monothelite teachings, but soon abandoned hope of uniting the church with this statement. Instead of conceding that Christ had two wills, Constans issued a new decree, known as the *Type of Constans*, which outlawed speaking of one or two wills in Christ.

Neither party was truly satisfied, and the division deepened. Theodore's successor in Rome, Pope Martin, presided over a council there (Lateran Council of 649) which condemned both Heraclius's *Ekthesis* and Constans's *Type*. Infuriated, Constans had Martin arrested, and the pope would eventually die in exile from his mistreatment. Maximus was also arrested, and Constans had his right hand cut off and his tongue cut out. He would survive his injuries for some time, and so not be a martyr proper, but his defense of orthodoxy earned him the title of "the Confessor."

Not surprisingly, Constans met little resistance after these actions. Nevertheless, after his death in 668, Pope Vitalian in Rome openly declared his dyothelite Christology. Despite many in the East who pressed the new emperor to enforce Constans's *Type*, Constantine IV deferred to the West's opinion on the matter—perhaps because he needed support from the West in his ongoing political struggles against the Arabs and against the Slavs.

Constantine summoned a new ecumenical council, Constantinople 680–81 (Constantinople III). The Chalcedonian Definition was reaffirmed with all of its anathemas, and with the interpretation that it precluded monoenergism and monothelitism: "And we proclaim equally two natural volitions or wills [*thelēma*] in him and two natural principles of action [*energeias*]."[60] With most of what we call the Middle East now under Arab rule, few were left in Old Rome or New Rome to defend monophysitism in any form.[61]

Although the western half of the Roman Empire had largely crumbled under Arian tribes, and although most of the monophysites of Egypt and the Far East had fallen under new empires, what was left of the Roman or

60. *Exposition of the Faith* (Constantinople III).
61. Only two members of the council voted in favor of monothelitism.

Byzantine Empire was now decidedly Chalcedonian. Even when the Holy Roman Empire is reforged by Charlemagne, European Christianity will retain and enforce a Chalcedonian Christology.

Miaphysite Christians Today?

Today, many Christian churches trace their history to what we have been calling monophysitism. These churches, however, find the term "monophysite" offensive and insist that they are miaphysite, for their understanding of Christ as one (= *mia* in Greek) person who united the two natures of divinity and humanity is derived from Cyril's teaching.[62] The exact difference between "mono-" and "mia-" in this debate has proved difficult to establish. All sides agree, however, that the semantics involved, within and between Greek and Latin, are multiplied when translating into Coptic, Syriac, and other Eastern languages.[63] The overlapping and often ill-defined terms like *physis*, *hypostasis*, and *ousia* lent themselves to misunderstandings that were fomented under the political pressure of the era. Even in the patristic period, there were those who claimed the debate stemmed more from misunderstandings than substantial disagreements.[64] The two sides disagree about how to best express the doctrine of the incarnation, and the two sides disagree about which aspect of Christology should be most protected.

The miaphysites believe Christ's oneness (one person) needs protecting. The Chalcedonians believe Christ's twoness (divinity and humanity) needs protecting. The Chalcedonians will claim that their formula of "one person in two natures" protects both.[65] The miaphysites will claim that placing Christ "in" two natures inevitably compromises Christ's oneness.

62. See the range of meanings for these terms in John A. McGuckin, *St. Cyril of Alexandria: The Christological Controversy; Its History, Theology, and Texts*, rev. ed. (Crestwood, NY: St. Vladimir's Seminary Press, 2004), 140. Cyril's language is complicated, but he does hold to dyophysitism, even before the Formula of Reunion, according to van Loon, *Dyophysite Christology of Cyril* (see chap. 7). Alternatively, after 433, Cyril (*Letter* 46.6) would still speak of "the one *physis* of the Son; but, as I said, incarnate." See discussion in Beeley, "Cyril of Alexandria and Gregory Nazianzen," 404.

63. Cf. the remarkable recent agreements between the Roman Catholic Church and the Oriental Orthodox Churches (see Ronald G. Roberson, "Oriental Orthodox–Catholic International Dialogue," in *Celebrating a Century of Ecumenism: Exploring the Achievements of International Dialogue*, ed. John A. Radano [Grand Rapids: Eerdmans, 2012], 304–14) and between the Eastern Orthodox and Oriental Orthodox Churches (see N. Alemezian, "The Oriental Orthodox Family of Churches in Ecumenical Dialogue," *ER* 61 [2009]: 315–27).

64. Evagrius, *Ecclesiastical History* 2.5.

65. Theodoret, *Eranistes* 2 (Ettlinger, 119), has the orthodox plead, "I am trying hard to avoid two cliffs, one of wicked mixture; and the other of wicked separation."

Whether either side will be able to convince the other remains a matter for ecumenical dialogue and prayer. For now, I will summarize the "orthodox," or Chalcedonian, position. In doing so, I will attempt to state the logic of Chalcedonian Christology in a way that I think is both true to the ancient architects of the Chalcedonian Definition and promising for current Christians considering Chalcedon's use in their own constructive theology.

The (Dyothelite) Orthodox Response

At the heart of most major theological thinkers in the patristic era is the apophatic approach. Apophaticism is the method of saying what one cannot say about God. This approach certainly should be balanced with positive statements about God, but classical Christian theology always confesses that God's own nature is mysterious and unknowable aside from God's own self-revelation.[66] Key examples of apophatic thinking can be found in the divine attributes: God is infinite (*not* finite), immortal (*not* mortal), invisible (*not* visible), and so on. These merely say what one should not say about God.

If one sees the ecumenical councils as apophatic statements, then more of the inner logic of the Christology involved becomes clearer. Here are things one *should not* say about Christ: do not say what-Nestorius-is-said-to-have-said (a.k.a. "Nestorianism" or dyoprosopitism); do not say what-Eutyches-is-said-to-have-said (a.k.a. "Eutychianism" or monophysitism).[67]

What *should* one say? Even the Chalcedonian Definition offers relatively little positive content. Most of the positive statements are statements both sides had already agreed on and understood as revealed in Scripture ("perfect in divinity and perfect in humanity . . . consubstantial with the Father as regards his divinity and the same consubstantial with us as regards his humanity"). The new contributions of the Chalcedonian Definition are apophatic statements ("no confusion, no change, no division, no separation"). The positive

66. The opposite would be kataphaticism, where one says all that can be said. Augustine's claim to "seek to understand" (*On the Trinity* 9.1) will be adopted by Anselm and the later scholastic tradition as "faith seeking understanding." This "seeking" permits the kataphatic expression of theology to be elevated. The Greek tradition in the East includes both apophatic and kataphatic elements, but the resistance to Western "developments" (such as the papacy and the *filioque* clause) prompted most Eastern thinkers to elevate the apophatic approach.

67. It is noteworthy that in ecumenical dialogue, the Eastern Orthodox and Oriental Orthodox Churches eagerly agreed on these points. See "An Agreed Statement," *GOTR* 10, no. 2 (1964–65): 14: "On the essence of the Christological dogma we found ourselves in full agreement. Through the different terminologies used by each side, we saw the same truth expressed. Since we agree in rejecting without reservation the teaching of Eutyches as well as of Nestorius, the acceptance or non-acceptance of the Council of Chalcedon does not entail the acceptance of either heresy."

confession of Christ is not new, but the prohibition against certain heresies is the explicit aim of the Definition.

Alternatively, the Nestorian and Eutychian expressions of Christology did aim to give clearly articulated positive statements about the incarnation. The logic of both is positive and comprehensible. This ability to comprehend the incarnation is very tempting. For example, Nestorius attempted to differentiate Jesus's humanity and the Word's divinity while still claiming one Christ. Nestorius's logic could be illustrated as follows:

$$
\begin{array}{r}
100\% \text{ Jesus} \\
+ \ 100\% \text{ Word} \\
\hline
= \ 200\% \text{ Christ}
\end{array}
$$

While Nestorian Christology uses a consistent math, it fails to represent the unity of Christ's personhood as revealed in Scripture.

On the other hand, Eutyches's logic could be illustrated with a similar formula, only altered to account for Christ's unity:

$$
\begin{array}{r}
50\% \text{ humanity} \\
+ \ 50\% \text{ divinity} \\
\hline
= 100\% \text{ Christ}
\end{array}
$$

Like Nestorianism, Eutychian thinking is logical and easily grasped, but it does not accurately reflect the biblical depiction of Christ who is both *fully* (100 percent) human and *fully* (100 percent) divine.

The Chalcedonian logic, when seen in this light, becomes either absurdly incomprehensible or profoundly mysterious—depending on whether your stance is critical or sympathetic. Chalcedon defines the incarnation in the following terms:

$$
\begin{array}{r}
100\% \text{ humanity} \\
+ \ 100\% \text{ divinity} \\
\hline
= \ 100\% \text{ Christ}
\end{array}
$$

Terrible math? Maybe, but it is terrific theology! How can we understand God becoming human? We cannot.

In his mock dialogue between Mr. "Orthodox" and Mr. "Eranistes" (= one who stitches scraps together), Theodoret has both parties agreeing on the absolute mystery contained in the doctrine of the incarnation:

Eranistes: "I say this union . . . is ineffable and inexpressible and surpasses all understanding."

Orthodox: "I also admit that the union cannot be explained. But I was taught by divine Scripture that each nature has remained intact even after the union."[68]

In other words, both parties agree that this doctrine "cannot be explained" (i.e., terrible math). Nevertheless, Christians must confess by faith what has been revealed.

What about all of the later "hair-splitting" theology about Christ's energies, wills, and whatever other terms ancient Christians found to fight about? Henry Chadwick once called this "the neuralgic problem of technical terms."[69] It must be remembered, however, that it was the heretics who attempted to overdefine Christology and sweep away the mystery. The orthodox party always retains some apophatic stance: *if* being human includes having an "energy," *then* Christ must have a human energy to be fully human. How to understand and "hair-split" human nature is not the issue. Instead, the ecumenical councils provide guidelines for what *not* to say:

* *do not say* less than human;
* *do not say* less than divine;
* *do not say* separation of human/divine; and
* *do not say* mixture of human/divine.

The Chalcedonian Definition is understood to be the guide for this apophaticism while also repeating the positive confession of the faith: Jesus is Lord.

Abstract Doctrine versus Concrete Images

What if we shifted from abstract formulas and mathematical axioms and offered some poetic images? Of course, God is Spirit, not flesh (John 4:24). Therefore, any material analogy will be inadequate to depict God. Nevertheless, even the most stringent anti-idolatry traditions, such as the book of Exodus, have still given depictions or imagery for God: like when God was revealed to Moses in the burning bush (Exod. 3). The bush itself was not God,

68. Theodoret, *Eranistes* 2 (Ettlinger, 112).
69. Chadwick, *Church in Ancient Society*, 520.

but God spoke from the burning bush. The burning itself, the fire, was not God, but a theophany—an appearance of God.

The early church found this analogy for how a created object (i.e., the bush) can hold, contain, participate in God (as manifested in the flame) to be helpful. Irenaeus will offer several analogies for how humans can also be a vessel for, bear, participate in God, such as a sponge in water, a wick in an oil lamp, an olive branch drawing the sap from the olive tree trunk and roots.[70] In these analogies, the sponge, the wick, and the branch all "participate in" something—the water, the oil, the sap. So with us when filled with the Spirit of God: we are like the sponge, wick, or branch, and we "soak up" God, as it were, like water, oil, or sap. We never stop being ourselves, and God never stops being God, but the two *substances* become one, in a certain way. Augustine, likewise, used the analogy of air and light: the air is not the light, but when it "contains" the light, the two are so united that we can distinguish them only "in theory."[71]

So with us and God: when we participate in God, we are mystically united to God. Again, by analogy, John of Damascus applied this kind of thinking, not to the mystical union of a Christian and the Spirit of God, but to the hypostatic union of humanity and divinity in Christ. This time, John used the analogy of a sword heated in a furnace until it is red-hot.[72] The sword is still a natural sword in substance, and the fire is still the natural substance of fire. And yet, the sword has been *infused* with fire (but not "confused" with it!). So with Christ: his humanity remains fully human, while his divine presence is now fused to it.[73] Think of the mount of transfiguration (Matt. 17:1–9): Christ's humanity remains, but is allowed to manifest his divinity, which shone like the sun—kind of like Moses after being in the presence of God, or the bush "burning" when God spoke through it. It is important to note that Jesus's *metamorphōsis* (the Greek word for "transfiguration" in 17:2) on the mountain is the opposite of what the Greeks said about Zeus. Zeus was a god who *changed his form* (= *metamorphōsis*) and looked human. Jesus still is human; his appearance only changes in that his divinity is allowed to shine through his humanity, like the sword filled with fire but remaining as a sword, or the bush burning but not burning up. His human nature does not

70. Irenaeus, *Against Heresies* 5.3.3 for a sponge (and a torch in fire); 5.10.1 (cf. Rom. 10:17) for an olive branch. The oil lamp and its wick are more implied than explicit: e.g., 3.18.3; 5.3.3. Cf. 3.17.2 for other illustrations.

71. Augustine, *City of God* 11.10; cf. Irenaeus, *Against Heresies* 4.120.5–6.

72. John of Damascus, *On the Orthodox Faith* 3.15.

73. Only with the caveat that this did not happen by a process of divinizing Christ's flesh over time; see John of Damascus, *On the Divine Images* 1.19.

become a divine nature, nor are the two natures confused. The two remain distinct, and yet the one participates in and is united to the other. Two natures united in one person.

To carry the metaphor further, the red-hot sword can simultaneously burn you and cut you. So it is with Jesus: he can touch you with his human nature and heal you with his divine nature (Mark 1:41). Likewise, he can simultaneously offer obedience to God as a human and forgiveness to us as God. In fact, he freely wills to do so both as a human and as God. Without the dual capacity (= two energies) and the dual desire (= two wills), Christ's salvific work appears to be incomplete, according to dyoenergist-dyothelites.[74]

While these analogies may be less precise than, say, the Chalcedonian Definition, they nevertheless may help to illustrate what Christians believe about Jesus. These images may be incomplete—and, to be sure, to push any analogy too far is dangerous—but they are not incorrect. If the previous debates about specific terminology become too abstract and unhelpful, then perhaps analogies and images such as these can help to clarify and still captivate. This is the power of images. Unless . . .

Is the use of an image for God forbidden? This question was raised by Christians in the wake of these christological debates, and the matter itself was understood as a christological question. Therefore, we can now turn to the christological heresy of iconoclasm.

Recommended Bibliography

Chadwick, Henry. *The Church in Ancient Society: From Galilee to Gregory the Great.* Oxford: Oxford University Press, 2001.

Clayton, Paul B., Jr. *The Christology of Theodoret of Cyrus: Antiochene Christology from the Council of Ephesus (431) to the Council of Chalcedon (451).* Oxford: Oxford University Press, 2007.

Green, Bernard. *The Soteriology of Leo the Great.* Oxford: Oxford University Press, 2008.

Hovorun, Cyril. *Will, Action and Freedom: Christological Controversies in the Seventh Century.* Leiden: Brill, 2008.

---

74. O'Collins, *Christology*, 201.

**Summary:
Iconoclasts**

**Key Doctrine:
Antirepresentationalism**

- Nonincarnate Jesus
- Jesus must not be depicted

Key Dates

- 730: Emperor Leo III bans icons
- 787: Council of Nicaea II affirms icons

9

Iconoclasts

Antirepresentationalism

If anyone does not accept this our Holy and Ecumenical Seventh Synod, let him be anathema from the Father and the Son and the Holy Ghost, and from the seven holy Ecumenical Synods!

—The Iconoclast Council of Hieria (754), anathema 19

That is how it is with the barking of the iconoclasts.

—Theodore the Studite

Once upon a time in Palestine, around 25 CE . . .
As Jesus was walking with his disciples, a messenger from the king of Edessa brought the Lord a letter, inviting him to the king's city and asking to be healed. Jesus declined King Abgarus's invitation to go to Edessa, saying he had another task to accomplish. Instead, Jesus allowed his portrait to be painted and sent back to the king. Christ's portrait displayed miraculous powers when it returned to Edessa, and it healed many.[1] This portrait, so the story goes, was the first icon of Christ.

1. Eusebius, *Ecclesiastical History* 1.13. No mention is made of the icon by Eusebius. That story is found in the later *Doctrine of Addai*.

195

Many generations later in Constantinople, around 729 . . .

The power-hungry, warmongering emperor Leo III ordered that the silver image of Christ standing over the palace gate be taken down. The good Christians of Constantinople responded with righteous indignation and struck down the palace workers attempting to carry out the impious order. In an unprecedented act of heretical wickedness, Leo then outlawed all holy icons. Leo's son, Constantine V, succeeded to the throne and even more aggressively carried out the *destruction of icons* (= iconoclasm). He plundered the churches and monasteries in order to melt down all the gold and silver he

Definition of Terms

Icon: from the Greek *eikōn*, "image"
Iconoclasm: destruction of icons
Iconodulism: respect of icons
Iconophilia: love of icons
Iconolatry: worship of icons

Note: "Iconodulism," "iconophilia," and "iconolatry" are often synonymous.

could find so as to fill his own treasuries. The saintly monks, nuns, and priests who tried to protect the church's sacred items were then persecuted and even martyred. This dark period finally ended years later, after Constantine died. His son, Leo IV, mercifully eased the persecution even though he still held to the heresy of iconoclasm. God next struck down Leo, leaving his nine-year-old son as heir. Since he was too young to reign, Leo's widow and the boy-emperor's mother, Irene (who was later canonized and known as Saint Irene), served as regent and finally restored the church's peace.

In 787 Irene convened the Seventh Ecumenical Council, Nicaea II, which denounced the iconoclasts for what they were: heretics. Iconoclasm, it was declared, is not simply bad practice. It is a christological heresy! Iconoclasm, according to the ecumenical council, is a denial of the incarnation.[2]

In the halls of academia, around 2015 . . .

Historians recognize the above summary of the traditional telling of the story as a heavily biased version of the iconoclast controversy. All of the iconoclast writings were ordered to be destroyed, and all of the histories that remain from this period are explicitly iconophile.[3] In the eighth century, however, both the iconoclasts and the iconophiles claimed to be orthodox, and they each claimed the others were the heretics. The debate took place

2. From the first session of Nicaea (787): "John, the most reverend bishop and legate of the Eastern high priests, said: This heresy is the worst of all heresies. Woe to the iconoclasts! It is the worst of heresies, as it subverts the incarnation [*oikonomian*] of our Saviour."
3. Nicaea (787), canon 9. On the histories written from this era, see Leslie Brubaker and John Haldon, *Byzantium in the Iconoclast Era (ca. 680–850): The Sources* (Aldershot, UK: Ashgate, 2001), 166.

over generations and interwove the usual threads of religion, politics, and rhetoric. While many of the details and intricacies of the political aspects of the iconoclast controversy cannot be adequately addressed here, the major events and persons involved can be briefly reviewed.[4] Before I do so, a few clarifications are in order.

Three Myths about the History of Icons

Because the iconoclast controversy stems from the eighth and ninth centuries, many today turn to this controversy with assumptions about the previous seven Christian centuries. Just how prominent icons were in these earlier periods is veiled in a lack of sources, which leaves the door open for misconceptions. In order to address this period and common assumptions about it succinctly, I will discuss three myths found today about the ancient period.

Myth #1: Judaism was strictly iconoclastic, and an anti-iconic Christianity would be truer to its anti-idolatrous roots. Instead, Judaism was very diverse in the Second Temple period, and many Jews did use figurative art, that is, images or *eikōn*s.[5] The most that can be said is that many Second Temple Jews were aniconic (avoided images). The problem for such labeling is that not all Jews practiced Judaism in the same way, just as early Christians practiced Christianity in a wide variety of ways. In fact, even our understanding of "iconoclasts" and "iconophiles" needs to be thoroughly revised to take into account that there was a range of motivations and expressions within both of these camps.[6]

Whereas many Jews in the Christian era were aniconic, few if any were iconoclastic (destroyers of images). What is more, archaeologists have discovered second-century synagogues in which were numerous murals of biblical scenes. Most important for Christian practice, the Old Testament injunction against images as idols did not apply to all images, as witnessed by the numerous instances of Israel's use of images and symbols.[7]

---

4. For a full time line, see Anthony Bryer and Judith Herrin, eds., *Iconoclasm: Papers Given at the Ninth Spring Symposium of Byzantine Studies, University of Birmingham, March 1975* (Birmingham, UK: Centre for Byzantine Studies, University of Birmingham, 1977), 178–79.

5. Steven Fine, *Art and Judaism in the Greco-Roman World: Toward a New Jewish Archaeology* (Cambridge: Cambridge University Press, 2005); and Heinz Schreckenberg and Kurt Schubert, *Jewish Historiography and Iconography in Early and Medieval Christianity* (Maastricht: Van Gorcum, 1992).

6. Jan N. Bremmer, "Iconoclast, Iconoclastic, and Iconoclasm: Notes toward a Genealogy," *CHRC* 88, no. 1 (2008): 1–17.

7. An argument championed by the iconophiles; see, e.g., John of Damascus, *On the Divine Images*.

Myth #2: Early Christianity was strictly iconoclastic until the "Constantinian Fall." While it is true that a high volume of art and images first appears in the archaeological records in the fourth century, there are examples of earlier Christian images.[8] The discrepancy in the records is attributed to two factors: (1) Christianity was an underground religion in the earliest centuries and therefore unsurprisingly left few traces; and (2) Christianity suddenly received an influx of wealth and patronage in the era of Constantine I, so it naturally began displaying higher amounts of art.

Early Christian apologists spoke against "images," but these attacks were aimed against non-Christian idolatry.[9] There are interesting exceptions. Tertullian referred to "the Shepherd" depicted on the communion cups in Rome (*On Modesty* 7.1; 10.12). To be sure, Tertullian's point is to disapprove of the *Shepherd of Hermas* as proper Scripture, but his comment concedes that Christians did display images in their liturgical vessels. More scandalous, some heretics dare to display a picture of Christ, according to Irenaeus.[10] Again, these references do not indicate that all Christians, especially "orthodox" Christians (which only begs the question), practiced iconodulism. They do indicate, however, that images were present in some early Christian communities. The real question is to what extent *icons* were present, which brings us to our third and last myth.

Myth #3: Icons were used in the earliest centuries in the same way they were used in the later centuries. While the first two myths are skeptical toward icons, this third point addresses a view that is too sympathetic to iconophilia. The letter from the Council of Nicaea (787) offers an illuminating point: the bishops encourage that "the brave deeds of the Saints be portrayed on

8. For a survey, see Paul Corby Finney, *The Invisible God: The Earliest Christians on Art* (Oxford: Oxford University Press, 1997), who discusses liturgical artifacts, burial art, and frescoes, and challenges the notion that pre-Constantinian Christians were aniconic. Such an assumption is an argument from silence. The evidence for the use of Christian images is especially prominent in catacombs and other architectural spaces devoted to Christian worship; see Richard Krautheimer, *Early Christian and Byzantine Architecture*, 4th ed. (New York: Penguin, 1986), 23–37. Also helpful is Jeffrey Spier, ed., *Picturing the Bible: The Earliest Christian Art* (New Haven: Yale University Press, 2008).

9. The most problematic example on this point is the fourth-century writer Epiphanius. See Olga Solovieva, "Epiphanius of Salamis and His Invention of Iconoclasm in the Fourth Century A.D.," *FH* 42, no. 1 (2010): 21–46, who finds his statements aimed at imperial imagery, not ecclesial or liturgical use of images.

10. Irenaeus, *Against Heresies* 1.25.6 (cf. 1.23.4; Epiphanius, *Panarion* 27.6.9–10; Augustine, *On Heresies* 7). Also cf. the later account of Veronica and the image of Christ (e.g., Eusebius, *Ecclesiastical History* 7.18; and the apocryphal *Vengeance of the Savior* 18, 24, 32–33, in Bart D. Ehrman and Zlatko Pleše, *The Apocryphal Gospels: Texts and Translations* [Oxford: Oxford University Press, 2011]). Also cf. the apocryphal *Acts of John* (2nd cent.), which mentions a picture of the apostle.

tablets and on the walls, and upon the sacred vessels and vestments, as hath been the custom of the holy Catholic Church of God from ancient times."[11] This affirmation illustrates how open the earlier Christian tradition was to interpretation on this issue. On the one hand, the iconoclasts said image veneration was new and idolatrous. On the other hand, the iconophiles said décor and art were ancient and orthodox practices. The iconoclasts, however, would probably concede that images like the one painted on the wall that moved Gregory of Nyssa to tears of devotion (Nicaea II, fourth session) had been around for centuries; nevertheless, the practice of venerating artwork was still deemed novel.[12]

There is simply no evidence that Christians of the earliest Christian centuries, even into the fourth and fifth centuries, used images and art as elements to be "venerated" (more on this below), as Christians of later centuries did. Even John of Damascus admits that there has been development from the Old Testament to the New, and from the apostolic era to later Christian practice:

> Where did you find clearly in the Old Testament or in the Gospel the name of the Trinity or *homoousion* or one nature of the divinity or three hypostaseis expressly or one hypostasis of Christ or two natures expressly? But nevertheless, since the holy Fathers define these terms from words found in Scripture that have the same force, we accept them and anathematize those who do not accept them. And I will show to you in the Old Testament that God prescribes the making of images . . . [examples given]. And in the Gospels the Lord himself . . . [the example of Caesar's image].[13]

Christianity develops, both in doctrinal terms and in devotional practice. Iconophiles like John of Damascus, therefore, have no reason to claim that the full liturgical practice of the seventh century was present in the first century. They instead emphasize that such developments are proper and necessary. The iconoclasts, of course, disagreed, and this is where we can turn from these general assumptions to some of the specific history from this controversy.

11. *Letter of the Synod to the Emperor and Empress* (NPNF[2] 14:572).

12. Theodore the Studite, *Second Refutation of the Iconoclasts* (preface): "At one time they blasphemously miscall the icon of our Lord an idol of deceit; at another time they do not say so, but say instead that the depiction is good, because it is useful for education and memory, but is not for veneration. For this reason they assign the icon a place high up in the church, fearing that if it is located in a lower place, where it could provide an opportunity for veneration, it may cause them to fall into idolatry" (cf. *Second Refutation* 27).

13. John of Damascus, *On the Divine Images* 3.11.

Definition of Nicaea II: On Icons

"We decree with full precision and care that, like the figure of the honoured and life-giving cross, the revered and holy images [Greek: *eikōnas*], whether painted or made of mosaic or of other suitable material, are to be exposed in the holy churches of God, on sacred instruments and vestments, on walls and panels, in houses and by public ways; these are the images of our Lord, God, and savior, Jesus Christ, and of our Lady without blemish, the holy God-bearer, and of the revered angels and of any of the saintly holy men. The more frequently they are seen in representational art [*eikōnikēs anatypōseōs*], the more are those who see them drawn to remember and long for those who serve as models, and to pay these images the tribute of salutation and respectful veneration [*timētikēn proskynēsin*]. Certainly this is not the full adoration [*latreian*] in accordance with our faith, which is properly paid only to the divine nature, but it resembles that given to the figure of the honoured and life-giving cross, and also to the holy books of the gospels and to other sacred cult objects. Further, people are drawn to honour the images with the offering of incense and lights, as was piously established by ancient custom. Indeed, the honour paid to an image traverses it, reaching the model; and he who venerates the image, venerates the person [*hypostasin*] represented in that image."

Images and Emperors

The scene from the eighth century mentioned above, where Emperor Leo III removes the image of Christ from the palace gate, is often identified as the beginning of the iconoclast controversy.[14] Leo's actions did spark a riot, and soon a bigger uproar would occur. After he banned icons, Leo confiscated all images found in the churches. The patriarch of Constantinople, Germanus I, and the pope in Rome, Gregory III, both condemned Leo's actions.

When Leo died in 740, Constantine V continued the iconoclast campaign, culminating in the council he summoned in 754, the Council of Hieria. Over

14. Cf. Theophanes, *The Chronicle* (724/25 CE). The title "iconoclast" is appropriate in that those involved literally broke and destroyed icons: "Accordingly, as many icons as were set in mosaic work they dug out, and those which were in painted waxwork, they scraped away; thus turning the comely beauty of the sacred temples into complete disorder. Among doings of this sort, it is to be specially noted that the pictures set up on tablets in memory of Christ our God and of his Saints, they gave over to the flames" (*Letter of the Synod to the Emperor and Empress* [*NPNF*² 14:571]). The only caveat is that the iconoclasts themselves would say they were destroying idols, not icons.

Martyr for Christ's Icon

Stephen the Younger had been baptized in Constantinople by Patriarch Germanus. He later became a monk and then a hermit, famed for his extreme displays of asceticism and piety. When he emerged from solitude after the Council of Hieria, he criticized the emperor and the council's iconoclasm. Constantine arrested Stephen, and then exiled him. After several different prisons, Constantine summoned Stephen back to Constantinople, where he interviewed the monk himself. Stephen refused to relent, and so the emperor had Stephen beaten to death and dragged through the streets of the capital city.

This version (*The Life of St. Stephen the Younger*, written in 807) of Stephen's martyrdom focuses on his defense of icons. Other records from this time, however, simply focused on the persecution of all monks at this time, Stephen being illustrative of the phenomenon (see Theophanes, *The Chronicle*, and Nicephorus, *Short History*). Regardless of the original "crime," Stephen was long remembered as a cherished martyr for icons, and his "birthday" (the day he was martyred), November 28, would be celebrated annually by Orthodox churches.

three hundred bishops were present, and they condemned icons as idols. Despite the large number, several important representatives were missing, namely, all of the apostolic patriarchs. Can there be an ecumenical council without Rome, Constantinople, Antioch, Jerusalem, and Alexandria?

Perhaps this can easily be explained. The sees of Jerusalem, Antioch, and Alexandria were all now under Muslim rule. The patriarchate of Constantinople was vacant at the time, and the bishop of Rome (the pope) never attended any of the ecumenical councils to date. On the other hand, the pope's representatives usually were invited and present, and the patriarchate of Constantinople was vacant precisely because of the iconoclast controversy itself. This council did not have the proper authorities in place.

Although the council declared itself ecumenical (see canon 19), the council's decision to ban anything made "by the evil art of painters" in the church met with much resistance.[15] Constantine V had little patience, however, for those who resisted the council's decision. The stories of the plundering of the monasteries and the public humiliation of monks and nuns are probably

15. The epitome/summary of the *Horos*, or Definition, of Hieria is available in an English translation in *NPNF*[2] 14 (quotation from 545). The statement was read in the sixth session, and extensive rebuttals were given (trans. Daniel J. Sahas, *Icon and Logos: Sources in Eighth-Century Iconoclasm* [Toronto: University of Toronto Press, 1986]), 52–169).

rhetorical exaggeration.[16] Even so, the iconophiles certainly felt persecuted for their beliefs, and in 765 one iconophile, Stephen the Younger, even died for his belief, becoming a martyr for his devotion to icons.

Constantine's actions went unchecked until his death in 775. Then his son Leo IV eased the persecution of iconodules, although he did not lift the ban on icons themselves. As mentioned in the opening section, when Leo IV died (780), Irene became regent for their nine-year-old son, Constantine VI. Apparently a lifelong closet iconophile, Irene worked to restore the church's images. In 787 she summoned an ecumenical council to reverse Hieria.

As in the First Ecumenical Council, the bishops would gather at Nicaea. There they would decide what teaching and practice would be deemed orthodox. This council would not only receive the approval of the emperor via his mother-regent, it would also be condoned by Pope Hadrian I, as well as the patriarchs of Antioch, Jerusalem, and Alexandria, and Patriarch Tarasius of Constantinople, who presided.

The council members made several declarations about icons. In sum, icons were declared to be *not* idols. The commandment against making an image of the Divine (Exod. 20:4) prohibits such images because God cannot be seen. The incarnation, however, was a game changer.[17] Since the first Christmas, icons as "artistic representation" can be spiritual aids that prompt Christians "to the memory of their prototypes, and to a longing after them." Therefore, while God alone is worshiped (*latreia*), icons deserve "salutation and honourable reverence [*proskynēsin*]."[18] Icons were thus defended by the council, and the defamation of icons was seen as a denial of God's incarnation, visibility, and tangibility. Iconoclasm, in short, was heresy.

Iconoclasm, Phase 2

The iconodules prevailed so long as an iconodulist emperor reigned. That changed, however, when Leo "the Armenian" came to power in 813. He,

16. Nicephorus, *Short History* 60, even acknowledges Constantine's belief that he was honoring God's will.

17. John of Damascus, *On the Divine Images* 1.6–16.

18. Definition of Nicaea (787) (NPNF[2] 14:550). The first commandment forbids one to "bow down" (*proskynē*) to other gods, but it does not reserve *proskynē* for God alone—other people and objects can be "venerated" in this way (cf. 1 Sam. 20:41 with David and Jonathan, where the Greek translation of the Old Testament, the Septuagint, uses the same Greek word; Heb. 11:21 on Jacob's staff). However, true worship, *latreia*, is reserved for "only" God (Luke 4:8; cf. Deut. 6:13); see *Letter of the Synod to the Emperor and Empress* (NPNF[2] 14:572).

Icons and Veneration of Saints

While the focus of this chapter is strictly on the Christology of icons, many iconoclasts objected to depictions of saints as well as, if not more than, depicting Christ. Are icons of saints to be venerated? In the eighth and ninth centuries, the answer was easy: yes. Saints are already venerated.

The communion of saints, affirmed in the classical creeds, simply asserts that all "holy ones" are united. How? The answer has always been, in Christ (Gal. 3:26–28). The *koinōnia*, or communion, shared by all saints is the unity of each believer with Christ—and thereby, with other believers.

The communion of saints was understood by the late patristic period to include communication with saints, even the most "holy ones," who are with Christ in heaven. Although those saints admittedly talked back only on the rarest and most miraculous of occasions, they could hear our prayers and intercede on our behalf. Even iconoclasts agreed on this point.

Therefore, when the iconoclasts objected to depictions of saints in the church, the iconophiles could easily respond by accusing them of opposing the heroes of the faith. If we already venerate, or honor, the saints, why not depict them along with Christ?

and after him his son, Michael II (820–29), reversed Nicaea II's decision and revived the practice of iconoclasm.

In 815 Leo convened a council in Constantinople. It met in Justinian's famous church, the Hagia Sophia, and issued its own *horos*, or "definition." This statement reaffirms the iconoclast Council of Hieria (754) and declares that council as orthodox and ecumenical. Nicaea II was denounced as "female frivolity," a reference to Empress Irene.[19]

Just as John of Damascus was the theological champion in the first phase of the iconoclast controversy, the iconophiles had another contender to represent their theology in this latest phase: Theodore the Studite, of the Stoudios Monastery in Constantinople. Theodore had already criticized Leo's son, the new emperor, Michael, for his unlawful divorce and remarriage. Michael exiled Theodore, and after his death, Michael's son Theophilos upheld iconoclasm. Soon, however, in an example of history repeating itself, the emperor died prematurely (842). His son, Michael III, was—as with the earlier controversy—too young to rule, and so the royal mother, Empress Theodora, served as regent, and (surprise, surprise) she was an iconophile. Theodora recalled

19. The quote is from the Definition issued at the Council of Constantinople (815). The translation can be found in Bryer and Herrin, *Iconoclasm*, 184.

Relics

A topic closely related to icons is that of relics. The martyrs had been venerated, or remembered with honor, since Stephen (Acts 7). Stephen's bones, however, were not discovered until the account of a miraculous revelation of their location in the fifth century. Earlier martyrs, however, did leave "relics," holy items, such as bones. One of the earliest accounts can be found in the *Martyrdom of Polycarp*, and numerous examples emerge in the fourth century, the most famous of which is the story of Helena, Constantine's mother, discovering the true cross of Christ, which was certainly venerated (see *Pilgrimage of Egeria* 5.7.c).

The theological justification is simple. Christians are not gnostic: the sanctification of Christians applies not only to their souls but also to their bodies. Therefore, participation in the divine nature (see 2 Pet. 1:4) includes the participation of the whole Christian, even one's bones. When the saint dies, the body and bones are honored and believed to retain divine power, even power to heal.

The scriptural justification for relics stems from multiple passages. First, when Moses stood in God's presence, his skin began to radiate (Exod. 34:35; cf. Mount of Transfiguration). Also, on many occasions God healed through the touch or "laying on of hands" of another person. Even Peter's shadow (Acts 5:15) and Paul's sweat-soaked handkerchiefs (Acts 19:11–12) retained sanctifying power. The most prominent example, however, of a relic of a holy person retaining divine power long after death comes in the scene from 2 Kings 13:20–21. The prophet Elisha had been dead for years, and his grave was opened up so as to inter another body—a common practice in that context. Suddenly, enemy soldiers came in sight. The grave digger unceremoniously tossed the dead man in the grave. When the body touched Elisha's bones, the dead man sprang back to life. There you have it . . . the power of relics!

The Seventh Ecumenical Council, which focused on icons, also issued a decree about relics:

Thus in the train of the impious heresy of the defamers of Christians, many other impieties appeared. Just as those heretics removed the sight of venerable icons from the church, they also abandoned other customs, which should now be renewed and which should be in vigour in virtue of both written and unwritten legislation. Therefore we decree that in venerable churches consecrated without relics of the holy martyrs, the installation of relics should take place along with the usual prayers. And if in future any bishop is found out consecrating a church without relics, let him be deposed as someone who has flouted the ecclesiastical traditions. (Canon 7 of Nicaea [787])

Theodore from exile, and iconoclasm was once again denounced, while Nicaea II (787) was declared the rightful, ecumenical council. This would mark the last instance of a Byzantine emperor opposing icons, and the iconophile position became the unquestioned orthodoxy of the church.[20]

Dueling Orthodoxies: Theological Accusations

Both sides hurled accusations at each other. Some were blatant misrepresentations. Others were valid concerns. In what follows, the alternating views respond to each other in a logical order, even though the chronological sequence in the eighth century was not so methodical and responsive. By breaking down the accusations and the responses in the following order, we can bring more of the theological rationale to light.

Iconoclast Accusation

You iconophiles practice idolatry.[21] Read the second commandment.

Iconophile Response

Not true. The second commandment is correct to forbid making images of God because "no one has ever seen God" (John 1:18a). That all changed, however, when "God the only Son, who is close to the Father's heart, . . . made him known" (John 1:18b). The incarnation made God visible.[22] Jesus is the Icon of God, as Paul says: "He is the image [*eikōn*] of the invisible God" (Col. 1:15). Whereas in Old Testament times people could not imagine, or image-in, what God looks like, now we can. God looks like Jesus (John 14:9). Besides, we do not worship the icon; we bow before it and worship God through it.[23]

---

20. Despina Stratoudaki White, "Patriarch Photios and the Conclusion of Iconoclasm," *GOTR* 44, nos. 1–4 (1999): 341–55. For the sake of space, I have left the Western and Frankish responses to icons aside. For this important issue, see Thomas F. X. Noble, *Images, Iconoclasm, and the Carolingians* (Philadelphia: University of Pennsylvania Press, 2009); and Bronwen Neil, "The Western Reaction to the Council of Nicaea II," *JTS* 51, no. 2 (2000): 533–52.

21. The first point John of Damascus responds to in *On Divine Images* (1.4; cf. 3.6). The iconodules are accused of worshiping "the creature instead of the Creator" (Definition of Hieria [754] [*NPNF*[2] 14:543]). A generation after Nicaea II, Theodore the Studite (*First Refutation of the Iconoclasts* 2; *Third Refutation* 55) is still combating this accusation. Even the later iconoclasts at the council of 815, however, admitted that icons were not idols.

22. John of Damascus, *On the Divine Images* 1.6–16.

23. See the Definition of Nicaea II (cited above). The iconophiles insist that, while the icon of Christ and Christ himself are clearly distinct, the one act of veneration is united in our experience. Therefore, *proskynē* given to the icon and the *latreia* given to Christ himself are simultaneously expressed (see Theodore the Studite, *Third Refutation of the Iconoclasts* sect. C;

(However, . . . we must admit that bowing before the icon, kissing the icon, praying to it, all looks suspiciously close to idolatry.)[24]

Now, it's our turn . . .

Iconophile Accusation

You iconoclasts teach novelty.[25] And everyone knows: novelty = heresy.

Iconoclast Response

Not true. The people of God have been abandoning idols since Abram left Ur (Gen. 12:1; Josh. 24:2). The New Testament never mentions the use of images in worship, and early Christians were against idolatry.[26] It seems that you're the ones who teach novelty, not us.[27]

(However, . . . we must admit that there is a lot of evidence of Christians using images since the second century.)

Now, it's our turn . . .

Iconoclast Accusation

You iconophiles mimic paganism.[28] Images in worship are syncretistic, borrowed from the Greeks and Romans.[29]

Iconophile Response

Not true. The pagans use prayers, but they pray to demons. We use prayers, but we pray to God. The two are similar, but not the same. Pagans believe that spirits dwell "in" their idols. We believe that God is manifested "through" our icons. God did not forbid *all* images (e.g., Num. 21:8–9), just certain kinds of images for certain reasons.[30] Iconism, God's self-manifestation through images, is inevitable for truly Christian faith (cf. the Scriptures, the sacraments, etc.).

---

and see Thomas Aquinas, *Summa Theologica* 3.Q25.art.3, for a later, Western explanation along these same lines).

24. John of Damascus, *On the Divine Images* 3.27–41, goes to great lengths to identify the "many kinds" of veneration.

25. The instances of iconophiles defending the antiquity of their practice are too numerous to list here.

26. See the five patristic instances of iconoclast precedents listed in Bryer and Herrin, *Iconoclasm*, 180.

27. "[The devil] gradually brought back idolatry under the appearance of Christianity" (Definition of Hieria [754] [*NPNF*[2] 14:543]); in the next sentence the use of icons is called "the new idolatry."

28. This was especially applied to depictions of saints (see Definition of Hieria [754] [*NPNF*[2] 14:544]).

29. The iconoclast council of 815 denounces iconophiles for using "the lighting of candles and lamps and the offering of incense, these marks of veneration being those of worship" (trans. in Bryer and Herrin, *Iconoclasm*, 184).

30. See John of Damascus, *On the Divine Images* passim; Theodore the Studite, *First, Second, and Third Refutation of the Iconoclasts*.

(However, . . . we must admit that a lot of our practices, such as burning incense, look suspiciously close to pagan worship of idols.)

Now, it's our turn . . .

Iconophile Accusation

You iconoclasts mimic Islam.[31] You are shamelessly trying to win over the Arabs in your fight with the Persians.[32]

Iconoclast Response

Not true. Muhammad began teaching that idols are bad, but the Scriptures have always taught that idolatry is bad. Ask the early Christian apologists: they argued strenuously that idolatry is an absurd act and a sin.

(However, . . . we must admit that when Justinian II placed the image of Christ on his coin in 695, the Muslim caliph was not pleased, and future emperors became more concerned with Muslim sensitivities on this issue.)

Now, it's our turn . . .

Iconoclast Accusation

You iconophiles are either Nestorians or Eutychians![33] When you depict Christ, you either depict Christ's human nature, separate from his divine nature (i.e., Nestorianism), or you mix the natures by depicting them both in the artist's material (i.e., Eutychianism).[34]

Iconophile Response

Not true. We use the Chalcedonian Definition in order to express the Christology of the icon: the icon does not merely depict Christ's humanity, nor does it depict a blend of the human and divine natures; instead, it depicts Christ's *hypostasis*.[35] In other words, Christ *himself* is represented,

31. Iconoclasts are called "Arabian wolves" (in *Letter of the Synod to the Emperor and Empress* [NPNF² 14:571]). In his *Chronicle* Theophanes repeatedly attacked the iconoclasts as "Saracens" and "Arabians." Note that Islam was not unanimously iconoclastic: while it was anti-idolatry, the evidence for "forceful destruction of images is usually quite late," according to Oleg Grabar, "Islam and Iconoclasm," in Bryer and Herrin, *Iconoclasm*, 45.

32. An accusation made by both ancients and moderns in regard to emperors from both phases of iconoclasm. Even Theophilos (r. 813–42), the last iconoclastic emperor (mentioned above), is suspected to have been motivated by the relationship with Islam. He spent much of his career at war with the Arabs.

33. The Definition of Hieria (754) (NPNF² 14:543–44).

34. For full discussion, see Matthew J. Milliner, "Iconoclastic Immunity: Reformed/Orthodox Convergence in Theological Aesthetics in Theodore of Studios," *ThTo* 62, no. 4 (2006): 501–14; and Theodor Damian, *Theological and Spiritual Dimensions of Icons according to St. Theodore of Studion* (Lewiston, NY: Edwin Mellen, 2002), 224–28.

35. The Definition of Nicaea (787) insists that the "person" (*hypostasis*) is represented and venerated—i.e., not the nature (*physis*). Later, Theodore the Studite would have to defend this

not just part of Christ—just as, with Christ's presence during his earthly ministry, the divine nature was united to the human nature in the person of Christ—the famous doctrine of the hypostatic union—and yet only the human nature is a visible nature. Icons are no more guilty of Nestorianism or Eutychianism than Jesus was. In Christ's earthly presence during his ministry, or in his iconic presence during our ministry, the union of divinity and humanity, while the two remain distinct, is actualized by Christ's personhood.[36]

(However, . . . we must admit that a sophisticated theological rationale is needed to explain the icon in such a way as to avoid these heresies.)

Now, it's our turn . . .

Iconophile Accusation

You iconoclasts are gnostics![37] You deny the goodness of matter and its ability to manifest God.[38]

Iconoclast Response

Not true. While we claim God can be manifested in the flesh of Christ and in the sacraments, we simply do not believe images should be considered as manifestations of God's presence.[39]

(However, . . . we must admit that the ability of the icon to evoke emotion and devotion from Christians seems to make icons a powerful aid for spiritual practice.)

In general, these represent the competing accusations of the two parties. Before concluding this discussion, let us attempt to hear "the gospel according to" each side in a sympathetic way in order to understand the shortcomings of strict and extreme iconoclasm, as seen from traditional iconophilia.

---

point at length; see esp. his *Third Refutation of the Iconoclasts*, which utilizes the hypostatic union of Chalcedon to fully articulate the theology of icons.

36. The argument of Theodore the Studite, *First Refutation of the Iconoclasts* 3–4.

37. An icon should be affirmed since it "provides confirmation that the becoming man of the Word of God was real and not just imaginary [*phantasian*]" (Definition of Nicaea [787]).

38. John of Damascus, *On the Divine Images* 2.13: "You abuse matter and call it worthless. So do the Manichees." The iconoclast council of 815 denounces iconophiles for using "dishonoured matter" to depict the Word (trans. in Bryer and Herrin, *Iconoclasm*, 184).

39. The iconophiles "senselessly dared to state that these icons were filled with divine grace," according to the Definition of the iconoclast council of 815 (trans. in Bryer and Herrin, *Iconoclasm*, 184). Theodore the Studite, *First Refutation of the Iconoclasts* 12, answered the question about divine presence in the icon with the rhetorical question, "What place is there where divinity is not present?"

Is God Iconoclastic?

If we sympathetically listen to the iconoclasts, we may find compelling arguments about the use and abuse of images. After all, even though the incarnation admittedly made God visible to us in the person of Christ, the second commandment is still the second commandment. When Christians ceased to observe other Old Testament laws (e.g., Sabbath, circumcision, food laws), they could justify their actions with New Testament teachings.[40] If we are to abandon the second commandment, why is there no such statement in the New Testament?

In reading the Scriptures one could argue that God is iconoclastic, even when looking beyond the simple injunctions against idolatry. Consider the scene in 2 Kings where Hezekiah cleansed the temple.[41] One of the icons displayed in the ancient temple was the bronze serpent Moses made in the wilderness (18:4). Hezekiah found that the people of God were actually worshiping this image as an idol. What did he do? He broke it! There you have it: iconoclasm. There are times when icons become idols and must be broken. Could early Christians interpret the temple of Jerusalem in the same way? The temple was always meant to point beyond itself to the transcendent God, who does not dwell in buildings made by human hands.[42] The temple itself, however, can be turned into its own form of idolatry, and it can be destroyed—it was in the sixth century BCE (586), and it was in the first century CE (70).[43] There you have it: God is iconoclastic. Isn't this evidence that we should be iconoclastic like God?

Protestants have been quick to side with iconoclasm. Protestants, beginning with Luther early in his career, and represented in extreme points with Zwingli, were iconoclasts. Zwingli painted over the murals on his church walls, and even went so far as to drag his pipe organ out into the churchyard and shatter it to pieces with an axe. Protestants want to know, how could the early church have been so blind to the second commandment? If we look back to the iconoclasm of the eighth century, during which Emperor Leo III

---

40. E.g., Mark 2:27; 7:19; Acts 10; 1 Cor. 10:25–31.

41. The point made by the iconoclast "heretic" in Theodore the Studite, *Second Refutation of the Iconoclasts* 38.

42. 1 Kings 8:27; 2 Chron. 6:18; Ps. 11:4; Isa. 66:1; Acts 7:48; 17:24.

43. The destruction of the temple has been a focal point for much anti-Semitism in Christian tradition, for it is said that the wrath of God came down on the Jews in full with this event. I want to be careful, therefore, to avoid such rhetoric. After all, even Christians worshiped in the temple in the first century—this is not simply aimed at Jews. Moreover, Christians were not the only ones with this interpretation of the destruction of the temple: see Josephus, *Jewish War* 2.455; 5.19; 6.110 (I am indebted to my colleague David Garland for helping me think through this issue and pointing me to Josephus's view).

declared a war against icons as a means of plundering churches and monasteries so that he could melt down the gold and silver to fill his own treasuries—actions eerily echoed by Henry VIII in the English Reformation—then it is easy to denounce iconoclasm as disingenuous, blasphemous, and heretical. When, however, we look to the abuse of icons, relics, indulgences, and other extremely problematic items in the late medieval Catholic tradition, then iconoclasm itself seems necessary. No doubt many of the eighth- and ninth-century iconoclasts agreed.

Perhaps a robust theology of icons could help us appreciate the tension between iconoclasm and iconodulism. Yes, any icon of God is capable of being made into an idol. And yes, God destroys idols: golden calves, bronze serpents, even the temple. In fact, remembering Paul's claim that Christ is *the Icon* of God (Col. 1:15), we could even say God carried out the greatest iconoclastic act imaginable by sending the Son to die on Calvary.

Yes, God is iconoclastic, but that is not all. God is also an iconophile. Even though the "temple" was destroyed, God also raised up this Icon after three days (John 2:19; cf. Mark 14:58).

Perhaps there are times when God calls Christians to iconoclasm, because icons are always in danger of being made into idols. But perhaps there is also a more incarnational and redemptive approach in which iconology is exactly that: being captured by the gaze of Christ himself through his various manifestations in the life of the church. Any dishonor of the Icon, then, would be a heresy.

Redeeming Iconoclasm

While the party-line statements of the iconophiles seem to outlaw any instance of iconoclasm, the theological arguments of Empress Irene's party simply focused on the rule and the exception which proves it. Icons are inherent to Christian faith.[44]

As just mentioned, Paul tells us in Colossians 1:15 that Christ "is the image [*eikōn*] of the invisible God" (cf. 2 Cor. 4:4). In a letter aiming to reconcile

44. In the second phase of the iconoclast controversy, the iconoclasts responded to this kind of argument by saying, "Well, then, God falls into contradiction and opposes Himself"—according to Theodore the Studite, *First Refutation of the Iconoclasts* 6 (cf. the whole dialogue of his *Second Refutation*). Clearly, Theodore is caricaturing his opponents' position, but it is suggestive that iconoclasm ignores the inherent tension of signs, symbols, and images in the Judeo-Christian tradition, a tradition that also opposes idolatry. Iconoclasts simply neglect this dialectic. For further elaboration of the relevance of past iconoclasm to contemporary theology, see Christopher Denny, "Iconoclasm, Byzantine and Postmodern: Implications for Contemporary Theological Anthropology," *Horizons* 36, no. 2 (2009): 187–214.

gentiles and Jews, Paul's language is provocative to say the least. Although all humans are made in the image of God (Gen. 1:26–27), Paul claims Jesus is *the* Icon of the invisible God, which must have sounded borderline blasphemous. To be clear, it is not said that Paul condones our making of icons. Instead, Paul claims *God* presented us with an icon, the Son of God, the spitting image of his Father. Paul is helpful in pointing out that the very heart of the Christian faith is a belief in icon-ism, that is, a belief in God's ability to be revealed. Even though God's own nature is "invisible," God chooses to be revealed. How? *Iconically*. God the Father is revealed through the Son, who simultaneously points beyond himself to the Father and manifests the Father's presence.[45]

Yet in this same passage, Paul can speak of Christ's own transcendent nature. For "in him" or "by him" "all things . . . were created" (1:16), and Paul goes on to say "in him all things hold together" (1:17). In other words, Paul's understanding of Christ's humanity and visibility does not negate Christ's divine omnipresence.

Can Paul take the next step and speak of Christ's manifest presence? Paul will tell the Colossians that he himself is "absent in body, yet with [them] in spirit" (2:5). Surely Jesus is also present in Colossae, despite being bodily absent and at the right hand of God the Father. In fact, Paul prays so that the "word of Christ [will] dwell" in the Colossians (3:16a). The word for "dwell" used here is *enoikeō*, from the Greek words *en-* and *oikos*, for "in" and "house." *En-oikeō* literally means "to in-habit" or "be in the house." How is Christ in the house(-churches) of the Colossians? Paul explains how: through such manifestations as "teaching" and "psalms, hymns, and spiritual songs to God" (3:16b). That is, Christ *inhabits* the liturgy of the house churches of Colossae. So then, Christ was not only the icon of God during his earthly ministry; Christ continues to be iconically present in the church's ministry.

If iconism is inherent to Christian faith, perhaps the use of images, signs, and symbols is unavoidable in the practice of our faith. Generations after Paul, Augustine, although using the Latin term *signus* instead of the Greek term *eikōn*, will find that words themselves are "visual signs." Words point to the referent they signify.[46] Even more delightful for Augustine, written words are icons of icons: the written words point to the (thought or spoken) words themselves, which in turn point to meanings or things signified by the words. While this seems like a tangent about semantics, Augustine insists that the nature of signs is vital to the Christian faith, for the written words (Scriptures) point to and reveal the Word (Christ).

45. See John 14:9, where Jesus declares, "Whoever has seen me has seen the Father."
46. *On Christian Doctrine* 2.3.

Augustine's argument aims to assist Christian teachers in their preaching of the Word. Even so, Augustine realizes that his insight into the nature of signs applies to much of Christian faith and practice. First, he admits that signs could be taken in an idolatrous and fleshly way, but he knows that a true Christian avoids this problem: "He . . . who either uses or honors a useful sign divinely appointed . . . does not honour the sign which is seen and temporal, but that to which all such signs refer."[47] Augustine names specific examples: "the Sacrament of baptism, and the celebration of the body and blood of the Lord," and he insists that "as soon as any one looks upon these observances he knows to what they refer, and so reverences them not in carnal bondage, but in spiritual freedom."[48] All signs, for Augustine, can point beyond themselves, and the sacred signs do so by signifying God. The church's sacred signs, therefore, can and do manifest God's presence to us. Icons are inherent to Christianity.

The connection between words as visual signs and other signs or images can also be found in Eastern writers, like (Pseudo-)Dionysius the Areopagite. Dionysius, in his *Mystical Theology*, states God's transcendence in radical terms that shock many Christians.[49] Anything, any word, that could be said about God could be turned into an idol. It also needs to be clarified that God's bodily appearances in the Old Testament are anthropomorphisms, but not pictures of God's actual nature. God is invisible and incorporeal. So then, *any* description of God is an anthropomorphism. God's emotions, God's titles, are all too small for the infinite God. God is not "a drunken warrior" as it says in Psalm 78:65. (Go ahead, look it up; I know you won't believe me otherwise. . . . Told you! Now, where was I? Oh yeah . . .) God is *like* a drunken warrior in this particular instance and in this particular way. So it is with *every* description: God is not *really* a rock, a fortress, a shepherd. God is like all of those things: unmovable, a shelter, one who protects. God, it must also be said, is *not* like those things: insensate, conquerable, carnivorous. Instead, the words and titles given to God are iconic: they point beyond the finite human meaning to the infinite divine Referent. God always transcends our descriptions of God. God even transcends our concept of God or divinity. Any time we say or write "God" we are at risk of creating a verbal or mental

---

47. *On Christian Doctrine* 3.9.

48. *On Christian Doctrine* 3.9. Cf. Tertullian, *Against Marcion* 4.40.3. Iconoclasts agreed on this point; they simply disagreed that nonsacramental signs can be iconic: "The only admissible figure of the humanity of Christ, however, is bread and wine in the holy Supper. This and no other form, this and no other type, has he chosen to represent his incarnation" (The Definition of Hieria [754] [*NPNF*[2] 14:544]); cf. Theodore the Studite, *First Refutation of the Iconoclasts* 10.

49. He even warns, "But see to it that none of this comes to the hearing of the uninformed" (1.2).

idol of God. Dionysius's understanding of symbols and images will be used during the iconoclast controversy to defend the use of icons.[50]

Although it is perhaps counterintuitive, Dionysius is not iconoclastic. We do not abandon language when undertaking what he calls "mystical theology." Instead, we understand our language iconically, as able to point beyond human conceptions to the God made known to us in human conceptions. The concepts, words, symbols, and images used in Scripture to describe God are not incorrect. They are simply inadequate. Even so, scriptural words and symbols are true, and they still manifest God.[51] So it is with all sacred signs and icons of God.

With an iconic understanding of Christian faith and practice, we can also account for the idea of orthodoxy itself. The beliefs themselves have been found to depend largely on their antithesis: words like "Trinity" and *homoousios* were not revealed in Scripture, but were responses to heresy. These words, however, were deemed necessary because they pointed to the right way to read Scripture, the right way to understand revelation. This "right way" is found in the concept of orthodoxy. The Greek adjective *orthos* means "straight." Perhaps orthodoxy itself is "right," not in itself or in precise words, but because these words are iconic—they point beyond themselves, right to God.[52]

With iconology we have come full circle from the first chapter. Marcion's supersessionist heresy focused on Christology and ontology (who is Jesus and what is his nature?), but other concerns were tied to Marcion's mistake. In addition to the ontological question, Marcion was answering the epistemological

50. Especially by Theodore the Studite (e.g., *Second Refutation of the Iconoclasts* 11). See additional sources and discussion in Denny, "Iconoclasm, Byzantine and Postmodern," 194. John of Damascus is using a similar argument in *On Divine Images* 1.17: "I say that everywhere we use our senses to produce an image of the Incarnate God himself, and we sanctify the first of the senses (sight being the first of the senses), just as by words hearing is sanctified. For the image is a memorial. What the book does for those who understand letters, the image does for the illiterate; the word appeals to hearing, the image appeals to sight; it conveys understanding" (cf. also 3.18–23 for "different kinds" of images).

51. Whereas the iconoclast claims, "It is a degradation . . . and a humiliation to depict Christ in material representations. It is better that He should remain in mental contemplation" (according to Theodore the Studite, *First Refutation of the Iconoclasts* 7). In this paragraph, my reading of the mystical tradition is indebted to Jean-Luc Marion, *God without Being*, trans. Thomas A. Carlson (Chicago: University of Chicago Press, 1991). Marion's understanding of the icon as "saturated phenomenon" (found in various books and essays of his) seems to me to answer Richard Rorty's antirepresentationalism. Also important for contemporary discussions is Marie-José Mondzain, *Image, Icon, Economy: The Byzantine Origins of the Contemporary Imaginary*, trans. Rico Franses (Stanford, CA: Stanford University Press, 2004).

52. Compare Averil Cameron, "The Violence of Orthodoxy," in *Heresy and Identity in Late Antiquity*, ed. Eduard Iricinschi and Holger M. Zellentin (Tübingen: Mohr Siebeck, 2008), 111–12, for a less optimistic view.

question: How do we *know* who Jesus is? Marcion's opponents, the orthodox, had an epistemology of knowing Christ through the whole of the Scriptures (not just a selection of them). So now, the iconoclasts have brought us to the ontology of this epistemology: we *know* God through God's self-revelation; but *what is* the nature of God's self-revelation? The iconoclasts' opponents, the orthodox, had a doctrine of revelation that claimed signs, symbols, and icons as vehicles of divine revelation and manifestation.

God chooses to speak and appear to us through the aural, the visible, and the tangible. In other words, God chooses to be revealed through icons. The same tension found in monophysite debates (see chap. 8) exists in the iconoclast controversy. How can the invisible God be one with a human being, Jesus, and yet the two natures be kept distinct? The analogy given was the burning bush: the bush was a real and natural bush, but God was manifested in and through it—as a flame that did not consume the bush. So in the incarnation (and this is key for the present discussion!) the *same Lord* manifested in the burning bush became incarnate in Christ. Now, although Christ has in a sense departed and ascended to heaven, the *same Lord* is known through the symbols and icons of the church.[53] The same Lord who forbade idolatry chose to be revealed in Christ.

Now that icons have brought us full circle in terms of epistemology and revelation, we can finally conclude by turning to one of the last christological heresies listed by late ancient heresiologists: the "Ishmaelites," or Muslims. Just as the early chapters on Marcion and the Ebionites brought into sharp relief the relationship between Judaism and Christianity, and just as the ontological and soteriological concerns were seen to intersect in most of the heresies encountered so far, now the Muslims will raise the question of how far christological boundaries can be pushed within one religion.

Muhammad and the Qur'an had a lot to say about Jesus.

Recommended Bibliography

Barber, Charles. *Figure and Likeness: On the Limits of Representation in Byzantine Iconoclasm.* Princeton: Princeton University Press, 2002.

Besançon, Alain. *The Forbidden Image: An Intellectual History of Iconoclasm.* Chicago: University of Chicago Press, 2000.

Brubaker, Leslie, and John Haldon. *Byzantium in the Iconoclast Era (ca. 680–850): A History.* Cambridge: Cambridge University Press, 2008.

---

53. This insistence on "the same Lord" is explicit in Theodore the Studite, *Third Refutation of the Iconoclasts* 26.

———. *Byzantium in the Iconoclast Era (ca. 680–850): The Sources*. Aldershot, UK: Ashgate, 2001.

Bryer, Anthony, and Judith Herrin, eds. *Iconoclasm: Papers Given at the Ninth Spring Symposium of Byzantine Studies, University of Birmingham, March 1975*. Birmingham, UK: Centre for Byzantine Studies, University of Birmingham, 1977.

Sahas, Daniel J. *Icon and Logos: Sources in Eighth-Century Iconoclasm*. Toronto: University of Toronto Press, 1986.

**Summary:
Muslims**

Key Doctrine: Reductionism
- Conspiracy Theory of Jesus
- Jesus was a prophet, misconstrued as God

Key Date
- 632: Death of Muhammad

10

Muslims

Reductionism

O people of the Book, the Messiah Jesus son of Mary was only the apostle of God and His word, cast unto Mary, and a spirit from Him.

> —Inscription in the Dome of the Rock Mosque
> (ca. 691; cf. Qur'an 4:171)

. . . as if God said to the prophet [Muhammad], "Avoid this way of arguing and debating; turn to a better way, the fairness of which will be witnessed by every sound reason and pure human fairness of one of us to another, and there shall be no inclination of one against their neighbor."

> —Fakhr al-Din Al-Razi (ca. 1200)

Thou art the Messenger of God, and I am Gabriel." These words were said to the prophet Muhammad in his first experience of revelation from heaven. The event scared him so badly he ran home and threw himself down, yelling to his wife, "Cover me! Cover me!" After finding out what happened, his wife consulted her cousin—an expert in visions.

The cousin heard the report and declared, "Verily Muhammad is the Prophet of this people. Bid him rest assured." Thanks to this cousin's reassurance,

Muhammad returned to the place where Gabriel appeared and began to receive the revelations that would eventually become the Qur'an. The reassurance of this cousin presents an interesting affirmation of Muhammad's teachings because this cousin was a Christian.[1]

Respect, Criticism, and Dialogue

Christians and Muslims, it is commonly assumed, belong to two distinct and separate religions.[2] Soon after the time of Muhammad, however, Islam was seen by Christians as a sect within Christianity. For example, John of Damascus (ca. 650–ca. 750) wrote his book *On Heresies*, listing all of the sects since apostolic times until his own day, and one of the last christological heresies named is that of the "Ishmaelites" (i.e., descendants of Ishmael), or Muslims.

Identifying Muslims as "Christian heretics" raises numerous questions. From a historical perspective, this view was first documented by John of Damascus, but it continued to be a Christian understanding of Muslims throughout the Middle Ages even until writers like Nicholas of Cusa (1401–64). From a political perspective, calling Muslims "Christian heretics" is not flattering, to be sure, for the Muslims are said to be—like all heretics—the "forerunner of Antichrist."[3] Nevertheless, identifying Islam as a sect of Christianity rather than a separate religion represents a more traditional Christian understanding. For example, as late as the sixteenth century, the famous scholar Desiderius Erasmus bemoaned the wars against the Muslim opponents of his day, for "those whom we call Turks are for the most part half Christian, and perhaps they are closer to true Christianity than many of us."[4] Seeing

1. This scene comes from the traditional story of Muhammad's life. See Muhammad ibn Ishaq, *A Life of Muhammad*, trans. Alfred Guillaume (London: Oxford University Press, 1955). Cf. W. Montgomery Watt, *Muhammad: Prophet and Statesman* (Oxford: Oxford University Press, 1964); and Martin Lings, *Muhammad: His Life Based on the Earliest Sources* (New York: Inner Traditions International, 1983). The quotations are from Lings (44).

2. The influential statement *A Common Word between Us and You*, issued by 138 Muslim scholars and leaders from around the world (October 13, 2007; http://www.acommonword.com), states, "Whilst Islam and Christianity are obviously different religions . . ." This, while "obvious" today, was not always so clear, as this statement itself will acknowledge (see quote below).

3. *On Heresies* 101. Earlier Christian writers usually invoke adjectives like "Godless," "God-forsaken," "God-hating," etc., for the Arabs, who are understood to be "Ishmaelites," "Hagarites," and even "Amalekites"; see Robert G. Hoyland, *Seeing Islam as Others Saw It: A Survey and Evaluation of Christian, Jewish and Zoroastrian Writings on Early Islam* (Princeton: Darwin Press, 1997). These writers, however, may know only of the Arab invasion and know nothing of Muhammad's teachings.

4. Cited in Cornelis Augustijn, *Erasmus: His Life, Works, and Influence* (Toronto: University of Toronto Press, 1991), 83.

the relationship between orthodox Christianity and Islam as a christological controversy forces us to reinterpret the historic debate between the two allegedly distinct religions.[5] Therefore, a brief word is in order about how best to talk about Islam in this chapter.[6]

As our early chapters on Marcion and the Ebionites indirectly raised the question about Christianity's relationship to Judaism, this chapter directly raises the question about Christianity's relationship to Islam. Our work, however, necessarily focuses on the historical origins of these religions and their past relationships. The current relationships and future dialogues are unfortunately beyond the scope of what can be adequately discussed here.

As with the chapters on the Nestorians and the monophysites, this chapter treads upon the ground of still-existing traditions. We are not just speaking theoretically about dead "heretics" of the past who cannot speak for themselves. While the current study can take into account what present Muslims say about their own tradition only in a secondary way, their views are still respected and appreciated in what follows. Should a Muslim read this chapter, it is hoped that he or she would feel as though this work is as sympathetic to Islam as it is to the other "heresies" treated in this work and even to the "orthodoxy" of classical Christianity, even if—as with the other "heresies"—I remain unconvinced by Islam's Christology. My aim is to retain both an intellectual honesty and a charitable attitude when reconsidering the historical sources.

Islam has traditionally treated Christianity in the same way that we are here treating Islam. That is, Islam has always understood Christians, along with Jews, as people of the Book who worship the one true God.[7] Christianity is within the bounds of Islam, except that it is usually understood to be a heretical form of the true faith.

By rejecting the understanding of Christianity and Islam as two distinct and separate religions (an understanding derived more from imperialistic and modernistic concerns than from either tradition), and by returning to traditional Christianity's and traditional Islam's understandings of each other, we can at least see the two on an equal playing field. What remains is for both to jockey for position: Which religion can claim to be the "true" religion? Which religion encompasses the other? Which is the heretical sect, and which is the

---

5. Similarly, Miroslav Volf, *Allah: A Christian Response* (New York: HarperOne, 2011), 146, compares the conflicts between the two with those between the "orthodox," on the one hand, and Sabellius and Arius, on the other.

6. For a fuller discussion about respectful engagement in historical studies, see Oddbjørn Leirvik, *Images of Jesus Christ in Islam*, 2nd ed. (Edinburgh: Continuum, 2010), 1–16.

7. Given the purpose and audience of this book, the relationship between Judaism and Islam will be left to the side.

John of Damascus (ca. 650–ca. 750)

John of Damascus wrote while serving in the court of the Arab caliph. Late in life he resigned from his office to become a monk in the Mar Saba monastery. From there he wrote several works, including works that speak against Islam (such as *On Heresies* and *Dialogue with a Saracen*). Although most famous for his stance against iconoclasm, John also took an approach to Islam that set the trajectory for most Christian writers to follow in the Middle Ages.

orthodox faith?[8] While neither side is likely to convince the other about how to answer these questions, both sides can agree to witness to what it believes to be truth while simultaneously recognizing and respecting the sibling relationship it has with the other.

For the sake of full disclosure I should confess my personal hope for Muslims to accept Jesus Christ as God incarnate who died for their sins and who rose from the dead to give them new life. Likewise, I assume that Muslims would hope for me to repent from blasphemous claims about multiple divine persons so as to adhere to monotheism strictly and truly. What follows, however, is not an attempt to convert, but an attempt to understand better the christological claims of Islam and how orthodox Christianity has responded.

One final word about a sympathetic rereading of the "heresy" of Islam: the trouble arises about how to treat the sources. When looking to Nestorianism and monophysitism, we chose to read the traditional orthodox sources critically in order to attempt to hear the marginalized "heretics" themselves with the hope of seeing how they could legitimately claim to be orthodox Christians. After all, no Nestorian or monophysite ever called him- or herself a Nestorian or a monophysite. The issue is not so simple with Muslims.

We will address the sources with the same critical eye as has been used in the rest of this book, but we will order the discussion so as to attempt to give a fair hearing to traditional Muslim concerns alongside the traditional Christian telling of the birth of Islam. The two versions will be narrated simultaneously in a split-screen approach in order to accentuate the similarities and the differences in the two versions. Then, the expansion of Islam will be rehearsed to understand better the historical encounter between it and

8. Ramon Lull (1232–1316) and Nicholas of Cusa (1401–64) recognized this point and attempted to see the two as *religio una in rituum varietate*; that is, "one religion" manifested in two "rites" or religious expressions. To be sure, Lull et al. viewed Muslims as in need of conversion to the true doctrine. See Jasper Hopkins, *Nicholas of Cusa's* De Pace Fidei *and* Cribratio Alkorani (Minneapolis: Arthur J. Banning Press, 1990), 4–5.

Christians in various regions. After the stage has been set, the discussion can then turn to a critical review of the sources in order to glimpse the points of contact between the "orthodox" Christian teachings about Jesus and the "heretical" Muslim Christology.

Islam's Origins according to . . .

. . . an Early Christian Account	. . . the Traditional Muslim Account
The Ishmaelites themselves descend from Abraham's illegitimate son, born from Hagar. Sometimes they are even called "Hagarites," after Abraham's mistress. But this people group who descended from Ishmael and lived in Arabia by and large remained ignorant or unfaithful when it came to the true religion of Israel—they were idolaters. Even when Christianity spread into Arabia, most of the Ishmaelites continued in their idolatry. That is, until a false prophet by the name of Muhammad arrived on the scene. He claimed that his new scripture had been sent from heaven. To his credit, he taught the truth that there is only one God, and so he led many of the Arabs to abandon their polytheistic idolatry. Unfortunately, he seemed to have been given bad information about how to read God's revelation (i.e., the Old Testament and the New Testament): he understood God to be unbegotten and barren, which he must have learned from an Arian somewhere. Again to his credit, he teaches that Christ was born of the virgin Mary, but he says that, as the Word and Spirit of God placed into Mary's womb, Jesus was nevertheless a created being. In fact, Muhammad was so uninformed about the Christian scriptures, he thought that Mary Mother of Jesus was the same "Mary" or "Mariam" who was sister to Moses and Aaron (cf. Qur'an 19:28). He also denies that Jesus truly died—a docetist!—for he claims that when the Jews tried to seize the "Prophet," God made it look as if Jesus was crucified, but Jesus was in fact a mere man and was taken directly up to heaven like Elijah. Muhammad even tells what happens after this assumption of Jesus into God's throne room: God asks Jesus why he claimed to be the Son of God; Jesus denies	Muhammad began receiving revelations from God, and he faithfully recited them to his people. There is only one true God, and this God wanted the Arabs to end their idolatry and return to the monotheism and moral life of their ancestor Abraham. They are, after all, descended from Abraham's firstborn son and true heir, Ishmael. After preaching this message for some time, Muhammad moved to Medina and found Jews and Christians who also—in their best moments—held to monotheism and kept the ethical code taught by Moses and Jesus. This Jesus was a special prophet, but he should not be considered God—there is only one God! God taught Muslims to say, "He is God the one the most unique. . . . He has begotten no one, and is begotten of none" (Qur'an 112:1–4). This is the only reliable revelation of God since ancient times; the Jews and Christians have corrupted what the original Law and Gospel said. For example, Christ was born of the virgin, but he wasn't God, as God himself said: "O people of the Book, do not be fanatical in your faith, and say nothing but the truth about God. The Messiah who is Jesus, son of Mary, was only an apostle of God and His Word which He sent to Mary: a spirit from Him. So believe in God and His apostles and do not call Him 'Trinity'" (Qur'an 4:171). The Jews, who at least hold to monotheism, rejected God's prophet Jesus and tried to crucify him. God, however, prevented such a crime, and Jesus was not killed—"though it so appeared to them" (Qur'an 4:157). Instead, "God raised him up" to heaven (Qur'an 4:158). When God asked Jesus whether he ever told people to worship him, he answered, "Could I say what I had no right to say? Had I said it You would surely have

. . . an Early Christian Account	. . . the Traditional Muslim Account
that he ever claimed that; and then God claims to have known that answer all along. Back to Muhammad's scriptures: if you ask who witnessed this revelation, the Ishmaelites can't give you an answer. This is clearly no Moses on Mount Sinai for the entire nation to see! Their own scripture teaches that witnesses are required for things like marriages and legal contracts, but they don't think Muhammad had any witnesses. They claim to accept the prophets of old, but they blame us for accepting Christ as the Son of God—even though the prophets predicted he would be so. When we tell them this, then they claim that the Jews corrupted the Scriptures and so the Old Testament can't be trusted. They accuse us of idolatry because we venerate the cross, but they go on a pilgrimage to the Ka'bah in Mecca, and they even kiss that curious black stone. This stone was allegedly used in some way by Abraham, but they disagree as to what exactly the patriarch did on that stone. To then list all of the specific teachings in the Qur'an would take too long, but suffice it to say that the whole of its teachings could not be accepted by any true believer.[a]	known" (Qur'an 5:116). As for the Qur'an, it is the revelation of God sent directly to the last and greatest of the prophets. Many in Mecca, Medina, and soon from the surrounding area heard Muhammad's teachings and knew what he said to be true. These revelations came to Muhammad over the span of approximately twenty-three years until he died. Very soon after his death, the revelations, or suras, were collected as one book, the Qur'an. When variants were discovered to result in erroneous readings, the caliph ordered that an exact copy be made of the original and forbade that any translations be made. Muslims are commanded to pray, fast, give alms, and once in their life make a pilgrimage to Mecca, where most attempt to touch or kiss the Ka'bah. This is a sacred place, for it is "the spot where Abraham had stood" (Qur'an 3:97). Over this, Abraham built the first place to worship God. All of the other teachings of the Qur'an revolve around the pillars of the faith—confession of belief in one God, prayers five times a day, fasting, alms, and pilgrimage to Mecca— which must be practiced or at least accepted by every true believer.[b]

[a]This paragraph is summarizing John of Damascus, *On Heresies* 101. Cf. Jacob of Edessa, *Letter to John the Stylite* 6 (cited in Hoyland, *Seeing Islam*, 166).
[b]This paragraph largely represents the view of the Qur'an itself. Traditional Muslim accounts have also been consulted. For the Qur'an 4:171, I have substituted "Word" and "Spirit," the more traditional translations, in order to demonstrate the parallels.

Despite a few crucial theological differences between these two accounts of Islam's origin, there remains a surprising amount of agreement on the basics of how Muhammad's movement began. There is even more agreement about the rapid expansion of Islam that came immediately after Muhammad's death. This expansion is worth reviewing here in order to understand the breadth of encounter between Islam and Christian groups in various areas.

Islam's Expansion

Before his death in 632, Muhammad had won over much of Arabia to his movement.[9] His followers were not just devoted to his monotheistic religion;

9. Muslim dating (Anno Hegirae) has not been included in this chapter.

they belonged to his Muslim society, like that described in the Constitution of Medina.[10] His successors would attempt to carry out the vision of spreading the Muslim faith throughout the world.

Leaving aside the impressive expansion into the Persian Empire, we will focus on the successes of the Arabs into western territories. Christian cities like Damascus and Edessa fell (in 636) to Muhammad's followers, and by 642 the whole of Syria and Egypt had been conquered. The strategic city of Constantinople would survive several siege attempts, but directly across the Bosphorus, the eastern territories would quickly succumb to Arab forces. By 669 Muslims advanced all the way across North Africa, and in 711 they launched a major invasion across the Strait of Gibraltar into Spain. The tug of war would continue in Europe for centuries.

In the tenth century the Frankish and Byzantine empires claimed major victories, and in 1095 Pope Urban II in effect launched the Crusades, as they are known today, by calling for a holy war (*bellum sacrum*) to save the Holy Lands. The Crusades continued for centuries to come, with the Ottoman Empire eventually taking Constantinople in 1453. The Ottomans remained a political threat to Europe well into the modern era. It was not until the rise of nation-states in the late nineteenth and early twentieth centuries that the empire began to dissolve, a process finally completed in the aftermath of World War I.

With such rapid expansion, the dividing line between the two religions sometimes became as clear as a political border drawn on a map.[11] In the earliest years of Islam, however, the line was not so clear. Many Christians in places like Egypt and North Africa welcomed the new political power and rejoiced to be liberated from the burdensome yoke of Byzantine rule.[12] The patriarch of Alexandria, for example, eagerly gave his city to the Arabs, who were seen as liberators when compared with the Byzantines.[13] Moreover, some of the sources depict Islam's beginning not so much as the

---

10. The Charter of Medina is traditionally dated to 622. Just how direct this constitution's impact was on later caliphs is debatable. Cf. the Constitution of Umar.

11. Fred M. Donner, *Muhammad and the Believers: At the Origins of Islam* (Cambridge, MA: Harvard University Press, 2010), 198, provides a map that helpfully visualizes this immense expansion.

12. E.g., (Pseudo-)Theophilus of Alexandria, *Arabic Homily*, 393 (cited in Hoyland, *Seeing Islam*, 172).

13. Jonathan Porter Berkey, *The Formation of Islam: Religion and Society in the Near East, 600–1800* (Cambridge: Cambridge University Press, 2003), 24, cites John of Nikiuto to argue that the Egyptians opposed Emperor Heraclius "because of the persecution wherewith he had visited all the land of Egypt in regard to the orthodox [= miaphysite] faith." See Hoyland, *Seeing Islam*, 132–35, for additional primary sources.

Figure 10.1. The Spread of Islam (© Baker Publishing Group)

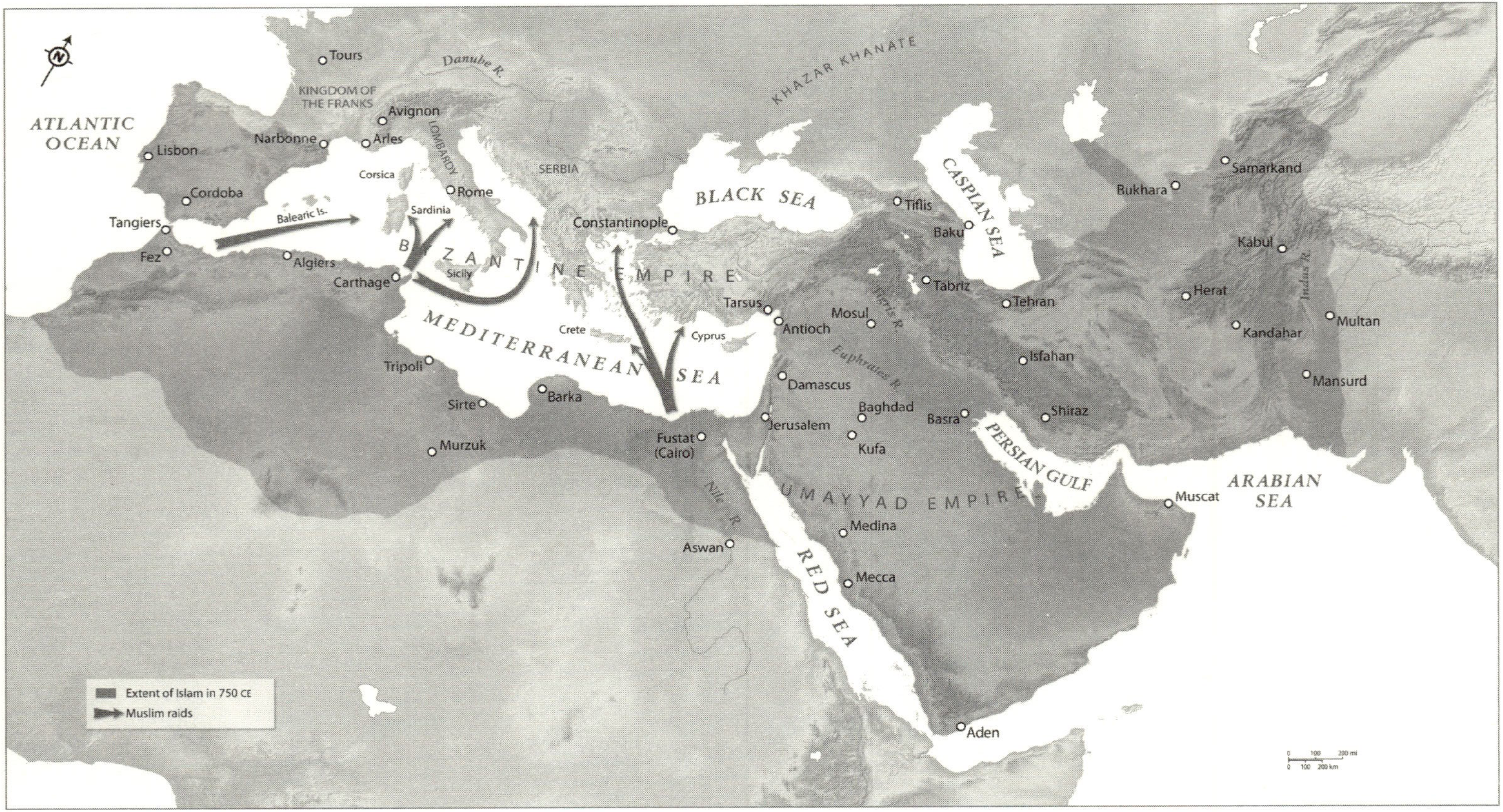

beginning of a distinct religion but as Muhammad's monotheistic reform movement, initially including Jews and Christians—a depiction in need of further discussion.

Siblings or Subordinates? Christians Who "Submit"

In recent decades, historians of religion have read both Christian sources and Muslim sources from the seventh and eighth centuries critically. The resulting picture is one where Christians and Muslims originally understood themselves as belonging to one faith. That is to say, both religions consist of a spectrum of convictions when it comes to their history. This brings us to the subject of diversity within either religion.

Since we can allow for diversity within each religion, and since we can undertake a critical reading of the origin of Islam within the wider history of religion at the time (which, admittedly, not everyone is comfortable doing), it is just at the point where Islam emerges as a diverse religious movement among many diverse religious movements that we can make an entry into understanding how Islam was seen as a sect within Christianity, that is, as a christological heresy.[14]

The traditional versions of Muhammad's life, the Qur'an's compilation, and Islam's origin all came under the critical eye of Western scholars especially in the last half century. Here are some of the claims made by these studies:

1. *Muhammad's biography* originates from sources that came two hundred years after the prophet. These sources appeared to be more interested in furthering the agenda of the Abbasid dynasty than in reporting accurate history.[15]

2. *The Qur'an*, which is traditionally said to have been compiled immediately after the death of the prophet, came to be seen as the later— some would say much later—work of scribes attempting to define what were and what were not authentic prophecies of Muhammad.

14. The Muslim scholars and leaders who authored the statement *A Common Word between Us and You* claim, "Muslims recognise Jesus Christ as the Messiah, not in the same way Christians do (but Christians themselves anyway have never all agreed with each other on Jesus Christ's nature), but in the following way: . . . *the Messiah Jesus son of Mary is a Messenger of God and His Word which He cast unto Mary and a Spirit from Him* . . . [quoting the Qur'an 4:171]. We therefore invite Christians to consider Muslims not against and thus with them, in accordance with Jesus Christ's words here."

15. Most recently, see Tom Holland, *In the Shadow of the Sword: The Birth of Islam and the Rise of the Global Arab Empire* (New York: Doubleday, 2012).

Figure 10.2. Christianity and Islam in Perspective

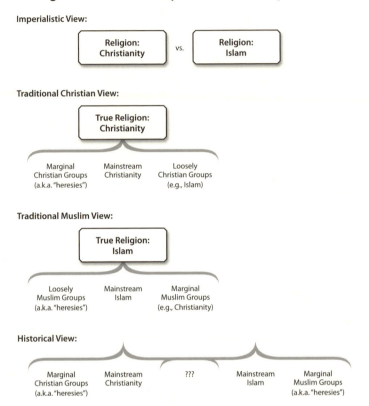

The inconsistencies in these prophetic statements demonstrate that the Qur'an was not originally a neatly bound collection of Muhammad's unified teaching, much less a dictated revelation from heaven.[16]

3. *The origin of Islam* is understood as a reform movement that combated idolatry and corruption in society. Whatever one thinks of the claim to revelation, Muhammad taught people to "submit" (which in Arabic is the root word for "Muslim") to the one true God. Jews and Christians, so long as they followed the ethical teachings of their scriptures, were accepted as part of this reform movement.[17] Absolute distinctions between the religions did not arise until the clash between an Islamic empire and the Byzantine Empire.

16. For a review of scholarly debate, see essays in Gabriel Said Reynolds, ed., *New Perspectives on the Qur'an: The Qur'an in Its Historical Context 2* (London: Routledge, 2011).

17. Donner, *Muhammad and the Believers*.

Many rejected these theories out of hand for religious reasons. Even recent scholars, however, have found the theories, while having an element of truth, too simplistic in their original form, and this second wave of scholarship has sided to an extent with the traditional Islamic position.

As for Muhammad's biography (point 1), many scholars have come to see the essential elements to be reliable, even if later agendas are sometimes detectable.[18] The primary question is just how to understand what effect the Christian presence in Muhammad's context has on our understanding of the prophet and his earliest movement.[19] Many Arabian tribes had converted to Christianity by Muhammad's time, and it is often assumed that there must be direct influence.[20] One source even claims that a Christian painted Jesus and Mary on the Ka'bah.[21] Similarly, others note how there are striking comparisons between Muhammad's earliest teachings and the heretical Christian sects present in his context.[22]

How did Muhammad learn about monotheism and biblical material? For scholars looking for an answer other than divine revelation, the answer must be a history-of-religions explanation: the later religion borrowed from the earlier. Robert Wright argues that the only explanation for the name "Allah," which is equivalent to the Aramaic/Syriac word for God (cf. Hebrew *El*), is that Syrian Christians worshiped "God"/"Allah" in Mecca, and Muhammad learned about this one true God from them.[23] A more nuanced view would allow for influence without dismissing Muhammad's own religious experience with this God of whom it is confessed, "There is no god but God."[24]

18. E.g., Donner, *Muhammad and the Believers*, 54, 66–69.

19. For Christianity in Arabia before Muhammad, see Hugh Kennedy, *The Prophet and the Age of the Caliphates: The Islamic Near East from the Sixth to the Eleventh Century* (Harlow, UK: Longman, 2004), 20; Lings, *Muhammad*, 16.

20. Hoyland, *Arabia and the Arabs: From the Bronze Age to the Coming of Islam* (London: Routledge, 2001), 147.

21. Lings, *Muhammad*, 17. Cf. John of Damascus, *On Heresies* 101, who claims there was a depiction of Aphrodite.

22. François De Blois, "Naṣrānī (Ναζωραῖος) and ḥanīf (ἐθνικός): Studies on the Religious Vocabulary of Christianity and of Islam," *BSOAS* 65, no. 1 (2002): 1–30, argues that "Nazarenes" survived despite the rest of the church forgetting the "Jewish Christian" group's influence (16). De Blois's point is convincing, allowing that "Jewish Christian" sects need not be identified with Epiphanius's Nazarenes and Ebionites (see chap. 2). Many scholars have noted that Manichaean, Nestorian, and monophysite churches were prevalent in the region. Cf. Origen, *Dialogue with Heraclides*; Eusebius, *Ecclesiastical History* 6.37; Augustine, *On Heresies* 83, for earlier *Arabici* as heretics.

23. Robert Wright, *The Evolution of God* (New York: Little, Brown, 2010), 340, citing Marshall G. S. Hodgson, *The Venture of Islam* (Chicago: University of Chicago Press, 1977), 1:155–56.

24. A treatment of Islam and Christianity along with Judaism would allow for a more complete picture; see Jan Hjärpe, "Jesus in Islam," in *Alternative Christs*, ed. Olav Hammer (Cambridge: Cambridge University Press, 2009), 71–74.

The Collection and Order of the Suras

The content and arrangement of the Qur'an is somewhat mystifying to most Christians. This is because the Christian Bible is arranged generally in narrative order, whereas the Qur'an is arranged according to the length of the suras, or chapters. That is, in the Bible the story begins "in the beginning" and proceeds along a historical and chronological trajectory (calling of Abraham, Abraham's children, the move to Egypt, the exodus, etc.). The Qur'an, on the other hand, contains very little sustained story, and thus cannot be organized in that way. Instead it is generally arranged from the longer suras to the shorter ones, with a few exceptions.

As for the Qur'an (point 2), the so-called inconsistencies of these suras have long been seen by Muslim scholars as different teachings given at different times and for different occasions, much like the idea of progressive revelation found in the Christian Bible. One does not find the kind of information in it that would be expected of later periods. Again, many today think the material common to both the Bible and the Qur'an is due to Muhammad's encounter with (Jews and) Christians. To be fair, however, the history-of-religions approach should not be taken to require that something borrowed from another faith or scripture must be dismissed as inauthentic religious expression.[25] The Qur'an itself claims to teach the same truths originally taught by Moses (i.e., the Jewish scriptures/OT) and Jesus (i.e., the Christian scriptures/NT): "[God] had revealed the Torah and the Gospel before this as guidance to men, and has sent the criterion of falsehood and truth."[26]

As for the original Muslim movement (point 3), historians have always recognized that Muhammad and his devoted followers saw Jews and Christians as people of the Book and as worshipers of the one true God.[27] The Qur'an (22:40) even provides for the defense of "monasteries [and] churches," along with the defense of mosques. So it is no surprise that we find much

25. Scholars have long known that previous sources informed Christian scriptures; see, e.g., 1 Kings 14:19 and Luke 1:1.

26. Qur'an 3:3–4.

27. Isho'yahb III, Epistle 14C.241 (cited in Hoyland, *Seeing Islam*, 181), who was first the bishop of Nineveh and then the catholicos (i.e., patriarch) of Adiabene, claims an affinity of Muslims toward Christians: "As for the Arabs, to whom God has at this time given rule over the world, you know well how they act towards us. Not only do they not oppose Christianity, but they praise our faith, honour the priests and saints of our Lord, and give aid to the churches and monasteries."

commonality in the original movement.[28] The Qur'an also teaches: "Do not argue with the people of the Book unless in a fair way, apart from those who act wrongly, and say to them: 'We believe what has been sent down to us, and we believe what has been sent down to you. Our God and your God is one, and to Him we submit.'"[29]

What is more, some passages in the Qur'an say Christians and Muslims are both to "submit" (i.e., the word for "Islam" or "to be a Muslim") to the true God and therefore to be part of the same religion:

> Say: ". . . We believe in God, and in what has been revealed to us, and in what had been sent down to Abraham and Ishmael and Isaac and Jacob and their offspring, and what had been revealed to Moses and to Jesus and to all other prophets by their Lord. We make no distinction between them, and we submit to Him and obey." And whoever seeks a way other than submission to God, it will not be accepted from him, and he will be a loser in the world to come.[30]

The question is just how the Muslims and—especially for our purposes—Christians responded when their differences came to the forefront of their relationships. The responses, it will be shown, varied.[31]

In general terms, scholars now understand the encounter between Muslims and Christians as unfolding in three stages.

Phase 1: An original community of Muhammad, where no boundaries were drawn between the people of the Book, that is, Jews, Christians, and Muslims.

Phase 2: A time when certain forms of trinitarianism and claims of Christ's divinity were forbidden but when the religious distinctions were still tolerated within the broader society.

Phase 3: The end of toleration, when Jews and Christians converted or were enslaved—a phase that actually occurred only in particular regions under particular political powers.

Christian responses varied accordingly in these phases.

28. Kennedy, *Prophet*, 45, notes how Muhammad was able to unite most of Arabia by forming alliances of the various tribes; the Christian tribes were allowed to remain Christian.

29. Qur'an 29:46.

30. Qur'an 3:84–85.

31. For the sources, see Hoyland, *Seeing Islam*; Hoyland, "The Earliest Christian Writings on Muhammad: An Appraisal," in *The Biography of Muhammad: The Issue of the Sources*, ed. Harald Motzki (Leiden: Brill, 2000), 276–97; and G. J. Reinink, "The Beginnings of Syriac Apologetic Literature in Response to Islam," *OrChr* 77 (1993): 165–87.

Varying Views of Christians in the Qur'an

Within the Qur'an various responses to Christianity can be found. The more inclusive views cited above need to be read alongside the more exclusivist statements. For example, the Qur'an also states, "O believers, do not hold Jews and Christians as your allies. They are allies of one another; and anyone who makes them his friends is surely one of them" (5:51). Some statements also clearly respond to Christian claims about the Trinity (albeit, an unorthodox view of the Trinity). For example, the Qur'an states, "O people of the Book, do not be fanatical in your faith, and say nothing but the truth about God. . . . Do not call Him 'Trinity'" (Qur'an 4:171; cf. 5:71–73; 112:1–4). Regarding how to harmonize these statements to the other, more inclusivist statements, one could choose one of the three following interpretations. (1) The seemingly inclusivist passages are not as inclusive as they seem. They teach tolerance in Muslim society and extend an invitation to people of the Book, but they must be read in light of the clear statements that deny salvation to anyone other than Muslims. (2) These passages are incoherent, and the inherent inconsistency invalidates the Qur'an. (3) The different passages stem from Muhammad's encounters with different Jewish and Christian groups at different times.

To further complicate matters, there is no clear-cut time line that accurately describes Christian-Muslim relations in every region, for practices varied from place to place. For example, Muslims in Syria continued to celebrate Christmas and Easter into the tenth century, much to the chagrin of Muslim teachers at that time, who recorded their complaints, and Muslims in Egypt and North Africa continued to celebrate these Christian holy days for centuries longer than their Syrian counterparts.[32] In addition, cutting across the three chronological phases of Christian-Muslim interaction, one finds variations along political and regional lines.[33]

One should not read the revised understanding of Islam described above to say that it was entirely a tolerant, interreligious peace movement while Christianity was an imperial force aligned with the imperial army. Both sides of this caricature misrepresent the encounter between Christians and Muslims.[34] The spread of military and political control by Muslim Arabs was violent, and

32. Berkey, *Formation of Islam*, 160, 251.

33. In general the more the source was aligned with the Byzantine Empire, the more likely the source viewed the Arabs as an anti-Christian force (see Hoyland, *Seeing Islam*, 53–115, 216–36). Also, the later source, the more likely it was to view the Muslims as demonic (ibid., 257–307).

34. Rodney Stark, *The Triumph of Christianity: How the Jesus Movement Became the World's Largest Religion* (New York: HarperOne, 2011), 207–8.

many Christians were persecuted by Muslims.[35] Nevertheless, such brutality was not characteristic of all Muslims or of all instances of their encounter with Christians, and it does not accurately represent Muhammad himself.[36] Also, the Christian responses varied from welcoming the Arab forces as liberators to marching against the Muslims in the Byzantine army. The primary point to be remembered here is that such a range of encounters emerged in the clash between the political powers beginning as late as 680.[37] Both sides exhibited a spectrum of behaviors: the various Christianities included some groups and individuals who viewed Muslims as a sect of Christians and therefore as allies; the various Islams included some groups and individuals who viewed Christians as people who submit to the one true God and therefore as within the bounds of Islam. While keeping these historical, regional, and political differences in mind, let us turn to some of the more universal agreements and disagreements found between Christians and Muslims, and see especially how both sides viewed Jesus.

Islamic Christology

According to the Qur'an, Muhammad is the "seal of the prophets," which many later Muslims understood to mean he was the final and most important prophet. He was not, however, the only one: before him were Abraham, Moses, and many other historic figures through whom the Almighty spoke. The message was always the same: there is one God, and people should obey God. Islam believes that until Muhammad, Jesus was the greatest—and one could even hear the Qur'an to say the most unique—prophet. Jesus is unique in the following ways.

- Jesus's birth was announced by the angel Gabriel.
- Mary was a virgin when she conceived Jesus. Jesus is "the Word and Spirit of God" placed in Mary's womb by God.[38]

35. See the sources in Hoyland, *Seeing Islam*, 336–86.
36. Karen Armstrong, *A History of God: From Abraham to the Present; The 4000-Year Quest for God* (London: Heinemann, 1993), 155–56: "Muhammad was fighting for his life, was evolving a theology of the just war in the Qur'an with which most Christians would agree, and never forced anybody to convert to his religion. Indeed the Qur'an is clear that there is to be 'no compulsion in religion.'"
37. The view of Donner, *Muhammad and the Believers* (cited above).
38. While most orthodox Christians after the Council of Constantinople (381) would avoid this coupling of "Word and Spirit of God" to describe Christ, it was common in the earlier centuries and remained in use in some quarters for some time after this council. In such cases, "Spirit" does not mean the third person of the Trinity, but describes God's nature as Spirit(ual),

- Jesus had creative power. As a child he once molded birds out of the dust of the earth, breathed into them, and made them come alive.[39]
- Jesus performed miracles, healed, and even raised the dead.
- Jesus proclaimed the gospel (cf. Moses, who proclaimed the law).
- Jesus preached only to the Jews, but his message was a universal one.
- Jesus was rejected by his people, who tried to crucify him.
- Jesus was taken up into heaven by God, where he now is.
- Jesus will come again for the day of judgment.

These teachings about Jesus sound surprisingly Christian to those not familiar with the Qur'an. Jesus's unique role, however, is not news to Muslims. Jesus is venerated by the followers of Muhammad.

Despite this relatively long list of beliefs about Jesus shared by Muslims and Christians, there are some apparent differences.

1. Jesus is not divine. He was a human prophet empowered by God.[40]
2. Jesus did not die on the cross. It merely appeared that way to the Jews.
3. Jesus did not rise from the dead. See the previous point; he never died.

While these points represent substantial disagreements with Christians and should not be dismissed as insignificant, they nevertheless do not represent absolute dividing lines between Islam and Christianity, at least not with Christianity as it was known in Arabia in the time of Muhammad.

Regarding the first point, Muslims confess that Allah is One (cf. Deut. 6:4). The notion of God's oneness is not simply mathematical (quantity); God is unique (quality). Arabic does not have a concept like divinity. Jesus is not Allah, for Jesus is human and creaturely and God is altogether transcendent. To call Jesus God/divine in Arabic would be to say Jesus is *a* god—something that all Christians would reject. Equally important is that Christians in the Church of the East (or "Nestorians") would make the same distinction: Jesus is not

---

for "God is Spirit" (John 4:24), not flesh. Cf. the Holy Spirit as *another* Advocate (John 14:16; cf. 1 John 2:1, where Jesus is a *paraklēton*).

39. Qur'an 3:49; 5:111; Mahmoud Ayoub, *A Muslim View of Christianity: Essays on Dialogue*, ed. Irfan A. Omar (Maryknoll, NY: Orbis, 2007), 114, comments on this passage: "In the Qur'an it is intended to show God's power as the creator through the agency of the divine Word, Jesus." Cf. *Infancy Gospel of Thomas* 2.2–4.

40. Qur'an 3:58–59; 4:171; 5:75; 112:1–4. Cf. *Gospel of Philip* 81, from Nag Hammadi, which represents the kind of variant Christian Christologies present in the East for centuries before and even after Muhammad: "He who creates cannot beget. . . . Now they say, 'He who creates begets.' But his [God's] so-called 'offspring' is merely a creature" (trans. *NHL*, 157).

divine; he is human; only the Word is divine. Even two-nature Chalcedonian thinking (that of the "Melkites") would insist on the same distinction while also emphasizing the union of these two natures.

Regarding the second point of disagreement, does Islam deny that Christ died on the cross? It is tempting to hazard a possible interpretation of the Qur'an; such a move, however, is the attempt of an outsider to tell Muslims how to read their own scriptures—something Christians tend to dismiss in regard to their own scripture, and so Jesus's golden rule cautions me against it.[41] Perhaps a more humble and respectful approach could be to put this in the form of a question. Is it possible that the Qur'an's statement that "it so appeared to them" (4:157) is not a denial of Jesus's crucifixion, but a denial of the persecutors' power over Jesus? The Qur'an states,

> And for saying: "We killed the Christ, Jesus, son of Mary, who was an apostle of God"; but they neither killed nor crucified him, though it so appeared to them. Those who disagree in the matter are only lost in doubt. They have no knowledge about it other than conjecture, for surely they did not kill him.

The whole passage is a declamation against the Jews who broke their covenant with God. This particular statement is a correction: the Jews believed they killed the Messiah; they believed they had power over God's messenger. The point is to deny Christ's enemies had any power. It is God who is sovereign. Rather than saying that God deceived the onlookers at the crucifixion with either a docetic-Jesus-hologram or a Jesus-stunt-double, what if the statement is claiming that God's Messiah laid down his own life; no one took it from him; and Jesus was given this power by the sovereign God?[42] Elsewhere in the Qur'an, Jesus himself says, "There was peace on the day I was born, and will be the day I die, and on the day I will be raised from the dead" (19:33). It seems that one can accept Jesus's death (and resurrection) as historical and be within the bounds of Islam.[43]

This reevaluation is offered here to illustrate the diverse understandings of Islam's early encounter with Christianity. We should not try to sweep crucial

41. Gabriel Said Reynolds, *The Qur'an and Its Biblical Subtext* (London: Routledge, 2010), contends that the medieval Muslim tradition should not be the governing hermeneutical lens for reading the Qur'an. It seems, however, that many Muslims disagree. Of course, many Christians also rely on earlier interpretations to guide them when it comes to interpreting the Bible, so novel interpretations of either scripture are unsurprisingly suspect.

42. Cf. John 10:17–18.

43. Suleiman A. Mourad, "The Qur'an and Jesus's Crucifixion and Death," in *New Perspectives on the Qur'an: The Qur'an in Its Historical Context 2*, ed. Gabriel Said Reynolds (London: Routledge, 2011), 349–57, reads the Qur'an to say Christ did die and was resurrected.

differences aside. It is simply important to remember that while many Christians have viewed Islam as a diabolical religion of the enemy, many others have found Muslims to share much in common with their own faith.

Christologies in Dialogue

In order to clarify the importance of this revised picture of early Islamic Christology, especially its importance for understanding the relationship between Muslims and Christians, let us imagine a dialogue. This fictive encounter will be set in Sufetula—a city in central North Africa (what is today Sbeitla, Tunisia) about one hundred miles south of Carthage and seventy miles west of the coast. Sufetula existed as a pre-Roman city, and it burgeoned under Rome and Constantinople. Christianity had a strong presence here, but it was conquered by the Arabs in 648. In fact, Kairouan was built near this city, quarrying some of its masonry to build the Uqba mosque there, claimed by some as the fourth-holiest site in Islam (after Mecca, Medina, and Jerusalem).

Outside Sufetula lived the indigenous Berber tribes, who at least partly sided with the Arabs. Even so, the alleged mass conversion of these tribes was not as final as it may sound. Traces of Christianity survived for centuries, and many of the converts to Islam would even become part of the Muslim Kharijites (a puritanist movement similar to Donatism in the region) and would fight the Arabs in later centuries.[44]

The dialogue partners will be an Arab officer ("M" for Muslim) whose assignment is to sweep the countryside looking for any remaining resistance, and a Christian farmer ("C" for Christian) who works a smallholding in a valley outside of town. *M enters on a horse, stage right . . .*

M: Hey, you there! This region has now been conquered. Do you submit?

C: Conquered? You mean you defeated that ragtag band of Roman soldiers holed up in their so-called fortress in town?

M: Yes, we besieged the city and defeated them easily.

C: God be praised! Those good-for-nothing soldiers caused all kinds of troubles. Does this mean we don't have to pay taxes to Rome anymore?

M: That's correct. You have to pay taxes to the caliph.

C: Who's the caliph?

M: He's our ruler, the successor to Muhammad (peace be upon him).

---

44. Donatism was a schismatic movement in North Africa that began in the early fourth century. Its adherents allegedly prioritized the holiness of the church over the oneness of the church.

C: Who's Muhammad?

M: Our founder and God's prophet. Do you submit?

C: Well of course I submit! I'm no soldier. Will you charge as much taxes as the Romans?

M: No.

C: God be praised! I submit.

M: Wait, you're not just submitting to our taxes. You must submit to Muhammad's teachings.[45]

C: Or what?

M: Or else.

C: Oh . . . Well then, what does Muhammad teach?

M: There is no god but God.

C: Okay, I submit.

M: Wait, it's not that simple! You must pray five times a day as well.

C: You mean like the five daily hours of prayer they have at the church?

M: Yes, like that.

C: Well, sure. I'm all for that, but it's a long walk to the basilica. Can I pray from here?

M: Yes, we recommend a prayer rug.

C: That's convenient. Okay, I submit.

M: I'm still not done. You must also give alms.

C: Alms to the poor? Now, to be honest it's hard to imagine many folks poorer than us, but the good bishop in town has been preaching about alms for years.

M: The point is to be just and charitable.

C: Amen to that. Okay, I'll give alms. Anything else?

M: Yes, you must fast, especially during the holy days.

C: Well, again, we're so poor we already "fast" more often than we would prefer. But like with alms, the right reverend bishop has been telling us that it's important to fast on the right days and in the right time of year. Sure. I'll fast.

M: You must also go on pilgrimage to Mecca.

C: Mecca?

45. Arab conquerors very often discouraged conversions, since the converts would in fact pay less taxes. Officially, forced conversions are forbidden, and yet the opportunity to convert should always be offered.

M: Mecca. It's the holy city where Abraham worshiped God, and where Muhammad (P.B.U.H.) learned there is only one God, and it's a long way away, and I know you're going to complain about how you don't have the money, and I'll bet you're going to say you're too old for such a long journey. There are exceptions for this one. The point is every person is ideally supposed to go to pay homage to this place where God was revealed. Can you agree in principle?

C: Hmm. Pious and practical. I like the way this Muhammad thinks. I submit "in principle."

M: To be clear, you must submit and confess Muhammad (P.B.U.H.) as the prophet of God who teaches all of these things.

C: "Confess . . ." That sounds like a big deal. I'm a baptized Christian. Is this a new religion?

M: Muhammad (P.B.U.H.) taught the same truth taught by Moses and Jesus.

C: Sounds like I could just say "I submit" without asking any more questions. But then again, you seem to want me to understand this new-but-not-new faith. I probably should find out what this Muhammad said about Jesus.

M: Jesus is very important to us: Jesus was born of the virgin Mary; he is the Word and Spirit of God sent into Mary's womb; he performed miracles and raised the dead; after he did his work on earth God raised him up to heaven, where he now waits to return for the judgment of the world.

C: Wow, you know a lot about the faith for a soldier. You all must be a devout people. All that you say about Jesus sounds like the same Jesus I know and love. Did the bishop submit? What about the church in town?

M: The bishop still teaches the Christians in the church. They have to pay a higher tax for being Christian.

C: And I bet I would have to pay a higher tax to go there.

M: That's correct.

C: What about the new basilica they're supposed to build on this side of the town? That would be a lot closer for me. Is that going to happen now that the emperor is no longer in charge?

M: No. You can't build any more churches. You can worship with us at the new mosque.[46]

C: What's a mosque?

46. Donner, *Muhammad and the Believers*, 214, notes early mosques that had Jewish and/or Christian elements in them.

M: It is where we worship and pray.

C: Sounds good. I submit.[47]

M: Good. God be praised. Go in peace.

C: God be praised, brother. See you in mosque on Sunday.[48]

M: Friday.

C: Friday?!

M: Yes, Friday. I've got to go. Someone will explain all this to you in time. Peace.

C: Peace.

M exits, stage left. And . . . scene.

It must be admitted that this imagined dialogue takes advantage of an illiterate rural individual who could not compare the new teachings on Christ with the Christian scriptures. Such was the case, however, for most of the population conquered by Islam. Few could read, and fewer could read the Latin of the urban churches in this particular region.[49]

Perhaps the Christian farmer would have been more persistent in asking about Christ's divinity. Then again, this particular Christian may have held to Arianism, which was introduced into North Africa by the Vandals long before Muslims arrived on the scene, and in that case the farmer would prefer to deny Christ as truly God/divine. The point is that the diversity of Christianity in the frontiers of the Byzantine Empire was great, and the general impression from reading the sources is that Christians seen as "friends with the Romans [i.e., Byzantines]" met with more problems than the non-Chalcedonians.[50] Regardless of all the variables in this dialogue, this imaginative exercise illustrates how easily Christians could see Islam as Christian, or at least as a righteous reform movement sent by God.

The generations of Christians born after this "submission" would have less and less access to Christian orthodoxy, and become more and more

---

47. Cf. Qur'an 3:52, where Jesus's disciples claim to be "Muslims" (ones who submit to God).

48. See the figure of Christ in a converted mosque from southern Tunisia in Elizabeth Savage, *A Gateway to Hell, a Gateway to Paradise: The North African Response to the Arab Conquest* (Princeton: Darwin Press, 1997), 205 and fig. 9.

49. See the helpful statement made by Donner, *Muhammad and the Believers*, 77. Philip Jenkins, *The Lost History of Christianity: The Thousand-Year Golden Age of the Church in the Middle East, Africa, and Asia—and How It Died* (New York: HarperCollins, 2009), 228–32, thinks the Egyptian and Syrian regions retained a Christian presence throughout the Middle Ages precisely because they—unlike the North African Christians—translated the Christian scriptures into the native language (Coptic and Syriac, respectively).

50. Theodotus of Amida, *Life* 58 (cited in Hoyland, *Seeing Islam*, 159).

assimilated into what will become mainstream Islam.[51] Fear of assimilation, not to mention the fear of apostasy, motivated other responses to Islam. We can now turn to those orthodox sources to see how they responded to Islam as a Christian heresy.

The (Christian) Orthodox Response

The orthodox response to Islam's view of Christ included many different kinds of answers.[52] Once again, for the sake of space a streamlined answer will be offered here in order to cut to the heart of the disagreement. Orthodox Christians heard the Muslim account of Jesus as something along the lines of (what we would call) a conspiracy theory. In response Christians pressed the debate along the lines of (what they explicitly called) inconsistency: in their view the Christian version was consistent, whereas the Muslim conspiracy was inconsistent and therefore easily discredited. Muslims claimed that early Christians conspired to corrupt the story of Jesus so as to make him a god.

Like all good conspiracy theories, the Muslim account of Christology requires the following. The standard account must be rejected as political propaganda meant to fool the masses. The people in charge (and probably the Catholic Church in cahoots) must be seen as conspirators who cannot be trusted. Third, all so-called evidence for the old view is probably falsified by the conspirators, while the real evidence was destroyed in the cover-up. With these elements in place, the conspiracy theory is unfalsifiable, and of course unverifiable. This unfalsifiability is not so much a problem in religion; after all, you've got to have faith. The charge of conspiracy theory also should not be taken entirely as derogatory of or exclusively applicable to Islam, for much the same could be said about Christian origins (cf. Matt. 28:11–15). An externally unfalsifiable theory must be discredited from within, by finding internal inconsistencies. Christians during the rise of Islam understood the Muslim version of Christ as inconsistent and therefore unconvincing. After all, Marcion had a similar such theory long ago (see chap. 1): the Scriptures had

---

51. Stark, *Triumph of Christianity*, 204: "It was a very long time before the conquered areas were truly Muslim in anything but name. The reality was that very small Muslim elites long ruled over non-Muslim (mostly Christian) populations in the conquered areas. This runs contrary to the widespread belief that Muslim conquests were quickly followed by mass conversions to Islam."

52. E.g., John Moschus, *Spiritual Meadow*, 100–102; and Sophronius, *Synodical Letter* (cited in Hoyland, *Seeing Islam*, 63, 69), claim the Muslim armies were God's punishment for immorality. Much later, the orthodox response is to crusade.

been falsified by the Jews, so you'll have to take one man's word and his new version of Scripture when it comes to knowing Christ.[53] It was unconvincing in Marcion's day, and the Muslim version appeared equally unpersuasive. Or, at least, it was unpersuasive to some literate Christians like John of Damascus who left a record of their objections.

Sometime after 700, John of Damascus wrote a dialogue with a "Saracen."[54] The aim is clearly not to report an actual conversation, but to teach Christians how to win a debate with Muslims. This is evident when the author interrupts the flow of the dialogue and directly addresses the reader. John advises the Christian how to begin such a debate:

> If you will be asked by a Sarac[en] this question: "What do you say that Christ is?" say to him: "Word of God." . . . And you also return the question to him: "What is Christ called in the Scripture?" . . . He will answer you: "In my Scripture Christ is called Spirit and Word of God." And then you again tell him, "In your Scripture are the Spirit of God and the Word said to be uncreated or created?" [. . . If he says "created," then ask,] "Before God created the Word and the Spirit did he have neither Spirit nor Word?" And he will flee from you not having anything to answer.[55]

John's confidence in this outcome is based on what he sees to be an internal inconsistency in the Muslim's view of Jesus: if Jesus is the Word of God, then he must be eternal with God or God did not have *Logos* (logic, reason, etc.) before Jesus. To be sure, Muslims likely did not understand "Word" (*Kelimāt*, which has a narrower meaning in Arabic) in the cosmic sense that Christians did.[56] Nevertheless, while this form of argument likely convinced few Muslims, it was compelling to Christians who saw Muslims as borrowing Christian concepts and narratives about Christ without holding to the consistent conclusions of those concepts and narratives. Muslims hold to a form of adoptionism, and the orthodox have already settled that debate long ago—no need to entertain it again.

53. Another example is the Nag Hammadi text *Apocalypse of Adam*, a gnostic treatise on how the revelation originally given to Adam and his descendants was lost but rerevealed to later prophets.

54. For background on the way Romans saw the "Saracens" of Arabia, see the late fourth-century historian Ammianus Marcellinus, *Roman History* 14.4.

55. *Dialogue with a Saracen* (quoted in Daniel J. Sahas, *Icon and Logos: Sources in Eighth-Century Iconoclasm* [Toronto: University of Toronto Press, 1986], 149).

56. However, see Ayoub, *Muslim View of Christianity*, 114: "Or is there not a mystery far greater than we have been able to fathom for the last fourteen hundred years? The verses describing Jesus in the Qur'an are not without mystery." Yet Ayoub denies that Christ was born of God ontologically (especially as the product of a sexual act; see 115).

Another area in which Christians viewed Muslim Christology as inconsistent and thereby unpersuasive is in the question about worship, especially as it relates to Christ. Islam's critiques of Christianity in regard to veneration (the preferred Christian term) or idolatry (the occasional Muslim claim) fall in the following order, starting with the least in importance.

First, Christians venerate/idolize relics, such as the cross of Christ, and this is a distraction from worship of God, if not idolatrous fetishism.[57] In response, as seen in the previous chapter, Christians understood these relics as spiritual aids, not distractions.[58] What is more, Muslims themselves practice the same thing in their veneration of the Qur'an and in their ritual pilgrimage to the Ka'bah in Mecca.[59] Relics and the corresponding iconic understanding of communication (see chap. 9) are inevitable for people who believe in God's self-revelation.

Next, Christians idolize Mary, according to Muslims. Again, traditionally Christians respond by saying Islam's understanding of Mary is inconsistent if not altogether confused: Mary is not Moses and Aaron's sister, for one thing; and, more substantially, Christians do not worship Mary but honor/revere her because of her role in bearing Jesus.[60] Islam's own veneration of Mary is difficult to understand, if she is the mother of a mere prophet, for no other prophets' mothers are so venerated.

The third area seen as inconsistent in Muslim teaching about Christ is in the use of scriptures. This is a question of epistemology for the Christians: how do you know what you know about Christ? Muslims claim the Christian scriptures were tampered with by the Jews and Christians (a claim in any conspiracy theory), and yet they seem to use Christian scriptures when it helps their case. Heretics have been doing this for generations (see chaps. 1 and 3).[61]

57. Muslim views on this in fact vary widely. The cross itself was believed to be worshiped by Christians, and that was a central contention. Relics and other holy signs are highly valued by many Muslims.

58. E.g., *Pilgrimage of Egeria* 5.7.c.

59. E.g., Germanus, *Epistle to Thomas, Bishop of Claudiopolis* (cited in Hoyland, *Seeing Islam*, 105–6), "With respect to the Saracens, since they also seem to be among those who urge these charges [idolatry] against us, it will be quite enough for their shame and confusion to allege against them their invocation which even to this day they make in the wilderness to a lifeless stone, name that which is called *Chobar* [i.e., Ka'bah]."

60. See Germanus, *Homily* 195 (cited in Hoyland, *Seeing Islam*, 107), who, when celebrating Constantinople's successful thwarting of the Arab siege (718), says, "[Christians, unlike Muslims,] with the eyes of faith see Christ as God and therefore confess that it is truly the Theotokos who bore him." Yet Mary is often honored by Muslims.

61. See Anastasius of Sinai, *Viae dux* 7.2.113 (cited in Hoyland, *Seeing Islam*, 95): "What a good student of the Jewish, Greek and Arab [i.e., Muslim] teachers is this Severus [the monophysite], who accepts in part the Scriptures and rejects a part of them, as do the adherents of the Manichaeans [i.e., the gnostics]."

The final and most important area of critique is when Muslims denounce Christians for worshiping Christ, when God proclaimed long ago to Abraham, Moses, and every other prophet that people should worship God and God alone. Christians, however, believe that they are in fact upholding this commandment (e.g., Exod. 20:2–3) because—unless you are a Marcionite or an Ebionite—as a Christian you believe that the God who spoke to Abraham and Moses is the same God incarnate in Christ Jesus. Worship of Jesus is not a question about polytheism or idolatry; to Christians it is a question about incarnational and sacramental forms of divine presence.[62] Muslims are inconsistent, according to medieval Christian writers, because they are perfectly willing to accept God's divine presence through the Word preached in a mosque, so they should be willing to accept that God could (and did) fully manifest himself as the Word—not just on the lips of the imam—but completely, in the flesh (see chap. 3).

These points are not listed here as if they settle the matter, for Muslims have responses to each claim about inconsistency. Today, Christians and Muslims will want to reframe these accusations into questions in order to promote better understanding.[63] In the early days of Islam, however, the perceived inconsistency of Muslim Christology allowed Christians to reject Islam as just another heretical sect of Christianity.

The Gospel according to Islam

As with the heresies covered in previous chapters, Christians in general do not think of heretics as having anything to teach the orthodox. For most Christians this would prove especially true in this last example, where Islam entails an entirely new religion. It is worth listening, however, to see if the Muslim faith, born out of a context of incredible diversity, has anything to teach Christians, for example, about too much diversity.

Muhammad's aversion to idolatry and injustice inspired him to lead a reform. While Christianity is not to blame for the polytheism in Mecca, it is telling that worship of "Allah" (the Aramaic/Syriac, and now Arabic, word for God used by Christians in Arabia) was carried out in Mecca and other contexts side by side with pagan cults. If it can be taken as historically reliable, we

---

62. See Anastasius of Sinai, *Viae dux* 1.1.9 (cited in Hoyland, *Seeing Islam*, 94): "Thus when we wish to debate with the Arabs, we first anathematize whoever says two gods, or whoever says that God has carnally begotten a son, or whoever worships as god any created thing at all, in heaven or on earth."

63. See Rowan Williams, "What Is Christianity? A Lecture Given at the Islamic University of Islamabad, 23 November 2005," *ICMR* 19, no. 3 (2008): 325–32.

could look at the example of the icon of the virgin Mary on the Ka'bah. Some Christians (see chap. 9) found the existence of such an image anywhere to be too much of a capitulation to the idolatrous practices of the non-Christians. Others who might accept icons might still bristle at Mary's position among a veritable pantheon of deities.

While today one may wish to debate this in terms of evangelistic method and cultural engagement, here we note simply that in Arabia the wide diversity of Christian practice as well as religions writ large made it difficult to find the boundary between Christianity and other religions.

Alongside worship of the one true God known in Christ, many Christian churches had added such an array of shrines, celebrations of saints, and attention to heavenly figures that the line between Christianity and polytheism became increasingly blurred. Even the sophisticated formulation of the doctrine of the Trinity, with its emphasis on the three distinct persons within the Godhead, would often prove difficult for average Christians to understand as truly monotheistic.[64] In his recent discussion of Islam, Christian theologian Miroslav Volf states an appreciation for the Qur'an's allegedly antitrinitarian statements: "What the Qur'an denies about God as the Holy Trinity has been denied by every great teacher of the church in the past and ought to be denied by every orthodox Christian today. I reject the idea that Muslim monotheism is incompatible with the Christian doctrine of the Trinity."[65] In other words, the Qur'an is not denying what the orthodox Christians teach (there is one God), but what the heretics teach (God's modes of being are in fact different gods, a chain of being from God). Muhammad's insistence about strict monotheism would have been a welcomed message to many Christians.

Another important value in Islam that could have easily been eclipsed in Byzantine Christianity was the call for justice. The Roman and then Byzantine Empire had long been known to practice nepotism and cronyism, and the entire political system functioned as little more than a sanctioned system of bribery. While Christianity had long preached justice and charity, many voices like John Chrysostom found Constantinople in particular and the imperial economy in general corrupt. Muhammad's umma, or Muslim community, with its idyllic view of a society that provides for the needs of all its members, must have appealed to many followers of Jesus.

---

64. The classic example is Ablabius's question to Gregory of Nyssa, "Why not say 'three Gods'?," which Gregory incorporated into the title of his response: *On Not Three Gods* (fourth century).

65. Volf, *Allah*, 14. Cf. Nicholas of Cusa: "In the manner in which Arabs (Muslims) and Jews deny the Trinity, assuredly it ought to be denied by all" (cited by Volf, *Allah*, 135–36).

The good news of Jesus Christ according to Islam is that the one true God sent his Word into the Virgin's womb, and Mary's Son was born, performed miracles, and taught the eternal truth—that is, the same message shared by every true prophet: people should repent from their wickedness and turn to God. The whole of Jesus's earthly ministry points us to God.

So far, the gospel according to Islam is appealing, and yet one question remains. Does all of this mean that in Christ "the fullness of deity dwells bodily" (Col. 2:9)?[66] If not, then Christians by and large suspect that this Christology is reductionistic: Jesus is "only" a messenger (Qur'an 4:171).

The orthodox Christians insisted on a full confession of Christ's iconic demonstration of God: Jesus's self-sacrifice and God's raising him from the dead. Only this, it is argued, can adequately account for a good Creator: God who made our bodies will redeem even our bodies, and the God who providentially wills this to be also brings it about, not by asking another to act as a stand-in, but by entering into our midst and "pitching his tent among us" (John 1:14). For the orthodox Christian who confesses faith in the one true God, Jesus is Lord—Immanuel.

Recommended Bibliography

Berg, Herbert, ed. *Method and Theory in the Study of Islamic Origins*. Leiden: Brill, 2003.

Cameron, Averil. "Interfaith Relations in the First Islamic Century." *BRIIFS* 1, no. 2 (1999): 1–12.

Griffith, Sidney H. *The Church in the Shadow of the Mosque: Christians and Muslims in the World of Islam*. Princeton: Princeton University Press, 2007.

Hjärpe, Jan. "Jesus in Islam." In *Alternative Christs*, edited by Olav Hammer, 71–86. Cambridge: Cambridge University Press, 2009.

Leirvik, Oddbjorn. *Images of Jesus Christ in Islam*. 2nd ed. Edinburgh: Continuum, 2010.

Samir, Samir Khalil. *111 Questions on Islam: Interview Conducted by Giorgio Paolucci and Camille Eid*. Edited, translated, and revised by Wafik Nasry. Cotranslated by Claudia Castellani. San Francisco: Ignatius, 2002.

---

66. Cf. Ayoub, *Muslim View of Christianity*, 113, who affirms, "Jesus is himself a divine sign, one to be celebrated with joy, marvel, and faith," with reference to Qur'an 3:45, where Jesus is "the Word of God."

Conclusion

Heresy according to the Gospel

Consequently, a proportionate number of heresies, with the utmost emulation, seek Jesus. Now all these heresies have their own peculiar Jesus.

—Hippolytus

For there must be also heresies among you, that they which are approved may be made manifest among you.

—Paul (1 Cor. 11:19 KJV)

Will the real heretic please stand up? After ten chapters reviewing ten heresies, we have found things ranging from misunderstanding to malicious misrepresentation, not to mention misguided beliefs. In some cases the heretics were not heretics after all. In some cases the orthodox were not so orthodox. This brings us back to the contested definition of these terms mentioned in the introduction, and so we will conclude by readdressing these concepts, but now informed by the detailed knowledge of the various heresies.

Responding to Heresy

How should one respond to heresy? According to some, we should avoid all contact. In Revelation the Ephesians are lauded for not tolerating evildoers and for hating the works of the Nicolaitans (2:1–7). Allegedly, the apostle

245

John refused to be in the same building with the heretic Cerinthus.[1] (Or was it Ebion?[2]) Ignatius advises Christians to "be deaf" to heretics: "Cover up your ears in order to avoid receiving the things being sown by them."[3] Similarly, Hippolytus's advice is to mimic the epic acts of Ulysses: when the sirens' song would lead him to destruction, he smeared wax in his ears; Christians should do the same when the heretics start talking.[4] Perhaps you would have been better off not reading this book!

What if you don't know whether the person is heretical or not? The older definition of heresy as novel falsehood that deviated from the apostolic truth has been shown not to work. To be sure, novelty is suspect, so Gregory of Nazianzus can mock the Apollinarians for teaching "a wisdom hidden ever since the time of Christ."[5] On the other hand, Gregory himself holds to the Nicene *homoousios*, certainly a novel term and perhaps even a novel concept. Falsehood itself is also a tricky question, since earlier writers did not have the benefit of sustained and ecumenical thinking on the subject. For example, Origen confessed the Rule of Faith, even the part about the Holy Spirit—which is very brief. He then admitted that the apostles never specified whether the Spirit was another "Son" or whether God created the Spirit.[6] In Origen's defense, hardly anyone spoke clearly and exhaustively about the Holy Spirit in the first three centuries. Nevertheless, by *later* standards he has deviated from the *original* truth—yes, you read that correctly.

One creative definition for heresy from the early church is that heresy is stubbornness. Cyril decried Nestorius for this: "We marveled at the hardness of heart of the man. He did not repent nor weep at the things which he dared to say against the glory of Christ."[7] Of course, Nestorius held out hope that another council would redeem his legacy—in fact, he believed Chalcedon did exactly that by affirming Christ's two natures. For his part, Cyril is no exemplar of submissiveness, but to his credit he did listen to John of Antioch and sign the Formula of Reunion. Would Nestorius have relented and signed such a statement if given the chance? (Admittedly, a big "if.") While this definition is appealing, stubbornness itself cannot be the main demarcation of heresy. When the orthodox are stubborn, like Athanasius (nicknamed *Contra Mundum*), we call it tenacity and perseverance.

1. Irenaeus, *Against Heresies* 3.3.4.
2. Epiphanius, *Panarion* 30.24.5.
3. *Letter to the Trallians* 9.
4. *Refutation of All Heresies* 7.1.
5. *Letter* 102.
6. *On First Principles* pref.4.
7. *Letter* 23.2.

One more definition of heresy from the ancient church does offer a fruitful way to think about the subject: schism. This was the original definition, when Paul used the word. "Indeed, there have to be factions [*haireseis*] among you," Paul said (1 Cor. 11:19). The division may be due to false teaching, but it may be due to poor practices (as in Corinth). The point is that disunity and disruption are the heretical calling cards.

Cyprian famously championed this understanding of heresy. For him, any schismatic is a heretic. He can claim the moral high ground: "We have not withdrawn from them," he explained, "but they from us."[8] The earlier writer Irenaeus focused on the teachings of those who have "gnosis" ("falsely so-called" according to his title and 1 Tim. 6:20). Beyond the doctrinal concerns, however, Irenaeus also pointed out the schismatic and exclusionary tendency of his opponents. They are the ones who withdraw from other Christians and claim to have the secret knowledge. They "hold themselves aloof from the communion of the brethren."[9] More scholarly work is needed to assess the evidence, but it appears the various gnostic groups did see themselves as a withdrawn minority sect, or the remnant community, as they might say.[10]

Before jumping to conclusions, however, a caveat must be made about defining heresy as schism. This definition only begs the question, which is the right church and which is the false church? and who gets to decide? During the Arian controversy, many Nicene bishops were appointed to rival an already established bishop. Is this schism? Not if the already established bishop is a heretic, according to the circular argument at work in this thinking. Given the problems in this line of thinking, we need to reassess our understanding of heresy.

Reappraisal of Heresy

Since none of the rhetorical characteristics of heresy work, perhaps we can attempt to offer a more historical description of the concept, along with its counterpart, orthodoxy. By asking how to respond to heresy in the previous section we have tacitly acknowledged a fairly startling realization. *Orthodoxy is a response to heresy.* Conversely, *heresy is an attempt at orthodoxy.* Circular reasoning? Allow me to explain.

Few historians today would argue that Chalcedon explicitly intended to reconcile the Antiochene and Alexandrian schools. This is too simplistic a

---

8. *On the Unity of the Church* 12 (ANF 5:425).

9. *Against Heresies* 3.11.9.

10. Examples include *Gospel of Judas*; *Second Treatise of the Great Seth* 59–60; *Tripartite Tractate* 108–13.

historical narrative. We can, however, recognize Chalcedon's ability to incorporate the concerns of both traditions. A singular emphasis on Christ's oneness on the one hand or his two natures on the other results, perhaps not in complete heresy, but in a less-than-complete expression of the mystery of the incarnation. True Nestorianism and Eutychianism both fall short of orthodoxy. Even so, we can acknowledge that both Nestorius and Eutyches attempted to express orthodoxy. Their attempts were simply found to be inadequate. Therefore, we have to clarify our definition: heresy is an *inadequate* attempt at orthodoxy.

How can heresy come before orthodoxy? We are not saying heresy preceded the gospel. Heresy is an inadequate attempt to articulate the gospel. Heresy, then, is a truncated gospel. It is preaching "a different gospel—not that there is another gospel, but there are some who are confusing you and want to pervert the gospel of Christ" (Gal. 1:6–7), and so it must be anathematized (1:9) as heresy. Notice that Paul does not claim his opponents teach falsehood. They simply neglect the full expression of what Christ has done.[11]

Next, we can infer that orthodoxy is a response to heresy. From a historian's vantage point it is obvious that orthodoxy was not a prepackaged set of doctrines. This is not news, but it needs to be clarified. J. N. D. Kelly describes Christianity on the eve of Chalcedon in ways that could probably be applied to many other contexts: "The Church at this epoch was feeling its way towards a balanced Christology."[12] Many Christians would wish to exchange Kelly's "feeling its way" language, which sounds too much like unguided groping in the dark, for a more devout description: the Spirit leads the church into all truth (John 16:13). Nevertheless, whether one sees this as a quest or a guided tour, the attempt to express truth doctrinally, it must be admitted, was the practice of a pilgrim church, a people of "the Way" (Acts 24:14). The doctrinal formulations never were clearly articulated in a primal creed, catechism, or systematic theology by Jesus or his original followers. Instead, orthodoxy as doctrinal proposition is a response.

Even ancient writers admitted to this way of thinking about orthodoxy. In a mock dialogue between an orthodox (dyophysite) and a heretic (i.e., monophysite), the fifth-century writer Theodoret has the protagonist back the antagonist into a corner: the heretic has to change his preferred terminology. When the orthodox protagonist outs the heretic for the semantic flip-flop, we hear this admission from the heretic: "The struggle with our adversaries forces me to do this." This is where orthodox writers typically accuse the heretics

11. Cf. Rowan Williams, *On Christian Theology* (Oxford: Blackwell, 2000), 79–92.
12. *Early Christian Doctrines*, rev. ed. (San Francisco: HarperSanFrancisco, 1978), 333.

of novelty. However, going against the reader's expectation, Theodoret has the orthodox spokesperson agree on the necessity to change terminology: "What you say is true, for it is what we say, or rather what everyone says who has preserved the apostolic rule intact."[13] In other words, while the concepts may need to change in response to one's opponents, the aim is to be faithful to the original content.

Another example can be found in the ninth-century iconoclast controversy. Theodore the Studite places the orthodox (iconophile) and the heretic (icono-clast) in a similar dialogue. The heretic insists that iconophilism is not found in Scripture, and the orthodox—somewhat surprisingly—agrees:

> Many teachings which are not written in so many words, but have equal force with the written teachings, have been proclaimed by the holy fathers. It is not the inspired Scripture but the later fathers who made clear that the Son is con-substantial with the Father, that the Holy Spirit is God, that the Lord's mother is Theotokos, and other doctrines which are too many to list. If these doctrines are not confessed, the truth of our worship is denied. But these doctrines were confessed at the time when need summoned them for the suppression of heresies which were rising up against the truth.[14]

In other words, when the orthodox party speaks of "two natures," or calls Mary the "Mother of God," or uses new terms like *homoousios*, it does so knowing full well that such terminology is a change, a response, for such concepts are not explicit in Scripture. Nevertheless, in response to "adversaries" who "force" them to do this by misinterpreting Scripture, the orthodox party must disambiguate.[15]

Unfortunately, when the orthodox attempt to clarify, they do not always attain their goal. Many heretics were responding to heretics, as Nestorius was responding to Apollinaris (or at least Apollinarianism), who was himself responding to Arius (or Arianism). Thus we see the earlier definition of heresy as an inadequate attempt at orthodoxy, even if later heresies are less inadequate. Therefore, we need to nuance our definition to say, not only that orthodoxy is a response to heresy, but that orthodoxy is *sometimes an inadequate response* to heresy, just as heresy was an inadequate attempt at orthodoxy.

In addition to heretical responses to heretics, another clear instance of an unacceptable response (at least as judged today) is the use of force. The violent

13. Theodoret, *Eranistes* 2.
14. *Second Refutation of the Iconoclasts* 7.
15. I borrow the concept of disambiguation, now popular on Wikipedia, from Benjamin Haupt, "Irenaeus' Citations of Scripture: Intentional or Careless Alterations?" (paper presented at the Society of Biblical Literature International Meeting, St. Andrews, Scotland, July 10, 2013).

and oppressive version of orthodoxy, especially when enforced by the state, has been noted throughout this book. Even apart from the physical and the political violence, we today often cringe at the rhetorical violence found in the orthodox response to heresy. Of course, no one played nice when it came to ancient debate, so this is to be expected. Nevertheless, an uncharitable attitude seems to lessen the effectiveness of orthodoxy. Irenaeus, for example, insists that when it comes to reporting the gnostics' view about their goddess, "We do not misrepresent their opinions on these points."[16] So does he misrepresent them on other points? Probably. He probably caricatures them. That is, he shows that heretical views, *when taken to their logical extreme*, are untenable. Perhaps this is an act of love, as Augustine would argue, to alert the potential heretic to potential pitfalls.[17] If so, then the notion of orthodoxy as a reaction to heresy could be constructive.

There is an obvious objection here. This dynamic definition of heresy is moral and religious relativism. In this way of thinking, couldn't just about anything be declared to be either heresy or orthodoxy, since any interpretation can be made plausible? Or worse, won't those in power inevitably impose their interpretation on their victims and call it orthodoxy? In response, I offer two points. First, I am simply being honest. Arius, for example, did not oppose a predefined orthodoxy and deviate from it. Second, I am still insisting that there is such a thing as orthodoxy. I am not saying that orthodoxy is simply "constructed" (culturally or otherwise) or imposed (violently, politically, etc.). I am saying it is encountered. This is not a relativistic definition of orthodoxy (the power asserted by the winners); orthodoxy is eventually defined.

I say "eventually" both in chronological terms and in phenomenological terms. Orthodoxy is eventually discovered chronologically—through the process of disagreement, dissent, and debate. Orthodoxy is eventually discovered phenomenologically—in the encounter with Christ (the Event par excellence)—while the second act of theological discourse reflects upon this encounter. This second act, however, is a process, not a prepackaged set of propositions. Let me give an example.

The trinitarianism of Nicaea and Constantinople was not simply the result of social and political struggle ("history written by the winners"), and neither was it given to the church by Jesus himself during his earthly ministry ("the unadulterated apostolic tradition"). Instead of either extreme view, one can trace the baptismal formula (Matt. 28:19), the apostolic preaching (1 Cor.

---

16. *Against Heresies* 3.25.6.
17. See Augustine's explanation of why reductio ad absurdum is necessary (*On Christian Doctrine* 2.31).

12:4–6; 2 Cor. 13:13), and the early Christians' attempts to articulate this clearly in the Rule of Faith all as early expressions of the basic ingredients for the trinitarian doctrine of 381. Orthodoxy, while not previously explicit in form, certainly existed in substance. R. P. C. Hanson's famous study of the Arian controversy, entitled *The Search for the Christian Doctrine of God* (referenced in chap. 5), took its title from this fact: "the search" for orthodox doctrine is not a defense of previously stated doctrine, nor a complete fabrication, but a search for something that is real and waiting to be encountered and discovered.

Once we have shifted away from orthodoxy as consisting of abstract propositions, we can reclaim orthodoxy both as something that can be formally articulated and as something that precedes such articulations. Jesus Christ is Lord (1 Cor. 12:3). The Spirit of God, we believe, has always led the church in worshiping Christ, and thereby coming to know and glorify the Father. When someone articulates an inadequate explanation (i.e., heresy) of the Christian belief underlying this Christian practice, other Christians respond with a correct, but sometimes still not fully adequate, response (orthodoxy). This later orthodox reaction and orthodox doctrinal formula are not altogether different from the prior orthodox belief and orthodox practice. It is simply later, reactive, and propositional. Orthodoxy attempts to express, with more clarity, the same good news.

Historically, some would summarize this way of speaking as saying, "Heresy is the mother of orthodoxy." Theologically speaking, it would be better to say that heresy is the unpleasant midwife of orthodoxy. The church, theologically speaking, filled with the Holy Spirit, is the mother of orthodoxy. This once again presses the question, Which is the right church, and which is the false church? And who gets to decide? As a last attempt to answer this question, let us turn to the location of heresy.

Redistricting the Heretics

Paul tells the "church of God that is in Corinth" (1 Cor. 1:2) how there must be heresies "among you" (11:19). They are present, "for only so will it become clear who among you are genuine," but these factionalists are nonetheless present in and part of the body when it "[comes] together as church" (11:18). Heretics are in the church!

Notice, we are not trying to answer the question about the personal salvation of any given heretic. Jesus said, "Follow me" (Mark 1:17). Paul said, "If you confess with your lips that Jesus is Lord and believe in your heart that God raised him from the dead, you will be saved" (Rom. 10:9). God looks on the heart (1 Sam. 16:7), and it is not in our power to decide whether the heretics really mean it when they say they follow Jesus. We are trying to discern how to identify heresy and orthodoxy.

How seriously are we to take this idea that the factious members of the church are nevertheless members of the church? This seems self-defeating. Cyprian cited Paul's statement about heretics in the church, but then supplemented Paul's remark with a prophecy from John the Baptist: "Thus the faithful are approved, thus the perfidious are detected; thus even here, even before the day of judgment, the souls of the righteous and of the unrighteous are already divided, and the chaff is separated from the wheat" (*On the Unity of the Church* 10, citing Matt. 3:12/Luke 3:17). Has Cyprian rightly located the timing of this separation? Very similar imagery is used by Jesus himself when he speaks of a wheat field that was also sown with weeds (Matt. 13:24–30). The workers ask whether they should pull the weeds, but instead they are told to wait for "harvest time" (13:30), or else they will uproot some of the good with the bad. The point seems to be that Jesus will be the one to "separate" on his return (cf. Matt. 25:32).

Are heretics still "among" us? Are they in the church? The author read by Cyprian every day, Tertullian, seemed to tacitly admit this about Valentinian gnostics: "If however even *among God's people* there is a sect more akin to the Epicureans than to the Prophets . . ."[18] Did Tertullian really admit that the heretics are "among the people of God"? This is probably more of a verbal slip than a theological admission of Tertullian's personal opinion. Nevertheless, I suspect that Tertullian's misstatement has proverbially left open the church door for heretics. If they can be spoken of as within the category of "people of God" by none other than the relentless heretic-slayer, Tertullian of Carthage, then perhaps we all will need to account for the heretics in some way when thinking about theology and even ecclesiology. Is there ever an appropriate time to separate from heretics?

Often, we have found the heresies to be partially true, but one-sided: heretics have lost the opposite dialectic of their "truth." Along similar lines, Brian Daley reviews examples of absurdities in early Christianity, such as "pedantic rationalists" who so philosophically emphasize God's transcendence that Christ is not God, and "pious fanaticists" who so biblically emphasize the exalted Christ that Christ is not human. In a via media, Brian Daley finds a wiser approach:

18. *On the Resurrection of the Flesh* 2.1 (emphasis added). For Cyprian reading Tertullian, see Jerome, *On Illustrious Men* 53.

And there were clearly some extraordinary thinkers in the early centuries of theological reflection—Athanasius, the three great Cappadocian Fathers, and Maximus Confessor in the East, as well as Augustine in the West—who are more difficult to identify, precisely because they seem to have avoided both extremes and to have reached out for a carefully constructed theological and Christological equilibrium.[19]

Many in the early church claimed orthodoxy to be "a middle way."[20] To be sure, finding the middle is not easy because one does not always know where the alternative boundaries lie. It is at this point that we discover why we need the heretics: without the necessary "heresies among you" we would never explore and discover the boundaries. The heretics are a gift to the church.

Conversely, it is important to warn the heretics so that they do not actually cross any given boundary. If their teachings appear—when taken to their logical conclusion—to cross certain boundaries, they should be warned about this pitfall. Is this fair? Not always. As we said above on this point, orthodoxy is often an uncharitable response to heresy. What we need is both a generous orthodoxy, as G. K. Chesterton called it, and a humble heresy. If the heretic would admit the possibility of crossing or even approaching boundaries, then perhaps these dangerous edges could be explored in communion with the orthodox sisters and brothers, with everyone properly belayed.

Remembering that no ecumenical council truly could be claimed to be ecumenical until the next ecumenical council dubbed it so, we must simultaneously hold to and paradoxically pursue orthodoxy with great patience and discernment. Again, this is not to say there is no orthodoxy and no heresy, as if we never say "*Anathema sit!*" (Gal. 1:8). The issue is, *when* do we say it? John of Damascus wisely cautioned, "For the moment I hesitate to say, as the divine apostle said, 'Let him be anathema!,' for [the heretic] may receive correction."[21] The original Creed of Nicaea was revised so as to drop the anathemas against Arianism once the creed began to be used locally in liturgical settings. An anathema is ultimately the role of the whole church.

Ideally, the whole church is best expressed in a truly ecumenical council, but even without the luxury of this ideal the church itself—however expressed—is the proper speaker of the anathema. On the one hand, the heretics ignore such denunciations at their own peril, but on the other, the devout who wish

19. "'One Thing and Another': The Persons in God and the Person of Christ in Patristic Theology," *ProEccl* 15, no. 1 (2006): 43.
20. E.g., John of Damascus, *On the Divine Images* 2.3.
21. *On the Divine Images* 2.6.

to hold to orthodoxy can do so without a witch hunt to oust every heretic from every pew. There must be heretics among you!

I suggest here merely that our theological posture toward heresy will have to take into account our historical indebtedness to the heretic in our midst. Heresy is a diverse concept, and some heretics will remain "among us" while others will withdraw from us, while others still will eventually be separated by us. Whatever and wherever these "separated brethren" are (to use Vatican II's terminology), they are our "brothers and sisters" nonetheless.

Although this book has been about Christology, we have ended by finding ecclesiology as the next logical step. The last frontier. While that subject lies beyond the parameters of the current project, we do need to conclude with a statement about schism, since that demarcates the point of contact between heresy and ecclesiology. What constitutes schism? Almost immediately and almost unanimously, theological discussions answer this question with an ecclesiology from above, that is, defining the church first and foremost at the macrolevel (i.e., *the* church) rather than at the local level (i.e., *a* church).

The idea of one true church, from which the schismatic heretics deviated, assumes that there once was such a thing as a visibly united church. The historical records, however, indicate the opposite: the original Christian movement was exceptionally diverse, and it exploded onto the Mediterranean world. To be sure, these Christians had a sense of mystical union (John 17:11) and spiritual fellowship (2 Cor. 13:13) with each other, and they tried their darnedest to communicate with each other. Such communication, however, was difficult and expensive. When various communities did succeed in communicating with one another, embarrassing scenes often occurred.

In the mid-second century, Polycarp of Smyrna and Anicetus of Rome discovered that they celebrated Easter on different days.[22] They could not come to an agreement, but they parted ways in peace. A few generations later, the bishop of Rome, Stephen, disagreed with Cyprian of Carthage over the practice of rebaptizing heretics: Cyprian did; Stephen did not. In their correspondence (see the *Letters* of Cyprian) the disagreement quickly turned into a stalemate. Stephen even excommunicated Cyprian, and all of the churches in Africa in communion with him. Cyprian, however, solicited the support of some Eastern bishops, so Stephen excommunicated all of them as well.[23] Cyprian had earlier stated that as bishop, he had no jurisdiction to command another bishop, nor vice versa. How then could this intramural standoff be resolved? It never was. Both Stephen and Cyprian died as martyrs, and the

---

22. Eusebius, *Ecclesiastical History* 4.14.1; 5.23–25.
23. See Cyprian, *Letters* 74, 75, 87; Eusebius, *Ecclesiastical History* 7.3–5.

churches continued in fellowship with one another. The so-called schism
between the two was of no real consequence at the local level, nor could it be
resolved at the translocal until the personalities involved were off the scene.

Of course, not all church problems were or could have been resolved so
easily, as seen in the Arian controversy. The various parties in that controversy
all accused the other of heresy and schism. Winrich Löhr insists that such
fourth- and fifth-century "church parties as such were an entirely historical
phenomenon. They had no real parallel in the second- or third-century church.
Their very existence was closely tied to what one may call the institutional
framework of the fourth-century church."[24] Löhr goes on to deem such categories as "unity from above," and by "above" he means imperial enforcement. Without Constantinianism the ecclesiology from above is a fish out of
water—and rarely can a Christian emperor be found today.[25]

The point of this concluding chapter can be put in the form of a question:
What if we abandoned this "from above" bias that has dominated church
history for so long? Instead, we could see the early Christians in all their diversity and decentrality. Are "heretics" in "the church"? Now, we realize that
this has usually been asked at the universal level and then moves to the local.
If, instead, the question started with the local congregation and then only
secondarily moved to the issue of how congregations relate to one another,
the conversation would change dramatically.

Historically there is now no denying that there are heretics in the church
universal, and pastorally many questions remain as to what to do when there
are "heretics among you" (however understood). If this depiction of ecclesiology looks too much like "spiritual anarchism," to use Adolf von Harnack's
disparaging description of the earliest state of Christianity, at least we have
abandoned any lingering Constantinian coercion or Theodosian tyranny.[26] All
hope and pray for a middle way between these two extremes. I simply offer
ecclesiology from below as a means of correcting the overly biased ecclesiology from above, both in terms of our historical method and in terms of our
theological assumptions.

Heresy, according to the gospel, is to teach another Christ. As we ask
who actually does this, we are inevitably asking who gets to decide. If there

24. Löhr, "A Sense of Tradition: The Homoiousian Church Party," in *Arianism after Arius:
Essays on the Development of the Fourth-Century Trinitarian Conflicts*, ed. Michel R. Barnes
and Daniel H. Williams (Edinburgh: T&T Clark, 1993), 82.

25. See Kallistos Ware, "Patterns of Episcopacy in the Early Church and Today: An Orthodox View," in *Bishops, but What Kind? Reflections on Episcopacy*, ed. Peter Moore (London:
SPCK, 1982), 1–24.

26. Adolf von Harnack, *The Constitution and Law of the Church in the First Two Centuries*,
trans. F. L. Pogson (London: Williams & Norgate, 1910), 198.

must be heretics among us, we had better think through how to answer these questions. The first question is not are you in the right church—that is the *difficult* question. The *first* question is, are you "in the grace of Christ" (Gal. 1:6; cf. 3:27–28)? Do you profess the same gospel (Gal. 2:7)? If so, then we may extend "the right hand of fellowship" (Gal. 2:9). That is the gospel according to orthodoxy.

Select Bibliography

Ancient Sources: Collections

Scripture

Unless otherwise noted, the translation is that of the NRSV. The Hebrew, Greek, and Latin come from the following critical editions: K. Elliger and W. Rudolph, eds., *Biblia Hebraica Stuttgartensia*, 5th ed. (Stuttgart: Deutsche Bibelgesellschaft, 1997); Michael W. Holmes, ed., *Greek New Testament: SBL Edition* (Atlanta: Society of Biblical Literature, 2010); Alfred Rahlfs and Robert Hanhart, eds., *Septuaginta* (Stuttgart: Deutsche Bibelgesellschaft, 2006); Robert Weber and Roger Gryson, eds., *Biblia Sacra Vulgata*, 5th ed. (Stuttgart: Deutsche Bibelgesellschaft, 1987).

Apocryphal Gospels

See Bart D. Ehrman and Zlatko Pleše, *The Apocryphal Gospels: Texts and Translations* (Oxford: Oxford University Press, 2011). For gnostic gospels, see "Nag Hammadi" below.

Ecumenical Councils

ACTS

Critical editions of the Greek/Latin text are in E. Schwartz et al., eds., *Acta conciliorum oecumenicorum* (Berlin: de Gruyter, 1927–). English translations are in *NPNF²* vol. 14. The translation for Chalcedon (451) is from Richard Price and Michael Gaddis, *The Acts of the Council of Chalcedon*, 3 vols. (Liverpool: Liverpool University Press, 2007); and Constantinople (553) is from Richard Price, *The Acts of the Council of Constantinople of 553*, 2 vols. (Liverpool: Liverpool University Press, 2009).

CREEDS, DEFINITIONS, CANONS, ETC.

Greek/Latin text and English translations are in Norman P. Tanner, ed., *Decrees of the Ecumenical Councils*, 2 vols. (Washington, DC: Georgetown University Press, 1990), used here for conciliar declarations, such as creeds, definitions, and canons.

Also cf. Jaroslav Pelikan and Valerie Hotchkiss, eds., *Creeds and Confessions of Faith in the Christian Tradition*, 3 vols. (New Haven: Yale University Press, 2003).

Nag Hammadi

When citing the gnostic texts from Nag Hammadi, I have simplified my references so as to include only what functions as section numbers given on the pages of James M. Robinson, ed., *The Nag Hammadi Library in English* (Leiden: Brill, 1996). Technically, the codex and line numbers should be given, but readers interested in looking up the context of any quote provided can simply turn to the text in Robinson and find the given number.

The Qur'an

Arabic text and English translation: Ahmed Ali, *Al-Qur'ān: A Contemporary Translation* (Princeton: Princeton University Press, 2001).

The Theodosian Code

Latin text: P. Krüger and T. Mommsen, eds., *Codex Theodosianus*, 3 vols. (Berlin: Weidmann, 1923–26). English translation: Clyde Pharr, *The Theodosian Code and Novels, and the Sirmondian Constitutions* (New York: Greenwood, 1969).

Ancient Sources: Individual Works

Anonymous. *Acts of Paul and Thecla*. Latin text: Oscar von Gebhardt, ed., *Passio S. Theclae Virginis*, TUGAL 22 (Leipzig: J. C. Hinrichs, 1902). English translation: An older translation is available online at http://www.fordham.edu/halsall/basis /thecla.asp; and a recent edition and bibliography is found in James K. Elliot, ed. and trans., *The Apocryphal New Testament* (Oxford: Oxford University Press, 1993).

———. *A Poem against the Marcionites/Carmen adversus Marcionitas*. Latin text: Karla Pollmann, *Das Carmen adversus Marcionitas: Einleitung, Text, Übersetzung und Kommentar* (Göttingen: Vandenhoeck & Ruprecht, 1991). The English translation is that of Sydney Thelwall in *ANF* 4:142–65.

Ammianus Marcellinus. *Roman History*. Latin text and English translation: J. C. Rolfe, *Ammianus Marcellinus*, 3 vols., LCL (Cambridge, MA: Harvard University Press, 1940–52).

Apollinaris. Greek fragments: H. Lietzmann, *Apollinaris von Laodicea und seine Schule: Texte und Untersuchungen* (Tübingen: Mohr/Siebeck, 1904). English translation of *An Exposition of the Faith (Kata meros pistis)*: *ANF* 5:40–47 (as Pseudo-Gregory Thaumaturgus, *A Sectional Confession of Faith*).

Arius. *Thalia*. Greek text: William Bright, *The Historical Writings of St. Athanasius according to the Benedictine Text* (Oxford: Clarendon, 1881). English translation:

Rowan Williams, *Arius: Heresy and Tradition*, rev. ed. (Grand Rapids: Eerdmans, 2002).

Athanasius. Greek text: Unless otherwise noted, Athanasius texts are from the series *Athanasius Werke*, ed. H.-G. Opitz et al. (Berlin: de Gruyter, 1935–). Cf. PG 25–26. English translation: Unless otherwise noted, the translations of Athanasius's works come from *NPNF*[2] vol. 4.

(Pseudo-)Athanasius. *Against Apollinaris (De incarnatione contra Apollinarem)*. Greek text: PG 26. English translation: William Bright, trans., *Later Treatises of Athanasius, Archbishop of Alexandria* (London: James Parker, 1881).

Augustine. *City of God*. Latin text: E. Hoffman, CSEL 40. English translation: Marcus Dods, *Saint Augustine: The City of God* (New York: Modern Library, 1993).

———. *Confessions*. Latin text: P. Knöll, CSEL 33. English translation: Henry Chadwick, *Saint Augustine: Confessions* (Oxford: Oxford University Press, 1998).

———. *On Christian Doctrine*. Latin text: W. M. Green, CSEL 80. English translation: R. P. H. Green, *Saint Augustine: On Christian Teaching* (Oxford: Oxford University Press, 1999).

———. *On Heresies*. Latin text and English translation: Liguori G. Müller, *The "De Haeresibus" of Saint Augustine* (Washington, DC: Catholic University of America Press, 1956).

———. *On the Trinity*. Latin text: W. J. Mountain and Fr. Glorie in CCSL 50–50A. For English translations, see *NPNF*[1] 3:1–228; and Gareth B. Matthews and Stephen McKenna, *Augustine: On the Trinity Books 8–15* (Cambridge: Cambridge University Press, 2002).

(Pseudo-)Barnabas. *Epistle of Barnabas*. Greek text and English translation: Michael W. Holmes, *The Apostolic Fathers*, 3rd ed. (Grand Rapids: Baker Academic, 2007).

Basil of Caesarea. *Against Eunomius*. Greek text and French translation: B. Sesboüé, G.-M. de Durand, and L. Doutreleau in SC 299, 305. English translation: Mark DelCogliano and Andrew Radde-Gallwitz, *Basil of Caesarea: Against Eunomius* (Washington, DC: Catholic University of America Press, 2011).

———. *Letters*. Greek text and English translation: Roy J. Deferrari, *Saint Basil: The Letters*, 4 vols., LCL (Cambridge, MA: Harvard University Press, 1926).

Boethius. *Against Eutyches and Nestorius*. Latin text and English translation: H. F. Stewart, E. K. Rand, and S. J. Tester, *Boethius*, LCL (Cambridge, MA: Harvard University Press, 1973).

Clement of Alexandria. *Stromata (Miscellaneous Items)*. Greek text and French translation: M. Caster et al. in SC 30, 38, 278, 279, 428, 446, 463. English translation: *ANF* vol. 2. Note: The *ANF* 2 editors elected to leave book 3 of the *Stromata* untranslated. A free online translation is available at www.earlychristianwritings.com and is taken from John Ernest Leonard Oulton and Henry Chadwick, *Alexandrian Christianity: Selected Translations of Clement and Origen* (Philadelphia: Westminster, 1954).

(Pseudo-?) Clement of Rome. *1 Clement*. Greek text and English translation: Michael W. Holmes, *The Apostolic Fathers*, 3rd ed. (Grand Rapids: Baker Academic, 2007).

Cyprian. *Letters*. Latin text: R. Weber in CCSL 3B, 3C. English translation: G. W. Clarke, *The Letters of St. Cyprian of Carthage*, in ACW 43–44, 46–47.

———. *Treatises*. Latin text: CCSL 3, 3A, 3D, 3E. English translation: Roy J. Deferrari et al., *Saint Cyprian: Treatises* (New York: Fathers of the Church, 1958).

Cyril. *Against Nestorius*. English translation: P. E. Pusey, *S. Cyril of Alexandria: Five Tomes against Nestorius*, Library of the Fathers 47 (Oxford, 1881).

———. *Against Those Unwilling to Confess the Theotokos*. English translation: George Dion Dragas, *Against Those Who Are Unwilling to Confess That the Holy Virgin Is Theotokos* (Rollinsford, NH: Orthodox Research Institute, 2004).

———. *Letters*. English translation: John I. McEnerney, *St. Cyril of Alexandria: Letters 1–50* (Washington, DC: Catholic University of America Press, 2007); and McEnerney, *St. Cyril of Alexandria: Letters 51–110* (Washington, DC: Catholic University of America Press, 2007) (used here). Cf. Lionel R. Wickham, ed., *Cyril of Alexandria: Select Letters* (Oxford: Oxford University Press, 1983).

———. *On the Unity of Christ*. English translation: John Anthony McGuckin, *On the Unity of Christ* (Crestwood, NY: St. Vladimir's Seminary Press, 2000).

———. *Twelve Anathemas*. Greek text and English translation: Lionel R. Wickham, ed., *Cyril of Alexandria: Select Letters* (Oxford: Oxford University Press, 1983).

———. *Works*. Greek texts: E. Schwartz et al., *Acta Conciliorum Oecumenicorum* (Berlin: Leipzig, 1927–).

(Pseudo-)Dionysius the Areopagite. *Mystical Theology*. Greek text and Latin translation: Mihai Nasta, ed., *Thesaurus Pseudo-Dionysii Areopagitae: Textus Graecus cum translationibus Latinis* (Turnhout: Brepols, 1993). English translation: Colm Luibhéid and Paul Rorem, *Pseudo-Dionysius: The Complete Works* (New York: Paulist Press, 1987).

Egeria. *The Pilgrimage of Egeria*. Latin text and French translation: Hélène Pétré, Éthérie: *Journal de voyage*, SC 21. English translation: George E. Gingras, *Egeria: Diary of a Pilgrimage*, ACW 38.

Epiphanius of Salamis. *Panarion (The Medicine Chest)*. Greek text: Karl Holl et al., *Epiphanius*, GCS. English translation: Frank Williams, *The Panarion of Epiphanius of Salamis*, rev. ed., 2 vols. (Leiden: Brill, 2009, 2013).

Eusebius of Caesarea. *Ecclesiastical History*. Greek text and French translation: G. Bardy, *Eusèbe de Césarée: Histoire ecclésiastique*, SC 31, 41, 55, 73. English translation: NPNF[2] 1:81–387.

———. *Life of Constantine*. Greek text: F. Winkelmann, *Eusebius Werke*, GCS; cf. F. Winkelmann et al., *Eusèbe de Césarée: Vie de Constantin*, SC 559. English translation: NPNF[2] 1:481–559.

Evagrius. *Ecclesiastical History*. Greek text: Adelheid Hübner, *Evagrius Scholasticus Historia ecclesiastica*, 2 vols. (Turnhout: Brepols, 2007). English translation: Michael

Whitby, *The Ecclesiastical History of Evagrius Scholasticus* (Liverpool: Liverpool University Press, 2000).

Gelasius. *On the Two Natures*. Latin text: E. Schwartz, *Publizistische Sammlungen zum acacianischen Schisma* (Munich, 1934).

Gregory of Nazianzus. *Letters*. Greek text: Paul Gallay et al., *Grégoire de Nazianze: Discours*, SC 247, 250, 270, 284, 309, 318, 358, 384, 405. English translation: NPNF[2] 7:437–82.

———. *Orations*. Greek text: J. Bernardi et al., *Grégoire de Nazianze: Lettres théologiques*, SC 208. (Select) English translation: NPNF[2] 7:203–434; cf. Lionel Wickham, trans., *On God and Christ: The Five Theological Orations and Two Letters to Cledonius* (Crestwood, NY: St. Vladimir's Seminary Press, 2002).

Gregory of Nyssa. Greek text: F. Mueller et al., *Gregorii Nysseni Opera* (Leiden: Brill, 1958–). English translation: NPNF[2] vol. 5; book 2 of *Against Eunomius* is now available in Lenka Karfíková, Scot Douglass, Johannes Zachhuber, and Stuart George Hall, *Gregory of Nyssa, Contra Eunomium II: An English Version with Supporting Studies; Proceedings of the 10th International Colloquium on Gregory of Nyssa (Olomouc, September 15–18, 2004)* (Leiden: Brill, 2007); also see N. D. March, "A Translation of Saint Gregory of Nyssa's *Antirrheticus adversus Apolinarium*" (ThM thesis, Holy Cross Greek Orthodox School of Theology, 2013).

Hippolytus of Rome. *The Refutation of All Heresies/Philosophumena*. Greek text: Miroslav Marcovich, *Hippolytus: Refutatio omnium haeresium*, PTS 25 (Berlin: de Gruyter, 1986). English translation: ANF 5:9–153; cf. Francis Legge, *Philosophumena, or, The Refutation of All Heresies*, 2 vols. (London: Society for Promoting Christian Knowledge, 1921).

(Pseudo-?) Hippolytus of Rome. *Against Noetus*. Greek text and English translation: Robert Buttersworth, *Hippolytus of Rome: Contra Noetum* (London: Heythrop, 1977).

Ignatius. *Letters*. Greek text and English translation: Michael W. Holmes, *The Apostolic Fathers*, 3rd ed. (Grand Rapids: Baker Academic, 2007).

Irenaeus. *Against Heresies*. Greek text and French translation: A. Rousseau et al., *Saint Irénée de Lyon: Contre les Hérésies*, SC 263–64, 293–94, 210–11, 100.1–100.2, 152–53. English translation: ANF 1:315–567; cf. D. J. Unger and J. J. Dillon, *Irenaeus, Against the Heresies, Book 1*, ACW 55 (New York: Paulist Press, 1992); Dominic J. Unger, *St. Irenaeus of Lyons: Against the Heresies (Book 2)*, ACW 65 (New York: Newman Press, 2012); and Matthew C. Steenberg and Dominic J. Unger, *St. Irenaeus of Lyons: Against the Heresies (Book 3)*, ACW 64 (New York: Paulist Press, 2012).

Jerome. *On Illustrious Men*. Latin text and Italian translation: Aldo Ceresa-Gastaldo, *De viris illustribus*, Biblioteca patristica 12 (Firenze Nardini Editore, Centro internazionale del libro, 1988). English translation: Thomas P. Halton, *Saint Jerome: On Illustrious Men*, FC (Washington, DC: Catholic University of America Press, 2000).

John Cassian. *On the Incarnation of the Lord*. Latin text: M. Petschenig, CSEL 13. English translation: *NPNF²* 11:551–621.

John of Damascus. *Dialogue with a Saracen*. Greek text and English translation: Daniel J. Sahas, *John of Damascus on Islam: The "Heresy of the Ishmaelites"* (Leiden: Brill, 1972).

———. *On Heresies*. Greek text: Migne, PG 95. English translation: Frederic H. Chase Jr., *Saint John of Damascus: Writings*, FC 37.

———. *On the Divine Images*. Greek text: Migne, PG 95. English translation: Andrew Louth, *St. John of Damascus: Three Treatises on the Divine Images* (Crestwood, NY: St. Vladimir's Seminary Press, 2003).

———. *On the Orthodox Faith*. Greek text: Migne, PG 95. English translation: Frederic H. Chase Jr., *Saint John of Damascus: Writings*, FC 37.

(Pseudo-)John of Ephesus. *Life of James*. Syriac text and English translation: E. W. Brooks, ed. and trans., PO 19:228–68 [citations refer to the page number in Brooks].

John Rufus. *Life of Peter the Iberian*. Syriac text and English translation: Cornelia B. Horn and Robert R. Phenix Jr., *John Rufus: The "Lives" of Peter the Iberian, Theodosius of Jerusalem, and the Monk Romanus* (Atlanta: Society of Biblical Literature, 2008).

Justin Martyr. *1 and 2 Apology*. Greek text: Charles Munier, *Apologie pour les chrétiens*, SC 507. English translation: Denis Minns and P. M. Parvis, *Justin, Philosopher and Martyr: Apologies* (Oxford: Oxford University Press, 2009).

———. *Dialogue with Trypho*. Greek text and French translation: Philippe Bobichon, *Justin Martyr, Dialogue avec Tryphon* (Fribourg: Academic Press Fribourg, 2003). English translation: Michael Slusser, Thomas B. Falls, and Thomas P. Halton, *St. Justin Martyr: Dialogue with Trypho* (Washington, DC: Catholic University of America Press, 2003).

Lactantius. *On the Death of the Persecutors*. Greek text and French translation: J. Moreau, *Lactance: De la mort des persécuteurs*, SC 39. English translation: J. L. Creed, *Lactantius, De mortibus persecutorum* (Oxford: Clarendon, 1984).

Leo the Great. *Letters*. Latin text: O. Günther, CSEL 35.1, 35.2. English translation: *NPNF²* 12:1–114; cf. E. Hunt, *St. Leo the Great: Letters*, FC 34.

———. *Tome*. Latin text and English translation: Norman P. Tanner, ed., *Decrees of the Ecumenical Councils*, 2 vols. (Washington, DC: Georgetown University Press, 1990), 1:77–82.

Maximus the Confessor. *Dialogue with Pyrrhus*. Greek: M. Doucet, *La dispute de Maxime le confesseur avec Pyrrhus* (Montreal: Université de Montréal, Institut d'Etudes Mediévales, 1972). English translation: Joseph P. Farrell, *The Disputation with Pyrrhus of Our Father among the Saints, Maximus the Confessor* (South Canaan, PA: St. Tikhon's Seminary Press, 2001).

Nestorius. *Bazaar of Heracleides*. English translation (from the Syriac text): Godfrey Rolles Driver and Leonard Hodgson, *The Bazaar of Heracleides* (Oxford: Clarendon, 1925).

————. *Fragments*. Greek text: Friedrich Loofs, *Nestoriana: Die Fragmente des Nestorius* (Halle: Niemeyer, 1905).

————. *Sermons*. English translation: Richard A. Norris Jr., *The Christological Controversy* (Philadelphia: Fortress, 1980).

Nicephorus. *Short History*. Greek text and English translation: Cyril Mango, *Nikephoros Patriarch of Constantinople: Short History* (Washington, DC: Dumbarton Oaks, 1990).

Novatian. *On the Trinity*. Latin text and German translation: H. Weyer, *Novatianus: De Trinitate/Über den dreifaltigen Gott* (Darmstadt: Wissenschaftliche Buchgesellschaft, 1962). English translation: Russell J. DeSimone, *Novatian*, FC 67.

Origen. *Against Celsus*. Greek text: M. Borret, *Origène: Contre Celse*, SC 132, 136, 147, 150, 227. English translation: Henry Chadwick, *Origen: Contra Celsum* (Cambridge: Cambridge University Press, 1953).

————. *Dialogue with Heraclides*. Greek: Jean Scherer, *Entretien d'Origène avec Heraclides*, SC 67. English translation: Robert J. Daly, *Origen*, ACW 54.

————. *On First Principles*. Greek/Latin text: H. Crouzel and Manlio Simonetti, *Origène: Traité des principes*, SC 252, 253, 268, 269, 312. English translation: G. W. Butterworth, trans., *Origen: On First Principles* (New York: Harper & Row, 1966).

Socrates. *Ecclesiastical History*. Greek text: G. C. Hansen, *Socrate de Constantinople: Histoire ecclésiastique*, SC 477, 493, 505, 506. English translation: NPNF[2] 2:1–178.

Sophronius. *Synodical Letter*. Greek text and English translation: Pauline Allen, *Sophronius of Jerusalem and Seventh-Century Heresy* (Oxford: Oxford University Press, 2009), 66–157.

Sozomen. *Ecclesiastical History*. Greek text: J. Bidez et al., *Histoire ecclésiastique*, SC 306, 418, 495, 516. English translation: NPNF[2] 2:239–427.

Tertullian. *Against Praxeas*. Latin text and English translation: Ernest Evans, *Q.S.Fl. Tertullianus, Treatise against Praxeas* (London: SPCK, 1948).

————. *On Fasting*. Latin text: Augusti Reifferscheid and Georgii Wissowa, CSEL 20 (1890). English translation: ANF 4:102–14.

————. *On Modesty*. Latin text and French translation: Charles Munier, SC 394. English translation: ANF 4:74–101 (used here); and W. P. Le Saint, ACW 28.

————. *On the Pallium*. Latin text and English translation: V. Hunink, *Tertullian: De pallio* (Amsterdam: J. C. Gieben, 2005).

————. *On the Resurrection of the Flesh*. Latin text and English translation: Ernest Evans, *Tertullian's Treatise on the Resurrection* (London: SPCK, 1960).

————. *Prescript against Heretics*. Latin text: A. Kroymann, CSEL 70. English translation: ANF 3:243–65.

(Pseudo-)Tertullian. *Against All Heresies*. Latin text: A. Kroymann, CSEL 70. English translation: ANF 3:649–54.

Theodore the Studite. *First, Second, and Third Refutation of the Iconoclasts*. Greek text: PG 99. English translation: Catherine P. Roth, *St. Theodore the Studite: On the Holy Icons* (Crestwood, NY: St. Vladimir's Seminary Press, 1981).

Theodoret of Cyrrhus. *A Compendium of Heretical Mythification*. English text (selections): Istvan Pasztori-Kupan, ed. and trans., *Theodoret of Cyrus* (London: Routledge, 2006), 198–220.

———. *Ecclesiastical History*. Greek text: A. Martin and P. Canivet, *Théodoret de Cyr: Histoire ecclésiastique*, SC 501, 530. English translation: NPNF² 3:33–159.

———. *Eranistes*. Greek text: Gérard H. Ettlinger, *Theodoret of Cyrus: Eranistes* (Oxford: Clarendon, 1975). English translation: Gérard H. Ettlinger, *Theodoret of Cyrus: Eranistes* (Washington, DC: Catholic University of America Press, 2003).

———. *Letters*. Greek text: Yvan Azéma, *Théodoret de Cyr: Correspondance*, SC 40, 98, 111. English translation: NPNF² 3:250–348.

Theophanes. *The Chronicle*. Greek text: Carl de Boor, *Theophanis Chronographia* (Hildesheim: G. Olms, 1963). English translation: Cyril A. Mango, Roger Scott, and Geoffrey Greatrex, *The Chronicle of Theophanes Confessor: Byzantine and Near Eastern History, AD 284–813* (Oxford: Clarendon, 1997); the citations will refer to year as calculated "CE."

(Pseudo-)Thomas. *Infancy Gospel of Thomas*. Text and English translation: April D. De-Conick, *The Original Gospel of Thomas in Translation* (London: T&T Clark, 2006).

(Pseudo-)Zachariah Rhetor. The original Greek is lost, but a Syriac abbreviated version has now been translated into English: Geoffrey Greatre et al., *The Chronicle of Pseudo-Zachariah Rhetor: Church and War in Late Antiquity* (Liverpool: Liverpool University Press, 2011).

Modern Sources

Abramowski, Louise, and Alan E. Goodman, eds. and trans. *A Nestorian Collection of Christological Texts*. 2 vols. Cambridge: Cambridge University Press, 1972.

Aland, Barbara. "Marcion-Marcionites-Marcionism." In *Encyclopedia of the Early Church*, edited by Angelo Di Berardino, 1:523–24. Oxford: Oxford University Press, 1992.

Alemezian, N. "The Oriental Orthodox Family of Churches in Ecumenical Dialogue." *ER* 61 (2009): 315–27.

Anatolios, Khaled. *Athanasius*. New York: Routledge, 2004.

———. *Athanasius: The Coherence of His Thought*. New York: Routledge, 2005.

Arendt, Hannah. *Love and Saint Augustine*. Edited by Joanna Vecchiarelli Scott and Judith Chelius Stark. Chicago: University of Chicago Press, 1996.

Armstrong, Karen. *A History of God: From Abraham to the Present; The 4000-Year Quest for God*. London: Heinemann, 1993.

———. *Islam: A Short History*. New York: Modern Library, 2002.

Augustijn, Cornelis. *Erasmus: His Life, Works, and Influence.* Toronto: University of Toronto Press, 1991.

Ayoub, Mahmoud. *A Muslim View of Christianity: Essays on Dialogue.* Edited by Irfan A. Omar. Maryknoll, NY: Orbis, 2007.

Ayres, Lewis. *Nicaea and Its Legacy: An Approach to Fourth-Century Trinitarian Theology.* Oxford: Oxford University Press, 2004.

Barber, Charles. *Figure and Likeness: On the Limits of Representation in Byzantine Iconoclasm.* Princeton: Princeton University Press, 2002.

Barnes, Timothy David. "The Exile and Recalls of Arius." *JTS* 60 (2009): 109–29.

———. *Tertullian: A Historical and Literary Study.* Oxford: Clarendon Press, 1971.

Barth, Karl. *Evangelical Theology: An Introduction.* Translated by Grover Foley. New York: Holt, Rinehart and Winston, 1963.

Bates, W. H. "Background of Apollinaris's Eucharistic Teaching." *JEH* 12, no. 2 (1961): 139–54.

Bathrellos, Demetrios. *The Byzantine Christ: Person, Nature, and Will in the Christology of Saint Maximus the Confessor.* Oxford: Oxford University Press, 2005.

Bauckham, Richard. *Jesus and the Eyewitnesses: The Gospels as Eyewitness Testimony.* Grand Rapids: Eerdmans, 2006.

———. "The Origin of the Ebionites." In *The Image of the Judaeo-Christians in Ancient Jewish and Christian Literature,* edited by P. J. Tomson and D. Lambers-Petry, 162–81. WUNT 158. Tübingen: Mohr Siebeck, 2003.

Bauer, Walter. *Orthodoxy and Heresy in Earliest Christianity.* Edited by Robert A. Kraft and Gerhard Kroedel. Philadelphia: Fortress, 1979.

Baum, Wilhelm, and Dietmar W. Winkler. *The Church of the East: A Concise History.* London: Routledge, 2010.

Beeley, Christopher A. "Cyril of Alexandria and Gregory Nazianzen: Tradition and Complexity in Patristic Christology." *JECS* 17, no. 3 (2009): 381–419.

———. "The Early Christological Controversy: Apollinarius, Diodore, and Gregory Nazianzen." *VC* 65, no. 4 (2011): 376–407.

———. *The Unity of Christ: Continuity and Conflict in Patristic Tradition.* New Haven: Yale University Press, 2012.

Behr, John. *The Case against Diodore and Theodore: Texts and Their Contexts.* Oxford: Oxford University Press, 2011.

———. *The Way to Nicaea.* Vol. 1 of *Formation of Christian Theology.* Crestwood, NY: St. Vladimir's Seminary Press, 2001.

Belcher-Hamilton, Lisa. "The Gospel according to Fred: A Visit with Mr. Rogers." *The Christian Century,* April 13, 1994.

Bennington, Geoffrey, and Jacques Derrida. *Jacques Derrida.* Translated by G. Bennington. Chicago: University of Chicago Press, 1993.

Berg, Herbert, ed. *Method and Theory in the Study of Islamic Origins*. Leiden: Brill, 2003.

Berkey, Jonathan Porter. *The Formation of Islam: Religion and Society in the Near East, 600–1800*. Cambridge: Cambridge University Press, 2003.

Besançon, Alain. *The Forbidden Image: An Intellectual History of Iconoclasm*. Chicago: University of Chicago Press, 2000.

Bethune-Baker, J. F. *Nestorius and His Teaching: A Fresh Examination of the Evidence*. Cambridge: Cambridge University Press, 1908.

Bevan, George A., and Patrick T. R. Gray. "The Trial of Eutyches: A New Interpretation." *ByzZ* 101 (2008): 617–58.

Blois, François de. "Naṣrānī (Ναζωραῖος) and ḥanīf (ἐθνικός): Studies on the Religious Vocabulary of Christianity and of Islam." *BSOAS* 65, no. 1 (2002): 1–30.

Blowers, Paul M. "Maximus the Confessor and John of Damascus on Gnomic Will (*gnōmē*) in Christ: Clarity and Ambiguity." *USQR* 63, nos. 3–4 (2012): 44–50.

Boyarin, Daniel. *Border Lines: The Partition of Judaeo-Christianity*. Philadelphia: University of Pennsylvania Press, 2004.

———. *The Jewish Gospels: The Story of the Jewish Christ*. New York: New Press, 2012.

Braaten, Carl E. "Modern Interpretations of Nestorius." *CH* 32 (1963): 251–67.

Brakke, David. *The Gnostics: Myth, Ritual, and Diversity in Early Christianity*. Cambridge, MA: Harvard University Press, 2010.

Bremmer, Jan N. "Iconoclast, Iconoclastic, and Iconoclasm: Notes toward a Genealogy." *CHRC* 88, no. 1 (2008): 1–17.

Brennecke, Hanns Christof. "Die letzten Jahre des Arius." In *Von Arius zum Athanasianum*, ed. Annette von Stockhausen and Hanns Christof Brennecke, 63–83. Berlin: de Gruyter, 2010.

Brent, Allen. *Hippolytus and the Roman Church in the Third Century*. Leiden: Brill, 1995.

Brown, Harold O. J. *Heresies: The Image of Christ in the Mirror of Heresy and Orthodoxy from the Apostles to the Present*. New York: Doubleday, 1984.

Brubaker, Leslie, and John Haldon. *Byzantium in the Iconoclast Era (ca. 680–850): A History*. Cambridge: Cambridge University Press, 2008.

———. *Byzantium in the Iconoclast Era (ca. 680–850): The Sources*. Aldershot, UK: Ashgate, 2001.

Bryer, Anthony, and Judith Herrin, eds. *Iconoclasm: Papers Given at the Ninth Spring Symposium of Byzantine Studies, University of Birmingham, March 1975*. Birmingham, UK: Centre for Byzantine Studies, University of Birmingham, 1977.

Burrus, Virginia. *The Making of a Heretic: Gender, Authority, and the Priscillianist Controversy*. Berkeley: University of California Press, 1995.

———. "Rhetorical Stereotypes in the Portrait of Paul of Samosata." *VC* 43, no. 3 (1989): 215–25.

Butler, Michael. "Neo-Arianism: Its Antecedents and Tenets." *SVTQ* 36, no. 4 (1992): 355–71.

Cameron, Averil. "Interfaith Relations in the First Islamic Century." *BRIIFS* 1, no. 2 (1999): 1–12.

———. "The Violence of Orthodoxy." In *Heresy and Identity in Late Antiquity*, edited by Eduard Iricinschi and Holger M. Zellentin, 102–14. Tübingen: Mohr Siebeck, 2008.

Caputo, John D. *On Religion*. London: Routledge, 2001.

———. *The Prayers and Tears of Jacques Derrida: Religion without Religion*. Bloomington: Indiana University Press, 1997.

Cerrato, J. A. *Hippolytus between East and West: The Commentaries and the Provenance of the Corpus*. New York: Oxford University Press, 2002.

Ceulemans, Reinhart. "Apollinaris of Laodicea in the Catenae as a Source of Hexaplaric Readings." *ZAC* 15, no. 3 (2011): 431–49.

Chadwick, Henry. *The Church in Ancient Society: From Galilee to Gregory the Great*. Oxford: Oxford University Press, 2001.

Chestnut, Roberta C. "Two Prosopa in Nestorius' *Bazaar of Heracleides*." *JTS* 29, no. 2 (1978): 398–409.

Clark, Elizabeth A. "Foucault, the Fathers and Sex." *JAAR* 56, no. 4 (1988): 619–41.

———. *Founding the Fathers: Early Church History and Protestant Professors in Nineteenth-Century America*. Philadelphia: University of Pennsylvania Press, 2011.

———. *The Origenist Controversy: The Cultural Construction of an Early Christian Debate*. Princeton: Princeton University Press, 1992.

Clayton, Paul B., Jr. *The Christology of Theodoret of Cyrus: Antiochene Christology from the Council of Ephesus (431) to the Council of Chalcedon (451)*. Oxford: Oxford University Press, 2007.

Collins, Paul M. *Trinitarian Theology, West and East: Karl Barth, the Cappadocian Fathers, and John Zizioulas*. Oxford: Oxford University Press, 2001.

Crone, P., and M. Cook. *Hagarism: The Making of the Islamic World*. Cambridge: Cambridge University Press, 1977.

Daley, Brian E. "Christ and Christologies." In *The Oxford Handbook of Early Christian Studies*, edited by Susan Ashbrook Harvey and David G. Hunter, 886–905. Oxford: Oxford University Press, 2008.

———. "'Heavenly Man' and 'Eternal Christ': Apollinarius and Gregory of Nyssa on the Personal Identity of the Savior." *JECS* 10, no. 4 (2002): 469–88.

———. "'One Thing and Another': The Persons in God and the Person of Christ in Patristic Theology." *ProEccl* 15, no. 1 (2006): 17–46.

Damian, Theodor. *Theological and Spiritual Dimensions of Icons according to St. Theodore of Studion*. Lewiston, NY: Edwin Mellen, 2002.

Dehandschutter, Boudewijn. "Heresy and the Early Christian Notion of Tradition." In *Heretics and Heresies in the Ancient Church and in Eastern Christianity*, edited by Joseph Verheyden and Herman Teule, 7–21. Leuven: Peeters, 2011.

DelCogliano, Mark. "Basil of Caesarea on Proverbs 8.22 and the Sources of Pro-Nicene Theology." *JTS* 59, no. 1 (2008): 183–90.

———. "The Eusebian Alliance: The Case of Theodotus of Laodicea." *ZAC* 12, no. 2 (2008): 250–66.

DelCogliano, Mark, and Andrew Radde-Gallwitz, eds. and trans. *St. Basil of Caesarea: Against Eunomius*. Washington, DC: Catholic University of America Press, 2011.

Denny, Christopher. "Iconoclasm, Byzantine and Postmodern: Implications for Contemporary Theological Anthropology." *Horizons* 36, no. 2 (2009): 187–214.

Desjardins, Michel. "Rethinking the Study of Gnosticism." *R&T* 12 (2005): 370–84.

Dickens, Mark. "The Church of the East: The Rest of the Story." *FH* 32, no. 2 (2000): 107–25.

Donner, Fred M. "The Historian, the Believer, and the Qur'an." In *New Perspectives on the Qur'an: The Qur'an in Its Historical Context 2*, ed. Gabriel Said Reynolds, 25–37. London: Routledge, 2011.

———. *Muhammad and the Believers: At the Origins of Islam*. Cambridge, MA: Harvard University Press, 2010.

———. "The Qur'an in Recent Scholarship: Challenges and Desiderata." In *The Qur'an in Its Historical Context*, ed. Gabriel Said Reynolds, 29–50. London: Routledge, 2008.

Dunderberg, Ismo. *Beyond Gnosticism: Myth, Lifestyle, and Society in the School of Valentinus*. New York: Columbia University Press, 2008.

Dunn, James D. G. *Jesus Remembered*. Grand Rapids: Eerdmans, 2003.

———. *Unity and Diversity in the New Testament: An Inquiry into the Character of Earliest Christianity*. Philadelphia: Westminster, 1977.

Dünzl, Franz. *A Brief History of the Doctrine of the Trinity in the Early Church*. Translated by John Bowden. London: T&T Clark, 2007.

Edwards, Mark. *Catholicity and Heresy in the Early Church*. Farnham, UK: Ashgate, 2009.

Ehrman, Bart D., and Zlatko Pleše. *The Apocryphal Gospels: Texts and Translations*. Oxford: Oxford University Press, 2011.

Elowsky, Joel C., ed. *John 1–10*. ACCS. Downers Grove, IL: InterVarsity, 2006.

Fairbairn, Donald M. "Allies or Mere Friends? John of Antioch and Nestorius in the Christological Controversy." *JEH* 58, no. 3 (2007): 383–99.

Ferreiro, Alberto. *Simon Magus in Patristic, Medieval, and Early Modern Traditions*. Leiden: Brill, 2005.

Fine, Steven. *Art and Judaism in the Greco-Roman World: Toward a New Jewish Archaeology.* Cambridge: Cambridge University Press, 2005.

Finney, Paul Corby. *The Invisible God: The Earliest Christians on Art.* Oxford: Oxford University Press, 1997.

Foster, Paul. "Marcion: His Life, Works, Beliefs, and Impact." *ExpTim* 121, no. 6 (2010): 269–80.

Fox, Kenneth A. "The Nicolaitans, Nicolaus, and the Early Church." *SR* 23, no. 4 (1994): 485–96.

Franzmann, Majella. "A Complete History of Early Christianity: Taking the 'Heretics' Seriously." *JRH* 29, no. 2 (2005): 117–28.

Freeman, Charles. *A.D. 381: Heretics, Pagans, and the Dawn of the Monotheistic State.* Woodstock, NY: Overlook Press, 2009.

Frei, Hans. *The Eclipse of Biblical Narrative.* New Haven: Yale University Press, 1974.

Frend, W. H. C. "Marcion." *ExpTim* 80, no. 11 (1969): 328–32.

———. *The Rise of the Monophysite Movement: Chapters in the History of the Church in the Fifth and Sixth Centuries.* Cambridge: Cambridge University Press, 1972.

Gager, John G. *The Origins of Anti-Semitism: Attitudes toward Judaism in Pagan and Christian Antiquity.* Oxford: Oxford University Press, 1983.

Gavrilyuk, Paul L. *The Suffering of the Impassible God: The Dialectics of Patristic Thought.* Oxford: Oxford University Press, 2004.

———. "*Theopatheia*: Nestorius's Main Charge against Cyril of Alexandria." *SJT* 56, no. 2 (2003): 190–207.

Gellner, David N. "Religion, Politics, and Ritual: Remarks on Geertz and Bloch." *SocAnth* 7, no. 2 (1999): 135–53.

Gemeinhardt, Peter. "Apollinaris of Laodicea: A Neglected Link of Trinitarian Theology between East and West?" *ZAC* 10, no. 2 (2006): 286–301.

Goldstein, Ronnie, and Gedaliahu A. G. Stroumsa. "The Greek and Jewish Origins of Docetism: A New Proposal." *ZAC* 10, no. 3 (2006): 423–41.

Grabar, Oleg. "Islam and Iconoclasm." In *Iconoclasm: Papers Given at the Ninth Spring Symposium of Byzantine Studies, University of Birmingham, March 1975,* edited by Anthony Bryer and Judith Herrin, 45–52. Birmingham, UK: Centre for Byzantine Studies, University of Birmingham, 1977.

Grant, Robert M. *Gnosticism: A Source Book of Heretical Writings from the Early Christian Period.* New York: Harper, 1961.

Graumann, Thomas. "'Reading' the First Council of Ephesus (431)." In *Chalcedon in Context: Church Councils, 400–700,* edited by Richard Price and Mary Whitby, 27–44. Liverpool: Liverpool University Press, 2009.

Green, Bernard. *The Soteriology of Leo the Great.* Oxford: Oxford University Press, 2008.

Greer, Rowan A. "The Man from Heaven: Paul's Last Adam and Apollinaris' Christ." In *Paul and the Legacies of Paul*, edited by William S. Babcock, 165–82. Dallas: Southern Methodist University Press, 1990.

Gregory, Andrew. "Hindrance or Help: Does the Modern Category of 'Jewish-Christian Gospel' Distort Our Understanding of the Texts to Which It Refers?" *JSNT* 28, no. 4 (2006): 387–413.

Griffith, Sidney H. *The Church in the Shadow of the Mosque: Christians and Muslims in the World of Islam*. Princeton: Princeton University Press, 2007.

Griggs, C. Wilfred. *Early Egyptian Christianity: From Its Origins to 451 CE*. Leiden: Brill, 2000.

Grillmeier, Aloys. *Christ in Christian Tradition*. Vol. 1, *From the Apostolic Age to Chalcedon (451)*. Translated by J. S. Bowden. London: Mowbray, 1965.

———. *Christ in Christian Tradition*. Vol. 2, *From the Council of Chalcedon to Gregory the Great (590–604)*. Translated by Pauline Allen and John Cawte. London: Mowbray, 1965.

Gunton, Colin. "And in One Lord Jesus Christ . . . Begotten, Not Made." In *Nicene Christianity: The Future for a New Ecumenism*, edited by Christopher R. Seitz, 35–48. Grand Rapids: Brazos, 2001.

Gwynn, David M. *Athanasius of Alexandria: Bishop, Theologian, Ascetic, Father*. Oxford: Oxford University Press, 2012.

———. *The Eusebians: The Polemic of Athanasius of Alexandria and the Construction of the "Arian Controversy."* Oxford: Oxford University Press, 2006.

Häkkinen, Sakari. "Ebionites." In *A Companion to Second-Century Christian "Heretics,"* edited by Antti Marjanen and Petri Luomanen, 247–78. Leiden: Brill, 2005.

Hanson, R. P. C. *The Search for the Christian Doctrine of God: The Arian Controversy, 318–381*. Grand Rapids: Baker Academic, 2005.

Harnack, Adolf von. *The Constitution and Law of the Church in the First Two Centuries*. Translated by F. L. Pogson. London: Williams & Norgate, 1910.

———. *History of Dogma*. Translated by Neil Buchanan. 7 vols. Boston: Little, Brown, 1905.

Haugaard, William P. "Arius: Twice a Heretic? Arius and the Human Soul of Jesus Christ." *CH* 29, no. 3 (1960): 251–63.

Haupt, Benjamin. "Irenaeus' Citations of Scripture: Intentional or Careless Alterations?" Paper presented at the Society of Biblical Literature International Meeting, St. Andrews, Scotland, July 10, 2013.

Haynes, Daniel. "The Transgression of Adam and Christ the New Adam: St. Augustine and St. Maximus the Confessor on the Doctrine of Original Sin." *SVTQ* 55, no. 3 (2011): 293–317.

Heine, Ronald E. "The Christology of Callistus." *JTS*, n.s., 49 (1998): 58–60.

———. "Hippolytus, Ps.-Hippolytus and the Early Canons." In *The Cambridge History of Early Christian Literature*, edited by Frances M. Young, Lewis Ayres, and Andrew Louth, 140–51. Cambridge: Cambridge University Press, 2006.

Hermann, Josef Vogt. "Noet von Smyrna und Heraklit: Bemerkungen zur Darstellung ihrer Lehren durch Hippolyt." *ZAC* 6, no. 1 (2002): 59–80.

Hildebrand, Stephen M. *The Trinitarian Theology of Basil of Caesarea: A Synthesis of Greek Thought and Biblical Truth*. Washington, DC: Catholic University of America Press, 2007.

Hjärpe, Jan. "Jesus in Islam." In *Alternative Christs*, edited by Olav Hammer, 71–86. Cambridge: Cambridge University Press, 2009.

Holland, Tom. *In the Shadow of the Sword: The Birth of Islam and the Rise of the Global Arab Empire*. New York: Doubleday, 2012.

Honigmann, Ernest. "Juvenal of Jerusalem." *DOP* 30, no. 5 (1950): 209–75.

Hopkins, Jasper. *Nicholas of Cusa's* De Pace Fidei *and* Cribratio Alkorani. Minneapolis: Arthur J. Banning Press, 1990.

Hovorun, Cyril. *Will, Action and Freedom: Christological Controversies in the Seventh Century*. Leiden: Brill, 2008.

Hoyland, Robert G. *Arabia and the Arabs: From the Bronze Age to the Coming of Islam*. London: Routledge, 2001.

———. "The Earliest Christian Writings on Muhammad: An Appraisal." In *The Biography of Muhammad: The Issue of the Sources*, edited by Harald Motzki, 276–97. Leiden: Brill, 2000.

———. *Seeing Islam as Others Saw It: A Survey and Evaluation of Christian, Jewish and Zoroastrian Writings on Early Islam*. Princeton: Darwin Press, 1997.

ibn Ishaq, Muhammad. *A Life of Muhammad*. Translated by Alfred Guillaume. London: Oxford University Press, 1955.

Iricinschi, Eduard, and Holger M. Zellentin, eds. *Heresy and Identity in Late Antiquity*. Tübingen: Mohr Siebeck, 2008.

Jackson-McCabe, Matt. "What's in a Name? The Problem of 'Jewish-Christianity.'" In *Jewish Christianity Reconsidered: Rethinking Ancient Groups and Texts*, edited by Matt Jackson-McCabe, 7–38. Minneapolis: Fortress, 2007.

Jacobs, Andrew S. "Jews and Christians." In *The Oxford Handbook of Early Christian Studies*, edited by Susan Ashbrook Harvey and David G. Hunter, 169–85. Oxford: Oxford University Press, 2008.

Jenkins, Philip. *Jesus Wars: How Four Patriarchs, Three Queens, and Two Emperors Decided What Christians Would Believe for the Next 1,500 Years*. New York: HarperOne, 2010.

———. *The Lost History of Christianity: The Thousand-Year Golden Age of the Church in the Middle East, Africa, and Asia—and How It Died*. New York: HarperCollins, 2009.

John Paul II and Mar Dinkha IV. *Common Christological Declaration of John Paul II and His Holiness Mar Dinkha IV, Catholicos-Patriarch of the Assyrian Church of the East*. http://www.vatican.va/holy_father/john_paul_ii/speeches/1994/november/documents/hf_jp-ii_spe_19941111_dichiarazione-cristologica_en.html.

Kaegi, Walter Emil. *Heraclius: Emperor of Byzantium*. Cambridge: Cambridge University Press, 2003.

Kelly, J. N. D. *Early Christian Doctrines*. Rev. ed. San Francisco: HarperSanFrancisco, 1978.

Kennedy, Hugh. *The Prophet and the Age of the Caliphates: The Islamic Near East from the Sixth to the Eleventh Century*. Harlow, UK: Longman, 2004.

King, Karen. *What Is Gnosticism?* Cambridge, MA: Belknap Press of Harvard University Press, 2003.

Kinzig, Wolfram. "The Nazoraeans." In *Jewish Believers in Jesus*, edited by Oskar Skarsaune and Reidar Hvalvik, 463–87. Peabody, MA: Hendrickson, 2007.

Klijn, A. F. J., and G. J. Reinink. *Patristic Evidence for Jewish-Christian Sects*. Leiden: Brill, 1973.

Knox, John. *Marcion and the New Testament: An Essay in the Early History of the Canon*. Chicago: University of Chicago Press, 1942.

Krautheimer, Richard. *Early Christian and Byzantine Architecture*. 4th ed. New York: Penguin, 1986.

Lapidus, Ira M. *A History of Islamic Societies*. 2nd ed. Cambridge: Cambridge University Press, 2002.

Leirvik, Oddbjørn. *Images of Jesus Christ in Islam*. 2nd ed. Edinburgh: Continuum, 2010.

Lewis, Nicola Denzey. *Introduction to "Gnosticism": Ancient Voices, Christian Worlds*. Oxford: Oxford University Press, 2013.

Lienhard, Joseph T. "Basil of Caesarea, Marcellus of Ancyra, and 'Sabellius.'" *CH* 58 (1989): 157–58.

———. "Did Athanasius Reject Marcellus?" In *Arianism after Arius: Essays on the Development of the Fourth-Century Trinitarian Conflicts*, edited by Michel R. Barnes and Daniel H. Williams, 65–80. Edinburgh: T&T Clark, 1993.

———. "Marcellus of Ancyra in Modern Research." *TS* 43 (1982): 486–503.

———. "Two Friends of Athanasius: Marcellus of Ancyra and Apollinaris of Laodicea." *ZAC* 10, no. 1 (2006): 56–66.

Lieu, Judith M. "'As Much My Apostle as Christ Is Mine': The Dispute over Paul between Tertullian and Marcion." *EC* 1 (2010): 41–59.

———. "Marcion and the Synoptic Problem." In *New Studies in the Synoptic Problem*, edited by P. Foster, A. Gregory, J. S. Kloppenborg, and J. Verheyden, 731–51. Leuven: Peeters, 2011.

Lings, Martin. *Muhammad: His Life Based on the Earliest Sources*. New York: Inner Traditions International, 1983.

Logan, Alistair H. B. *The Gnostics: Identifying an Early Christian Cult*. London: T&T Clark, 2006.

Löhr, Winrich A. "Arius Reconsidered: Part 1." *ZAC* 9, no. 3 (2005): 524–60.

———. "Arius Reconsidered: Part 2." *ZAC* 10, no. 1 (2006): 121–57.

———. "A Sense of Tradition: The Homoiousian Church Party." In *Arianism after Arius: Essays on the Development of the Fourth-Century Trinitarian Conflicts*, edited by Michel R. Barnes and Daniel H. Williams, 81–100. Edinburgh: T&T Clark, 1993.

Loofs, F. *Nestorius and His Place in the History of Christian Doctrine*. Cambridge: Cambridge University Press, 1914.

Loon, Hans van. *The Dyophysite Christology of Cyril of Alexandria*. Leiden: Brill, 2009.

Lüdemann, Gerd. *Heretics: The Other Side of Early Christianity*. Translated by John Bowden. Louisville: Westminster John Knox, 1996.

Lüling, Günter. *A Challenge to Islam for Reformation: The Rediscovery and Reliable Reconstruction of a Comprehensive Pre-Islamic Christian Hymnal Hidden in the Koran under Earliest Islamic Reinterpretations*. Delhi: Motilal Banarsidass, 2003.

Luomanen, Petri. "Ebionites and Nazarenes." In *Jewish Christianity Reconsidered: Rethinking Ancient Groups and Texts*, edited by Matt Jackson-McCabe, 81–118. Minneapolis: Fortress, 2007.

———. "'Let Him Who Seeks, Continue Seeking': The Relationship between the Jewish-Christian Gospels and the Gospel of Thomas." In *Thomasine Traditions in Antiquity: The Social and Cultural World of the Gospel of Thomas*, edited by J. Ma. Asgeirsson, A. D. DeConick, and R. Ero, 119–53. NHMS 59. Leiden: Brill, 2006.

———. "Where Did Another Rich Man Come From? The Jewish-Christian Profile of the Story about a Rich Man in the 'Gospel of the Hebrews' (Origen, *Comm. in Matth*. 15.14)." *VC* 57, no. 3 (2003): 243–75.

Luttikhuizen, Gerard P. "Elchasaites and Their Book." In *A Companion to Second-Century Christian "Heretics,"* edited by Antti Marjanen and Petri Luomanen, 335–64. VCSup 76. Leiden: Brill, 2005.

———. *The Revelation of Elchasai: Investigations into the Evidence for a Mesopotamian Jewish Apocalypse of the Second Century and Its Reception by Judeo-Christian Propagandists*. Tübingen: Mohr Siebeck, 1985.

Lyman, J. Rebecca. "Arius and Arians." In *The Oxford Handbook of Early Christian Studies*, edited by Susan Ashbrook Harvey and David G. Hunter, 237–57. Oxford: Oxford University Press, 2008.

———. "Hellenism and Heresy." *JECS* 11 (2003): 209–22.

———. "Natural Resources: Tradition without Orthodoxy." *AThR* 84 (2002): 67–80.

————. "A Topography of Heresy: Mapping the Rhetorical Creation of Arianism." In *Arianism after Arius: Essays on the Development of the Fourth-Century Trinitarian Conflicts*, edited by Michel R. Barnes and Daniel H. Williams, 45–62. Edinburgh: T&T Clark, 1993.

Lyotard, Jean-François. *The Confessions of Augustine.* Translated by Richard Beardsworth. Stanford, CA: Stanford University Press, 2000.

————. *The Postmodern Condition: A Report on Knowledge.* Translated by Geoff Bennington and Brian Massumi. Minneapolis: University of Minnesota Press, 1984.

Marion, Jean-Luc. *God without Being.* Translated by Thomas A. Carlson. Chicago: University of Chicago Press, 1991.

Marjanen, Antti. "Gnosticism." In *The Oxford Handbook of Early Christian Studies*, edited by Susan Ashbrook Harvey and David G. Hunter, 203–20. Oxford: Oxford University Press, 2008.

Markschies, Christoph. *Gnosis: An Introduction.* Translated by John Bowden. London: T&T Clark, 2003.

Marmion, Declan, and Rik Van Nieuwenhove. *An Introduction to the Trinity.* Cambridge: Cambridge University Press, 2011.

Matter, Jacques. *Histoire critique du gnosticisme.* Paris: F. G. Levrault, 1828.

McGowan, Andrew. "Marcion's Love of Creation." *JECS* 9, no. 3 (2001): 295–311.

————. "Tertullian and the 'Heretical' Origins of the 'Orthodox' Trinity." *JECS* 14 (2006): 437–57.

McGrath, Alister. *Heresy: A History of Defending the Truth.* New York: HarperCollins, 2009.

McGuckin, John A. "The Christology of Nestorius of Constantinople." *PBR* 7, nos. 2–3 (1988): 93–129.

————. *St. Cyril of Alexandria: The Christological Controversy; Its History, Theology, and Texts.* Rev. ed. Crestwood, NY: St. Vladimir's Seminary Press, 2004.

McLeod, Frederick G. *Theodore of Mopsuestia.* New York: Routledge, 2009.

Meeks, Wayne A., and John T. Fitzgerald. *The Writings of St. Paul.* 2nd ed. New York: Norton, 2007.

Meier, John P. *A Marginal Jew: Rethinking the Historical Jesus.* Vol. 1, *The Roots of the Problem and the Person.* New York: Doubleday, 1991.

Meijering, E. P. "Athanasius on God as Creator and Recreator." *CHRC* 90, nos. 2–3 (2010): 175–97.

Meyer, Marvin W. *The Gnostic Discoveries: The Impact of the Nag Hammadi Library.* San Francisco: HarperSanFrancisco, 2005.

————. *The Gnostic Gospels of Jesus: The Definitive Collection of Mystical Gospels and Secret Books about Jesus.* San Francisco: HarperSanFrancisco, 2005.

Milliner, Matthew J. "Iconoclastic Immunity: Reformed/Orthodox Convergence in Theological Aesthetics in Theodore of Studios." *ThTo* 62, no. 4 (2006): 501–14.

Moll, Sebastian. *The Arch-Heretic Marcion*. Tübingen: Mohr Siebeck, 2010.

Moltmann, Jürgen. *The Trinity and the Kingdom of God*. San Francisco: Harper & Row, 1981.

Mondzain, Marie-José. *Image, Icon, Economy: The Byzantine Origins of the Contemporary Imaginary*. Translated by Rico Franses. Stanford, CA: Stanford University Press, 2004.

Mourad, Suleiman A. "The Qur'an and Jesus's Crucifixion and Death." In *New Perspectives on the Qur'an: The Qur'an in Its Historical Context 2*, edited by Gabriel Said Reynolds, 349–57. London: Routledge, 2011.

Murphy, Austin G. "Re-Reading the Johannine Prologue." *ProEccl* 14, no. 3 (2005): 306–23.

Neil, Bronwen. "The Western Reaction to the Council of Nicaea II." *JTS* 51, no. 2 (2000): 533–52.

Noble, Thomas F. X. *Images, Iconoclasm, and the Carolingians*. Philadelphia: University of Pennsylvania Press, 2009.

Norris, Frederick. "Paul of Samosata: Procurator Ducenarius." *JTS* 35 (1984): 50–70.

Norris, Richard A., Jr., ed. *The Christological Controversy*. Philadelphia: Fortress, 1980.

O'Collins, Gerald. *Christology: A Biblical, Historical, and Systematic Study of Jesus*. Oxford: Oxford University Press, 2009.

Pagels, Elaine. *The Gnostic Gospels*. New York: Random House, 1979.

Parvis, Sara. "Christology in the Early Arian Controversy: The Exegetical War." In *Christology and Scripture: Interdisciplinary Perspectives*, edited by Angus Paddison and Andrew T. Lincoln, 120–37. London: T&T Clark, 2007.

Payton, James R., Jr. "John of Damascus on Human Cognition: An Element in His Apologetic for Icons." *CH* 65, no. 2 (1996): 173–83.

Pearson, Birger A. *Ancient Gnosticism: Traditions and Literature*. Minneapolis: Fortress, 2007.

———. *Gnosticism and Christianity in Roman and Coptic Egypt*. New York: T&T Clark, 2004.

———. *Gnosticism, Judaism, and Egyptian Christianity*. Minneapolis: Fortress, 1990.

Pearson, Lori. "Schleiermacher and the Christologies behind Chalcedon." *HTR* 96, no. 3 (2003): 349–67.

Pelikan, Jaroslav. *Mary through the Centuries: Her Place in the History of Culture*. New Haven: Yale University Press, 1996.

———. "Montanism and Its Trinitarian Significance." *CH* 25, no. 2 (1956): 99–109.

Pelikan, Jaroslav, and Valerie Hotchkiss, eds. *Creeds and Confessions of Faith in the Christian Tradition*. 3 vols. New Haven: Yale University Press, 2003.

Perkins, Pheme. *Gnosticism and the New Testament*. Minneapolis: Fortress, 1993.

Pettersen, Alvyn. "Truth in a Heresy? 3: Arianism." *ExpTim* 112, no. 5 (2001): 150–54.

Pontifical Council for Promoting Christian Unity. "Guidelines for Admission to the Eucharist between the Chaldean Church and the Assyrian Church of the East." Rome: Pontifical Council for Promoting Christian Unity, 2001.

Prestige, G. L. *God in Patristic Thought*. London: SPCK, 1956.

Price, Richard. "The Council of Chalcedon (451): A Narrative." In *Chalcedon in Context: Church Councils 400–700*, edited by Richard Price and Mary Whitby, 70–91. Liverpool: Liverpool University Press, 2009.

Pritz, Ray. *Nazarene Jewish Christianity: From the End of the New Testament Period until Its Disappearance in the Fourth Century*. Jerusalem: Magnes Press, Hebrew University, 1988.

Räisänen, Heikki. "Marcion and the Origins of Christian Anti-Judaism: A Reappraisal." *Temenos* 33 (1997): 121–35.

Rasimus, Tuomas. "Ophite Gnosticism, Sethianism and the Nag Hammadi Library." *VC* 59 (2005): 235–63.

———. *Paradise Reconsidered in Gnostic Mythmaking: Rethinking Sethianism in Light of the Ophite Evidence*. Leiden: Brill, 2009.

Raven, Charles E. *Apollinarianism: An Essay on the Christology of the Church*. Cambridge: Cambridge University Press, 1923.

Reed, Jonathan L. *The HarperCollins Visual Guide to the New Testament*. San Francisco: HarperOne, 2007.

Reinink, G. J. "The Beginnings of Syriac Apologetic Literature in Response to Islam." *OrChr* 77 (1993): 165–87.

Reynolds, Gabriel Said. "Introduction: The Golden Age of Qur'anic Studies." In *New Perspectives on the Qur'an: The Qur'an in Its Historical Context 2*, edited by Gabriel Said Reynolds, 1–21. London: Routledge, 2011.

———, ed. *New Perspectives on the Qur'an: The Qur'an in Its Historical Context 2*. London: Routledge, 2011.

———. *The Qur'an and Its Biblical Subtext*. London: Routledge, 2010.

Rippin, Andrew. "Literary Analysis of Qur'ān, Tafsīr, and Sīra: The Methodologies of John Wansbrough." In *Approaches to Islam in Religious Studies*, edited by Richard C. Martin, 151–63. Oxford: Oneworld, 2001.

Roberson, Ronald G. "Oriental Orthodox–Catholic International Dialogue." In *Celebrating a Century of Ecumenism: Exploring the Achievements of International Dialogue*, edited by John A. Radano, 304–14. Grand Rapids: Eerdmans, 2012.

Robinson, James M. *The Coptic Gnostic Library: A Complete Edition of the Nag Hammadi Codices*. Leiden: Brill, 2000.

Roukema, Riemer. *Jesus, Gnosis and Dogma*. London: T&T Clark, 2010.

Sahas, Daniel J. *Icon and Logos: Sources in Eighth-Century Iconoclasm*. Toronto: University of Toronto Press, 1986.

Samir, Samir Khalil. *111 Questions on Islam: Interview Conducted by Giorgio Paolucci and Camille Eid*. Edited, translated, and revised by Wafik Nasry. Cotranslated by Claudia Castellani. San Francisco: Ignatius, 2002.

Saritoprak, Zeki. "How Commentators of the Qur'an Define 'Common Word.'" in *A Common Word and the Future of Christian-Muslim Relations*, edited by John Borelli, 34–45. Washington, DC: Prince Alwaleed Bin Talal Center for Muslim-Christian Understanding, 2009.

Sarot, Marcel. "Patripassianism and the Impassibility of God." *STK* 72 (1996): 73–81.

Savage, Elizabeth. *A Gateway to Hell, a Gateway to Paradise: The North African Response to the Arab Conquest*. Princeton: Darwin Press, 1997.

Schaff, Philip, and David S. Schaff. *History of the Christian Church*. Vol. 1. New York: Scribner's Sons, 1910.

Scholer, David M. *Nag Hammadi Bibliography, 1970–1994*. Leiden: Brill, 1997. See also the supplemental bibliographies of Scholer published annually in the journal *Novum Testamentum*.

Schreckenberg, Heinz, and Kurt Schubert. *Jewish Historiography and Iconography in Early and Medieval Christianity*. Maastricht: Van Gorcum, 1992.

Schweitzer, Albert. *The Quest of the Historical Jesus: A Critical Study of Its Progress from Reimarus to Wrede*. Translated by W. Montgomery. London: Adam and Charles Black, 1910.

Simon, Marcel. *"Verus Israel": A Study of the Relations between Christians and Jews in the Roman Empire (AD 135–425)*. 2nd ed. Translated by H. McKeating. London: Valentine Mitchell, 1996.

Simonetti, Manlio. *Studi sull' Arianesimo*. Rome: Editrice Studium, 1965.

Skarsaune, Oskar. "The Ebionites." In *Jewish Believers in Jesus*, edited by Oskar Skarsaune and Reidar Hvalvik, 419–62. Peabody, MA: Hendrickson, 2007.

Smith, J. Warren. "Suffering Impassibly: Christ's Passion in Cyril of Alexandria's Soteriology." *ProEccl* 11 (2002): 463–83.

Solovieva, Olga. "Epiphanius of Salamis and His Invention of Iconoclasm in the Fourth Century A.D." *FH* 42, no. 1 (2010): 21–46.

Spier, Jeffrey, ed. *Picturing the Bible: The Earliest Christian Art*. New Haven: Yale University Press, 2008.

Spoerl, Kelley McCarthey. "Apollinarius and the First Nicene Generation." In *Tradition and the Rule of Faith in the Early Church: Essays in Honor of Joseph T. Lienhard, S.J.*, edited by Ronnie J. Rombs and Alexander Y. Hwang, 109–27. Washington, DC: Catholic University of America Press, 2010.

———. "The Liturgical Argument in Apollinarius: Help and Hindrance on the Way to Orthodoxy." *HTR* 91, no. 2 (1998): 127–52.

Stang, Charles M. "The Two 'I's of Christ: Revisiting the Christological Controversy." *AThR* 94, no. 3 (2012): 529–47.

Stark, Rodney. *The Triumph of Christianity: How the Jesus Movement Became the World's Largest Religion*. New York: HarperOne, 2011.

Stead, G. Christopher. "Arius in Modern Research." *JTS* 45, no. 1 (1994): 24–36.

———. *Doctrine and Philosophy in Early Christianity: Arius, Athanasius, Augustine*. Aldershot, UK: Ashgate, 2000.

———. "Rhetorical Method in Athanasius." *VC* 30 (1976): 121–37.

———. "The Word 'from Nothing.'" *JTS* 49 (1998): 671–84.

Steinhauser, Kenneth B. "The Acts of the Council of Aquileia (381 C.E.)." In *Religions of Late Antiquity in Practice*, edited by Richard Valantasis, 275–88. Princeton: Princeton University Press, 2000.

Strecker, Georg. *The Johannine Letters: A Commentary on 1, 2, and 3 John*. Edited by Harold Attridge. Minneapolis: Fortress, 1996.

Streett, Daniel R. *They Went Out from Us: The Identity of the Opponents in First John*. Berlin: de Gruyter, 2011.

Studer, Basil. *Trinity and Incarnation: The Faith of the Early Church*. Edited by Andrew Louth. Translated by Matthias Westerhoff. Edinburgh: T&T Clark, 1993.

Teal, Andrew. "Athanasius and Apollinarius: Who Was the Chicken and Who Was the Egg?" *StPatr* 46, no. 3 (2010): 281–88.

Thomassen, Einar. *The Spiritual Seed: The "Church" of the Valentinians*. Leiden: Brill, 2006.

Tiessen, Terrance L. "Gnosticism as Heresy: The Response of Irenaeus." *Didaskalia* 18, no. 1 (2007): 31–48.

Tillich, Paul. *Dynamics of Faith*. New York: Harper & Row, 1957.

van den Broek, Roelof. "Gnosticism I: Gnostic Religion" and "Gnosticism II: Gnostic Literature." In *Dictionary of Gnosis and Western Esotericism*, vol. 1, ed. Wouter J. Hanegraaff, 403–16, 417–32. Leiden: Brill, 2005.

Verheyden, Joseph. "Epiphanius on the Ebionites." In *The Image of the Judaeo-Christians in Ancient Jewish and Christian Literature*, edited by P. J. Tomson and D. Lambers-Petry, 182–208. WUNT 158. Tübingen: Mohr Siebeck, 2003.

Volf, Miroslav. *Allah: A Christian Response*. New York: HarperOne, 2011.

Wahlde, Urban C. von. "The Johannine Literature and Gnosticism: New Light on Their Relationship?" In *From Judaism to Christianity: A Festschrift for Thomas H. Tobin, S.J., on the Occasion of His Sixty-Fifth Birthday*, edited by Patricia Walters and Thomas H. Tobin, 221–54. Leiden: Brill, 2010.

Wansbrough, J. *Qur'ānic Studies: Sources and Methods of Scriptural Interpretation*. Oxford: Oxford University Press, 1977.

———. *The Sectarian Milieu: Content and Composition of Islamic Salvation History*. Oxford: Oxford University Press, 1978.

Ware, Kallistos. "Patterns of Episcopacy in the Early Church and Today: An Orthodox View." In *Bishops, but What Kind? Reflections on Episcopacy*, edited by Peter Moore, 1–24. London: SPCK, 1982.

Watt, W. Montgomery. *Muhammad: Prophet and Statesman*. Oxford: Oxford University Press, 1964.

Webb, Stephen H. *Jesus Christ, Eternal God: Heavenly Flesh and the Metaphysics of Matter*. Oxford: Oxford University Press, 2011.

Welburn, Andrew J. "Reconstructing the Ophite Diagram." *NovT* 23, no. 3 (1981): 261–87.

Wesche, Kenneth Paul. "The Union of God and Man in Jesus Christ in the Thought of Gregory of Nazianzus." *SVTQ* 28, no. 2 (1984): 83–98.

Wessel, Susan. *Cyril of Alexandria and the Nestorian Controversy: The Making of a Saint and of a Heretic*. Oxford: Oxford University Press, 2004.

White, Despina Stratoudaki. "Patriarch Photios and the Conclusion of Iconoclasm." *GOTR* 44, nos. 1–4 (1999): 341–55.

Wiles, Maurice. *Archetypal Heresy: Arianism through the Centuries*. Oxford: Oxford University Press, 1996.

Williams, D. H. "Constantine, Nicaea and the 'Fall' of the Church." In *Christian Origins: Theology, Rhetoric and Community*, edited by L. Ayres and G. Jones, 117–36. London: Routledge, 1998.

———. *Evangelicals and Tradition: The Formative Influence of the Early Church*. Grand Rapids: Baker Academic, 2005.

———. "Monarchianism and Photinus of Sirmium as the Persistent Heretical Face of the Fourth Century." *HTR* 99, no. 2 (2006): 187–206.

Williams, Michael A. "Life and Happiness in the 'Platonic Underworld.'" In *Gnosticism, Platonism, and the Late Ancient World: Essays in Honour of John D. Turner*, edited by Kevin Corrigan and Tuomas Rasimus, 497–523. Leiden: Brill, 2013.

———. "A Life Full of Meaning and Purpose: Demiurgical Myths and Social Implications." In *Beyond the Gnostic Gospels: Studies Building on the Work of Elaine Pagels*, edited by Eduard Iricinschi, Lance Jenott, Nicola Denzey Lewis, and Philippa Townsend, 19–55. Studies and Texts in Antiquity and Christianity. Tübingen: Mohr Siebeck, 2013.

———. *Rethinking "Gnosticism": An Argument for Dismantling a Dubious Category*. Princeton: Princeton University Press, 1996.

Williams, Rowan. *Arius: Heresy and Tradition*. Rev. ed. Grand Rapids: Eerdmans, 2002.

———. *On Christian Theology*. Oxford: Blackwell, 2000.

———. "What Is Christianity? A Lecture Given at the Islamic University of Islamabad, 23 November 2005." *ICMR* 19, no. 3 (2008): 325–32.

Woodberry, J. Dudley. "Contextualization among Muslims Reusing Common Pillars." *IJFM* 13, no. 4 (1996): 171–86.

Wright, Robert. *The Evolution of God*. New York: Little, Brown, 2010.

Yamauchi, Edwin M. *Pre-Christian Gnosticism: A Survey of the Proposed Evidences*. 2nd ed. Grand Rapids: Baker, 1983.

———. *A Separate God: The Christian Origins of Gnosticism*. San Francisco: Harper-Collins, 1993.

Young, Frances M. "Exegetical Method and Scriptural Proof." In *Studia Patristica* 19, edited by Elizabeth A. Livingstone, 291–304. Leuven: Peeters, 1989.

———. *From Nicaea to Chalcedon: A Guide to the Literature and Its Background*. 2nd ed. Grand Rapids: Baker Academic, 2010.

Index

11-16-15
2-17-16   1/21/20
  4   23
  2   2